ON CIRCUIT

1924–1937

Frontispiece

[page 114

AYLESBURY 1928

ON CIRCUIT

1924-1937

BY

Sir Frank Douglas MacKinnon

LORD JUSTICE OF APPEAL; BENCHER OF THE INNER TEMPLE; HONORARY FELLOW OF TRINITY COLLEGE, OXFORD

Cambridge

AT THE UNIVERSITY PRESS

1940

CAMBRIDGE UNIVERSITY PRESS
Cambridge, New York, Melbourne, Madrid, Cape Town,
Singapore, São Paulo, Delhi, Tokyo, Mexico City

Cambridge University Press
The Edinburgh Building, Cambridge CB2 8RU, UK

Published in the United States of America by Cambridge University Press, New York

www.cambridge.org
Information on this title: www.cambridge.org/9781107605084

First published 1940
First paperback edition 2011

A catalogue record for this publication is available from the British Library

ISBN 978-1-107-60508-4 Paperback

To my
MARSHALS
whose companionship did
so much for my happiness
on these Circuit journeys

PREFACE

When the war, and the black-out, put an end to most forms of innocent diversion, I found consolation of an evening by compiling this account of my Circuit experiences. It is based upon the journals I used to keep, but omitting their more personal passages.

When I mentioned this enterprise to my friend Sir George Branson he told me that he had been lent by Mr W. Grantham, K.C., a Circuit Journal kept by his father. Mr Grantham lent it to me. He also lent me some Circuit Notes made by Baron Huddleston, of which he had made a copy when marshal to his father. I have inserted some extracts from "Huddleston *Notes*", and "Grantham *Notes*". Huddleston was a Judge from 1875 to 1890, and Grantham from 1886 to 1911, so that their notes refer to these periods respectively.

I have received, through Mr Norman Birkett, K.C., its Leader, the permission of the Midland Circuit to print the extracts I have made from the Circuit Records.

F. D. M.

BEACONSFIELD
5 March 1940

On CIRCUIT: 1924–1937

1924

The last big case I was concerned with at the bar, in July 1924, was before Mr Justice Bailhache. It was a dispute between an American Insurance Company and an English one, and the issue was about the technicalities of arbitration under the law of New York. As it happened London was full of American lawyers. The American and the Canadian Bar Associations were here on an organized visit. So there was no lack of expert witnesses available. I spent my evenings attending dinners in their honour—we had three at the Inner Temple—and my days examining, or cross-examining, our guests in the witness-box. I remember saying to one, whom I had made my friend overnight, "There is little I can ask you, Mr Wickersham, but I cannot deny myself the pleasure of being able to say that I once cross-examined an Attorney-General of the United States".

The case ended at the end of term. Mr Justice Bailhache bade us good-bye, though not with the ancient formula *Cras Animarum*: that was not his style. I went off for a well-earned vacation, little thinking that I should never see him again, and still less that I should be his successor in the following October. On 6 September I went with two friends and a knapsack to walk in the Pyrenees. The first day we spent at Lourdes. It was my third visit, and I found the spectacle as interesting as ever. And so to Luz, Bareges, to the top of the Pic du Midi de Bigorre, and to Gavarnie. Then over the long pass to Ordessa and the Val d'Arazas, on the Spanish side, the most beautiful spot in the Pyrenees. Back to Gavarnie and by a strenuous passage to Cauterets. And so to Pau, St Engrace, Mauléon, Ahusquy and Bayonne.

On Monday, 29 September, I got home, very brown and very fit. My wife, who had been attending to my letters, said: "There are a lot of letters for you, and there is one you ought to answer. It is from the Lord Chancellor." "What on earth does he want?" I said. "Well," she said, "he is proposing to make you a judge." I was indeed astonished, and said I had no idea there was any vacancy. On which she told me that while I was away Mr Justice Bailhache had died suddenly. The French papers would not record that, even if I had read them. No one can ever have had such an invitation from a Lord Chancellor with more complete surprise than I did.

The Lord Chancellor was Lord Haldane, in the first Labour Government. In fact I was the only judge of the High Court whom he appointed under that administration. I was sworn in as a Judge of the King's Bench Division, before him, at the House of Lords, on 7 October 1924. Ten years before, almost to a day, in the same room, and before the same Lord Chancellor, I had taken the oath as one of His Majesty's Counsel.* On this second occasion I was told to wait upon him in a judge's robes. My own could not be ready in time; so I went rather too amply adorned in the robes of Mr Justice Shearman, who was larger than I am.

My new robes were ready for me to wear when I was sworn in before the Lord Chief Justice, in his Court, on 13 October 1924. One part of my equipment I kept for a very short time, and then returned it unused to the makers. This was the black cap. Very soon after my appointment Lord Darling finally retired from the Bench, and when he did so he gave me the black cap he had used throughout his judicial career. I have carried it throughout mine (and sometimes used it on grim occasions), and when I went to the Court of Appeal in 1937 I handed it on to Mr Justice Wrottesley upon his appointment to the King's Bench. If he, and perhaps others, should continue the transmission, this black cap is likely to accumulate associations of horror. But I hope that theatrical piece of ritual, a legacy of a macabre past, may be abandoned in a more enlightened age. And then the thing may go to a museum.

I little realized when I was at the bar how large a proportion of his time a Judge of the King's Bench spends away on circuit. I had

* That ceremony was not the same as the one when John Campbell was sworn in as King's Counsel in June 1827. He records in his diary: "We were in the Chancellor's private room in the House of Lords. They made us kneel down and swear that we did not believe in the damnable doctrine of Transubstantiation." *Life of Lord Campbell* (1881), Vol. I, p. 446.

myself never even joined a circuit. I started as a pupil of Lord Justice Scrutton. He had once joined the South-Eastern Circuit, but he never went on it. (When he became a judge, however, he was the best judge in a criminal case of his time, perhaps of any time.) In his chambers there was no connexion with any circuit. I had very little money, and to join a circuit as he had done would have wasted some of it. And as I hoped to get work chiefly in the Commercial Court I never joined one at all. As a result, of course, I was never privileged to be a Recorder.

Lord Haldane, I presume, honoured me by his selection because he had listened with approval to arguments of mine in the House of Lords and the Privy Council. If he had bethought him that perhaps the most serious work of a King's Bench Judge is to try prisoners at the Assizes and at the Old Bailey, and had enquired how far experience qualified me for that task, I am sure he would never have appointed me at all. As a youth I was once fined for riding a bicycle without a light. I had for some years occasionally sat at Petty Sessions as a county magistrate, and sometimes attended Quarter Sessions under the chairmanship of Lord Parmoor. These were the only occasions on which I had ever been inside a criminal court. Moreover my experience of juries, and their ways, was negligible. I do not suppose I addressed a jury more than half a dozen times during my twenty-seven years at the bar.*

In these circumstances it was with very considerable trepidation that on 18 October 1924 I left London for Carlisle† upon the Northern Circuit, with the prospect of having to try prisoners as my first duty. But I had two pieces of good fortune. My first marshal—first of a numerous and charming company—was John Maude, who already knew all that I did not. And secondly, there was Sir Herbert Stephen, that most experienced and kindly Clerk of Assize. Their help, especially in the matter of sentences, was invaluable. For the rest,

* Lord Wright's practice at the bar was very similar to mine, but on a more prosperous scale. He did join the North-Eastern Circuit, and therefore, like Lord Justice Scrutton (whose pupils we both were), had been at least once in a criminal court in the barristers' seats. There is only one reason for his getting the better of me, at the bar, and since, that, if it were suggested, I should strenuously contest, viz. that he was at Trinity College, Cambridge, and I at Trinity College, Oxford.

"The fault, dear Brutus, is not in our stars,
But in ourselves, that we are underlings."

† In 1435 the Act, 14 Hen. VI, cap. 3, provided that in Cumberland "in Time of Peace and of Truce" the Assizes shall be held at Carlisle.

I sat with my finger in the index of Archbold, and I hope my uneasiness was not too apparent.

I had one other very great piece of good fortune, when I started going on circuit. A judge is attended by a cook and two man-servants, who are his Circuit butler, and the marshal's man. I was able to make an alliance with John P. Devany as my Circuit butler. He had great experience, as he had been Circuit butler to Lord Russell of Killowen, when Lord Chief Justice. Devany was my very kind friend, and for about ten years he did a great deal for my happiness. When he said he must retire, owing to advancing years, it was a great loss to me.

The Circuit butler valets the judge, and waits at table. The marshal's man, who valets the marshal, is his assistant. In Grantham's *Notes* he records that the marshal's man used to have the privilege of selling the daily Cause Lists, and that at Liverpool this was very profitable.

But before I faced any prisoners there was the Grand Jury, and I had only the vaguest idea what I ought to say to them. What I did say was perhaps unusual. I spoke of the impressiveness of being received as His Majesty's Judge of Assize in their ancient city, and I added: "I do not know it for a fact, but I suspect that when my great-grandfather emigrated from Scotland he probably passed through Carlisle on foot. I am sure his reception here cannot have been as stately as mine has been, but I hope it may have been as cordial."

It was perhaps well that I did not go farther back in recalling visits of my namesakes, if not my ancestors, to Carlisle. When that city was surrendered to the Young Chevalier on 17 November 1745 a good many MacKinnons were in his invading army that went on to Derby. I doubt if I had a direct ancestor among them. For the first of them that I know of had gone from Skye to Arran at least by 1700, if not before, and three generations were farming in Arran until my great-grandfather, in 1780, came away to England on his way to Italy and later to the Argentine.

After Culloden, in August 1746, the Assize at Carlisle was a terrible affair. The Commission was opened on 12 August by four judges, headed by Chief Baron Parker. They found 382 prisoners to be tried, mostly captured refugees from the battle. It was thought impossible to try so many. So it was decreed—by what power or authority I cannot imagine—that, with the exception of some greater offenders, they should draw lots to provide one out of every twenty to be tried, the other nineteen agreeing to submit to transportation. Some having accepted these terms, the prisoners were reduced to 127, against whom true bills were found by the Grand Jury. The Court then adjourned until 9 September. Eventually 96 were sentenced to the horrible death that was then the penalty for High Treason. Of them 31 were thus executed, including Sir Archibald Primrose, in October. All the rest, except two who had died in prison, were transported for life.*

My first prisoners at Carlisle all pleaded "Guilty", and the business of the Assize was over by lunch time. So early I learned that though on circuit one may have to sit much longer than in town—on the next Saturday, at Lancaster, I sat till 5.30—there are times of holiday. In this afternoon we had a walk to the Crown Inn, Wetheral, on the Eden. And for the next two days I enjoyed the hospitality of a High Sheriff, that pleasant experience I have so often repeated.

Judges' Lodgings are of two types, either an official house permanently kept and furnished by the county, or a furnished house hired for the period of the Assize from its owner. At Carlisle my Lodgings were of the latter sort, in a modern villa, comfortable enough but not impressive. At Lancaster there is a fine seventeenth-century house to the north of the Castle and the church. The panelled dining-room on the first floor is magnificent. In front of the house is an open space sloping down hill. When I came there the General Election was in full swing—for Lord Haldane remained in office less than a month after recommending my appointment—and the contest in Lancaster was keen. I received one day from the Labour Party a very polite message to say that, with my permission, they desired to hold an open-air meeting in the space before the Lodgings in the evening, but that if it would be in the least an annoyance to me they would cancel it. Of course, I agreed.

In Huddleston's *Notes* I find: "A dozen of port is sent to the Judges at Lancaster, supposed to be bought by the interest of a sum left by an old lady for that purpose." But in Grantham's *Notes* there is a memorandum from the Under-Sheriff, dated 5 March 1906, which gives a different explanation. "Years ago a present of Port wine for

* *Carlisle in 1745* (London, 1846), pp. 245–259. There is no MacKinnon in the list of the 127 on p. 248. Some of them may have drawn a favourable lot: there are plenty of the name in the United States and Canada.

the use of the Judges was sent either annually or periodically to the lodgings at Lancaster by the Duke of Buccleugh. The origin of this present is quite unknown, and it has been discontinued for many years. A great deal of the Buccleugh property in the neighbourhood of Lancaster has been sold, and whether this had anything to do with its discontinuance I do not know."

The Sheriff's trumpeters in Lancashire are the best in all the counties. They wear a picturesque uniform; their trumpets are keyed so that they can play all sorts of tunes as duets; and from attending four times a year at lengthy Assizes at Liverpool and Manchester they get so much practice that they play admirably. The banner on one trumpet bears the arms of the Duke of Lancaster, old John of Gaunt; that on the other the arms of the Sheriff. "D'ye ken John Peel" is a tune they play with obvious gusto: and on the last day of the Assize at Manchester they play "Auld Lang Syne" with much feeling.

In *Denman's Digest, or Archbold Abridged* (1912, p. xlviii) I find: "It was resolved by the Judges, on 12 April 1904, that the sheriff's trumpeters should not be dispensed with. There can be no doubt in the minds of those familiar with the subject that the time-honoured institution of heralding the approach of the King's representative by the sound of trumpets has a tremendous effect in impressing the populace with the importance of the proceedings. The day of the abolition of trumpeters would be an evil one."

From the Lodgings at Lancaster it is a short distance up a steep footpath to the Castle. The roadway goes by a longer and more gentle ascent. When the High Sheriff and his Chaplain come to escort the Judge to the Court the trumpeters attend with a fanfare. Then they walk up the footpath, while the carriage drives its longer course, and are ready at the Castle for a second tune.

The "carriage" is now almost always a motor-car. In Lancashire, at this time, it was the most enormous Daimler I have ever seen. It had belonged to the first Lord Leverhulme, when he was High Sheriff, and at the end of his year of office he gave it to the county for the Judges' use. When I first rode in it in 1924 it was painted a bright vermilion with immense coats of arms on each panel. A year later I found that the then High Sheriff had had it repainted a more demure colour, and the coats of arms reduced to a more modest size. And being an heraldic enthusiast he had taken great pains to get the coat of John of Gaunt precisely correct. There was something about the label of difference, which he told me but I have forgotten, of which he was particularly proud. I believe it had been incorrectly tricked for centuries.

Lancaster Castle is a magnificent building, and the two Courts in it are very fine. The Crown Court has, in the dock, grim relics of the bad old days. On the back of the dock is an iron device into which the fingers of a man's hand can be put. Another piece of iron on a hinge comes round the wrist and can be made fast, so that the palm of the hand is exposed. Alongside is a brazier, and a branding iron with the letter M at the end of it.

Now these things are there in obedience to an Act of Parliament of 1487. And they are connected with that preposterous absurdity "the Benefit of Clergy" which disfigured the English criminal law down to the nineteenth century. Down to 1826 the penalty for every felony was death. But this was subject to the operation of the Benefit of Clergy. Originally this arose from the immunity of the cleric from the jurisdiction of the Secular Courts. And as clerics were alone literate, or were supposed to be, the Benefit of Clergy came to be allowed to anyone who, upon conviction, could show his ability to read in the dock. A woman, of course, could not even by a fiction be a clerk; but by an Act of Philip & Mary women were allowed the like privilege. Until then all women convicted of felony had to be hanged. In the seventeenth century the convict's test was always his ability to read the first verse of the 51st Psalm—or even to recite it, with the book open at the wrong place or upside down. This was known as "the neck verse". But by an Act of 1707 the claim was allowed, without reading, to anyone convicted of a clergyable felony. An example of this ritual—and of the strange lack of decorum that might occur at an Assize in the old days—is recorded in *Manningham's Diary* (Camden Society, 1868) on 24 February 1601. The Assizes were being held at Rochester, before Serjeant Daniel (later Judge of the Common Pleas, 1604 to 1610) as Commissioner. "There was one had his booke given him at the prisoners barr, where the ordinary useth to heare and certifie there readinge. And one Mr Gylburne start up sayinge 'He will reade as well as my horse'; which wordes Serjeant Daniel, having before allowed the cleargy, tooke very ill, telling him playnely that he was too hasty: and yet caused the prisoner to be brought nearer that Gylburne might hear him reade, and he reade perfectly."

Under this amazing system there was a time when the most brutal murderer, with sufficient wits, could go scot free. The natural reaction was to cut down the privilege, and this was first done by the Act of 1487. This provided that any convict who successfully claimed the Benefit of Clergy should be branded on the thumb with M for murder, and T for other felonies. One found to be thus branded, i.e. convicted for a second time, was to be denied the Benefit of Clergy unless he was actually in Holy Orders. This is the meaning of the sentence at the end of many old trials, "He prayed his Clergy, and was burnt in the hand".

The instruments in the dock at Lancaster are there by reason of this Act of 1487. The T iron has been lost. I believe this is the only Court in England in which there is such a survival. But I find in *History of the County Buildings of Northampton* (1885), by C. A. Markham, that until comparatively recently there was a similar iron handcuff, and branding irons, in the splendid Crown Court at Northampton. And I think I remember that in the Museum at Chester I saw the branding irons that were formerly in the Court there.

The branding had to be done by the Gaoler in open court. I believe that the Judge's marshal (whose last surviving duty was to swear the Grand Jury) had then to go to the dock, and when the horrid rite was accomplished, to report—"Good mark, my Lord". In fact, however, judges would often mitigate the barbarity of the laws they had to administer by hinting, presumably through the marshal, that a lukewarm or even a cold iron might be used. In the report* of a case in 1759, before Lord Mansfield, counsel "observed that the punishment of burning in the hand is constantly and notoriously done, in the face and with the knowledge of the judges themselves, with a cold iron". From a like motive, when the penalty for stealing in a shop to the value of 5*s*. was death (as it was until the nineteenth century), a judge would often encourage a jury to find that a valuable article was only worth 4*s*. 11*d*.

In 1547 the Benefit of Clergy was taken away altogether upon conviction for murder, highway robbery, horse-stealing, and burglary. Thereafter, and especially in the eighteenth century, successive Acts declared various offences to be felonies without Benefit of Clergy. So that by the end of the reign of George III there were 160 offences in

* *Rex* v. *Beardmore* (1759) 2 Burrow 792.

this category. I repeat that until 1826 the penalty for every felony was death. It was the enactment that these 160 offences should be without Benefit of Clergy that made them effectively capital. But manslaughter, however heinous, remained a clergyable felony until 1822.

These various Acts left fewer occasions for the branding under the Act of 1487. In 1717 transportation for seven years was substituted for the branding. And in 1779 a judge was empowered to substitute whipping, or a fine, in place of it. The Act of 1487 was repealed in 1827.

There is a surviving echo of the Benefit of Clergy in the ritual of criminal trials to-day. The difference between a felony and a misdemeanour is now arbitrary and irrational. When a person has been found guilty of a felony, the Clerk of Assize addresses him*: "Prisoner at the bar, you have been found guilty of felony. Have you anything to say why the sentence of the Court should not be passed upon you?" But he makes no such enquiry in a case of misdemeanour. In the old days the question was "Have you anything to say why sentence of death according to law should not be passed upon you?" And the question really meant "Do you claim Benefit of Clergy?" I have heard the modern question many hundred times. The convict, if he answers at all, usually protests that he is really innocent. If any of them had ever had the wit to say "Yes, I claim my clergy. Give me the book open at the neck verse", I should have been tempted to knock a month or two off my intended sentence in recognition of his historical erudition.

When I write "my intended sentence" I am not using precise language. No judge says "I sentence you" to so and so. He always says "The sentence of the Court is" so and so. A Judge of Assize sits by virtue of a Commission to him and a number of others. And it authorizes trials by "you or any two of you, of whom the Judge of our Supreme Court of Judicature shall be one". As the circuit officials are among those commissioned, the quorum of two is normally constituted by the Judge and the Clerk of Assize. But any sentence is properly the sentence "of the Court".

There was, in the old days, another difference between a felony and a misdemeanour, besides the fact that in the former the convict

* In the technical phrase he "calls upon him".

had to be "called upon", but in the latter not. In a charge of felony until 1897 the jury were not allowed to separate from the moment they were sworn until they delivered their verdict. This by the Act of 1897 survives in a charge of murder. But with a misdemeanour the jury might separate when the Court adjourned. The Tichborne Claimant was at first indicted for forgery as well as perjury, the forgery being his signing Tichborne bonds "R. C. D. Tichborne". Forgery was a felony, but perjury was only a misdemeanour. The rule that in a case of felony the jury must not separate still existed in 1872. As the trial of the Claimant was certain to be a lengthy affair—though no one can have foreseen how lengthy—it would have been an intolerable thing for the jury to be locked up together night after night. So the charge of forgery was dropped, and he was only tried on the indictment for perjury. The trial began on 23 April 1873 and the verdict of "Guilty" was returned on 28 February 1874. This was the 188th day of the actual hearing, but if the charge of felony had been persisted in the jury would have had to live together in an hotel, locked up every night, for 310 nights.

In the old days, also, when the jury retired to consider their verdict they were given in charge of a bailiff who was sworn by the Clerk of Assize in the terms*—"You shall well and truly keep every person sworn of this Jury in some private and convenient room without Meat, Drink, Fire, Candle, or Lodging...". The jury was in fact starved and frozen into agreement. At the trial of the seven bishops in 1688, when the jury were about to retire, the Lord Chief Justice (Sir Robert Wright) said, "Gentlemen of the Jury, Have you a Mind to Drink before you go?" The jury said, "Yes, my Lord, if you please". Upon which "Wine was sent for, for the Jury".

The jury were locked up all night. The solicitor for the bishops sat on the stairs to watch lest any minion of the Crown supplied food to jurors favourable to the prosecution and so enabled them to starve out the others. At four in the morning some basins of water for washing were allowed to enter: the jurymen drank it all. Ultimately they were eleven to one. The biggest of the eleven said: "I am the

* *The Office of the Clerk of Assize* (1682), p. 48. The remainder of the Bailiff's oath survives to-day almost *verbatim*—"and you shall not suffer any person whatsoever to speak to them, or any of them; neither shall you yourself speak to them until such time as they be agreed of their Verdict, unless it be to ask them whether they be agreed of their Verdict; so help you God".

largest and strongest: here I will stay till I am no bigger than a tobacco pipe before I say Guilty." The one dissentient collapsed at six in the morning. At the sitting of the Court at 10 a.m. the verdict was "Not Guilty", and the Stuart dynasty was doomed.*

Lord Campbell writes in his journal† in August 1854, *à propos* of his part in the Lords over the Common Law Procedure Act of 1854: "On one important enactment I have been thwarted and defeated. I wished to do away with the barbarous custom of imprisoning and starving juries to compel unanimity." He tried to provide that if at the end of 12 hours ten of the jury were agreed their verdict should have effect. The Commons disagreed and proposed that after 12 hours, if there was no unanimity, the jury should be discharged, and a fresh trial take place.

In a case in 1858 (*Cooksey* v. *Haynes*, 27 L.J. 371) where a jury who had retired "covertly procured victuals and liquor", the Court ordered a new trial, saying that "it concerns the interests of justice itself that such gross indecencies in the administration of it should not be allowed". It was only in 1870 that an Act provided that a jury when out of Court might be provided with a fire, and with reasonable refreshments "to be procured at their own expense".

Eventually the present practice was introduced by which, if the jury is in hopeless disagreement, after the lapse of a time which is in the Judge's discretion, he can discharge them and order the case to be tried again before another jury.

I spoke just now of the marshal's last surviving duty—to administer the Oath to the Grand Jury. This was still his privilege in 1924, and for seven years after. It gave him a fine speaking part. He must be dull indeed who was not a little uplifted when he had to rehearse so fine a piece of English. First he addressed the Foreman thus: "You, Sir, as Foreman of this Grand Inquest of our Sovereign Lord the King and the body of this County of —— shall diligently enquire and true presentment make of all such matters, offences, and things as shall be given you in charge, or shall otherwise come to your knowledge, as touching this present service. The King's Counsel, your fellows', and your own, you shall observe and keep secret. You shall present no person out of envy, hatred, or malice; neither shall you leave any

* Macaulay's *History* (1860), Vol. II, p. 384.

† *Life of Lord Campbell* (1881), Vol. II, p. 325.

one unpresented through affection, fear, gain, reward, or the hope or promise thereof; but you shall present all things truly and indifferently as they shall come to your knowledge, according to the best of your skill and understanding. So help you God."

When the Foreman had been perhaps a little dazed by this allocution, the marshal swore the rest of the Grand Jury, four of them at a time, thus: "This same oath which your Foreman hath taken on his part, you, and each of you, shall well and truly observe and keep on your parts respectively. So help you God."

The Foreman's Oath is obviously an ancient formula. I possess a little book, *The Office of the Clerk of Assize: containing the Form and Method of the Proceedings at the Assizes.... The Second Edition*—1682, which gives it almost verbatim* at p. 31. [The First Edition of 1660 is very rare. I only know of one copy, given by Lord Halsbury to the Inner Temple Library.]

I have another, earlier, little book, *The Book of Oaths, and the Severall Forms thereof Ancient and Modern.... Printed at London...* 1649. In that "The Oath of the Grand Inquest" is given thus: "Ye shall truly enquire, and due presentment make of all such things as you are charged withall on the Queene's behalf; the Queene's Councell, your owne, and your fellowes, you shall well and truly keepe; And in al other things the truth present. So help you God, and by the Contents of this Booke." I presume the Queen was Elizabeth.

I was told that in Lancashire they were pleased to have the phrase in the Foreman's Oath run "this County Palatine of Lancaster". At Manchester my marshal (not John Maude, but his successor) essayed to gratify them thus. But by an unhappy slip of the tongue he made it "this County Palestine of Lancaster". And there were reasons why the slip was particularly unfortunate in Manchester. As a contrast in swearing I recall an occasion at Liverpool, in October 1925, when I had to try a Chinese sailor for alleged manslaughter on a British ship on the high seas. Nearly all the witnesses were Chinese. As each of them entered the witness-box he was handed a cheap saucer by my clerk, who said to him, through the interpreter, "Break the saucer". The man smashed it on the floor. My clerk then said, and

* I find an even closer identity with the modern form in another of my old books—Scroggs, *The Practice of Courts Leet and Court Baron* (4th ed. London, 1728). It is the Oath for the Foreman of a Court Leet.

the interpreter repeated in what I assumed to be Chinese: "The saucer is broken. If you do not speak the truth, your Soul shall be broken like the saucer."

The Judge's marshal, who, like the Clerk of Assize, the Under-Sheriff, and all circuit officials, was paid by fees extracted from acquitted prisoners and litigants, had sometimes other duties than supervising the branding and swearing the Grand Jury. At the York Lent Assizes, 1803, two youths named Heald and Terry were tried for the murder of an old woman. Both were found guilty and sentenced to death. The execution was fixed, as was then the practice, a few days later. On the appointed morning Terry assured the Chaplain of the gaol that Heald was innocent. The Chaplain thought he ought to tell the Judge of this, and did so. "But his Lordship was so perfectly satisfied of Heald's guilt that he ordered the sentence to be put in execution. His Lordship, however, humanely sent his marshal to attend the prisoners, with a discretionary power to respite the execution should any circumstances appear to him, respecting Heald, that would justify the measure."* The marshal was convinced that Terry was not speaking the truth, so they were both left to their fate.

I sat in the Crown Court at Lancaster. I found myself wondering whether it was in that Court, or in the adjacent Civil Court, that Boswell moved for his writ *Quare adhaesit pavimento*. I went in to inspect the Civil Court, which is as fine, or even finer, than the Crown Court. It is adorned with a most interesting collection of heraldic achievements and "javelins". One rarely sees javelins and javelin men (the High Sheriff's bodyguard in his livery carrying ornamental halberds) nowadays. The crest of each Sheriff was worked into the metal head of the halberd, or "javelin". And a great collection of them is ranged all round the circular space facing the bench in this Court. I do not know whether they have been collected from country-houses, or whether it was the practice for each Sheriff to deposit one at the end of his year of office. If they came there by a deliberate collection I wish that the same thing might be done in other counties. I have fairly often seen a Sheriff's javelins in an old country house, e.g. a whole row in a rack at Denham Place, a few miles from my home in Buckinghamshire, when it was the home of the Ways. I do

* Medland and Weobley, *Remarkable Trials* (1808), Vol. I, p. 11.

not know what became of the javelins when the place was sold. But one of them might have started the collection I should like to form at Aylesbury.

Yet another piece of good fortune on this, my first, circuit was that at Liverpool I was joined by Mr Justice Avory. After Carlisle and Lancaster I had got over my trepidation about trying prisoners. He tried them at Liverpool. But if I had still any concern when I resumed the task at Manchester I might have had the help of the most experienced judge of crime there ever was, and of the kindest of friends. It was a particularly good piece of fortune for another reason. Judges choose their circuits at the beginning of term for the term following. And they choose in order of seniority. The Northern Circuit, with its long periods at Liverpool and Manchester, is the least desirable there is. So it is rare for a senior judge, as Mr Justice Avory then was, ever to be seen upon it. Indeed the usual rule is that the two junior judges find themselves sent to Liverpool and Manchester, and they continue to go there until by the appointment of two new judges they cease to be the juniors. I believe that it was from his strong sense of duty that on this occasion Mr Justice Avory chose to go to Liverpool and Manchester, when he might have taken a lighter and pleasanter task, e.g. to go to Cambridge, Norwich, Bury St Edmunds and Chelmsford. I am afraid I was never so moved. And as I ceased to be the junior judge in three months after my appointment, I have only been to Liverpool and Manchester once again, in October 1925, and once, in April 1930, on the additional Spring Assize that takes place only at Liverpool and Manchester, and at Leeds.

Though the first or second South-Eastern is now the most desired circuit, there was apparently a time when, as the Home Circuit, it was the least popular, as the Northern is now. In his *Life* of Chief Justice Richardson, Campbell* tells how in 1634, when on the Western Circuit, he made some remarks on wakes and church ales in a charge to a Grand Jury. This affronted Laud, as an interference with ecclesiastical affairs, and he brought it before the Privy Council. In consequence Richardson was "put from riding the Western, and forced to go the Essex circuit, reputed the meanest of all others, which no justice but the puisne justice or serjeant used to ride". The "Essex Circuit" means the old Home Circuit.

* *Lives of the Chief Justices* (1874), Vol. II, p. 19.

I never completed the whole of the Northern Circuit by going to Appleby. And when I left the King's Bench in 1937 the Courts at Appleby, Bury St Edmunds, and Oakham were the only three Assize Courts in England and Wales in which I had not sat. I regret that very much, for I know all three towns as charming places to visit, and the Courts I have inspected. That at Oakham is perhaps the most interesting one in the whole Island.

At one time it was the custom for a judge to choose a particular circuit and always go upon it. Lord Campbell says that Chief Justice Dyer (Judge 1559–1582) "always, according to the fashion of the time, *rode* the same circuit, and he chose the Midland" (*Lives of the Chief Justices*, Vol. I, p. 225). And he says that Sir Peter King, when appointed Chief Justice of the Common Pleas in 1714, "broke through the old custom for a judge to continue to ride the same circuit, for he visited all the circuits in turn" (*Lives of the Chancellors*, Vol. VI, p. 86). I doubt if it can have been a very old custom in 1714. In the *Diary** of Mr Justice Rokeby (Judge of the Common Pleas 1689, and of the King's Bench 1695–1699) he records that between 1689 and 1697 he went 6 times on the Western circuit, 5 on the Oxford, 3 on the Norfolk, 2 on the Home, and 1 on the Midland. I am very glad that the old custom was abandoned. It would be intolerably monotonous to go always on the same circuit.

An Assize at Appleby in the old days had one curious feature. King John granted the Shrievalty of Westmorland to Robert de Veteripont as an hereditary office, and it descended to his heirs. Once it came to an heiress. "The famous Countess of Pembroke, being hereditary Sheriff of Westmoreland, attended the Judges in that capacity at the Assizes."† By the seventeenth century the office was inherited by the Tuftons, Earls of Thanet. And they usually entertained the Judges at Appleby Castle. Roger North, in his *Life* of his brother, Lord Keeper Guildford, says of him when on the Northern Circuit as Chief Justice of the Common Pleas: "The Earl of Thanet is the hereditary Sheriff of that county [Westmorland]; the only one of that Quality in England, and had ordered a sumptuous Entertainment to be given by one Mr Gambetes, his Steward, to the Judges."‡ But Baron

* *The Diary of Mr Justice Rokeby* (1688–1697) (Privately printed, 1887).

† Campbell, *Lives of the Chief Justices*, Vol. III, p. 63.

‡ *Life of Francis North, Lord Keeper of the Great Seal* (1742), p. 141.

Alderson records* a strange incident in the spring of 1825. "At Appleby, the hereditary High Sheriff, Lord Thanet, in his own absence, had omitted to appoint a deputy, and no Grand Jury being able consequently to be summoned, business was brought to a standstill. The Court was adjourned from day to day"—and the Judge roamed the hills. "No appointment arriving from Lord Thanet, though anxiously expected, instead of going into Court, he continued his rambles." Apparently the Assize eventually had to be abandoned. What happened to the prisoners, or what happened to Lord Thanet, is not stated.

In 1850 the last Earl of Thanet died. By his will he bequeathed the Shrievalty to Mr Tufton, who was his illegitimate son. Thereupon there was passed the Act 13 & 14 Vict. cap. 30. This recites the grant of the office by King John to Robert de Veteripont and his heirs, that it had descended to Henry, Earl of Thanet, lately deceased, and that he had purported to bequeath it to Mr Tufton. It cancels the grant, and puts Westmorland in the same position as other counties. I believe "Mr Tufton" was consoled with a baronetcy.†

I think this is the only example of a hereditary Shrievalty in an English county. But when the Bishop of Durham was in his full power, and the Assizes at Durham were held under his Commission, the office of Sheriff of his County Palatine was hereditary in successive Sir Hedworth Williamsons.

Baron Alderson, who was on the Northern Circuit when at the bar, records one curious thing about Lancaster. "At Lancaster [in 1827] Bayley J. after hearing me lead these two causes, offered to call me within the bar, or in other words to make me a King's Counsel at Lancaster, a privilege which the Judges possess at this place. I have declined the honour for the present circuit, but I mean to accept it next time, if offered, and so I told him."‡

And one more quotation from the same book may be given. "In the spring of 1834 he went the Northern Circuit with Mr Justice Taunton. The following description of their entry into Lancaster seems

* *Selections from the Charges of Baron Alderson with an Introductory Notice of his Life*, by Charles Alderson (1858), p. 35.

† Cf. *Life of Lord Campbell* (2nd ed. 1881), Vol. II, p. 310.

‡ *Selections from the Charges of Baron Alderson etc.* (1858), p. 38. The same offer had been made by Mr Justice Bayley to Brougham in 1823. See Atlay, *Victorian Chancellors*, Vol. I, p. 267 *note*.

almost...to belong to a past age.— We had a most imposing procession to-day. The Sheriff met us on horseback himself, with a *cortège* of eighty persons, all mounted on grey horses. We were placed in a coach drawn by six greys, and seven outriders on greys also, and followed by a second carriage behind; in this way we entered the town.'"*

Mr Justice Avory and I had no such splendours. But if Baron Alderson, with a prophetic eye, had seen us ninety years later in Lord Leverhulme's colossal red Daimler he would surely have been astonished.

At Liverpool the Lodgings are in the big house in Newsham Park, once the mansion to which that park belonged. The servants preserved a tradition that Queen Victoria, when on a visit to the house, slept in one of the very Victorian beds. Whether Mr Justice Avory or I used it I forget. The distance from St George's Hall made it necessary for us to have luncheon taken down there every day, instead of returning to the Lodgings as in most places. But that was a small disadvantage compared with the benefit of spending the night in complete quiet and in comparatively rural surroundings.

At the end of the day I usually left my colleague to drive back alone, while I had a walk in the town and then back to Newsham Park. The walk in the town nearly always took me down to the Landing Stage. For I never tired of the scene provided by the arrival of the great ferry boats, the dexterity with which they were manœuvred, and their constant departure packed with vehicles and human beings. I wonder if the scene is as animated now that the Mersey Tunnel exists?

On the walk back to Newsham Park I found, to the south-east of it, a region of streets of small Victorian houses. The builder was apparently inspired by the nearness of Newsham House to call his streets after judges. And so there are Coleridge, Grantham, Ridley, Hawkins, Hannen, Bigham, and Channell Streets. I think the most depressing of all was Hawkins Street.

In Grantham's *Notes* there is a memorandum, dated 5 March 1906, by the Under-Sheriff of Lancashire. "Before 1835 Lancaster was the only Assize Town. Liverpool was added in 1835, and Manchester in 1864. When Lancaster was the only Assize town the Assizes lasted

* *Selections from the Charges of Baron Alderson etc.* (1858), p. 63.

for a considerable time. . . . No records can be found in the Sheriff's office which throw any light upon what the custom was with regard to the reception of the Judges when they travelled by road. Tradition has it that the judges were met by the High Sheriff about a mile from Lancaster. Whether or not the Sheriff was always on horseback on these occasions seems obscure, but at any rate occasionally he was, and he rode in front of the Judge's carriage, preceded by his Javelin men and a company of gentlemen of the county in their carriages. The Javelin men in the old days were generally tenants, or sons of tenants, of the Sheriff, and probably must have been mounted, if only as a means of locomotion. At any rate as late as the end of the forties on two occasions they rode in the Sheriff's procession from his residence to the neighbouring town when he was going thence by train to Lancaster to meet the Judges. But the Judges at that time came by train and were met at the station, the Javelin men being on foot, as they are now. Trumpeters and Javelin men are still employed in Lancashire, but the latter are no longer tenants but ex-soldiers or ex-policemen. They wear the Sheriff's livery colours. The Sheriff's Officers, or bound bailiffs, used to attend the Assizes dressed in red coats, but now they send one of their men instead. . . . With respect to the Grand Jury it has always been the custom in Lancashire for the Sheriff to invite gentlemen to attend, and, upon 23 accepting, to place them upon the Grand Jury panel. It is the practice, I believe, in other counties to summon a large number of magistrates and other gentlemen to attend, and to impanel the first 23 who answer. On the first evening of each Assize at Liverpool and Manchester the Sheriff entertains the Grand Jury at dinner, and at Lancaster he entertains them at luncheon."

By 1924, when I first went to Lancashire, the javelin men had disappeared. I suppose a very opulent Sheriff may occasionally revive them, as I have known happen elsewhere. The dinners and luncheons to the Grand Juries were still continuing. As in the course of his year of office this meant eight dinners, and three luncheons, with a minimum of twenty-five people at each of them, it is easy to understand that the Shrievalty of Lancashire is the most burdensome, financially, in the whole country. Though Grand Juries were abolished in 1933, I believe these entertainments to the class of gentlemen who used to constitute them continue.

At Manchester the Lodgings are equally far away from the Courts, in a big house at Upper Broughton. The neighbourhood is rather depressing. Kersal Moor, which is near by, is an open space on which one can walk after breakfast: but the melancholy which Lant Street shed upon the soul can be as nothing compared with that induced by Kersal Moor.

The Courts at Manchester were built by Alfred Waterhouse, R.A. He laid an even heavier hand on Manchester than he did upon Balliol, Caius, and Eaton Hall. Attached to the Courts is a house which was designed to be, and for a time was, the Judge's Lodgings. We went into that dreadful erection every day for lunch. There came a time when Mr Justice Kennedy, an old Northern Circuit man, said he could not endure life in that house. So he stayed on in the house at Newsham Park, and came over by train from Liverpool to Manchester every day. Whether he designed it I do not know; but this was the best possible method to deliver his brethren from the curse of the Waterhouse Lodgings. The rivalry, not to say jealousy, between Manchester and Liverpool is of long standing. And Manchester could not have its Judges of Assize preferring to live in Liverpool. So the house at Upper Broughton was purchased, and the Judges have only to endure the horrors of Waterhouse Gothic at luncheon.

Assizes at Liverpool and Manchester, with the multiplication of motor cases, and of divorce suits, tend nowadays to be unbearably lengthy. We were perhaps more fortunate in that we were only a fortnight at Liverpool, and nineteen days at Manchester, with a week in London in between. On Sunday, 7 December, I got home by a train that conveniently took me direct to High Wycombe.

1925

In January 1925, by what I thought a stroke of good luck, I went on the South Wales Circuit. English Judges of the High Court had only been going on circuit in Wales for ninety-five years. I don't know how justice was administered in Wales before 1542, or whether it was administered at all. The Act of Union of 1536 (27 Hen. VIII) made five new Welsh counties—Denbigh, Montgomery, Radnor, Brecon, and Monmouth. In 1542 the Act 34 & 35 Hen. VIII provided that Courts of Justice called "The King's Great Sessions in Wales" should sit twice a year in each Welsh county except Monmouth; whereby Monmouth was returned to England.

The Act appoints four circuits, two for North Wales, and two for South Wales, with three counties in each. There were two judges for Montgomery, Flint, and Denbigh (to which Chester was afterwards added), two for Anglesey, Carnarvon and Merioneth, two for Brecon, Glamorgan, and Radnor, and two for Cardigan, Pembroke, and Carmarthen. To these posts members of the bar were appointed, who could continue practice at the bar when they were not on duty in Wales. And they were also allowed to appoint deputies, if their other engagements made a visit to Wales inconvenient. It was common for leading barristers to hold these appointments, and a good many Law Officers have been Chief Justices of Chester. This went on until 1830. In that year the Great Sessions for Wales were abolished, and the North and South Wales Circuits were created. Since then one Judge of the King's Bench has gone to the North Wales counties, and one to those in South Wales (excluding, in modern times, Glamorgan). They meet at Chester, for the Assize there, and then go on together to Cardiff or Swansea for the Assize of Glamorgan.

The Judges of the Great Sessions in Wales were often people of inferior capacity, and the Courts were not held in much estimation. Atlay, *Victorian Chancellors* (Vol. II, p. 141), says that "till 1830 all the more important Welsh cases, civil and criminal alike, were tried at Hereford and Shrewsbury". An example is the charge of seditious libel against Shipley, Dean of St Asaph, in 1783. It stood for hearing at Wrexham in November 1783 before Kenyon and Daines Barrington, was adjourned till 1784, and then by *certiorari* was removed from the Great Sessions to the King's Bench. It was tried before Mr Justice Buller at the Summer Assizes at Shrewsbury in 1784, when Erskine made a very notable defence.

Both the North and South Wales Circuits are very pleasant, especially in the summer, for the surroundings and the scenery. There are two drawbacks. The Lodgings in some of the smaller places are very bad. And a judge with any energy is uncomfortably conscious of the deplorable waste of his time. When in 1830 the Welsh counties were added to the English system the tradition of the independence and separation of English counties was applied, even though many of the Welsh counties were merely the artificial creations of 1536, and most of them were exceedingly small. So it was arranged that a judge should go to an Assize town in every county, e.g. to Ruthin and Mold, which are only eight miles apart. Difficulties of locomotion in 1830 may possibly have justified the multiplication of twelve Assize towns in North and South Wales. But the time has long passed when these counties should be grouped together. Power was created by an Act of 1876 to issue an Order in Council grouping counties together for the Autumn Assize. That is a modern addition to the two ancient Assizes in the spring and summer. Under this an Order has long been in existence under which in October a single judge goes only to Carnarvon, Ruthin, Chester, Carmarthen and Brecon, and is joined by a second judge at Cardiff or Swansea. But at the other two Assizes the old waste of judicial power and judicial time, by going to these many places with very little work at any of them, continues—as I think, scandalously. In the *Life* of Baron Alderson, from which I have already quoted, it is recorded* that in 1856 he wrote a memorandum as to his proposals for reforming the Circuit System. *Inter alia* he says: "The following seem to me to be capable of being discontinued, or united with others, without inconvenience:—Appleby, Huntingdon, Rutland, Monmouth, and at least six counties of Wales." As I write, that was said eighty-three years ago. But twice a year still judges waste their time by going to those six counties! That Baron Alderson was

* *Selections from the Charges of Baron Alderson etc.* (1858), p. 155.

right may I think be shown by some of the experiences I shall have to record.

Haverfordwest, where I started, is a strange contrast to Liverpool and Manchester in every way. The Lodgings were in the meanest and most uncomfortable house I have ever been in. There was no bathroom. And there was no sort of illumination except gas from brackets on the walls with the old-fashioned burners that I remember as in use about 1880. I could not help saying to the Under-Sheriff that if the County of Pembroke desired to retain the dignity of an Assize town it ought to provide His Majesty's Judge of Assize with the elementary decencies of life. To which he replied: "Why, my Lord, this is the town house of the Philippses of Picton Castle!" So it may have been once. But I cannot believe they can have lived in it since the eighteenth century.

Haverfordwest is dignified in a way that many great cities are not. For by sect. 124 of the Act of 1542 it is provided that the town shall be a county in itself.* So when the Commission was read in Court I might have found myself faced by two Grand Juries, one for the County of Pembroke, and one for the town. But there were no prisoners from the town, and therefore no Grand Jury. So I received a pair of white gloves from the town. The same thing happened shortly afterwards at Carmarthen, which is also, by favour of Henry VIII, a county borough.

Haverfordwest and Carmarthen thus share a dignity which, among ancient Assize towns, is only enjoyed by Bristol, Exeter, Lincoln, Newcastle-on-Tyne, Norwich, Nottingham, Worcester, and York. Chester and Gloucester are also Counties of Cities, but they do not, like the others, have a separate Commission of Assize. The County of Haverfordwest, which had a population of 6113 in 1931, enjoys a distinction which none of these cities does. For it has a Lord Lieutenant! Finally, Haverfordwest enjoys the distinction of having Borough Quarter Sessions with no Recorder to preside thereat. The only place in the same position was the borough of St Albans until 1874.

There were only three prisoners from the county, of whom two pleaded guilty: and there were no civil cases. So the whole business finished on the first day, and I had a holiday on the morrow. This gave

* By sect. 111 of that Act Haverfordwest was given a Member of Parliament, and kept the privilege until 1832.

me the chance I had long desired, of seeing St David's Cathedral. And that surpassed even the high expectations I had formed from what I had read and heard. In one respect it is perhaps unique. The whole floor of choir and nave is on a steady incline; not, as is common, a series of levels with steps between, but a continuous gradient, so that if you put a ball down at the high altar it might roll to the western door.

At Lampeter the Lodgings were a comfortable little country house outside the town. As there were no prisoners, I had another pair of white gloves. There was one civil case, which was over in a few hours. I went to dine with the dons at St David's College, which was very much like dining at the high table at a small Oxford college.

Down to 1889 the Assizes for this county were always held at Cardigan, but in that year they were transferred to Lampeter as being more convenient of access. In the *Life* of Baron Alderson (p. 56) it is recorded that when he was at Cardigan in the summer of 1832, the defendant, in an action set down for trial there, sent him a statement of his case with a £10 note enclosed.

At Carmarthen there were five prisoners from the county, and none from the town, and one simple civil case. Four of the prisoners pleaded guilty. So the whole business only took two short days. But there was another civil case down for hearing that was a heavy one: it was settled on the second day. If all the five prisoners had had to be tried, and both civil cases heard, the five working days I had been advised to allot to Carmarthen would have been barely enough. As it was, I had three days' holiday. This illustrates the difficulty of arranging the Circuit System for a succession of small country towns in North or South Wales.

At Brecon the Lodgings were in a bad and uncomfortable house in the town, but nothing like so bad as the dreadful house at Haverfordwest. There were only two prisoners, both of whom pleaded guilty, and one short civil case. My resulting day off I employed in walking up the Brecon Beacon, and seeing the admirable Priory church.

Next day was a Saturday, and we were due to go to Presteign. But at Presteign there was no business at all, either criminal or civil, and I cancelled the Assize. As I was due at Chester on the Tuesday, it was no use trying to go back to town. So from Saturday to Monday we went to stay with a particularly charming High Sheriff at a beautiful house on the Wye, and on the Monday went for one night to Presteign.

Presteign is a village in size. There is probably not a house in it that could be hired for the Judges' Lodgings. So there is an official house, as in a big English city. And it is next door to the Court, or rather part of the same building, so that you can walk into the Court from it, as you can at Aylesbury, Stafford, Northampton, Derby, and Warwick. The house is fairly comfortable, but rather grim, and made the more so by being adorned with rows of lithographed portraits of past Sheriffs. The Court is a curious little place, with the woodwork grained and varnished, and with sawdust spread upon the floor.

At the end of a branch line, and at one corner of its minute county—you can step into England in a few yards—Presteign is an absurd place for an Assize town. It once shared the dignity with New Radnor. For sect. 118 of the Act of 1542 enacts that the County or Shire Court of the County of Radnor is henceforth to be one time at New Radnor and the next at "Preston", and so on, "and never from henceforth be kept or holden at Rather Gowey". Rather Gowey is now called Rhayader.

The thing that I found most interesting in Presteign was a grave in the churchyard. The head-stone reads thus:

> To the memory of Mary Morgan, who young and beautiful, endowed with a good understanding and disposition, but unenlightened by the Sacred truths of Christianity, became the victim of sin and shame and was condemned to an ignominious death, on the 11th of April 1805, for the murder of her bastard Child.
>
> Rous'd to a first sense of guilt and remorse by the eloquent and humane exertions of her benevolent Judge, Mr Justice Hardinge, she underwent the Sentence of the Law on the following Thursday with unfeigned repentance and a fervent hope of forgiveness through the merits of a redeeming Intercessor.
>
> This Stone is erected not merely to perpetuate the remembrance of a departed penitent, but to remind the living of the frailty of human nature when unsupported by Religion.
>
> Thomas Brudenell Bruce, Earl of AILESBURY

And on a small stone at the foot is this inscription, which I fancy was not written by the unctuous pen of the noble Earl.

> To the memory of
> MARY MORGAN
> who suffered April 18th 1805
> Aged 17 years.
>
> *He that is without sin among you, let him first cast a stone at her.*
> The 8th Chapter of John, part of ye 7th verse.

The story told by these stones is tragic enough: but the additions of local tradition make it more tragic still. For they tell you that the man who seduced the poor girl was upon the Grand Jury that found a true bill for murder against her. And that the junior of the circuit, who defended her, rode off to London with desperate haste to try to get a reprieve before the day fixed by the "benevolent Judge" (as was then the practice) for her execution. He had only a week. He got the reprieve, and rode feverishly back to Presteign. He arrived on the fatal day, but an hour too late. She had suffered the ignominious death—at the age of 17.

If these events had happened at Dorchester in 1805, might not Thomas Hardy have made a story out of them?

There is another memorial rather like this. It is far away in Suffolk, in the graveyard between the two great churches at Bury St Edmunds.

> Reader
> Pause at this humble stone;
> it Records
> The Fall of unguarded Youth
> By the allurements of Vice
> and the treacherous snares
> of Seduction.
> SARAH LLOYD
> on the 23rd of April 1800
> in the 22nd year of her Age
> suffered a just but ignominious
> Death
> for admitting her abandon'd Seducer
> at the Dwelling house of
> her Mistress
> in the night of 3rd Octr
> 1799
> and being the Instrument
> in his hands of the Crime
> of Robbery and House-burning.
> These were her last Words
> May my example be a
> Warning to Thousands.

The "benevolent Judge" of Mary Morgan was George Hardinge (1744–1816), called to the bar at the Middle Temple, 1769, Senior Justice of Brecon, Glamorgan, and Radnor, 1787–1816. When he was in the House of Commons, during the dispute with the American colonies, he produced with all solemnity the fatuous argument that they were not being taxed without representation. "For all the grants of land in America were to be held of the Manor of Greenwich in the County of Kent, and therefore the Knights of the Shire for the County of Kent represented all the Americans."* Clearly he was an ass: and equally clearly he was not a benevolent judge. For he had the power himself to reprieve her, and recommend her to the Royal Mercy. He has the full responsibility of having "left her for execution" a week after her conviction.

By an odd chance I came across Hardinge's own epitaph, which is in the church at Kingston-on-Thames, on a joint memorial to his parents and himself. It is a fine example of the fulsome. "Their eldest son, George Hardinge was born in 1744, also educated at Eton,

* *Life of Lord Campbell* (1881), Vol. 1, p. 16.

and an Excellent Scholar. He was successively Solicitor-General and Attorney-General to the Queen, a Member of the House of Commons, and Chief Justice of Brecknock, Radnor, and Glamorgan. His Eloquence at the Bar, and in the Senate, was Conspicuous, and in the Seat of Judgment it was Dignified. He was Active, Zealous, Persevering and Benevolent, and by his Incessant Exertions a Powerful Friend. Adorned with Attic Wit, Various in Accomplishment, Cheerful, Animated, Radiant, Singularly Gifted to Charm by his Conversation and Correspondence, He is Deeply Deplored. He died in 1816 in the 72nd Year of his Age, and he is Buried in this Chancel Near to his Friends."

I do not know how the Earl of Ailesbury came to be concerned to point the moral of poor Mary Morgan's fate at Presteign. But he had a foible for epigraphy. For it was he who, at an earlier date, erected the column in Savernake Forest. On the two faces of it he records his gratitude—to his uncle for leaving him the estate, to George III "who unsolicited conferred upon him the honour of an Earldom", and to Providence for restoring "that excellent and beloved Sovereign" to sanity.

When I arrived at Chester I had sat in Court, in these small places in South Wales, 21 hours in all. A judge who was in London during the same period would have sat in Court 75 hours, i.e. 15 days of 5 hours each. I had therefore lost 54 hours of working time by days of enforced idleness or in travelling. And yet I had fixed the various Commission Days on the best advice I could get as to the time needed. If, indeed, all the prisoners had pleaded "Not Guilty", and none of the civil cases had been settled, I should probably not have had nearly time enough. As I have said before, I agree with the view of Baron Alderson, expressed eighty-three years ago, that at least half of the Welsh Assizes should be suppressed, and the counties grouped together. There is the more reason than in his day for two reasons. Means of communication have become immensely improved. And the local prisons have been nearly everywhere abolished. Sect. 71 of the Act of 1542 provided that each Sheriff should have a gaol for prisoners of his Shire town. But there was no gaol to be "delivered" in any of the five little towns I had been in. And before I went there I was asked to approve of the Court not sitting at Lampeter before noon, on the ground that the prisoners, if there were any, would have to be brought from Swansea Gaol, and there was no train by which they could conveniently arrive before that hour.

The way in which the grouping of counties should be effected may be a matter for argument. After a good many years of experience of both the present circuits, and taking into account the modern means of communication, I think my suggestion would be as follows. All the work from Flint should be transacted at Chester, and that from Montgomery at Shrewsbury. Cardiff should remain the Assize town for Glamorgan, and also (for another reason) for Monmouth. For the rest of Wales I would have four Assize towns, viz. Aberystwyth for Merioneth and Cardigan, Carmarthen for Pembroke and Carmarthen, Llandrindod Wells for Brecon and Radnor, and Bangor for Anglesey, Carnarvon and Denbigh. This means five Assize towns, instead of twelve as at present. Of course there would be furious opposition to such a proposal from vested interests, and sentimental enthusiasms. But my concern is for efficiency and economy.

At Chester I joined Mr Justice Talbot, who had been round the North Wales Circuit. This was the first of many occasions on which I had as companion that charming man, and very great judge. He was my immediate senior in the list of judges, and when, at our choice of circuits, he named his, I used, with his encouragement, to choose the same, if the second place was available. He was always my good friend. I believe he thought I was not sufficiently enthusiastic in my admiration for Winchester College—the great passion of his life—but he even forgave me that. With a taste for epigram one might be tempted to say that he is the best judge whose name is known to the fewest readers of the *Daily Mail*. On that, or on any other test, Talbot was the best judge I have known.

If any man was ever qualified by heredity to be a lawyer and a judge, it was he. Towards the close of his year of office as Treasurer of the Inner Temple I moved a resolution at a parliament, as we call the business meeting of the Benchers. Of course I consulted him about it beforehand, and such was his modesty that I had some ado to persuade him to let me move it. It was carried unanimously, and as result there hangs in the Parliament Chamber a framed scroll of parchment, beautifully inscribed by Mr Grailey Hewitt. It reads thus: "Be it remembered that the Honourable Sir George Talbot, a Judge of the King's Bench Division of the High Court of Justice, was Treasurer of the Inner Temple for the year 1936. He was the eldest son of the Right Honourable John Gilbert Talbot, by his wife, the Honourable Meriel Sarah, eldest daughter of George, Lord Lyttelton. Sir George Talbot was therefore, on his father's side, sixth in descent from Charles, Lord Talbot, Lord High Chancellor from 1733 to 1737, and Treasurer of the Inner Temple in 1727. On his mother's side, he was thirteenth in descent from Sir Thomas Littleton, Judge of the Common Pleas in 1466, and of the King's Bench in 1475, the renowned author of the Treatise on Tenures, and the first known Reader of the Inner Temple. He was also, on his mother's side, ninth in descent from Sir Thomas Bromley, Lord High Chancellor from 1579 to 1587, and Treasurer of the Inner Temple in 1574." Is there any other country in the world, with such a continuity of history and of institutions as makes such a record possible?

The Courts at Chester are in the Castle, which is also the headquarters of the garrison. On the opening day of the Assize an officer salutes the Senior Judge at the gate of the Castle and hands him a written "state" of the garrison. A similar ceremony takes place at Exeter, but with a difference. There on the first morning the officer calls on the Judges before they leave the Lodgings, presents the "state", and asks permission for the troops to be let out of barracks. This dates from a time long ago when some soldiers indulged in a riot during the Assizes. In consequence the troops are always supposed to be confined to barracks unless the Judge gives his dispensation.

I find some earlier examples of the bandying of civilities between the Bench and the Army in Mr Justice Rokeby's *Diary*.* "Gloucester, July 1696. There were severall companys of foot soldiers quarter'd in Glocester, which was kept in ye nature of a garrison, and every night ye military officers brought us ye word in ye evening, which was supposed to be a respect to us, as comeing with ye King's Commission." At Monmouth, five days later, "Part of y^e^ [same] regiment was quarter'd in this Town, & Capt. Pointz, ye Cheife Commander here came to me to receive ye Word. I told him I did suppose we were to receive the word from them, but he told me in regard we represented ye King's person, he was to receive the word from us, and accordingly I gave him ye word: King William."

The Lodgings at Chester were an inadequate villa outside the

* *The Diary of Mr Justice Rokeby* (1688–1697) (Privately printed, 1887), p. 47.

town. There was only one small sitting-room, with one writing table, for the two judges and their two marshals. And this was divided by folding doors from a small room used by our clerks, whose conversation was constantly audible through the partition.

When we went on to Cardiff we had plenty of room. For we were lodged in the enormous Mansion House. The Lord Mayor of Cardiff uses this for receptions and other civic functions, except when the Judges are there, but does not live there all his time. I think the only "Mansion Houses" in which a Mayor resides continuously during his year of office are in London, at York, and at Doncaster. But the last-named is not an Assize town.

The Mansion House at Cardiff was large and comfortable, though certainly not beautiful. It had at least one billiard-table, on which I tried to play: and I should not be surprised to hear that it had two.

The modern Courts at Cardiff are very fine. Indeed I think they are the best in the whole kingdom. And Cardiff can pride itself on having as magnificent a set of public buildings, in as spacious a site, as any English city. There is, of course, no single building to compete with St George's Hall at Liverpool. But the range of fine buildings, in a wide avenue with lawns and trees, is admirable, and will be better still when the whole scheme is completed.

✧ ✧ ✧

In the old days there were two circuits a year, in Hilary term and in Trinity term. In Victorian times a third, in Michaelmas term—at most places for the trial of prisoners only—was added. Still more recently an extra fourth Assize, in Easter term, was created for Liverpool and Manchester, and for Leeds, alone. In May 1925 I went on this circuit, for a fortnight, to Leeds. But as I went to Leeds again in July, as part of the regular North-Eastern Circuit, anything I find to remember about Leeds may be left till then, or later.

✧ ✧ ✧

In July 1925 I went with Lord Finlay on the "North-Eastern Circuit", i.e. Newcastle, Durham, York and Leeds. That is a modern name, and a modern thing. It only dates from 1876. Before that there was only the "Northern Circuit", upon which the Assize towns originally were York, Durham, Newcastle, Carlisle, Appleby, and Lancaster. Anciently Lancaster was the only Assize town in Lancashire. In 1835 Liverpool was added. In 1864 York was transferred to the Midland

Circuit, and a third Assize started in Lancashire at Manchester. There was another peculiarity about the old "Northern Circuit". As I have said, there used to be two regular circuits in a year, in Hilary term and in Trinity term—winter and summer. But on the Northern Circuit it was only in the summer that the two judges went to all the above six towns. In Hilary term they went only to York and Lancaster. In the four northernmost counties there was therefore only one Assize in the year. And as a committed prisoner was very rarely allowed bail, a man eventually acquitted might well languish for 10 or 11 months in gaol. A gaol in the winter in Durham, Newcastle, Carlisle or Appleby must have been an uncomfortable place. The worst was probably that at Durham, which belonged to the Bishop.

Sir Samuel Romilly in his diary,* on 24 October 1807, being in Durham as Chancellor of the Palatine Court of Chancery, says he assisted the magistrates on a question whether a man should be allowed bail. "I thought... that the prisoner would, if the facts should appear to be the same on his trial, be entitled to his acquittal, and that he ought to be bailed; which was accordingly done. If bail had not been accepted for this man, he must have remained in gaol for ten months; as the next assizes at Durham, where they are held only once a year, will not be till late in August. After having suffered an imprisonment of eleven months (for he has been above a month in prison already) it would have been declared by the verdict of the jury that he was not deserving of any punishment." A foot-note adds, "At the ensuing assizes in 1808 this man was acquitted".

The reason, or the excuse, for this treatment of the four northern counties was the difficulty of travelling, and its dangers, especially in the passage from Newcastle to Carlisle. Macaulay, in his famous chapter on the state of England in 1685, says: "No traveller ventured into that [border] country without making his will. The Judges on circuit, with the whole body of barristers, attorneys, clerks, and serving men, rode on horseback from Newcastle to Carlisle, armed and escorted by a strong guard under the command of the Sheriffs. It was necessary to carry provisions; for the country was a wilderness which afforded no supplies. The spot where the cavalcade halted to dine, under an immense oak, is not yet forgotten. The irregular vigour with which criminal justice was administered shocked observers whose

* *Life of Sir Samuel Romilly* (3rd ed. 1842), Vol. II, p. 79.

lives had been passed in more tranquil districts. Juries, animated by hatred and by a sense of common danger, convicted housebreakers and cattle stealers with the promptitude of a court-martial in a mutiny; and the convicts were hurried by scores to the gallows."

Roger North, in his *Life* of his brother, later Lord Keeper and then Chief Justice of the Common Pleas, says: "He took the opportunity one Summer [about 1680] to turn by the North, which begins at York and concludes at Lancaster; but in the Winter it is usual to omit the Counties of Durham, Northumberland, Cumberland, and Westmoreland....From Newcastle his Lordship's Rout lay to Carlisle. The *Northumberland* Sheriff gave us all Arms, that is a Dagger, Knife, Penknife, and Fork, all together. And because the hideous Road along by the *Tyne*, for the many and sharp Turnings, and perpetual Precipices, was for a Coach not sustained by main force impassable, his Lordship was forced to take Horse and to ride most part of the way to Hexham."*

A writer in 1705 says: "Alanson's Banck was the last place we were to be in Scotland; its only remarkable for the Custom house, and a Change built longwayes, like an Almshouse. Hither the Judges of the Northern Circuit generally resort, that they may say they have been in Scotland."†

James Boswell, writing at Carlisle, 21 August 1778, describes the arrival of the Judges from Newcastle. "It is the custom for the High Sherif to ride to ——, seven miles from the town, to meet the judges: and he is accompanied by as many Gentlemen as chuse to attend him. Formerly, and till within these few years, He used to go to the extremity of the County. The Sherif has as many servants of his own as he chuses to bring, and his friends send every one a servant. These used formerly to be drest in the Sherif's own livery, so that there were new liveries every year, which was a great expense. But now one livery serves year after year till the clothes are worn out. The livery on this occasion was brown faced with red. Each servant carries a long pole with a Javelin of gilt at the end of it, and a bunch of red fringe round the pole where the javelin joins it, and they are called Javelinmen. This Sherif was not a popular man, so was but poorly attended.

* *Life of Francis North, Lord Keeper of the Great Seal* (1742), pp. 134, 139.

† *A Journey to Edenborough in Scotland*, by Joseph Taylor, of the Inner Temple (Edinburgh, 1903), p. 153.

He had not twenty Javelin men, and few Gentlemen. An old gentleman of the county, Mr Appleby Dacre, told us that when he was Sherif he was attended by 250 Javelin men, whose liveries cost £3 apiece, so that the cost of that alone was seven hundred.... I was determined to see everything, since I had come to see an English Assize for the first time. So I mounted a hack and rode out with the Sherif.... At the little publick *hut* (for I cannot call it *house*) where we waited, there was wine for any body who chose to take it. In a little the Judges arrived in a post-chaise and four, upon which the Sherif with his white rod approached the carriage, the other Gentlemen following, and all paid their compliments to the Judges; and then the Sherif conducted them to his Coach and four, which had followed the riders empty, together with two or three chaises with Gentlemen in them. The Sherif sat backwards, and the Judges fronted him. The Judges were Willes* and Hotham.† Willes... was all bustle, and talk, and laugh, and by no means answered the notion I had formed of an English Judge. Hotham was a decent, grave, polite, young man. Willes, in the hearing of all around, begged the Sherif to order his servants to drive as fast as they could. There was a levity in this. The Sherif gratified him and kept us at a hard canter, I may say a gallop, till we were within a quarter of a mile of the town. The Sherif told me Willes said 'I dont love to go jigmagowe', and several times repeated his request to be driven fast.... I should have mentioned that the Under-Sheriff went forward to where the Judges dine, and comes up with them. Willes stopped the Coach a little from the town, and made it drive more composedly."‡

To drive nowadays from Newcastle to Carlisle, by the great Roman road alongside the Wall, would be easy and pleasant enough. But the growth of population made the old Northern Circuit an impossible thing, and the new North-Eastern Circuit, covering Northumberland, Durham, and Yorkshire, had to be created. The more natural way is to start at Newcastle, and work southwards. But in June, when Lord Finlay and I left London, it was the Newcastle race week. Newcastle could not stand the combined strain of the Races and an Assize: even the prisoners on bail would to a man—or woman—refuse to surrender. So we began at Durham, and went on to Newcastle, York, and Leeds.

* Sir John Willes (1685–1761), Chief Justice of the Common Pleas 1737.

† Beaumont Hotham (1737–1814), Baron of the Exchequer 1775. Second Lord Hotham 1813.

‡ *Boswell Papers.* Isham Collection. Vol. XIII, p. 137 *seq.*

The King's Judges of Assize only began to sit at Durham in 1536. And from then until 1836 they sat there not by virtue of the King's Commission, but that of the Prince Palatine, the Bishop of Durham. He issued his Commission to the same judges whom the King had sent to Newcastle and York. The Courts were the Bishop's: the building was at the side of the Palace Green on the west, where there is now the University Union Society. And the prison was the Bishop's, of which Howard in 1780 wrote: "Felons have no court.... The men are put at night into dungeons: one 7 feet square for three prisoners: another the *Great Hole*, 17 feet by 12, has only a little window. In this I saw six prisoners, (in 1776) most of them *transports* [i.e. waiting to be shipped to the Plantations], chained to the floor. In that situation they had been many weeks; and were very sickly. Their straw on the stone floor almost worn to dust."* The Bishop also appointed the Sheriff, and, as I have said, at one time it was held by many successive Sir Hedworth Williamsons.

He must be very lacking in imagination who is not impressed, or even moved, by being His Majesty's Judge of Assize at Durham. The spectacle of the Cathedral and Castle, as seen from the railway station, is the finest in England. And the Judges of Assize are lodged in the Castle itself. As you come to the gate, in the Sheriff's car, a bell is rung to warn someone—surely the Seneschal—of your approach. Within there is now not only mediaeval splendour but such modern comfort as is possible with walls of immense thickness; Norman arcades, and a perfect bathroom; the great staircase of black oak, and electric reading lamps from wall-plugs. As senior judge I had the suite of rooms at the eastern end, by the great staircase, a fine parlour and bedroom, and a bathroom lately made in an embrasure of the enormous Norman wall. When the Bishops gave up the Castle, and were left with the humbler splendours of Bishop Auckland, they reserved the right to use this suite if they wished to stay a night in Durham. This resulted once, as they tell you, in a little contest between Bishop and Judge of Assize. For the Bishop intimated his desire, and claimed his right, to use the rooms when the Assizes were on. The Judge gave way, and slept elsewhere. They say that the Bishop who did this was Westcott: I had thought he was one of those ecclesiastics to whom the epithet "saintly" is usually applied. They

* *The State of the Prisons* (2nd ed. 1780), p. 379.

also tell you that if the Judge had been less polite, and better informed, he might have prevailed. For he could have said to the Bishop, "You may have a right to use these rooms. But the furniture in them does not belong to you. I will evacuate the bedroom for you: but I shall take the bed with me." So I was told. In fact I think it might be a nice question who owns the furniture (some of which is very fine) if someone stole a piece of it, and an indictment against him had to be framed.

Sir Samuel Romilly was in 1805 appointed Chancellor of the Palatine Court of Chancery by the Bishop of Durham. In his autobiography, having pointed out the defective jurisdiction of the Court and the consequent smallness of its business, he adds: "But though a Chancellor of Durham has not the comfort of reflecting that his services are of much public utility, he may, if he be fond of such things, enjoy the grandeur, and magnificence, and homage which attend him. The Castle of Durham, the episcopal palace, is, when the Chancellor arrives, given up to him by the Bishop. It is his house; the servants attend upon him as the lord of it; a costly dinner is given to the dignitaries of the church, to the counsel, the officers of the court, and the neighbouring gentlemen; and this, though at the Bishop's expense, is, by a kind of legal fiction, considered as the Chancellor's dinner. The invitations are sent in his name; he presides at the table; and when the Bishop is at Auckland, the Chancellor invites and receives him as his guest. . . . It was night when we got there. . . . We found we had been long expected; and as we drove through the gates into the spacious court, and the porter sounded the great bell, we saw the servants hurrying out with lights. In the midst of bows and compliments, and by numerous attendants, we were conducted through long lighted galleries into a drawing-room, where some of the officers of the court and their wives were waiting to receive us, and 'My Lord' and 'Your Honour' ushered in every phrase that was uttered. . . . But to me all this ceremonial was not more ridiculous than it was irksome."*

Before 1836 the Bishop, and Prince Palatine, had an enormous income. Sir Walter Scott, in his diary, gives an account of a dinner in the hall of Durham Castle, given by Bishop Van Mildert to the Duke of Wellington: "We dined about a hundred and forty or fifty men, a distinguished company for rank and property. . . . We dined in the old

* *Life of Sir Samuel Romilly* (3rd ed. 1842), Vol. I, p. 431.

baronial hall, impressive from its rude antiquity....The bright moon streaming in through the old Gothic windows contrasted strangely with the artificial lights within; spears, banners, and armour were intermixed with the pictures of old bishops, and the whole had a singular mixture of baronial pomp with the grave and more chastened dignity of prelacy."*

We went to the Cathedral on Sunday, and in that building an Assize Service is a moving thing. I am sure I never took part in a more impressive ceremony than at the end of the service, when the choir and clergy walked first down the nave, and the High Sheriff and Judges after them. The ecclesiastical party turned off to the South door, and the judicial to the North; both turned inwards before leaving, and bowed to one another. A little later, relieved of our robes, we went to luncheon with the Dean, Bishop Welldon. And so I first entered that house which has become very familiar to me since one of my oldest friends, and fellow undergraduate at Trinity College, Oxford, became Dean in place of Welldon.

Welldon's luncheon parties (I went to several of them) had always one feature. He had a butler, whom I believe he had enlisted in India, who delighted in making amazingly elaborate table decorations, with patterns of coloured sand, grains of wheat, and other substances. The effect was rather like those patterns that one used to see in the lower part of the window of a corn-merchant's shop. I confess the result was hideous, but the labour involved must have been immense. And at least the butler's labours provided a conversational opening at a party that was apt to be a little difficult and constrained. The other regular thing was that after luncheon the Dean took us along the underground passage, some fifty yards long, to his kitchen. Which is indeed the most magnificent kitchen in the land.

At Newcastle the Judges are lodged at the Mansion House in Savile Row, and are entertained there by the Corporation. This is the only city which is so hospitable.† Everywhere else the Judge has to take his own cook, and provide food for himself and his retinue. In the old days a judge had to pay the expenses out of his own purse, but he collected fees for trying cases. Mr Justice Rokeby, from whose

* Lockhart, *Life of Scott* (1848), Vol. IX, p. 159. This was in October 1827.

† According to Grantham's *Notes*, the Judges at Bristol in his time were lodged in two hotels at Clifton alternately, "the Corporation paying all expenses". Nowadays one takes one's own cook to the Mansion House.

Diary I have quoted already, has a good many entries that illustrate this. In July 1695, on the Oxford Circuit, he notes: "In this circuit ye towns of Abingdon, Shrewsbury, and Stafford pay for ye Judges' horsemeat." In his second circuit, March 1689–1690, he was to have gone the Oxford with Mr Justice Eyre. He says: "I went only to Reading and Oxford, & then ye King's pleasure was signified to me to returne to London, and Justice Eyre went ye rest of ye circuit alone. We had hired a Coach betwixt us, but Justice Eyre refusing to take it along with him, I came home in it, and after ye circuit was over ye accts were stated, and Justice Eyre demanded that I should pay halfe of ye charges of his own Saddle horses, & of his clerk of ye chamber, & of his groome and sumpter. I thought it was not reasonable, but upon his p̄posal I referred it to Justice Powell and Justice Ventris, who judged it against me: and I was out of purse this circuit 19 *li* and above." In March 1690–1691 he was on the Norfolk Circuit with Chief Justice Holt: "I hired a coach & 4 horses to myselfe this circuit, & took my chamber clerk in ye coach with me, & hired a horse for Jo: to carry a portmantle, and I was out of pocket this circuit in ye whole about 34 *li*." On the Norfolk Circuit in March 1692–1693: "I hired a coach...and by reason of ye badness of ye wayes I was forced to take six horses." And on the Oxford Circuit, in July 1696: "In this circuit I hired a coach and four horses, and took my chamber clerk in ye coach with me. I hired also two horses for John and Joshua, my two servants, and I was out of purse in ye whole (above all yt came in) above 54 *li*:—

Coach hire	24.10.0
travelling charges into & out of ye circ^t	12. 0.0
My share for housekeeping charges	11. 0.0
Hire of two horses & their meat &c.	7. 8.0
	54.18.0"

Lord Campbell* prints the accounts of Chief Justice King and Mr Justice Dormer as Judges of Assize on the Northern Circuit in January 1720, that is at York and Lancaster only. Their joint expenses for the whole circuit are £107. 4*s*. 6*d*. They take credit for sums received for entries, recoveries, and fines, amounting to £68. 13*s*. 4*d*. This left a balance of £38. 11*s*. 2*d*., of which each judge paid half.

Nowadays a judge receives nothing for entries, recoveries, and

* *Lives of the Chancellors*, Vol. VI, p. 89.

fines, or in any other way from his circuit work. But he does receive a daily allowance from the Treasury for his expenses. I have heard of judges finding themselves with a deficit at the end of a circuit, but I can only suppose that they must have entertained on a very lavish scale, or had very wasteful servants. In my experience of thirty-six circuits in thirteen years my balance was always on the right side. And to that extent my remuneration in the Court of Appeal is now slightly less than it was in the King's Bench: while the monotony of life, now that I have lost the diversions of circuit, is greater.

I do not know when the present amount of the daily allowance for expenses was fixed. If, like Judges' salaries, it has not been increased for a century, one might suppose that when money went so much farther the Judges might have had a handsome balance on the right side. But in the old days Judges on circuit entertained on a very lavish scale. It was customary at nearly every town to give a dinner to the Grand Jury and another dinner to the magistrates. After his first circuit as Lord Chief Justice, Lord Campbell writes in his diary, 9 April 1850: "The most arduous duty on the circuit was entertaining the magistrates at dinner, a duty we had to perform at every assize town." In Huddleston's *Notes* there are many references to this old custom, which was falling into disuse, because, with increase of travelling facilities, magistrates went home, and few wanted to stay to dine. Apparently the Judge gave an oral invitation in Court, and those who wished to attend gave in their names to the Judge's butler. It was also a tradition that they could come in morning dress, which survived from the time when they had played a part in the mounted cavalcade attendant on the Sheriff when he met the Judges. Huddleston notes that at Devizes in 1877, not a single magistrate came, at Norwich in 1876 one magistrate and the Sheriff's Chaplain. (He notes elsewhere that it is usual to ask the Chaplain, but not the Sheriff, to the Magistrates' Dinner. This may have been because a Sheriff, during his year of office, is not allowed to act as a magistrate). At Aylesbury in 1876, and at Maidstone in 1876 only three came. Grantham adds a note that these dinners were by his time everywhere given up.

Dinner as a meal was once *the* meal of the day. And the vast quantities of food provided can nowhere be better realized than in the *Diary of a Country Parson* (1758–1802). Luncheon as a meal was only invented about 1820. It is significant that one of Huddleston's *Notes* is: "The adjournment for luncheon used to be from 15 to 20 minutes, but since 1882 has been for half an hour." And another is: "The Judges' Luncheon is usually brought to the Court, unless the lodgings adjoin it." Nowadays adjournment for an hour is not unknown, and the Judges almost always return to the Lodgings for it.

An allowance to the Judge for his circuit expenses is at least as old as 1627. Sir James Whitelocke, in that year, records:* "The allowance of Justices of Assize in their circuits, as it was proportioned at the first making thereof,

A puisne judge for his	dyet per diem	0.18.4
	men, ten, allowed eatche 16d	0.13.4
	horses, thirteen, eatche 16d	0.17.4
		2. 9.0
Ad for the second judge as mutche		2. 9.0"

In fact I think an allowance to the Judges for their maintenance on circuit began in the reign of Elizabeth. In earlier times it was apparently the duty of the High Sheriff to provide them with food. Dugdale, *Origines Juridiciales* (1671), p. 335, prints "The copy of a Letter from the Lords of Her Majestie's Most Honourable Privy Council to the Shireeves of the Several Counties in England, for easing them in the charge of entertainment of the Justices of Assize and Gaol Delivery, with Dyet, in their respective Circuits, 21 Feb. 1573." This refers to complaints "of the great burthen and charge sustained in the said Office of Sheriffwick by reason...of the large diets and other charges of the Justices of Assize and Gaol Delivery, yearly increasing in such sort....Therefore to remedy this matter it is determined by Her Majesty...that the Sheriffs shall not after this Lent Assises have the charges of the Justices' diets; but that the said Justices shall have of her Majesty several sums of money out of her Coffers, for their daily Diets, during the time that heretofore the Sheriffs have been chargeable withall within their Counties:...and yet it is meant that you shall against the Summer Assises...aid and assist the Servants of the said Justices that shall require your advice or help, to make provision for their Masters Diets, and for lodgings and House-room at as reasonable charges as may and ought to be for the Queens

* *Liber Famelicus* (Camden Society, 1858), p. 109.

Majesties Service....For these next Assises it shall suffice that you make provision for two messes of meat well furnished, and in case over and besides that, you shall demand any further allowance of the Justices Diets, it is not meant you shall have any allowance for the same afterwards; you see what Order it hath pleased her Majesty to take herein. Your loving Friends, W. Burghley, E. Lyncoln" [and nine other Privy Councillors].

As the city of Newcastle pays for the Judges' meat, and not merely, like Abingdon, Stafford, and Shrewsbury, in 1695, for his horsemeat, the Judge's balance on the North-Eastern Circuit is not likely to result in a deficit. By a paradox you can, and do, ask your host, the Lord Mayor, to dine with you, along with the senior Aldermen, Town Clerk, City and County Sheriffs, the Bishop, the senior Naval and Military Officers, and the Clerk of Assize. After dinner there is a ceremony which is very pleasant for the two Judges. The Lord Mayor proposes their health, and presents each of them with a gold coin, traditionally a Jacobus to the Senior, and a Carolus to the Junior Judge. Whether the supply of "Broad-pieces" of James I and Charles I is giving out from this special demand I know not: but I became the happy possessor of a most beautiful Rose Noble of Edward II.

The origin of this pleasant custom is supposed to be the perils of that journey from Newcastle to Carlisle of which I spoke before. The Corporation used to provide an armed guard, but at some date the Judges agreed to hire their own guard, and the Corporation provided the money. The offering is still called "Dagger Money". The tradition of Jacobus and Carolus would suggest that the arrangement was made in Stuart times. But in the reign of Charles I at least one judge received an older coin. Sir James Whitelocke was on the Northern Circuit in July 1626,* and he records that he received "of the Maior of Newcastle, at leave taking, a spur royal in gold". That was a coin of the reign of Elizabeth: on the reverse it had a star resembling the rowel of a spur.

Lord Campbell, who was on the Northern Circuit as Chief Justice in the summer of 1852, says in his diary: "The Corporation of Newcastle entertained us free of expense while we were within their jurisdiction, and at our departure the mayor, according to ancient usage, presented to me a gold Jacobus to buy a dagger with which

* *Liber Famelicus* (Camden Society, 1858), p. 107.

I might defend myself from Scottish freebooters as I passed along the border." Huddleston's *Notes* say that "when they leave Newcastle, the Mayor presents one judge with a gold Carolus and the other with a Jacobus.... Verbal thanks are tendered merely."

When I was given my Rose Noble and stood up to say "Thank you", it occurred to me to recall the origin of the custom, as it had been told to me. "But what was the peril, and who were the marauders, against whom the Judges had to be guarded? I can hardly doubt that they were raiders from over the border. I hope, my Lord Mayor, you will think that Fate has been kind to both England and Scotland, when we observe that the two Judges to whom you have just presented these beautiful coins are named MacKinnon and Finlay—two intruding Scots."

I have since found that the same fancy once occurred to James Boswell. By the favour of Lord Lonsdale he was elected Recorder of Carlisle in 1788. In 1787 Dr John Douglas (formerly a Snell Exhibitioner of Balliol—that passport of so many Scots into England) had been appointed Bishop of Carlisle. Boswell made this epigram:*

Of old, ere wise Concord united this isle,
Our neighbours of Scotland were foes at Carlisle;
But now what a change have we here on the border,
When Douglas is Bishop, and Boswell Recorder.

The hospitable entertainment of the Judges at Newcastle is also a thing of long standing. The travelling Joseph Taylor of the Inner Temple, in 1705, says:† "The Major is allowed 700 *l.* per Ann. for his Table, and every judge that comes thither is all the while treated at the publick charge, and carried one day to Shields by water, and nobly entertain'd there, to support which Expence, the Major is allowed 100 *l.* by the Town."

This form of entertainment is also referred to by Roger North in his *Life* of his brother, Lord Keeper Guildford, when, as Chief Justice of the Common Pleas, he was on the Northern Circuit at Newcastle: "The magistrates were solicitous to give him all the Diversion they

* Pottle, *Boswell's Literary Career* (Oxford, 1929), p. xlii. Lord Campbell, on the Northern Circuit in 1852, wrote: "Tait, the Dean of Carlisle, gave us a splendid entertainment, and presented a rare instance of a Scotsman promoted in the church of England." Tait was afterwards Archbishop of Canterbury. And what was to Campbell a "rare instance" has now become common form.

† *A Journey to Edenborough in Scotland* (Edinburgh, 1903) p. 87.

could: and one was the going down to Tinmouth castle in the Town Barge. The Equipment of the vessel was very stately; for, ahead, there sat a four or five Drone bag-pipes, the North country organ, and a Trumpeter astern; and so we rowed merrily along" (p. 136).

At York the Lodgings are a very fine old house in Lendal. It was built about 1730 by Dr Wintringham upon part of the graveyard of St Wilfred's. It has been the Judges' Lodgings since 1806, when it took the place of an old house in Coney Street that previously fulfilled that purpose. The Lendal house has a fine dignified front, with a double staircase up to the *piano nobile*. The panelled dining-room at the back is a magnificent room, and finer than the rather similar room in the house at Lancaster. On the afternoon of their arrival the Judges are waited upon by the Lord Mayor, attended by the Town Clerk, the Mace-Bearer and the Sword-Bearer. The last functionary wears an immense fur hat.

Next morning, when the Assize opens, you go a little way up the street to the Mansion House, where the Lord Mayor lives during his year of office. Here he entertains the Judges, and a large company of both sexes, at breakfast in the big room upstairs. Each judge, already encumbered with his complete robes, and a full-bottomed wig, is presented with a large bouquet on his arrival. This was no doubt once regarded as a protection against the gaol fever, which on a good many occasions killed judges.

It was a pleasant function, but I am not at my best, conversationally, at breakfast; and I think it is difficult, without practice, to eat bacon and eggs in judicial ermine and a wig. After breakfast we went to service at the Cathedral.

Of two judges one tries the prisoners in the Crown Court, and one hears cases in the Civil Court. At the next place they reverse the roles. The Judge who tries the prisoners is said to be "In Commission". As I was in Commission at York, I was conducted, after the Assize Service, to the ancient and most picturesque Guildhall, behind the Mansion House, there to open the Assize for the City. For here, as elsewhere, there is a double Assize, City and County. There were, however, no City prisoners, and therefore no Grand Jury. I received white gloves, and was handed over by the City Sheriff to the County Sheriff to be conducted by him to the Castle for the County Assize. There, strangely enough for York, there were only two prisoners, and by the afternoon I was trying a civil case. We got back to London on a Thursday evening, and were due to go to Leeds on the Monday after. So it was no use to try to sit in London on the Friday: and, as luck would have it, the Eton and Harrow match was on the Friday and Saturday.

According to Grantham's *Notes*, at York "the Judges go from the station with the City Sheriff to open the Commission at the Guildhall, then to the Castle to open the Commission for the County, and then to the lodgings. Next morning the Judge in Commission charges the City Grand Jury at the Guildhall, then goes at 9 to the Lord Mayor's breakfast, and after it goes to charge the County Grand Jury at the Castle." If this was still the practice in his time, it shows that opening the Commission on the day of arrival lasted longer than I had supposed.

One incident during this circuit led me to write the following letter, which was printed in *The Times Literary Supplement*, 13 August 1925, under the heading "A Scottish and Yorkshire Use":

The Judges who go on the Summer Assize receive from the Sheriffs of the various counties, or their under-sheriffs, lists of gentlemen suggested as fit and proper persons to be Sheriffs in the future. These lists are on 14 November used at that sitting of the King's Bench (as the successor of the Court of Exchequer) at which the Chancellor of the Exchequer presides. A list of three names for each County is then made, which later goes before His Majesty in Council to be pricked.

I have recently received such lists from the Sheriffs in Northumberland, Durham, and Yorkshire. The Yorkshire list was indorsed "Lites", a word which aroused my curiosity. Two under-sheriffs of great experience told me that the list in Yorkshire was always so called, but they did not know its meaning or origin. Further enquiry of the King's Remembrancer's office elicited that the Yorkshire list alone has always borne this superscription.

Having now leisure, and access to the Oxford English Dictionary, I found there, as I expected, the explanation of the word. Leet, substantive 2, is explained as "Now chiefly Scottish". Two definitions are given: "(1) A list of persons designated as eligible for some office." For this ten quotations, ranging from 1441 to 1884, are given, all of them Scottish; and (2) "*Plural*—the candidates forming a leet." For this three Scottish quotations of the 16th century are given. And there is added this note. "The only use which is known to us outside Scotland is with reference to the annual election of Wardens of the Trinity House, Hull. Four 'lites' are nominated, from whom the two wardens are chosen."

I am interested to find that there is one other use outside Scotland, that it is also in Yorkshire, and that the same spelling is used for the Sheriff's list of his suggested successors as for the Candidates at the Hull Trinity House.

I made a mistake in the date, 14 November. I should have written 12 November. For St Martin's day is 11 November, and this annual appearance in Court of the Chancellor of the Exchequer is "on the morrow of St Martin". Early in November 1925 I received this intimation.

The Clerk of the Council presents his compliments to Mr Justice Mac-Kinnon, and has the honour to state that the Lords of the Council will meet in the King's Bench Division of the High Court of Justice, on Thursday, the 12th day of November next, at 2 o'clock p.m., on which occasion his Lordship's attendance is requested.

Privy Council Office, Whitehall, 31st October 1925.

I was glad to attend and take part in so ancient a ceremony. As I remember this function, as a spectator and youthful barrister, the proceedings were longer and more contentious. Gentlemen desiring exemption appeared by counsel, and their claims were argued. Nowadays I believe more care is exercised to put down only the names of those willing to serve. There are few claims to be released, and on this occasion in 1925 no counsel appeared.

The final selection of the next year's High Sheriff is made by the King in Council, by his pricking with a bodkin the paper against the name of one of the three for each county, usually, I believe, the first. I had always supposed that this was a very ancient usage dating from the days when Kings could not write. Lord Campbell shared that belief, for I see that he says* that when as Chancellor of the Duchy he attended Queen Victoria to "prick" a Sheriff of Lancashire, he was asked by the Prince Consort as to the origin of the ceremony, and he answered: "In ancient times, Sir, when sovereigns did not know how to write their names."

On further investigation I found that the usage could not have been continuous from very early times. For from 1299 to 1340 Sheriffs were elected by the counties and not appointed by the Crown. In 1299 the Statute, 28 Edw. I, cap. 8, enacted: "Le Roi ad grante a soen poeple quil eient eslection de leur viscontes en chescun conte—sil voelent." And in 1340 it was provided by 14 Edw. III, cap. 7, that the Sheriffs

* *Life of Lord Campbell* (1881), Vol. II, p. 217.

should be chosen yearly by the Lord Chancellor, the Lord Treasurer, the President of the King's Council, the Keeper of the Privy Seal, and the Chief Baron of the Exchequer, with the two Chief Justices "on the morrow of All Souls at the Exchequer". Except for the change from the morrow of All Souls (3 November) to the morrow of St Martin (12 November) this was the ceremony I attended on 12 November 1925.

Subsequent enquiry from Mr Colin Smith, Deputy Clerk of the Council, showed me that the "pricking" was not really ancient. But I was surprised to find that it is really comparatively modern. It appears that the Record Office has Sheriff Rolls from Henry VIII onwards, with a fragment of a Roll of Henry VI. This fragment, and all the Rolls of Henry VIII, Edward VI, and Mary, have black dots against the name of the selected Sheriff on the left-hand side. And these Rolls were not signed by the Sovereign. It is only in Elizabeth's reign that the pricking begins, but her Rolls do bear her signature.

On the day when I had Mr Colin Smith's letter telling me these facts I happened to sit at dinner next to that prodigy of learning, the late Provost of Eton. I told him about the pricking of Sheriffs, and how I had learned that it only began with Elizabeth. Upon which he made this brilliant suggestion: "Depend upon it, she was one day at her needlework and they came and worried her with the Sheriff Roll. In her hasty way she would not wait for the standish, and instead of putting black dots she pricked holes with the implement in her hand. And so made the precedent that has been followed ever since."

If this were in truth the origin of the pricking, it would not be very surprising: many ancient things in England start from as casual a beginning. But to prick a paper, instead of putting a mark on it, is known elsewhere. The attendance of men in chapel used to be so recorded. Thomas Hughes attributes that practice to his mythical St Ambrose College, and so does Cuthbert Bede to his Brazenface. The Proctors record votes in Convocation by using the "prickers", which they take from the knobs in which they are kept.*

As for the bodkin, Mr Colin Smith told me this. His Majesty does not use an ancient implement, but a new one is not procured except upon Royal command. The one in use in 1925 is believed to have been made for Queen Victoria when she came to the throne. This has quite

* Baxter and Gibson, *Oxford University Ceremonies* (1935), p. 60.

a substantial steel blade ending in a sharp point. Its handle is a gilt knob bearing the insignia of the Privy Council. Its predecessor, a lighter implement, is in the King's possession: it is believed to date from the reign of George III.

The Sovereign was not (and, no doubt, is not) bound to appoint one of the three people nominated on the morrow of St Martin. He could appoint another, who was called the Pocket Sheriff. Henry Purefoy writes,* on 22 January 1747: "I have received advice from a ffreind in London that the three Gentlemen who were prikt down for Sherifs for the County of Bucks have all got of, and that Mr Campbell Price of Westbury or myself will certainly be the Pocket Sheriff." In fact Purefoy was pricked as Sheriff a year later, in February 1748.

In such a case presumably the three nominees, having failed in the Court, subsequently got themselves excused by back-stairs influence. John Stone writes† to Lord Fermanagh, 12 November 1724: "Your Lordship's kind notice of my being first in the Sheriff's list for Oxon and the way to get off is most oblinging. My Brother served it but a little before his death, which makes it more Servere the same Estate should so soon be charged again with it....I am told that after the three are named in the Court of Exchequer it is too late to be got off by any other than a Privy Councillor's speaking to the King...and that the Lord Chancellor is the fittest person to be applied to. If your Lordship can find means to acquaint him of the hardship I lie under in this particular, I may very well hope that he will be, as long as he is Chancellor."

✧ ✧ ✧

In October 1925 I went again on the Northern Circuit, joining at Liverpool Mr Justice Wright, who had been to Carlisle and Lancaster. It was an autumn of prolonged frost: on one expedition for a week-end with friends in the Lakes, and on another into Derbyshire, I had magnificent walks on the hills upon frozen snow in brilliant sunshine.

I again spent a good deal of time, as I had done a year before, in reading the early records of the old Northern Circuit, which the junior lent me. I believe the circuit has decided not to publish them. I hope

* *The Purefoy Letters* (Eland, 1931), Vol. II, p. 365.

† *The Verney Letters* 1717 *to* 1799 (1930), Vol. II, p. 116.

it will forgive me if I say that the existing records begin on 9 August 1763 and continue without a break. Down to 1876 they are of course the common record of the two present circuits, Northern and North-Eastern.

The earlier parts I found extraordinarily interesting. Richard Burke, whose untimely death broke his father's heart, signs them as junior in 1785, and a letter from him is inserted, dated "Worcester, 12 March 1786", in which he takes leave of the circuit, and announces that he has joined the Oxford Circuit. In 1786 James Boswell, who had just been called to the English bar by the Inner Temple in Hilary term 1786, is junior, and he is directed to reply to Burke's letter. He has inserted a copy of his nonsensical effusion dated "York, 18 March 1786". Then a similar change happened to Boswell, and there is inserted a letter from him, dated "Chelmsford, 28 July 1786", taking leave of the Northern Circuit in his turn, and announcing that he has transferred himself to the Home Circuit. When Boswell finishes his term of office as junior he inserts his account with the circuit duly balanced. If you add up the two sides of it, you will find that he has made an error of one shilling in his own favour.

I had only time to read the first three volumes of these records, and they end with Boswell's letter of resignation in July 1786. Later on, if he did not rejoin the circuit, his connexion with it was renewed. For he was made Recorder of Carlisle in 1788, and held that office until June 1790. And I think he must have rejoined the circuit. In a letter to Temple of 23 August 1789 he tells him how he was robbed of his wig at Lowther Castle. "I suspected a wanton trick, which some think witty." And he says: "I left Auchinleck with intention to join the Northern Circuit at Carlisle."

I wonder what Boswell and his contemporaries would have thought of women barristers, and of their being members of the Northern Circuit. Though they are members they do not attend the Bar Mess, and they have for themselves a "Northern Circuit Women's Bar Mess". At Manchester, upon their invitation, my marshal, the Clerk of Assize, and I dined with them at their first Guest Night. I understood that they have begun Records of their own. I hope that some day they may be as entertaining as the men's Records, even though they begin about 160 years later.

Another happy recollection of this circuit at Manchester is that of a long Saturday morning spent at the Chetham Hospital. It is one of the most delightful places I ever saw, and I have been surprised to find how many people who have often passed its door have never entered it. Soon after my return to London I was singing its praises to Lord Sumner, who said: "I regret to say that though I was for years at the Manchester Grammar School close by I was never inside the Chetham hospital."

The Library was to me the chief delight; it was happy in its librarian, Mr Philips, whose knowledge of its contents was only surpassed by his enthusiasm for the whole place, and his courtesy in showing it. If I had two Rylands libraries, I would gladly exchange them for one Chetham library. The Hall is very fine, the Audit Room is magnificent, and the Reading Room most beautiful. As for the furniture in the Audit Room and the Reading Room, it is enough to make a collector die of envy.

The business of an Assize is marked with a ceremonial that is a very ancient inheritance, though it has gradually been simplified and shortened. Before leaving London the Judge or Judges sign and deliver a series of Precepts to each Sheriff of a county, and of a county borough, upon the circuit. I print an example of one of these in Appendix A, at the end of this book. The Clerk of Assize sends these to the various Sheriffs, and with each he sends another document, signed by himself, with his surname only. I give an example of this in Appendix B.

The authority to hold an Assize is the King's Commission. And the Assize is opened by the reading of the Commission, or the material parts of it, in Court by the Clerk of Assize. I print an example of a Commission in Appendix C. The Commission is now a single document. In the old days Assizes were held by virtue of six different Royal Mandates. These were: (1) The Patent of Assize. (2) The Patent of Association. (3) The Writ of Admittance. (4) The Writ of *Si Non Omnes*. (5) The Commission of *Oyer* and *Terminer*. (6) The Commission of Gaol Delivery. The forms of these, in Latin,* as issued in the reign of Charles II may be found in *The Office of the Clerk of Assize* (2nd ed. 1682) at pp. 4–11.

By the middle of the eighteenth century the forms appear to have

* All formal legal documents, including indictments, were in Latin until its use was abolished by an Act of 1730. That is the reason why so many Latin tags, such as *Mandamus, Certiorari, Nisi prius,* survive in legal phraseology.

been altered. In 1749 it was written: "The Judges on *Circuits* sit by Virtue of five several Commissions: (1) A Commission of Oyer and Terminer, (2) A Commission of general Gaol Delivery, (3) A Commission of Assize, (4) A Commission or Writ of *Nisi Prius*, and (5) A Commission of the Peace in every County of their Circuit."*

Down to 1914 this multiplicity of forms continued. The late Sir Arthur Denman, Clerk of Assize of the South-Eastern Circuit, told me that from his appointment in 1887 until 1913, the forms in use were: (1) A Commission of Oyer and Terminer, (2) Commission of Association, (3) Commission of Assize, (4) Commission of Gaol Delivery, (5) Writ of Association, and (6) Writ of *Si Non Omnes.* He added that in 1887 the Commission of Oyer and Terminer had the Great Seal, in yellow wax, covered up with leather, attached to it, but in 1888 it, and all the documents, had a paper embossed seal instead.

In 1914 the present single "Commission" was invented. It was the work of a small committee of which I believe Mr Justice Bray was chairman, and for its wording he was chiefly responsible.

The day on which a Judge, or the two Judges, travel to an Assize town is always called "Commission Day". This is the day specified in the Judge's Precept to the High Sheriff (Appendix A). In the old days the Judges on arrival went straight to the Courts, and the Commission was read. Nowadays that always takes place on the morning after their arrival, which is really the opening day of the Assize.

In Boswell's account of his going with the Sheriff to meet the Judges arriving at Carlisle in August 1778, which I quoted before, he says: "Willes stopped the Coach a little from the town, and made it drive more composedly. They drove to the Town hall and there their Commission was read; that is to say *read short*, as Willes called out to do, so that a word here and there only was uttered. The Sherif then conducted their Lordships to lodgings provided for them at his expence. And there the Mayor, Aldermen and Recorder, preceded by their Mace, waited on their Lordships."† The following day he went into Court, and heard the calling of the Grand Jury, etc.

When the Judges on arriving went straight to the Court for the reading of the Commissions they had of course to be in their robes.

* *The Crown Circuit Companion*, by Stubbs and Talmash (2nd ed. 1749), p. 2.

† *Boswell Papers*. Isham Collection. Vol. XIII.

I have no doubt that on that 21 August 1778 Chief Justice Willes and Baron Hotham had put on their robes and wigs at "the place where they dined", from whence the Under-Sheriff had conducted them in the post-chaise and four.

This old practice is no doubt the reason why, before you leave London, the first Under-Sheriff always enquires of one's clerk whether the Judge desires to be met at the station "in state or privately". I have never heard of any Judge in modern times choosing the former alternative. If he did, the High Sheriff in uniform, with his Chaplain, would meet him. And the Judge would have to wear his wig and robes. I believe Lord Chief Justice Coleridge, who died in 1894, used so to adorn himself in the railway carriage as he neared his destination, but he was the last to do so. And I have seen in some guide-book (I think at Northampton) that the station-master would reserve a waiting-room on the arrival platform in which the Judges robed. This was about 1850.

And I find that others sometimes did it besides Lord Coleridge. In Grantham's *Circuit Diary* he records: "17 Jan. 1887. I arrived at Norwich, robed in the station-master's room at the station, and drove to open the Commission at the Guildhall." And "13 March 1889. We reached Cardiff in the train via Abergavenny, and opened the Commission in a crammed court at 4 p.m." In November 1889 he speaks of arriving at Bodmin by train in the afternoon, "where after a very cold journey I had to robe at once, open the commission, and go to church".

Huddleston, in his *Notes*, says: "Sometimes it is convenient to open the Commission before going to the Lodgings, for instance the City Commission at Lincoln, in which case the Judge robes at the station, where a room is provided by the Under Sheriff for the purpose: sometimes the Judge robes in the train, as at Newtown in Montgomery." In another Note, he says: "It is usual to go to church *after* opening the Commission, sometimes even after charging the Grand Jury, while they are considering bills."

A disaster about a "Commission Day" of the old sort is recorded by Lord Campbell* in a letter of 14 August 1818. The incident is interesting as illustrating the extraordinary devotion to technicalities, which the legal mind used to exhibit. Writing on that day at Gloucester

* *Life of Lord Campbell* (1881), Vol. I, p. 352.

he speaks of "the scrape we have got into by Garrow* not arriving in time to open the Commission. Such a thing I believe has never happened...and what the result will be it is impossible to tell. The Under-Sheriff was despatched to consult the Lord Chancellor.... My own opinion is that the civil causes cannot be tried at all, but that the gaol delivery may proceed. At Monmouth...Wed. evening at eight o'clock when the business finished we mounted our horses. We reached Gloucester a little before one, and found the judge had got there only a few minutes before us. Whether he was aware of the necessity of being here before twelve o'clock, or whether he had gone to sleep, or what was the cause of his dilatoriness I am at a loss to explain. He might have left Monmouth an hour sooner."

The Lord Chancellor was Lord Eldon, so it is possible to believe, what would otherwise be incredible, that he decided that a new Commission for a later date must be issued. The Judges and the bar waited about in idleness at Gloucester for more than a fortnight, and the Assize was eventually begun on 31 August.†

Nowadays on the morning after "Commission Day" the Judge in Commission wears his full red robes and full-bottomed wig, and carries the black cap. The other Judge (unless there is to be an Assize Service to attend) wears his black robes and bob-wig, and carries his three-cornered hat. At the Courts the Judge in Commission is conducted to the Crown Court by the Sheriff and his Chaplain, while the other Judge is taken to his room by the Under-Sheriff.

When the Judge in Commission comes into Court he stands at his desk, on which his three-cornered hat has been placed. His clerk then makes two proclamations: "All Persons having anything to do before my Lords the King's Justices‡ of Assize, Oyer and Terminer, and general Gaol Delivery draw near and give your attendance."

"My Lords the King's Justices‡ do strictly charge and command all persons to keep silence whilst the Commission of our Sovereign Lord the King is produced and read."

The Clerk of Assize then reads a condensed version of the Commission (Appendix C). I venture to think that some Clerks of Assize

* Sir William Garrow (1760–1840), Baron of the Exchequer 1817.

† *Life of Lord Campbell* (1881), Vol. I, p. 354.

‡ In these proclamations, when there is only one Judge, his clerk is apt to change this to "My Lord the King's Justice". This is incorrect. The Commission is to a number of persons (see *infra*), and the plural should be used.

cut it down too much, and lose some of its magniloquence in a poor paraphrase. If you want to hear it done well, and dramatically, you should attend the opening of an Assize on the Midland Circuit, and hear it read by Mr George Bancroft.

When in his reading he comes to "Our Judges for the time being of our Supreme Court of Judicature" the Clerk of Assize substitutes the name of the Judge who is standing above him, and turns and bows to him. The Judge in return raises his three-cornered hat to his head, and replaces it on the desk. This is the only semblance of use of the hat that now survives. I have said that the Judge in the Civil Court carries it with him on the way to the Courts. But he does not take it into Court. In London it is never used. But it was at one time. When Mr Justice Stareleigh sat at the Guildhall (in the absence of the Chief Justice of the Common Pleas, owing to indisposition) to try a civil case on 14 February 1828, he came into Court and "put his little legs underneath his table, and his little three-cornered hat upon it".

When the Clerk of Assize has read the Commission, the Judge's clerk says "God Save the King", and the Judge then takes his seat. A message is sent to the other Judge, who has been waiting in his room, that the Commission has been opened, and he then goes into his Court to start work.

The Judge's clerk, in the Crown Court, then says: "Mr High Sheriff of this County, be pleased to return the several precepts and writs to you directed and delivered or returnable here this day that my Lords the King's Justices may proceed thereon." The High Sheriff, who is on the bench next to the Judge, on his right, hands to the Judge a roll or packet of papers tied up with coloured tape, usually green. The Judge receives it with a bow and hands it down to the Clerk of Assize. (As to the contents of this roll I will say something later.)

Until 1933 the Judge's clerk then said: "Gentlemen* of the Grand Jury, be pleased to answer to your names and save your fines." The Clerk of Assize then read out twenty-three names, and each in turn said "Here". On some circuits it was usual to add the name of his abode to the man's name. In Wales it was not done. I believe English Clerks of Assize by their well-meant efforts of pronunciation were apt

* When, in later days, ladies appeared on a Grand Jury this became "Members of the Grand Jury".

to cause unseemly amusement. When the twenty-three were called, and had answered, the Judge's clerk said: "Gentlemen of the Grand Jury, be pleased to observe your Foreman's Oath."

Then came the turn of the Judge's marshal, as I have before described it. The Judge's clerk then said: "Gentlemen, are you all sworn?", to which I never heard any response. The clerk then said: "My Lords the King's Justices do strictly charge and command all persons to keep silence whilst the charge is given to this Grand Jury upon pain of fine and imprisonment."

The Judge then addressed the Grand Jury. When he finished the Grand Jury retired to their room. And the Judge retired to his, where he put off his full-bottomed wig, and replaced it with his bob-wig. Now that Grand Juries are no more, he so retires after receiving the roll of papers from the High Sheriff. He used to have to wait in his room (and perhaps smoke a pipe) until the Grand Jury were ready with a true bill. Now he can begin trying prisoners directly he has changed his wig.

I think this change of wig may be a modern concession to judicial comfort. When Lord Campbell became Lord Chief Justice in 1850 he went on the Midland as his first circuit. He writes in his diary on 9 April: "I have returned from the circuit, having made my *début* as a judge.... I suffered from nothing except wearing a full-bottomed wig having been disencumbered of it for nine years. My head ached and my faculties were cramped by the pressure of it, but I hope that use will again reconcile me to this barbarous encumbrance." This must surely mean that he had to wear it at all times on the bench. If he had only done so for the limited time that the present mode requires, he could hardly have made so much outcry.

As to Grand Juries, I think the reform in 1933 went too far. I would certainly have abolished the Grand Jury at Quarter Sessions, both in counties and boroughs, and I would still more certainly have abolished it at the Old Bailey. There it was an absurdity, and a source of great expense. But for reasons other than its intrinsic usefulness (which was negligible) I would have retained the Grand Jury at County Assizes. It was a good thing for county justices to meet the Judges of Assize as they had been doing for centuries. They liked the privilege, and so far as I know there was no real reason why it should not have been continued.

The methods of the Grand Jury will soon be forgotten. So it may be worth while for me to put on record that when they returned an indictment (with their indorsement "A true bill", or otherwise) it had to be handed direct by the Foreman, or one of the Grand Jurors, to the Clerk of Assize. No one must touch it on the way, or he might tamper with it. As in most Courts the Grand Jury came into a gallery, there were devices by which the indictment could pass from one hand to the other. The most usual was a long rod, like a fishing-rod, with a clip at the end. By this means the document was handed direct to the Clerk of Assize.

I have described the present ritual of the opening of the Commission. In the old days it was much more elaborate, and must have occupied a great deal more time than the 15 or 20 minutes now required. In my little book of 1682, *The Office of the Clerk of Assize*, it is set forth thus:

First, when the Court is set, the Cryer must make three Proclamations.

[This means "Oyez, oyez, oyez". This is still done at the opening of Quarter Sessions, at any rate in Buckinghamshire.]

Then the Clerk of Assize must cause him to say as followeth, *viz.* My Lords, The King's Justices do straitly charge and command all manner of persons to keep silence, and hear the King's Majesties Commissions of Assize and *Nisi prius* openly read, upon pain of imprisonment.

Then must the Clerk of Assize read (1) The Commission of Assize, (2) The Commission of Association, (3) The Writ of Admittance, (4) The Writ of *Si non omnes*. And then the Clerk of Assize must say, *God save the King*, and the Cryer shall repeat the same with a loud voice after him. Note, That the Writ of Admittance, and the Writ of *Si non omnes* shall be only read at the first County in the Circuit, and not in any other.

[The four documents are given (pp. 4–7) in closely printed black letter, and in Latin. The reading of them would be a very long business. It is not surprising that by 1778 Chief Justice Willes had got in the habit of calling "Read it short".]

Then the Cryer must make one Proclamation [i.e. "Oyez"], and say, If any man will be essoined in Assize of *Novel disseisin*, Assize of *Mort-dauncester*, Certificate of Assize, *Juris Vtrum*, or *Attaint*, let him come forth, and he shall be heard.

Then the Cryer must make another Proclamation, and say, All manner of Persons that have any Writs of Assize, or Records of *Nisi prius* to be put into the Court, put them in forthwith, or none shall be received.

Then must the Cryer make a Proclamation [i.e. "Oyez"], *and say*, My Lords, the King's Justices do straitly charge and command all manner of persons to keep silence, and hear the King's Majesties Commissions of *Oyer* and *Terminer*, and general Gaol-delivery for this County of *H.* to be openly read, upon pain of imprisonment.

Then must the Clerk of the Assizes read the Commission of *Oyer* and *Terminer*, and general Gaol-delivery, that done, say, *God save the King*; and the Cryer shall repeat the same after him with a loud voice.

[The Commissions of Oyer and Terminer and of General Gaol Delivery are printed in Latin, at pp. 8–11. The former is the longest of the whole six.]

Then the Clerk of Assize shall cause the Cryer to make another Proclamation, and say after him thus, My Lords, the Kings Justices do straitly charge and command all manner of persons that none dare be so hardy or presume to raise or inhaunce the prizes of Victuals, or Horse-meat to greater value than they were at before the coming of the King's Justices, upon pain of Imprisonment.

Then the Clerk of Assize shall cause the Cryer to make another Proclamation, and say, Sheriff of the County of *H.* return the Precepts and Writs of Assize, and *Nisi prius* to you directed and delivered returnable here this day, that my Lords the King's Justices may proceed thereon.

Then the Sheriff delivers a Roll of all the names of the Justices of Peace, *&c.* to the Judge, and then the Judge takes notice of the Sheriff, and speaks to him to be covered, but till then the Sheriff may not be covered.

Then the Clerk of Assize shall cause the Cryer to make another Proclamation, and say, All Justices of the Peace for this County of *H.* answer to your names at the first call, and save your Fines.

Then the Clerk of the Assize must name them as they are returned in the Calendar, and the Cryer must call them by their several names and additions one after the other in this manner.

H. Lord *F.* Lord High Chancellour of *England* one of his Majesties Justices of the Peace for this County.

T. Earl of *S.* Lord High Treasurer of *England*, another of his Majesties Justices of the Peace for this County.

J. Earl of *S.* another of his Majesties Justices of the Peace for this County.

J. Earl of *B.* another of his Majesties Justices of the Peace for this County.

A. Earl of *E.* another of his Majesties Justices of the Peace for this County.

Sir *H. G.* Baronet, Master of the *Rolls* in the High Court of *Chancery*, another of his Majesties Justices of the Peace for this County.

[All Privy Councillors were, and are, in the Commission of the Peace for every county. That is why people like the Lord High Treasurer are included.]

Sir *J. M.* Knight of the *Bath* and Baronet, another of his Majesties Justices of the Peace for this County.

Sir *H. G.* another of his Majesties Justices of the Peace for this County.

And so of all the rest.

If the Justice of Peace that is called do appear, then the Cryer must say *Vous aves*, Sir *J. G.* and the Clerk of Assizes must mark his appearance in the Calender.

[This part of the ritual was still being performed in 1778. In Boswell's account, of which I have already quoted so much, he says: "On 22 August I went into the Court on the Crown's side held by Judge Willes, and heard first the Justices of the peace of the County called over, each of whom that was present put a shilling into a little bag held out by the Crier, who said to each 'Vous Avez'. The Judge asked all of them to dine with him. Then the Grand Jury were called over. Sir James Lowther was their Foreman.... He had travelled night and day from London to be present at the Assizes.... Judge Willes read a Charge to the Grand Jury, neat but common place, blaming neither Ministers nor Generals for our bad success in America, but the profligacy of the Nation, and recommending reformation." The shillings were, I think, part of the perquisites of the Clerk of Assize.]

When they are called, then the Clerk of Assize shall cause the Cryer to say, All Mayors of Burroughs within this County of *H.* answer to your names as you shall be called every man at the first Call, and save your Fines.

E. L. Gent. Mayor of this Burrough of *Hertford.*

J. G. Gent. Mayor of the Burrough of St. *Albans.*

Then the Clerk of Assize shall cause the Cryer to say, All Coroners of our Soveraign Lord the King within this County of *H.* answer to your names as you shall be called every man at the first call, and save your Fines; then the Clerk of Assize shall farther say, the Cryer repeating the same after him with a loud voice.

E. B. Gent. one of the Coroners of this County of *Hertford.*

F. C. Gent. another of the Coroners of this County.

Then the Clerk of Assize shall direct the Cryer to call all Stewards of Leets and Liberties within this County, as they be retorned in the Calendar in the same manner as the Coroners were called.

Then the Clerk of Assize shall cause the Cryer to call the chief Constables of Hundreds in the same manner as abovesaid; and after them the Bailiffs of Hundreds, and Liberties within this County, as the Clerk of Assize shall name them to him.

Then the Clerk of Assize must cause the Cryer to make another Proclamation, and say, All Justices of Peace, Coroners, Stewards of Leets and Liberties, and other Officers that have taken any Inquisitions, or Recognizances, whereby you have let any man to bail, put in your Records thereof forthwith, that my Lords, the King's Justices may proceed thereon.

Then the Gaoler must give the Clerk of Assize an account of what Prisoners have been bailed by any Justices of the Peace after they were committed, and by what Justices they were bailed, that the Clerk of Assize may call to the Justices of Peace that bailed them for their Recognizances.

Then must the Clerk of Assize cause the Cryer to make another Proclamation, and say, You good men that be returned to enquire for our Soveraign Lord the King, and the body of this County of *H.* answer to your names every man at the first call, and save your Fines.

But if there do not appear enough, before any of them be sworn, to make up a Jury, then must the Clerk of Assize call them over again, Sir *A. B.* Baronet, the Cryer repeating the same after him, and if he do not then appear, then the Clerk of Assize must examine the Bailiffs who summon'd Sir *A. B.* to be here this day upon this service; when the Bailiff answers that he did, then the Clerk of Assize shall bid the Marshal give him the Book, and when the Bailiff has laid his hand on the Book, the Clerk of Assize shall say, You shall true answer make to such questions as the Court shall demand of you, so help you God; and when he is thus sworn, the Clerk of Assize shall say to him, By the Oath you have taken, did you summon Sir *A. B.* to be here this day upon this service; if he shall say, Yes: Then the Clerk of Assize shall ask him, When? where? and whether in person or not? and what he did say? and if his answer satisfies the Court, that the Judge doth excuse him, then the Clerk of Assize shall mark him spared; and so the Clerk of Assize shall ask for every one that did not appear at the first Call.

If there doth not appear a full Jury at the second Call, then the Sheriff must return some of the Free-holders of the same County, that are present, even the Justices of Peace upon the Bench, if he please.

Note, There ought to be at the least thirteen upon the Grand Jury, that there may be a Casting Vote, and so from that number to twenty three, for that County is best serv'd when the Gentlemen thereof, that are ingenious and learned, are assembled upon such an account.

Note also, that in calling the Justices of Peace, Coroners, Stewards of Leets & Liberties, Chief Constables, & Bailiffs of Hundreds, and Grand Juries, and other Juries, their appearances are usually marked with this mark(.) and when they are sworn, then they are usually marked with this mark(. .) or some such other mark, and their defaults left blank in the Margin, except the Judge set a Fine upon any of them for not appearing, then that is set down in the Margin.

Then the Grand Jury must be called in order, every one by his name, and addition as they be returned.

When the Jury be full, then the Marshal shall swear them after this manner, The Fore-man by himself must lay his right-hand on the Book, and then the Marshal shall give the Oath.

[The oaths of the Foreman and the rest of the Grand Jury are practically verbatim with those I have given earlier.]

The rest of the Grand Jury by three at a time in order, are sworn.

When all the Grand be thus sworn, then the Clerk of Assize doth say to the Cryer, Count these; and as he names them, the Cryer shall count them, concluding after the last name, Good men and true, stand together and hear your Charge.

Then the Clerk of Assize shall direct the Cryer to make Proclamation, and say, My Lords the King's Justices, do straitly charge and command all manner of persons to keep silence whilst the charge is in giving to the Grand Jury, upon pain of Imprisonment.

Then must the Grand Jury nominate a Bailiff to attend them.

All this, for the most part, is finished the first day in the forenoon; [Unless the Court began at a very early hour I am surprised that all this could be finished by noon. It must however be remembered that the number of county justices would be very small. I see from our Buckinghamshire Quarter Session Records that there were only about 40 justices in the county in 1710. There are now over 260. But the weakest aspect of the Bench everywhere now is that it is too numerous.] and when the Court rises, the Clerk of Assize directs the Cryer to make three Proclamations, and Adjourn in this manner:

All manner of persons that have appeared here before my Lords the King's Justices at these Assizes and General Gaol Delivery may take their ease at present, and attend here again at two of the Clock in the afternoon, and then he saies, *God Save the King*.

But note, If the Court of *Nisi prius* be sitting, then the Clerk of Assize shall direct the Adjournment thither.

When the Court is Adjourned the Trumpets shall sound, and the Sheriffs men two by two with their Holberds in their hands, and the Under-Sheriff following them with their White wands in their hands, shall attend the Judge in the Sheriffs Coach, where the Sheriff often rides with him from the Court to his Lodgings.

In my later book of 1749 the account of the ceremonial is shorter, and some parts of it have been omitted, e.g. the proclamations about *Novel Disseisins*, and raising or enhancing the prices of Victuals. But it is said that the Clerk of Assize "reads the several Commissions before-mentioned", which are five in number. And that he "calls the *Nomina Ministrorum*, namely, the Justices of the Peace, Coroners, Stewards, Bailiffs, Constables &c." The account ends, after the charge to the Grand Jury, "this is the most Part of the Business of the morning of the first Day".

In the second half of the eighteenth century there was one addition. Before the charge to the Grand Jury there was read "His Majesty's Proclamation against Vice, Profaneness, and Immorality". I have not discovered when this practice began, or when it was given up: nor have I ever seen its terms. Apparently it lasted much longer than one might suppose. For Huddleston's *Notes* say: "After the Grand Jury is sworn the proclamation against Vice and Immorality is read."

Both these accounts describe the reading of the Commission as taking place, as it does now, on the opening morning of the Assize. I can only suppose that the practice of doing it on the night before, as at Carlisle in 1778, or, as it should have been, at Gloucester in 1818, was introduced after 1749, with a view to saving time the next morning. I do not know when there was a reversion to the older practice.

Presumably in the older time the Commission Day named in the Judge's Precept to the Sheriff was the first working day of the Assize, and in 1818, when Garrow was an hour late, it was the day before, as it is now. Otherwise the decision of Lord Eldon, apparently based on the necessity of the Commission being opened on a fixed day, is all the more incomprehensible!

Technically an Assize still begins on the Commission Day specified in the Judge's Precept to the Sheriff. And any sentence of imprisonment runs from that day. If Commission Day on which a judge travels to an Assize town is a Monday, and the Commission is read and trials begin on Tuesday, and if on the Wednesday the Judge wishes to pass a nominal sentence he must make it *three* days. The prisoner has been in imprisonment for Monday, Tuesday and part of Wednesday. If on the Wednesday he said "one day's imprisonment", the man would technically have a claim against the Governor of the prison for false imprisonment.

It was not long before I had the curiosity to find out what were the contents of the packet handed to me by the High Sheriff in response to my clerk's demand. On the first occasion when I opened it I found nothing but blank paper. The Under-Sheriff, with many apologies, explained that he had been delayed in making up the packet and had arranged to deliver it later to the Clerk of Assize. I expect he never knew of any judge displaying my curiosity.

I opened another roll at Chester in February 1926, and found that its contents were as follows: (1) The Precept signed by the Judges, which I have printed in Appendix A. On the back of it was an indorsement, signed and sealed by the Sheriff, which I add at the end of that

Appendix. (2) Attached to the foregoing, a sheet of paper signed and sealed by the Sheriff, headed

"CHESHIRE WINTER ASSIZES
2 February 1926

CHESHIRE } The names of the Grand Jury to enquire for our Sovereign
to wit } Lord the King for the body of the said County."

with the names of 24 Grand Jury men and their places of abode. (3) The Precept from the Clerk of Assize, set out in my Appendix B. This was indorsed on the back as shown at the end of that Appendix. (4) Attached to the last three lists (*a*) a printed list of 36 special jurors, two copies on white paper, and five copies on blue paper; (*b*) a printed list of 120 common jurors, in two sets of 60 each (six copies); (*c*) a very long written list headed "*Nomina Ministrorum* for the year 1926". First came the names of the two Judges and the Lord-Lieutenant of the county. Then followed, under various headings: *Peers etc.* (11 Peers and 4 Privy Councillors), *Baronets* (16 names), *Knights* (15 names), *Esquires* (452 names), *Clerks* (one parson), *Ladies* (33 names), *Mayors* (9 names), *Coroners* (5 names), *Chief Constables* (9 places), *Sheriff's Officers* (3).

The preparation of this list of *Nomina Ministrorum* must have been troublesome. When I again examined a Sheriff's offering at Shrewsbury in June 1926, I found that before the names of the Peers, there were the Archbishop of Canterbury, the Lord Chancellor, and the Archbishop of York, in that order. So to include them was, I believe, the practice in many counties.

In October 1932 I had a letter from the Lord Chancellor to say that he had been asked by some of the Under-Sheriffs to release them from the further task of making the *Nomina Ministrorum*, required by the Precept of the Clerk of Assize, but not by that of the Judges. I replied that I thought that no harm would be done to anyone if their request was complied with. And I mentioned my experience of finding nothing but blank paper. The Lord Chancellor made an order; and there have been no *Nomina Ministrorum* since 1932.

At the end of the day, if there is more work to be done on the morrow, the Judge's clerk makes proclamation, when the Court adjourns: "All persons having anything further to do before My Lords the King's Justices may now depart hence, and give their attendance here to-morrow morning at half past ten of the clock." And when the Court rises on the last day, he proclaims: "All persons having anything further to do before my Lord's the King's Justices may now depart hence and give their attendance forthwith at my Lord's lodgings. God save the King and my Lords the King's Justices." I believe this last behest is because theoretically the Judge is available to anyone who has a right to his services until he leaves the county. I am glad that I have never known anyone to be so inconsiderate as to obey it and come to the Lodgings.

When I said that the three-cornered hat is never used in London I overlooked one occasion. When on 9 November the Lord Mayor comes into the Court of Appeal, to invite their Lordships to his dinner, the Lords Justices wear their hats on top of their wigs. This I believe is to disabuse the Lord Mayor of any notion that they do not remain covered in his presence. In the Court of the Lord Chief Justice the Judges similarly wear their black caps, which gives them a still more bizarre aspect. The King's Remembrancer, who sits beneath them, takes no part in the proceedings. But at one stage he ostentatiously puts his three-cornered hat on his wig, to make the Lord Mayor realize that he too can be covered in his presence.

I have said that in the old days Judges used to wear the three-cornered hat in Court, as Mr Justice Stareleigh was doing in 1828. Lord Campbell,* in his *Life* of Kenyon, has this: "It was observed for a number of years before he died, that he had two hats and two wigs—of the hats and the wigs one was dreadfully old and shabby, and one was comparatively spruce. He always carried into court with him the very old hat and the comparatively spruce wig, or the very old wig and the comparatively spruce hat. On the days of the very old hat and the comparatively spruce wig he shoved his hat under the bench, and displayed the wig; but on the days of the very old wig and the comparatively spruce hat, he always continued covered. I have a very lively recollection of having often seen him sitting with his hat over his wig." And he adds a foot-note: "Till the middle of the last century the Chancellor is always represented with his hat on. In early times it was round and conical; and such was Lord Keeper Williams's, although he was a bishop. In Anne's reign three-cornered hats came up. The black cap of the common law judges, which has remained

* *Lives of the Chief Justices*, Vol. IV, p. 145.

unchanged for many ages, is square. With this they used always to be *covered*; but they wear it now only when passing sentence of death." On Sir John Holt's fine monument in Redgrave church, Suffolk, his statue has his black cap on his knee. It is exactly like that of a judge of to-day, except for being one or two inches smaller. He died in 1710.

1926

In January 1926 I went on the North Wales Circuit. It was as pleasant and varied an experience as I had had in South Wales a year before. But I was not surprised to find the same waste of judicial time as I did then. At Welshpool there were no prisoners, and one civil case; at Dolgelley no prisoners, and one civil case; at Carnarvon four prisoners, and one civil case, which had to be postponed owing to the illness of a witness; at Beaumaris three prisoners, all of whom pleaded guilty to trifling offences; at Ruthin four prisoners, and one civil case; and at Mold two prisoners, who pleaded guilty, and one civil case. In the result by the evening I got to Chester I had spent in Court 37 hours, on days on which if I had been in London I should have sat for 85 hours, a loss of 48 working hours. This was not quite so bad as a year earlier in South Wales—21 hours in Court as against 75 in London, a loss of 54 hours. In North Wales again I found there were no gaols to be delivered. If not on bail, prisoners were brought from Liverpool prison to Welshpool, Carnarvon, Beaumaris, and Mold, and from Shrewsbury prison to Dolgelley and Ruthin.

In Barry O'Brien's *Life* of Lord Russell of Killowen, L.C.J., there is a detailed account of his experience of work on the North Wales Circuit in July 1900, just before his death in August of that year. He left town on Thursday 5 July for Newtown, which takes the place of Welshpool in the summer. He had white gloves, and no civil work, at Newtown, Dolgelley, and Beaumaris, and very little to do at Carnarvon, Ruthin, and Mold. On the same sort of calculation I reckon that, including the purely formal dealings with Grand Juries at the maiden assizes, he spent less than 20 hours in Court as against 65 hours if he had been sitting regularly in London. The only difference is that under the present system the first two Assizes, at Newtown and Dolgelley, would have been cancelled, and he would only have left town for Carnarvon on Tuesday, 10 July.

It is difficult to realize that it was only in the year 1908 that a judge was empowered,* and directed, to cancel an Assize if there was no business at all to be done at it. Before that date he travelled to the town, went to an Assize Service, had the Commission opened, harangued the magistrates assembled as potential Grand Jurors, and received white gloves. Under that system on each of the four occasions when I have been on the Midland Circuit I should have gone through this ritual at Oakham! In Grantham's *Circuit Diary* in February 1891 he goes to a "maiden assize" at Oakham, harangues the Grand Jury, and receives white gloves.

At each of these six Welsh towns, being very desirous of walking, I tried to buy the One Inch Ordnance Map of the district. Only Welshpool and Carnarvon were sufficiently civilized to supply them. In a country town one surely ought to be able to buy Ordnance Maps at the Government shop, the Post Office. I thought one could. But when I tried at one or two Post Offices I found I might as well have enquired for a Sanskrit dictionary. Not only had they no Ordnance Maps for sale, but they appeared to be unaware of their existence, or even of the meaning of the words "Ordnance Maps".

That there were to be no prisoners at Welshpool was known before I left town, and I was asked by the Clerk of Assize whether I thought the Grand Jury should be summoned to attend. I said I thought they should. When they appeared in Court I told them I had done so, and that I hoped that they, or at least a majority of them, would approve my decision. I said I thought it was desirable for the gentlemen of the county to attend and meet His Majesty's Judge of Assize, even if it was only to receive his congratulations upon the law-abiding virtues of their county. I added that they might remember, as an illustration of the antiquity of such attendance, the account in *The Spectator* of Friday, 20 July 1711 (nearly 215 years ago), of Sir Roger de Coverley's arrival at the Assizes. Way was made for him "for his reputation in the country" to take his place on the bench next the Judge: and he took occasion to whisper in the Judge's ear "that he was glad his Lordship had met with so much good weather in his circuit". But I doubt if Addison can ever have been present in an Assize Court. "The Court was sat before Sir Roger came", and after he had got to his seat next the Judge, "I was listening to the proceedings of the Court with much attention." But "after about an hour's sitting I

* By the Act 8 Edw. VII, cap. 41.

observed to my great surprise, in the midst of a trial, that my friend Sir Roger was getting up to speak". And speak he did, apparently without any protest from the Judge, though "the speech he made was little to the purpose...and I believe was not so much designed by the Knight himself to inform the Court, as to give him a figure in my eye, and keep up his credit in the country". I cannot believe that even in 1711 a Judge of Assize would tolerate the interruption of a trial by a county magistrate, whatever his age and his "reputation in the country", and permit him to deliver an aimless oration designed to impress his friend, and to "keep up his credit in the country".

Addison here uses the word "country" as meaning "county", which was usual until the nineteenth century. In the old ritual "Culprit, how wilt thou be tried?" said the Clerk of Assize. And the prisoner answered "By God and my country". Whereon the jury were told that he "has put himself upon his country, which country ye are". The use is the same in Jane Austen's novels. In *Mansfield Park* Rushworth is introduced as "a young man who had recently succeeded to one of the largest estates and finest places in the country". And after Maria's divorce she and Mrs Norris retired "to an establishment formed for them in another country".

At Carnarvon we were lodged in the Rectory, which is on the edge of the Roman Segontium: the remains of one of its gates are in the garden, and Roman coins are often dug up. The morning after we arrived we awoke to find about nine inches of snow on the ground, a rare event for those parts. For the Assize Service we went to St Mary's church, against the town walls. It is an interesting building, admirably restored. The vestry, in a bastion of the wall, makes a beautiful room. On the wall I saw hung up the rusted clapper of the old bell, with a legend attached that it fell off in 1910 while the knell of an executed murderer was being tolled. In the yard before the church was a fine tree: no one could tell me if it was a holly, or an ilex, or what. If it is a holly, it is one of the largest I ever saw, and illustrates the theory that as the holly grows great it can afford to dispense with its protective prickles.

Beaumaris is almost as insignificant as an Assize town as Presteign. The Lodgings were in a small, old-fashioned, villa at the corner of the terrace on the sea front. The carriage, to drive the few yards to the Court, was a Victorian barouche drawn by the two funeral horses of the town. There was a faded photograph on the piano in the drawing-room of the Lodgings, which showed Lord Russell of Killowen in his robes descending the steps on Monday, 16 July 1900. Awaiting him, at the bottom of them, was the same vehicle, and I suspect the same horses, that awaited me on Monday, 25 January 1926.

The Court at Beaumaris is an extraordinary little barn-like structure, with its date 1614 on one gable. When I took my seat on the exiguous bench I found the Grand Jury in a pen on my left. As their swearing in began I suggested that it would be convenient if each gentleman would sit down after he was sworn: but it appeared that this was impossible, for there were no seats and no room for any. When they retired to their arduous labours—there were two people charged with a venial bigamy, and one with stealing to the value of *7s. 6d.*—I retired to the "Judge's Room". This was a small wooden cupboard, in which there was just room for me to sit on a Windsor chair, and, as is my wont, to smoke a pipe. Suddenly, from the pressure of spectators in the Court, a door from my cupboard, or part of the structure, gave way, and I became the cynosure of curious eyes. Perhaps it was as well that the charming gentleman who was High Sheriff of Anglesey was more gorgeously apparelled than any Sheriff I ever saw—in the uniform of a General of the Head Quarters Staff—and the average splendour of the ceremonial was thereby raised to near the level of St George's Hall, Liverpool.

In the churchyard at Beaumaris I noticed the grave of "John Pritchard, Tide-Waiter" who died in 1854. If there is a tide-waiter at Beaumaris now, he enjoys a sinecure. West of the church is a small disused prison of an incredibly forbidding aspect. As the business in Court was all over long before lunch, we had a free afternoon and walked to Penmon Priory. The great stone wall was, I believe, constructed by a Bulkeley, of the great house at Beaumaris, to form a deer park. In the Priory Buildings is a magnificent dove-cot with hundreds of nests in the walls. Best of all are the Norman nave and transepts, and in the South transept a wonderful Runic cross: it had been rescued from the ruins where it had been used by the Norman builders as a lintel. Not far away, inside the vast wall of the old deer park, is a second fine Runic cross.

And so to Ruthin, and then to Mold. From Ruthin to Mold is less than 10 miles. So, when we moved, my marshal and I went by foot along the old road, which is now grass-grown, through the hills. Of course we could not buy a map, but we met an intelligent boy who started us on the right way, and it was later easy to find. It comes out to the new road by the oddly named "Loggerheads" Inn; and close to that we inspected a very ancient water-mill still noisily worked by a pleasant miller, and by the stream.

Mold was distinguished by providing as good Lodgings as any in the Kingdom, the charming country house called Rhuol. As Flint is the smallest of all counties, except Rutland, one might have expected some awful place like the Haverfordwest house. As it was I had never been in better Lodgings, and, except perhaps at Salisbury and Oxford, I have not since.

I liked the church at Mold, which is late Perpendicular. The floor slopes all its length, as at St David's, but less steeply. This inscription, on an elegant cartouche seemed to me interesting:

WILLIAM WYNNE, of Tower, D.D.
Sometime Fellow of All Souls College in Oxford,
And Rector of Llanvechan in this Diocese,
departed this life 3rd March 1776,
Aged 77.

In conformity to ancient usage,
from a proper regard to decency,
and from a concern for the health of his
Fellow-Creatures, he was moved to give
particular directions for being buried
in the adjoining churchyard
and not in the Church.

And, as he scorn'd flattering of others
while living, he has took care to prevent
being flattered himself when dead,
by causing this small memorial to be
Set up in his life-time.

God be merciful to me a sinner.

The quondam Fellow of All Souls was ahead of the time in these very proper sentiments. I regret to say that a Bencher of the Inner Temple was buried in the Inner Temple vault under the Temple Church as late as 5 August 1852, and a Bencher of the Middle Temple, in the Middle Temple vault, on 28 May 1853. Thoresby, the Leeds historian, being at Berwick-on-Tweed on 11 September 1681, records in his *Diary* his surprise at "the Scotch mode for Aldermen and persons of some rank to be buried in the churchyard" instead of inside the church.

And so to Chester, where I met Mr Justice Fraser, coming from Presteign. We were in the same poor house that I was in a year ago, but I am glad to say this was the last occasion on which it was used. On the Sunday we went to service at the Cathedral. In the afternoon we went to tea with the Bishop and Mrs Paget and were then taken all over the Cathedral by the Bishop and the Dean. Anyone who went to Chester at that time knew that the Dean had done wonders, and made his Cathedral a model for all others to try to copy. I had already spent much time in it, but perhaps that made me enjoy even more the privilege of going round with him. One of our marshals was bred in the Roman Church, and as we were walking home afterwards he said: "If all the English Bishops and Deans were like those two, I should be seriously shaken in my proper allegiance."

Cardiff, I am afraid, I disliked as a city even more than I did a year ago. Perhaps its chief disadvantage is that right through it from north to south runs a quadruple barrier of two railway lines, the Castle grounds, and the river, and there is only one way across this barrier. The best form of diversion and exercise we found was to take a bus to Penarth and there walk by the sea. But the sun set early, and there was not much time to walk at Penarth.

The police guard, when the Judges arrive at the Courts at Cardiff, is always a very fine set of men. I believe a good many of them were Rugby internationals. They were at this time under the command of Sergeant Macdonald, a magnificent Highlander, and bigger than any of them. We heard that on this occasion he had expressed his satisfaction at having two Scottish judges—or at least with good Scottish names. One day I asked him in to my room, where Mr Justice Fraser joined me, and we had a talk with him. I believe he liked me. But it was rightly my brother Fraser that he loved. For he talked to him in Gaelic.

On my first visit to Cardiff I said of the manifold splendours of the Mansion House that I should not be surprised to hear that it had two billiard-rooms. On this visit I verified the fact: there were two.

During this circuit I read with interest Lord Cockburn's *Circuit Journeys*. A Scottish friend, to whom I mentioned the notes I made of my circuit experiences, gave me the book. I have long possessed, and more than once read, Cockburn's *Memorials of his Time*, and his *Journal*. There are few things better than his character sketches of the old Scots Judges in the former, and among them notably the account of Lord Braxfield, which opens with the sentence, "But the giant of the Bench was Braxfield. His very name makes people start yet."

Circuit Journeys I had not come across, and I was interested to find in it a precedent, *longo intervallo*, for the record I was keeping.

The Scottish Circuits, in Lord Cockburn's time, differed in one important matter from ours. His journal is full of complaints of the inns in which he had to stay; for there were no Judges' Lodgings. The ceremonial, provided for us by the High Sheriff and his trumpeters, they had with a difference. The Judges went in procession with trumpeters, officials, and soldiery, but they walked the streets in their robes *on foot*. Considering how often it rains in Scotland, there must have been many miserable times for this function. In Cockburn's *Journal* (Vol. I, p. 173) there is a sketch by John Lockhart of Lord Pitmilly walking in a circuit procession at Glasgow, holding an umbrella over his head.

The Scots Judge of Lord Cockburn's time also had no marshal, or his equivalent. In *Circuit Journeys*, speaking of old times and the changes since 1800, he writes: "The slowness of movement, and badness of up-putting, prevented ladies from accompanying lords as habitually as they do now. But to make up for this, every judge carried about a lately fledged advocate as his humble friend. To be seen travelling circuit with my Lord was thought such a feather in a youth's cap, that his friends never allowed him to decline the honour. Decline being aide-de-camp to the general! But, Lord, it was dull! I never knew one victim that enjoyed the sacrifice. There could, for weeks alone together, be no cordiality between age and youth, patronage and dependence, levity and dignity. Even Hope's kindness, and cumbrous efforts to be jolly, could not save it from oppressiveness. With most others it was the *peine forte et dure*. The sedate driving, the two hours pauses every stage, the disrespect of taking refuge in a book, the positive insult of walking off alone, the condescending remark of my Lord, only so much the worse when it was intended to be gay, the respectful acquiescence of 'the young man'. Och! Och! it was dreadful. Nearly fifty years have not effaced Lord MacKenzie's sufferings under Lord Craig."

I might have read this passage with concern and alarm, if I had thought that it had any application to the charming young men—many of them "lately fledged advocates"—who honoured me by their company as marshals. But I cannot believe that Charles M—— remembers as *peine forte et dure* that Sunday walk in the snows of the Derbyshire hills. Or that Harold C—— found my cumbrous efforts to be jolly did not save him from oppressiveness. If it were so, they, and many more, were very apt dissemblers. And certainly I was never able to observe "the respectful acquiescence of the young men". That there "can be no cordiality between age and youth" is not true nowadays.

Owing to the absence of any roads on which a carriage could go, the Scots Judges in early days rode round their circuits on horseback. So it was in England, but the change was made in England much earlier than in Scotland. For in Scotland it was continued as a dignified habit, when it was really no longer necessary. As late as 1744 Lord Dun felt constrained to resign his judgeship, because he was no longer able to ride.

✧ ✧ ✧

In July 1926 my duty was to join Mr Justice Avory at Stafford, the last town on the Oxford Circuit, and then go to meet Mr Justice McCardie at Birmingham, the last town on the Oxford and Midland Circuits: Birmingham only became an Assize town in 1884. But shortly before I was due at Stafford I had a letter from Mr Justice Avory to say that the work at Shrewsbury was unusually heavy, so that he would be glad if I would join him there. This was a happy chance: for there is no more delightful town than Shrewsbury, and I went there very contentedly on 30 June.

The permanent Lodgings at Shrewsbury are a very fine Queen Anne house in Belmont, high over the river, with a garden sloping down to the town walls. The broad hall, running from back to front, and the dining-room are finely panelled in oak, and the proportions of all the rooms are good. But there are fine old houses everywhere in Shrewsbury, especially in *culs de sac* like Quarry Place, and Swan Hill Court, and I spent much time in wandering about and wishing that I had a master key, and a cap of invisibility, that I might see their interiors. Perhaps the most stately of all of them is the great house on which you can gaze through its broad gate on the town walls, just opposite the surviving tower on the wall. These fine houses, so far as my enquiries told me, were nearly all occupied by elderly maiden ladies.

The Castle was thus occupied until lately, but has now been taken over by the Corporation and well restored. The great hall, furnished with good modern oak fittings as a Council Chamber, is admirable. Over the main gate of the gaol, near the railway station, is a bust of William Wilberforce. It gives him features by no means unpleasant, and suggests that Charles Lamb was unkind to him when, in his description of Peter Peirson, he wrote: "His cheeks were colourless, even to whiteness. His look was uninviting, resembling (but without his sourness) that of our great philanthropist."

The churches of Shrewsbury I found delightful, despite the havoc that has been played in them. Shrewsbury is beautiful enough now, with its old houses and what remains of its churches. But what a town it would be if the Abbey, St Chad's, St Julian's, and St Alkmund's were all intact as in the fifteenth century, and there were no such modern monstrosities as that ghastly hospital and girls' school, which flank the approach to the hideous Kingsland Bridge, and spoil the view of the town from across the river.

The two Courts at Shrewsbury are good. But usually there is only one judge now, so the second Court, in which I sat, is used for meetings of the County Council, and they had taken away the witness-box. If a witness has to stand somewhere on the floor of the Court, without the elevation of a box to inspire him to audibility, he has an incentive to mumble that most witnesses seldom require in any case.

Fortunately the heaviest of the civil cases, which I was trying, was settled half-way through, and I had a pleasant afternoon up at the School watching a cricket-match. On the Sunday evening I went to the School Chapel and to supper with my friend, Canon Sawyer, the Head Master. There I met the head of the School, and as a result received from him next day, at Stafford, a Latin letter. "Tibi licet", it ran, "ab archididascalo postulare ut mentes nobis horas postmeridianas e studiis laxet. Nos igitur, alumni, perarduo defatigati labore, te precamur ut privilegio tuo utaris...." When I received it the circumstances were unfavourable to Latinity. My marshal, *horresco referens*, had taken his degree at Cambridge in what I believe is called the Engineering Tripos. My colleague refused to help me, his marshal pretended to be unable. From what I saw of Stafford I doubt if it contained a Latin dictionary. So I had to essay a reply unaided. But however doggish the result, my young friend would not scruple to hand it to the Head Master; and he would hardly deprive them of their half-holiday as a punishment for my errors.

At Stafford—as at Aylesbury, Derby, and Presteign—the permanent Lodgings are under the same roof as the Courts, and except to go to the church on the opening day, we had no use for the Sheriff's car. The rooms are spacious, if rather gaunt, but the building is too closely beset by others, and lacks light and air. There is a door of communication with the fine modern County Council Buildings. And they are notable for containing by far the finest collection of county prints, both portraits and topographical, that I have ever seen anywhere. I believe this was due to the skill and enthusiasm of Mr Joy, the Clerk to the Council. Stafford may be congratulated on outdoing all other counties in this respect.

In the Crown Court there is a monument on the wall to Mr Justice Talfourd, the friend of Charles Lamb and of Charles Dickens. At the Spring Assizes in 1854, while in the act of addressing the Grand Jury, he died suddenly upon the bench in this Court. "By a curious coincidence, six years after Talfourd's death, to the very day, Baron Watson, the old Waterloo veteran, was taken with a fatal seizure in Court at Welshpool, shortly after charging the grand jury of Montgomeryshire."*

Stafford I thought a most uninteresting town, and the country round it very dull. Lord Campbell, when a young man on the Oxford Circuit, wrote,† in March 1819: "Here we are at Stafford, the dullest and vilest town in all England." St Chad's has fine Norman work in its small nave. No one would expect its existence from the hideous West front on the street. The only fine old house is the one which has been turned into the Post Office, and its interior gutted. Our sole diversion was to go out one afternoon to Ingestre, and walk round the outside of the house. Before it was burnt and rebuilt it must have been a fine place; but the rebuilding was at a dangerous age, and the detail is bad. The small Classical church, close to the house, with its fine woodwork and its family monuments I found most interesting.

* Atlay, *Victorian Chancellors*, Vol. II, p. 110.

† *Life*, Vol. I, p. 355.

The work at Stafford finished in four days, so that I could get up to town and go to Lords for the Eton and Harrow match on the Saturday. At that same Assize in March 1819, Campbell said: "There are considerably over 100 prisoners to be tried." That is the sort of thing that one often comes across in accounts of Assizes in the old days. And the number of civil cases seems equally large. In Mr Justice Rokeby's *Diary* he records that on the Western Circuit, in the summer of 1693, there were 268 causes tried, including 65 at Exeter. Campbell, in April 1812, speaks of 64 causes and 67 prisoners at Gloucester. Two things must be remembered. As to prisoners, the jurisdiction of Petty Sessions to try offenders summarily, and of Quarter Sessions to try them on indictment, was infinitely smaller than to-day. Very many of the numerous prisoners would be charged with offences which would now be dealt with at Quarter Sessions, and still more at Petty Sessions. As to civil causes, there were then no County Courts, and there was no machinery for getting summary judgment under the modern Order 14. A great many civil cases at the Assizes would be undefended, and a great many of trifling importance.

Atlay, *Victorian Chancellors* (Vol. I, p. 101) writes: "During the five years ending in 1827 no fewer than 30,000 out of the 90,000 causes entered annually at Westminster were for sums not exceeding £20; the lists at assizes were swollen with cases which today would not go beyond the County Court Registrar; the cost of recovering sums under £50 was often ludicrously out of proportion to the amount at issue. Many banks and commercial houses systematically submitted to loss and robbery rather than prosecute their claim in a court of law."

On the Sunday afternoon, in sweltering heat (and in the costume of Lords, which made it worse), I went to Birmingham to join Mr Justice McCardie at the Lodgings at Edgbaston. They are in a very large Victorian house, which is comfortable enough, but is hideous. The furniture throughout is the purest Victorian I have ever seen: a selection of the best pieces would make an inimitable display. At the back of the house is a garden with an excellent lawn, on which we played bowls nightly, and in a fortnight improved a good deal on our first erratic essays. Some judges are not so old that they must decline upon bowls, and McCardie and I would have been glad to have had the lawn marked and netted for lawn tennis. As it was we did play a good deal at friendly houses near by, despite a heat wave for our first week.

I am afraid I do not greatly admire Birmingham. The fine part of the town, near the Town Hall and the Courts, is limited, and the rest of its vast expanse is ugly and dull. Edgbaston is a strangely rural suburb, or rather an island, with the city all round it. Except for the park at Nottingham, on a much smaller scale, I know nothing like it in any great city. Aston Hall is a splendid relic, but its surroundings are very depressing, and it cannot compete with Temple Newsham at Leeds. There is a dangerous temptation to use a place like this as the dumping ground of inferior things that overflow from the municipal Art Gallery and Museum. The long gallery at Aston is very fine, but it would look much better if its wonderful panelling were left bare of the inferior pictures hung along it. And though "the first electro-plating machine" may be of interest in a technical museum, it is out of place in a Jacobean interior.

A pleasant relaxation was to drive to Lichfield one afternoon. On the way we stopped to see the church at Sutton Coldfield. Close to the south side of it is the grave of Mary Ashford, for whose death Richard Thornton was tried, and acquitted, at Warwick Assizes in 1817. Whereupon there ensued those astonishing proceedings in the last Appeal of Murder, which may be read in the report of *Ashford* v. *Thornton* (1 B. & Ald. 405). The gravestone has a long inscription which we found quite illegible. I detected the words "female virtue" near the beginning, and I suppose it may have pointed a moral like the stone of Mary Morgan at Presteign.

The church is a good one. Round the chancel is some fine Renaissance woodwork, which Sir Gilbert Scott cast out of Worcester Cathedral, when that unhappy building, under his hands, ἐσκιδμωρεύθη.

And so, through a pleasant country, to Lichfield, where Alderman Wood met us at the Johnson House, and showed us all its treasures. I had not been there for a long time, and I did not know, or I had forgotten, that those treasures were as good as they are. There can be no such collection of Johnsonian relics anywhere, except at Buffalo, where my friend Mr R. B. Adam has the greatest collection of all. The house is admirably kept, and Lichfield may be proud of this monument to its greatest citizen. Of his statue, outside, they cannot be proud. And why, oh why, did they allow the late Mr Fitzgerald to put up an alleged statue of Boswell? It is bad enough that every day, as I cross from the Law Courts to the Temple, I have to avert my gaze lest I should be affronted by a sight of the dwarfish mulatto that disfigures the eastern end of St Clement Danes. Mr Fitzgerald wrote a number of bad books, but you need not read them: it is not so easy to avoid his bad statues when they are allowed to be set up in public places.

On the second week-end we motored by Henley-in-Arden, Stratford-on-Avon, Chipping Campden, Broadway, Tewkesbury, Worcester, and Bromsgrove. I had been to them all before. Stratford was full of Americans in horn spectacles: if you have seen its sights once, you do not want to see them again, and we did not stop. But Chipping Campden's church, and its street, you cannot see too often. Sir Baptist Hicks's monument is magnificent. And since I was there they had put on show the wonderful old English cope, and altar frontals, in a glass case. At Tewkesbury, if your eye travels only to the top of the Norman arcade, you have a sense of being abroad, from its loftiness. Looking up higher you lose the illusion, from the lowness of the vault above. At Worcester we remembered the woodwork we saw at Sutton Coldfield, and marvelled again at its rejection for that which was put in its place. At Bromsgrove I sought out an epitaph I remembered in the churchyard. The *Oxford Dictionary* does not record a word which it contains: if it did, I fancy this tombstone would be its only authority. Thus it runs:

> A quondam beauty here is laid in dust,
> One (tho' but young) was prudent, pious, just;
> So modest, gracious, meek, so void of hate,
> No injury she could retaliate;
> But tears to Earth, her sighs to Heaven sent,
> Ne'er bitter language showed her malecontent;
> She pious councel dyeing gave to all,
> To be with Christ she longed. And her soul
> Is now in heaven, in whom every grace
> Was proto-varnish't with an Angel's face.

She died 5 August 1685, aged 18.

◇ ◇ ◇

For the autumn of 1926, by some extraordinary piece of good luck, I was allowed to choose the first South-Eastern Circuit, that is Cambridge, Norwich, Ipswich, and Chelmsford. This is perhaps the most desired of all, and it usually fell to one of the senior judges. To be able to go there two years after my appointment to the Bench was very unexpected.

It was hard on Cambridge men not to be able to go to their own University town until they had been many years on the Bench. Mr Justice Branson, an old Cambridge rowing blue, had to wait eleven years before he was allowed to go to Cambridge Assizes, and Lord Wright, a quondam Fellow of Trinity, never had the chance to do so in the seven years that he was a Judge of first instance. I was able to do something to remedy this grievance later on. There is a very old rule that in his second year on the Bench a judge may assert a claim to go upon the circuit of which he was a member when at the bar—a rule of which I could never take advantage. In January 1936 I moved a resolution at a Judges' meeting that this rule should be enlarged, by adding the alternative of going on the Oxford Circuit, for a graduate of Oxford, or on the first South-Eastern for a graduate of Cambridge. This was carried unanimously, and the grievance of a Cambridge man of not being able to go to Cambridge until he had served for very many years has been mitigated. The Oxford Circuit was always easier to get, and Oxford men did not have to wait so long to go there. But it was only 5½ years after my appointment that I was able to go to Oxford.

To Cambridge I went on Thursday, 14 October. As is well known, the Judge of Assize is lodged in the Master's Lodge at Trinity.

I believe this has been the practice since the reign of Elizabeth. From time to time the College has tried to protest against the burden, but the contest has been with the Crown, which claimed the right to have His Majesty's judges housed in the Lodge, rather than with the judges themselves. The most signal occasion of this was when in 1866 the Autumn Assize was invented. The College intimated to Baron Martin, the prospective judge of the Autumn Assize, that he must not expect to be entertained on this occasion, that the College had often protested against the practice, and they claimed that it could only apply to the two ancient Assizes in Spring and Summer. Thereupon the Home Secretary intervened, and the College had to submit. The matter was then settled by the following document:

Instrument conceding to Her Majesty's Judges of Assize the use of certain apartments and offices in Trinity College and certain allowances etc. whenever they shall hold courts of Assize for the Town and County of Cambridge.

The Crown and the College

A question having arisen between the Crown and Trinity College with respect to the lodging of H.M's. Judges of Assize at Trinity College We, the Master, Fellows, and Scholars of Trinity College, in order to prevent any misunderstanding do freely and voluntarily concede (without prejudice to any legal right alleged or existing either on behalf of the Crown or the College) that H.M. Judges of Assize whensoever they shall hold Courts of Assize or Gaol Delivery for the Town and County of Cambridge shall have the use of all the apartments and offices as specified in the accompanying schedule which have been usually appropriated to them at the spring and summer assizes together with such allowances as they have heretofore received out of the Steward's office.

In witness whereof we, the said Master, Fellows, and Scholars have affixed the common seal of the College to the present writing this 12th day of June 1866.

Schedule.

1. Senior Judge's Room, with dressing-room & closet adjoining.
2. Junior Judge's Room, with dressing-room adjoining.
3. The large Dining Room.
4. The Servants' Hall.
5. The Judges' Kitchen.
6. The Judges' Cellar.
7. The room above the Servants' Hall, known as the Judges' Steward's room, and in common with the Master the use of the Pantry.

Another bone of contention used at one time to arise between the College and the Judges themselves. This was when a judge brought his wife with him. This trouble became acute in 1883, when Mr Justice Watkin Williams (who died in a spectacular way at Nottingham a year later) brought a wife, and a marshal with a wife. Mr Justice Denman, a quondam Senior Classic and Fellow of Trinity, was delegated by the Judges to settle the question. And I believe he arranged that in future judges should not bring wives. On the two occasions on which I have been at the Cambridge Assizes my wife has slept at the Bull, but of course joined me for any meals she desired at the Lodge.

The Lodge is very spacious, and I hope the advent of the Judge does not now cause much inconvenience to the Master. The only room of whose use it deprives him is the enormous dining-room. Beyond it, as I remember, there was a suite of two bedrooms and a bathroom set aside for the Judge and his marshal. I do not know if these are the Senior Judge's room, and the Junior Judge's room, as in the Schedule above, and as in the time when two judges came. If so, I do not know where, under that regime, there was room for two marshals. But the rooms may have been rearranged under the modern system of a single judge. The bedrooms are hung with a considerable collection of portrait prints of deceased judges.

The High Sheriff having conveyed me to the great gate of Trinity I there parted from him, and advanced with my marshal towards the Master's House on the other side of the great court. As we came through the gate, the Master with two other dons (presumably upon some signal from the porter) came out of his front door, and towards us. We met in the middle of the court, and after we had exchanged greetings I was escorted to the Lodge.

In the *Diary* of Mr Justice Rokeby, Cambridge, 12 March 1694/5, he wrote: "The coach could not conveniently go into Trinity Colledge, where I lay, soe ye Sheriff provided me a chair, which carryed me through ye Court to ye Coach." I have been told by an elderly Trinity man that it was a tradition that the Judge used to be carried across the court in a sedan chair. He said he had never seen this ceremony, but he had seen the chair, and he remembered it being used on a wet night for a lady who was dining at the Lodge. I wonder if it is still stored away somewhere in the College.

On reaching the Lodge we were taken into the vast dining-room to the right of the hall. That was my only sitting-room, but it was large enough for anything. Just after we entered a butler appeared with a tray of glasses of mulled port. It was five in the afternoon. But I am all for the observance of ancient ritual. And the drink was concocted after a most admirable recipe, so that inclination combined with duty.

Next morning there was a serious ceremony for a modest graduate of the University of Oxford. Three separate parties were announced in succession. I think the first was the High Sheriff and Chaplain, and the second the Mayor, with some Aldermen and the Town Clerk. But the most impressive was the Academic party. The windows of the great room give a full view of the court, and across it I saw advancing Bedels with maces—Esquire Bedels, I found, for they have not abolished them as we did at Oxford in 1856—and all the Vice-Cancellarian pomp. I confess to some shyness, as the butler announced, "The Vice-Chancellor, Proctors, and Heads of Houses". But it soon passed away.

Bentley's Rudeness

When Sir Peter King, Chief Justice of the Common Pleas, went to the Cambridge Assizes in 1720 the controversy between the Heads of Houses and Bentley, Master of Trinity, was acute. The Vice-Chancellor wrote as follows, to excuse himself and the Heads from waiting on the Judge at Trinity:

My Lord. I would have waited on your Lordship, but for the terrible apprehensions I am under, that my poor wife, who is lately brought to bed, will shortly breathe her last. Under this anxiety, I am forc'd, by letters from Cambridge, to bear in mind the affairs of that University. Thither your lordship is quickly going, and believe me, my Lord, none upon earth are more ready to pay you respect and honour than we are. But, my Lord, the Master of Trinity has taken a resolution, and put it in practice, to make the Vice-Chr and Heads wait in the open Court among the mob, or at least be taken into a comon room among the footmen, when they come to pay their duty to you. Till he shall come to a better mind (which in this and all other respects I wish he may) I beg leave to depend on your Lordship's and Mr Justice Blencoe's goodness, that you will favourably interpret this behaviour of the University, and accept your usual present from the hands of the Bedell; if the Heads are not allowed the constant customary convenience in waiting upon you. Pardon this trouble, my Lord, and the confusion I am in.

I am, with the greatest respect,
Your Lordship's most obedient, humble Servt
T. Gooch*

Great Russell Street
July 28, 1720

I do not know what was "the usual present". At Oxford the Vice-Chancellor gives the Judge a glorified pair of gloves. At Cambridge, Trinity College gives him six bottles of port, but I don't think the Vice-Chancellor now gives him anything. The Oxford gloves, the Cambridge port, the Newcastle "dagger-money", and the York febrifuge, are now, I think, the only presents a Judge of Assize receives. In the old days there were more. Campbell, in his *Life* of Sir Matthew Hale,† says that from time immemorial the Dean and Chapter of Salisbury used to present six sugar loaves to the Judges of Assize in that city. Country gentlemen often gave them venison. Mr Justice Rokeby, in his *Diary*, writes: "Monmouth, July 1692, Sir Char. Kemys gave me a buck which he never used to ye Judges before." At Stafford, August 1695: "We had 3 brace of bucks and 5 sheep give us." And

* Sir Thomas Gooch, Bt., Master of Caius College, 1716–1754. Bishop of Bristol, Norwich, Ely.

† *Lives of the Chief Justices*, Vol. II, p. 205.

in August 1696, on the road from Worcester to Stafford "we stayed by ye way onely att Wolverhampton, drunk a glass of sack in ye coach (att ye door of an Inn) given us (as is customary) by ye Constables of ye Town".

Nobody ever gave me any venison. But the practice seems to have continued sufficiently late for Grantham to think it desirable to record in his *Notes* that when presents of venison are made to the Judges the recognized tips to the donor's keeper are "10*s.* 6*d.* for a haunch, 15*s.* for half a buck, and 21*s.* for a whole buck".

I am glad that no such difficulty as that in 1720 prevented my being waited on by the Vice-Chancellor and Heads. The Cambridge Proctors wear a gown unlike that of their Oxford brethren. And on such a ceremonial occasion as this they are attended by two men in top-hats, each burdened by a huge volume to which he is joined by brass chains. I think I was told that one volume was a Bible, and one the University Statutes. I hope for the sake of the men in top-hats that this duty is not very frequent: the books appeared to be very heavy, and the chains irksome.

Then, with the High Sheriff and his chaplain, to Great St Mary's. But the University ruled there. The Sheriff's chaplain remained in his pew, and the sermon (a very good one) was preached by a Pro-Proctor.

Huddleston, with apparent satisfaction, records in his *Notes*: "The Vice-Chancellor at Cambridge claims precedence over the High Sheriff and to sit in court on the right of the Judge. Hawkins J. refused to acknowledge the claim." Hawkins J. may have been right, but neither he nor Huddleston was an Oxford or Cambridge man, or they might have treated the matter with more consideration.

There were only three or four unimportant crimes to be tried, and the business was finished in one day. When a witness from near Littleport was being examined, this piece of dialogue occurred:

Q. How long have you known Mrs ——?

A. About two years.

Q. Do you know her well?

A. Only to give her the seal of the day.

I pricked up my ears at this. George Borrow often uses the phrase. Opening *Wild Wales* I came, in five pages, to—"I got up and gave him the sele of the day in English".

The use seems to be purely East Anglian. Wright's *English Dialect Dictionary* (Vol. v, p. 307) has: "Seal...Sub. 2. Also written Sele: (1) Time, season....Phrases, 'the seal of the day' (to you—a friendly salutation)." And the quotations are mostly from Norfolk and Suffolk.

Next day was Saturday, and I was free. In the morning I met my friend, S. C. Roberts, and he showed me over the Pitt Press. It is strange how Oxford and Cambridge insist on subtle contrasts in the names of things common to them. Mr Roberts is Secretary to the Syndics of the Press. But at Oxford they are Delegates, not Syndics. Oxford has a Registrar, but at Cambridge he is the Registrary. And, of course, Oxford has Quads and Common Rooms, while Cambridge has Courts and Combination Rooms.

And then I found one thing (I do not say there are no others) in which Cambridge is superior to Oxford. For in the market-place I found a perfectly admirable stall of old books at very reasonable prices. We have nothing like it at Oxford. The man who kept it (a Jew in a bowler hat) I had known by sight for years as a constant attendant at Sotheby's and Hodgson's auctions. He was a real benefactor to Cambridge. I tried to suggest that he would do well to transfer his stall to Oxford, for there were there more numerous readers of books as good as his: but he was not to be tempted, or he did not believe me.

The Saturday afternoon I spent delightfully in the Pepys Library at Magdalene with the Master of Magdalene. There is nothing like it in Oxford, or anywhere in the world.

The more I know of Samuel Pepys the greater miracle he appears to be. Suppose the Diary had not survived, or had never been deciphered, what should we have thought of him? A great official and administrator, a man of very diverse interests, an enthusiast for art, music, and literature, of an exquisite taste, honoured, respectable, austere? But the Diary exists, and in a flash one's mind reverts to the tale of Deb Willett, and all its tragi-comedy; or thinks of him tousling "la femme de Bagwell". The contrast suggests to me two disconcerting speculations to which I do not know the answer. Firstly, if other eminent people had a similar gift of stenographic candour, should we have more of such incredible contradictions? And secondly, is it possible that many women are as complaisant as all women appear to have been to Pepys? Still less do I know the answer to the most difficult question of all—Did Pepys foresee that some day his Diary might be deciphered and published to the world? And, foreseeing that, was he content that it should come about?

A good part of Sunday morning I spent in King's Chapel, that stupendous building, and part in admiring brickwork (of which we have none in Oxford) at St John's, Queens', and St Catharine's. At night I dined with the Master in hall at Trinity, and when doing so rather reluctantly followed the convention of a black silk gown and bob-wig. It is a fine hall, but not quite so good, I think, as the hall of Gray's Inn, which it so much resembles. The new Combination Room (I nearly wrote Common Room) is a noble chamber, and when age has toned its colouring it will be a fine monument of the twentieth century.

On Monday morning we departed to Norwich. At my departure I was waited upon by the Vice-Master and two dons, the mulled port was again brought in and we drank a stirrup cup. And so to the Sheriff's car at the gate.

In Huddleston's *Notes* he says that the Heads of Houses attend again when the Judge departs. If so the practice has become obsolete.

In Grantham's *Notes* there is a memorandum by the Under-Sheriff of Norfolk dated November 1905: "About 60 years ago the Sheriff of Norfolk had from 18 to 20 Bound Bailiffs or Officers.... The Sheriff being bound by law to have 20 javelin men to attend upon and escort the Judges at the Assizes [as to this see *infra*, p. 127] the officers of the Sheriff were appointed by him as javelin men. They received from the Sheriff a livery including boots and overcoats, and a sum of 5*s*. a day during attendance, and a gratuity towards a dinner at the finish of the Assizes. Early in the morning of the Commission Day the Sheriff dispatched two of his bailiffs, one called the long messenger, and the other the short messenger, to ascertain the hour he might expect the judges. The Long Messenger thereupon went at or near the border of the County to meet the judges in their carriage, and ascertain from them the hour at which they expected to arrive at Norwich, and also to receive from them any directions they might have to give to the Sheriff. He immediately travelled as fast as possible [this, doubtless, means on horseback] to the place where the short messenger was posted, which was generally about 10 miles from Norwich, and delivered the judges' directions to him. The Short Messenger thereupon proceeded as fast as possible to the Sheriff with the instructions of the judges, the long messenger slackening pace. The Sheriff, with his Chaplain, Javelin Men, Footmen, Trumpeters with their banners, carriage and four, his marshal on horseback (who was usually one of his chief tenants) and two outriders, was in readiness at the hotel to receive the Short Messenger. Upon the judges arriving at about a mile or two from the City they were met by the Sheriff and his retinue, who escorted them to the Shire Hall to open the Commission, the City Sheriff in his carriage following in the rear, who then took the judges to the Guildhall to open the City Commission. The County Sheriff and the City Sheriff then took the Judges to their lodgings at St Catherine's Plain (now the Catholic Convent), the bells of St Peter's Church ringing all the time. A considerable number of persons usually went out of the City on the road, to see the judges come into the City. The High Sheriff gave two public invitation dinners at each Assize, one called the Commission Dinner, at which from 60 to 80 gentlemen of the City and County were invited to the old Royal Hotel or the old Norfolk Hotel, and the other dinner to the Grand Jury and such other gentlemen who were present in court as the High Sheriff thought proper to invite to meet the Grand Jury."

This appears to indicate the practice of about 1840. In 1781, as appears from a passage I quote, *infra*, p. 158, it was customary for the Norfolk Sheriff to give a county ball at each Assize.

As the Judges went straight to open the Commissions they must clearly have arrived in Norwich in their full robes and wigs. I should like to know where they put these on: I can't believe they wore them throughout their day's journey.

At Norwich on my visits I was lodged in a pleasant house in the Precincts, where the organist lived. There were only four prisoners from the County. But the Recorder, by some mistake, had fixed his Quarter Sessions for the same day as the Assize, a coincidence that would cause much inconvenience, even if it were permissible. I did not pretend to be in a hurry to leave so charming a city as Norwich, so I encouraged the Recorder to cancel his sessions, and tried his seven prisoners myself. Quite apart from this there are separate Commissions of Assize for the County, and for the City, as a county borough. As a result I was partly in the care of the City Sheriff. And he provided a coach, with a body that swayed very much on its springs, two great horses, and a footman standing up behind.

The Cathedral, St Helen's Hospital, St Andrew's Hall, The

Stranger's Hall, and the Castle—all of these I knew before, but it was a delight to see them again. The Cathedral was still under the old sort of regime, which had not been moved to copy the new methods of the Dean and Chapter of Chester. That has long been altered, and the Cathedral now, under its present Dean, is as admirable as any. The cleansing of monuments, colouring of heraldry, and, above all, the colouring of the wonderful bosses in the cloisters, has transformed the whole place with added beauty. One afternoon we motored to Yarmouth. It was the height of the herring season, and you could smell the town a mile away. The thousands of Scotch girls were at their lightning task of gutting the millions of fish and packing them in salt in barrels. I never saw so astonishing a spectacle. But I felt at the time that I never wanted to see a herring again.

One of the counsel who appeared before me at Norwich was Mr F. K. North of Rougham Hall, near King's Lynn. He is the descendant of Roger North (1653–1734), whose *Lives* of his brothers, *Examen*, and *Autobiography* I have found such pleasant reading.* In the last there is some account of his experiences on circuit, whither he went in his usual close attendance on his brother Francis, when he was Chief Justice of the Common Pleas. At Exeter he saw a trial of some wretched old women as witches. "The trial was before Judge Raymond, a mild, passive man, who had neither dexterity nor spirit to oppose a popular rage, and so they were convict and died.... Another instance of this sort happened in Somersetshire before my brother, which was not the result of error and ignorance, as this, but of mere malice. A young woman was indicted for being a witch, and bewitching a child. The evidence was the child's fits upon the witch's approach, as commonly the case is, and the child or girl of about twelve years of age that was bewitched spat up pins in her fits, but straight, and not, as usually, crooked pins.... At last the judge spoke to the justice that examined the matter at first, to say what he thought upon his view of the fact. He said that he verily believed that they were stuck right down in the top of her stomacher, and that in her convulsing strains, which were not extending, but bringing down her head to her breast, she took them out with her mouth and spit them into folks' hands, and then pretended to ease. This account was so facile of belief that it took, and cleared the poor young woman."

* I might also mention his *A Discourse of Fish and Fish-Ponds, by a Person of Honour* (1715), which I also possess.

It seems almost beyond belief that things of this sort were happening only about 250 years ago. For Francis North was Chief Justice of the Common Pleas from 1673 to 1681, when he became Lord Keeper—and as a result Roger North at once transferred his practice from the common law to the chancery bar. The procedure of the time also seems odd to us. I do not know what would be thought now if a Judge of Assize were to call upon a J.P. who had heard a case at Petty Sessions, and committed the accused, "to say what he thought upon his view of the fact". But in the old days the committing Justice was often called as the principal witness against an accused.

One other pleasing incident on circuit Roger North records in his *Autobiography*. "It happened in Dorsetshire once that the High Sheriff had ten sons carried halberds, and wore his livery, and his eldest son was captain of the band. Great notice was taken of this, and being complimented by the judges upon it, said if they were too good to serve the King and their father they were no sons of his, and he would disown them." Dr Jessopp, in a note, refers to *Hutchin's History of Dorset* (1774, Vol. I, p. 263), who says that this was Thomas Gollop, of North Bowood and Strode, High Sheriff in 1670. Hutchin's version is that he was attended by ten of his eleven sons as javelin men, who were led by their uncle, his younger brother.

I do not know when the trade union rules of the bar about circuits became fixed. Roger North apparently was not in his day limited to his own, or to any particular, circuit. For he says: "I went but three circuits, the West, North, and the Norfolk, the two last but once, so that in the west we were as at home; for lodgings and acquaintance, and all incidents, were by our frequent coming there, so established, that we had no trouble or uncertainty about our accommodations."

It may be, however, that he is only referring to his going on circuit as his brother's constant companion, and not as a practising barrister. In his *Life* of the Lord Keeper (1742, p. 116) he says that when he became Chief Justice he chose the Western Circuit, and, as I have said before, it was then the practice for a judge always to go on the same circuit. But this cannot have been an invariable rule. "For he took the opportunity one summer to turn by the North, which begins at York and concludes at Lancaster" (p. 134).

We went on to Ipswich, as dull and uninteresting a town as Norwich was bright and delightful. The Lodgings were in an ugly villa on the Woodbridge Road. There were only two prisoners, one of whom was

a hopeless lunatic who was at once found unfit to plead. And there was one civil case, which was settled after an hour's hearing.

Essex was less virtuous than Suffolk, and at Chelmsford there was work for eight full days. But Chelmsford is a pleasant enough town to stay in, and the Lodgings were very comfortable. They are so close to the church and the Courts that it is almost absurd to use any vehicle, and whenever it was fine I went to the Court on foot. Considering how near Chelmsford is to London I think it preserves the air and amenity of a country town to a surprising degree. I felt the contrast to Reading, which is six miles farther from London, but seems its mere suburb.

We enjoyed some pleasant hospitality, and some sight-seeing. When we dined with the High Sheriff, who was also M.F.H., every man present, except my marshal and myself, was in the pink of the Essex Hunt. As for the sights, the best of them were three wonderful examples of red brickwork—New Hall, close to Chelmsford, Faulkbourne Hall, and Spains Hall. The brick newel stair and brick window tracery at Faulkbourne are as fine work in that material as ever I saw. Henry VIII's front at New Hall is magnificent, and the architect who put on the new wing has done nothing to spoil it.

As to Essex there is in the Grantham *Notes* a memorandum by Mr Chas Gepp, Under-Sheriff of that county, dated 21 November 1905: "Previously to the year 1823 it appears to have been the custom for the High Sheriff of Essex to be responsible for two public dinners at the Assizes, at which on two successive days he entertained the Grand Jury. And by custom he was in the habit of sending Wine for the table of the Judges and to the Clerk of Arraigns [I expect this means the Clerk of Assize], the Under Sheriff, the Gaoler, and other subordinate officers. There was also a custom that he should provide fuel and beer at the Judges' Lodgings. Having regard to all these expenses in addition to the usual ones occasioned by the exigencies of his office, it is not surprising to learn that the expenses of the High Sheriff at the two assizes were said to average £1300 and upwards. It may be mentioned here that the expenses which the High Sheriff is now liable for need not amount to a third of that sum, and in fact many High Sheriffs in recent years have carried out the duties of the office for a sum considerably less even than £400. In the year 1823 at a meeting of the Magistrates and Gentlemen of the County it was resolved to discontinue the Public dinners at the Assizes in as far as they were entertainments by the High Sheriff, and it was determined that they should in future be conducted altogether as ordinaries, at which the High Sheriff should if he so pleased preside: every expense being included in the equal amount of charge made upon every individual who was present, and to which ordinaries the High Sheriff should be requested to abstain from making any addition whatever. With regard to discontinuance of the provision of wine for the table of the Judges, and fuel and beer at their lodgings, the meeting stated: 'It is our opinion no ground would be thereby afforded for calling in question the respect and deference entertained for the persons and authority of the Judges of the land.'

"At present I have been unable to find any contemporary account of the entry of the Judges into the town preceded by the Sheriff's cortege...nor does it appear when the practice of the Sheriff going on horseback with his javelin men was discontinued, but as far as I can form any opinion the practice was discontinued a considerable time before London and Chelmsford were connected by railway in 1841.

"In 1823 it was determined that the trumpeters should be provided with a cocked hat, and a green coat cut straight with a green cloth cape, and cuffs, and the javelin men with a cocked hat, and drab coat loose with a falling cape and cuffs of green cloth, the buttons upon the coat to be white and impressed with the County arms. It is strange that nothing was said about their nether garments, but top boots and spurs would no doubt have been mentioned, if the Javelin men were still a mounted escort. The costume of the Javelin men in my time, to the best of my recollection, comprised a green livery with a certain amount of gold lace about it. They had silk hats with cockades, and the Javelin which gave them their name. The employment of the Javelin men was continued some little time after the Act of 1859. [This made it no longer obligatory for the Sheriff to provide twenty javelin men in each English, and twelve in each Welsh county. See *infra*, p. 127.] I fear there is nothing recorded in Essex similar to that which is alluded to in the statement of the Under-Sheriff of Norfolk with regard to the two Bailiffs, the long and the short messenger. Tradition says, however, that the High Sheriff of Essex and his mounted men were in the habit of going as far out of the town as The Old White Horse in Widford to meet the Judges and escort them into the Town. The distance from The Old White Horse to the Shire Hall in Chelmsford would be about 1½ miles."

1927

In January 1927 I went again to North Wales. The result of my usual calculation was that by the time I got to Chester I had spent only 20 hours in Court, whereas if I had stayed in London for the same period I should have done 70 hours' work. The absurdity of not grouping together these little counties is increased by the provision in an Act of 1925 which provides that cases in one county may be sent by Petty Sessions to the Assizes of a neighbouring county. It has always been absurd enough to have separate Assizes at Ruthin and Mold, seeing that the distance between them is 10 miles by the high road, 9 miles as a sensible judge walks over the hills, and 8 miles as the crow flies. In fact I had five prisoners at Ruthin, but two of them had just been committed for an offence perpetrated at Bangor in Carnarvonshire. And at Mold there were five prisoners. The work at Ruthin took 5 hours, and at Mold 6 hours, so it is obvious that all were simple and trifling cases.

One of the theoretical advantages of local Courts and Assizes is that cases are tried by jurors of the neighbourhood. I had a curious example of the practical disadvantage of this at one of the small towns. A man brought an action to restrain his next-door neighbour from committing a nuisance. Upon the evidence I do not think any reasonable being could have the slightest doubt, and I am certain that any jury from anywhere away from the locality would have found a verdict for the Plaintiff. To my amazement, and disgust, they found for the Defendant. I asked the Under-Sheriff what this meant. I was told that the Plaintiff was very unpopular in the place, while the Defendant was well liked. The Plaintiff may have earned his unpopularity; he did not get justice.

A year or two later, with reference to some suggestions I had made for reforming the Welsh circuits, a lawyer of great experience, and a Welshman, wrote me a letter in which he said: "The great advantage, to my mind, of grouping the counties for civil causes, is that it tends to avoid a local jury. In my experience, the local jurors, whether special or common, know all about the cases beforehand, and all sorts of influences are brought to bear on them during the hearing of a case, if it lasts more than one day."

It is only in Wales that I have had juries return verdicts which I was certain were wrong and perverse. This civil case was one occasion, and there were two when the manifestly guilty were acquitted. After one of the latter cases had been reported in the papers, I had a letter from a stranger in which he said: "My Lord. As you were trying the case of —— at —— last week it occurs to me that you may be interested to hear of another verdict of a Welsh jury long ago at ——, in proof that times change not. When I was a boy, over 70 years ago, my father told me that when he was constructing the Chester to Holyhead railway there was a serious daily loss of jumpers, i.e. steel bars about 6 feet long. The police made a search, and found a whole stack of them in a workman's cottage. The man was tried. The defence was 'that he was wont to use a walking-stick, and had taken them home absent mindedly'. The jury acquitted him all right."

The maxim *Judex damnatur, cum nocens absolvitur* ought not to be applied to judges on Welsh circuits.

At Beaumaris, a year ago, I had observed the outside of the small gaol, which has long been disused. Part of it forms the local police station, and on this visit I got the inspector to show me over it: for I had heard that it still contained an old-fashioned treadmill. It is a grim building, largely constructed of enormous slabs of slate. The treadmill was there, under a penthouse in the yard, but it had long been rusted up, and judge, marshal, and inspector were not heavy enough to make it budge an inch. When I next went to Beaumaris, in June 1932, I took occasion to speak to the Grand Jury about their small prison and its treadmill, suggesting that it ought to be preserved as an historical relic. I had a message later that my idea found favour, a good many of the Grand Jurors had never heard of the treadmill, but they were all interested, and were going to take steps to have it cared for.

I do not know if this gaol is the one of which Howard gives an account in his *State of the Prisons* (1780), but it well may be. According to that the gaoler had a salary of £5 from the Sheriff, and could exact 5*s*. from each felon and each debtor. He had also a licence to sell beer. Each felon was allowed a shilling loaf a week and one pound of butter. A debtor had no allowance at all. "This gaol is also the county bridewell. There are five rooms for debtors, and two for felons. A court, but no water." In June 1774 there were in it only two debtors, in July 1779 four debtors and one felon. There was no chaplain, and no surgeon.

The day on which my marshal and I walked from Ruthin to Mold there was a tremendous gale. And on the top of Moel Famman (1850 feet) it was tremendous indeed. On its top there is a great pyramid of stone, the ruins of a tower put up in honour of George III's jubilee. On an ordinary day it is an easy thing to climb. My marshal, a stout young man, and a member of the Alpine Club, tried to do that: but the wind beat him utterly.

Mold again was delightful, not for itself (for it is an ugly little town), but because of the comfort and beauty of the house in which a kindly lady allowed the County of Flint to house the Judge of Assize. On this circuit I had been in one place in Lodgings which for their squalor, dirtiness, and general discomfort, were the worst I ever saw—even worse than Haverfordwest. It was indeed a pleasure to come at Mold to almost the most desirable Lodgings there are anywhere. If there is to be grouping of the Welsh counties, and if this house is to continue to be available, I could wish that Mold may still be an Assize town.

And so to Chester, where I met Mr Justice Finlay, arrived from Presteign. He astonished me with the news that he had actually had a prisoner to try at Presteign! This was a momentous event. The county authorities, conscious of the necessity, had the Lodgings re-decorated, and a bathroom installed. The great day came. The Judge went to church, the trumpets blew, the Commission was read, the stage was set. Then the prisoner, a travelling tinker, who had been let out on bail, was called on to surrender. *He did not turn up!* So Presteign, fluttered for a moment by the unusual spectacle of an Assize, sank back to its accustomed and secular repose.

At Chester I found that the hope I formed a year ago, of a change of Lodgings, was realized. We were lodged in a delightful house on the road to Eccleston, south of the city. It stands on a small rocky cliff above the Dee, and this cliff had been made into a natural rock garden. It was too early to see the beauty of this, but it was full of pleasant things and later in the year must be delightful. Below the garden were meadows along the river, and through them a path to Eccleston.

At Mold a man, committed from Petty Sessions in Flint, was tried for manslaughter, and was quite properly acquitted. The victim, knocked down by the car of the accused, died in hospital at Chester. The Coroner's jury found a verdict of manslaughter on which he had to appear at Chester Assizes. This was one of the absurdities that used* to happen from the duplicated activities of Petty Sessions and the Coroner. At Chelmsford the autumn before there had been a man in my calendar charged with murder on an Essex Coroner's Inquisition. But being also committed at Petty Sessions, he had been tried and convicted at the Old Bailey, and his execution was actually fixed for the day when the Assize opened at Chelmsford.

The man at Chester duly surrendered, put in his plea of "Autrefois Acquit", and a verdict upholding it was returned by the jury. His counsel, finding a passage in Archbold, asked for an order that his client might "depart without day". To which I assented, but the learned gentleman was unable to gratify my curiosity to know the true meaning of the phrase, or if it would make any difference if I merely said he could go away.†

Nowadays, when a verdict of "Not Guilty" is returned, the Judge says to the acquitted man—"You are discharged". The door of the dock is opened, and he goes away free. It was not always so simple. In 1682, "If the Jury say *Not Guilty*, then the Clerk of Assize must say to the Prisoner, *Down upon your knees, and say God save the King and this Honourable Bench*".‡ I suppose the man had to do that. But he was not then at liberty. Down to nearly the end of the eighteenth century all officials were paid by fees. And a prisoner on his acquittal had a debt to discharge to the Keeper of the prison, where he had been awaiting trial (for bail was rarely granted), and another debt to the Clerk of Assize, and a third to the Under-Sheriff. Howard, in his great work *The State of the Prisons* (1780), says that he was first moved to undertake it by discovering, as High Sheriff for Bedfordshire in 1773, that acquitted prisoners often had to go back to prison and remain there "till they should pay *sundry fees* to the gaoler, the clerk of assize, &c." In 1774 he gave evidence as to this before a Committee of the House of Commons, and in the same year an Act was passed

* But has now been abolished by sect. 20 of the Coroners Amendment Act 1926.

† For the comment upon this of one who was present see that most learned work, *Personal Actions at Common Law* (1929), by Ralph Sutton, at p. 87.

‡ *The Office of the Clerk of Assize* (2nd ed. 1682), p. 50.

reciting that "Persons in custody for Felonies, though they are acquitted on their trials, are nevertheless frequently detained for certain Fees to the Sheriffs, Gaolers, or Keepers of Prisons, which is both oppressive and unjust". It therefore enacted that the county funds should pay such fees, not exceeding 13*s.* 4*d.* This Act, however, did not mention the fees of the Clerk of Assize, or, at Quarter Sessions, the Clerk of the Peace. And Howard complains (2nd ed. 1780, p. 20) that acquitted prisoners were still being sent back to prison for these fees to be exacted. In his detailed account of every prison in England and Wales he specifies the fee which the Gaoler is entitled to demand from a felon. And at p. 435 of his second edition he gives a List of Fees due to Clerks of Assize on each of the circuits. These vary very much. On the Home Circuit on an acquittal the Clerk of Assize was only entitled to 8*s.* 4*d.* But on the Western Circuit the amount was £1. 10*s.* 8*d.* On most of the circuits the fee varied on an acquittal by the petty jury, and an *Ignoramus* by the Grand Jury: and on some of them the fee on acquittal of a charge of murder was higher than on a lesser felony.

The High Sheriff of Cheshire on this occasion had revived the ancient splendours of his office. He had the old coach gloriously repainted. And he had sixteen javelin men in a livery of blue and yellow, each carrying an immense javelin, or halberd, newly constructed. I admired the display, and particularly the halberds. On which, as this was the last Assize of his year of office, he offered to give me one of them. I accepted it gratefully, and he had it sent to my home, where I have it in the hall as an adornment.

I find in the Grantham *Notes* of Chester: "This is one of the few towns in which javelin men are still kept up." The tradition may have influenced the revival by this gentleman in 1926–1927.

We had arranged to go to the Cathedral on the Sunday, and not on the first day of the Assizes. As it happened, however, there was so little work that we finished it all in three days, by the Thursday evening. We were not due at Cardiff until the following Wednesday. So we went back to London on the Friday, and missed the service at Chester altogether.

I like an Assize Service in a Cathedral. The first one at which I was ever present was when I was an undergraduate, and did not know I was going to the bar. This was on Sunday, 4 February 1894, when

Lord Coleridge, Lord Chief Justice, was the Judge, and Benson, Archbishop of Canterbury, was to preach the "Humility" sermon. It became known afterwards that there had been a controversy between the Judge and the Archbishop as to precedence. Each asserted his pre-eminence, and the unfortunate Vice-Chancellor, Boyd of Hertford, was the unwilling centre of their conflict. He solved the difficulty by arranging for them to arrive separately at the church, and each be escorted alone to his place. And when these facts were known, we appreciated the added significance of a passage in the Archbishop's sermon: "May I not speak in this presence of the veneration with which England has ever regarded her great Judges, on this account, that the love of justice has been continuously felt to be a passion with them—a high atmosphere in which egotism has shrunk and faded. 'I magnify my office' is the language of one who esteemed himself 'less than the least'. He is sacrificed to his work, not decorated with it."

An Assize Service on a week day in the parish church is usually a dull affair. There is often no choir, and the pretence of singing hymns, by the handful of a congregation, is absurd: though I remember one or two occasions in Wales where policemen provided a noble chorus. I doubt the propriety of the selection, which is often made, of a hymn of Charles Wesley about the Last Day. At "robed in majesty and power", or "the judge is come", I have seen a glance directed at my scarlet and ermine: and "attentive to the trumpet's sound" is suggestive of the Sheriff's fanfare waiting outside.

Between the best and the worst Assize sermon that I have heard the difference is great, but the average is of a uniform dullness. My friend Mr Arundell Esdaile told me of an Assize sermon preached in 1624 by a Sheriff's Chaplain named Lawrence. It was printed with the pleasing title, "A golden trumpet to rouse up a Drowsie Magistrate".

Roger North, in his *Autobiography*, says: "'Size sermons used to entertain the company, for seldom any was without something so remarkable as to be discoursed of either to the advantage or disadvantage of the preacher. The parsons on those occasions think they must harangue judge, juries, officers, and all orders of men. Once the Doctor had finished his catalogue, and at last looked about and said, 'But now as to the lawyers. Stay, I think there is none of them here.' And so went on to other matters."

Roger North also writes: "The cathedral towns were our greatest refreshment, for there were good company, and the clergy were our good friends, besides we made Sundays there if possible, because of the music and the pleasure of the cathedral." I quite agree with him, and have done the same.

In the *Diary of John Rous* (Camden Society, 1856) in 1631, he says: "Summer Assizes at Bury had one Mr Scot, of Ipswich, that preached before the Judges, who made a sore sermon in discovery of corruptions of judges and others. At Norwich Mr Greene was more plaine, insomuch that Judge Harvy [Francis Harvey, Judge of the Common Pleas, 1624–1632] in his charge broke out thus—'It seems by the sermon that we are corrupt, but know that we can use conscience in our places, as well as the best clergie man of all'."

In the *Diary of Thomas Cartwright, Bishop of Chester* (Camden Society, 1843), he says that at Lancaster, on 11 August 1687, he went with the High Sheriff to meet the Judges. And "12 August. I went with Judge Powel [Sir John Powell, 1633–1696] to the Church; Sir Richard Allebone [1621–1688, made a judge by James II in 1687, because he was a Papist] and the Catholics went at the same time to the school-house, where they had mass and a sermon; we had none of the best; 'twas preached by Mr Turner whom I chid for his extemporary prayer, and sermon, of both of which he promised amendment for the future. I heard Sir Richard Allebone give the charge, in which he took notice, that no protestants but myself, my Lord Brandon, and Sir Daniel Fleming, came out to meet them, which was a great disrespect to the King's Commission."

One thing that may be noted at Assizes Services is that the Bidding Prayer is in slightly different terms at almost every place. This presumably is due to local tradition, and because the proper form is not specified in the Prayer Book. A bidding prayer was once the preliminary to every sermon, and its terms were enjoined in the Injunctions of 1559, and in the Canons of 1604. No. 55 of the Canons of 1604 is as follows:

The forme of a Prayer to bee used by Preachers, before their Sermons

Before all Sermons, Lectures, and Homilies, the Preachers and Ministers shall move the people to joyne with them in praier in this forme, or to this effect, as briefly and conveniently as they may.

Ye shall pray for Christ's holy Catholic Church, that is, for the whole

Congregation of Christian people dispersed throughout the whole world, and especially for the Churches of England, Scotland, and Ireland. And herein I require you most especially to pray for the King's most excellent Majestie, our Soveraigne Lord James, King of England, Scotland, France, and Ireland, Defendour of the Faith, & Supreme Governour in these his Realmes, and all other his Dominions and Countries, over all persons, in all causes, as well Ecclesiastical as Temporall. Ye shall also pray for our gracious Queene Anne, the noble Prince Henry, and the rest of the King and Queenes Royall Issue. Ye shall also pray for the Ministers of God's holy word & Sacraments, as well Archbishops and Bishops, as other Pastours and Curates. Yee shall also pray for the King's most honourable Counsell, and for all the Nobilitie and Magistrates of this Realme, that all and every of these in their severall Callings, may serve truely and painefully to the glory of God, and the edifying and well governing of his people, remembering the accompt that they must make. Also yee shall pray for the whole Commons of this Realme, that they may live in true Faith and feare of God, in humble obedience to the King, and brotherly charitie one to another. Finally, let us praise God for all those which are departed out of this life in the Faith of Christ, and pray unto God that we may have grace to direct our lives after their good example: that this life ended, wee may be made partakers with them of the glorious Resurrection in the life Everlasting, Alwayes concluding with the Lords prayer.

That is a fine piece of English, and much to be preferred to the debased version that is so often substituted.

Lord Sankey once told me that he had encountered a Sheriff's Chaplain who introduced a striking novelty in his bidding prayer. Either he thought that a judge should be treated as well as a bishop, or he lost his head; but, whatever his reason, having called for prayer "for Edward, Bishop of this Diocese", he proceeded a little later to make the same demand "for John, Judge of this Assize".

J. Alderson Foote, K.C., in his admirable book *Pie Powder* (1911), says: "I once heard a Sheriff's Chaplain include the Judge's Marshal in the bidding prayer."

I doubt if there can ever have been two such Assizes as those at Swansea in the autumn of 1926, and at Cardiff in February 1927. Mr Justice Fraser and Mr Justice Wright sat till close on Christmas 1926, and the former then returned to Swansea on 11 January 1927. He finished the business there on 8 February, the day before Mr Justice Finlay and I arrived at Cardiff. And we were confronted with a calendar of 305 prisoners, of whom about 270 were miners charged with riot during the great Coal Strike. My primary concern was with the civil list, which I finished in about 10 days. I then helped with the prisoners until 5 March, when I went back to town. Mr Justice Finlay got away from Cardiff on 29 March. That I deserted him for so long was pardoned by his good nature, and was induced by the practical difficulty that the same counsel were briefed on each side in all the remaining cases.

There was a sad monotony about all these cases. Towards the end of the Strike a few men began to break away, and return to work at various collieries. Feeling was strong against them, and they were guarded by police escorts. Crowds assembled in the evening, as the man, or men, came back from work, stone-throwing began, and a fight between the police and the crowd followed. The prisoners charged at the Assizes were those identified by the police on various occasions as having taken part in the disorder; for it was never possible to arrest anyone at the time. And if it had been practicable to increase these identifications, there might have been thousands charged instead of hundreds.

There was also a monotony about the defences in these cases. I could not help suspecting that some of the accused might well have been acquitted, if they had said: "Yes, I admit I was present, but I was not culpable. I was out on my proper affairs, when the crowd swept down on me, and I became unwillingly involved in it. I threw no stones, and took no part in the rioting." The defence did not in any case seek to deny that there had been a riot. But apparently all these men and women (there were a good many women in the dock, and in many cases they behaved worse than the men) shared the view of old Mr Weller as to the proper line of every defence. Except a very few—e.g. one man who had a wooden leg, and whose identification was overwhelming, and one man who was arrested with his pockets full of stones—every one of the prisoners set up an *alibi*. Each gave evidence that he was at least 3 miles away (usually in bed), and he called friends and relatives, in varying numbers, to corroborate him. The juries disbelieved the majority of these stories, and convicted.

There was constant reference in the police evidence to the fact that the crowd sang "The Red Flag". For years I had seen in the papers such a sentence as "The meeting broke up with the singing of the Red Flag". But never, in any paper, or anywhere else had I been able to find the words of this poem. I mentioned this to Mr Artemus Jones, K.C., who appeared for all the prisoners. Next day he sent me a copy of the song which one of his clients had written out. Here it is:

The Red Flag

The People's flag is deepest red,
It shrouded oft our Martyrs dead;
And ere the limbs grew stiff and cold,
Their hearts' blood dyed its every fold.

Chorus Then raise the scarlet standard high!
Within its shade we live or die.
Though cowards flinch, and traitors sneer,
We keep the Red Flag flying here.

Look round! The Frenchman loves its blaze,
The sturdy German chants its praise,
In Moscow's vaults its hymns are sung,
Chicago swells the surging throng.

It well recalls the triumphs past,
It gives the hope of peace at last;
The banner bright! The symbol plain
Of Human right, and Human gain!

It suits today the weak and base,
Whose minds are fixed on pelf and place,
To cringe before the rich man's frown,
And haul the sacred emblem down.

With heads uncovered swear we all
To bear it onward till we fall:
From dungeons dark, or gallows grim,
This song shall be our parting hymn.

Burnet said of *Lilliburlero* that "perhaps never had so slight a thing so great an effect". But literary taste must indeed be depraved, if these deplorable lines carry any inspiration! I hope it was venial to try my hand at a parody, and to send back to Mr Artemus Jones this:

The Red Bag

The Lawyer's Bag is deepest red,
From blood of clients, dried and dead;
They hymn its praises as they die,
Or sink to welcome bankruptcy.

Chorus Then flaunt the scarlet sack! Let briefs
Swell out its ruddy folds in sheafs;
Let Courage spur the Litigant
And keep our bloody Bag from want.

Look round! Where Lawyers most resort,
From King's Bench Walk to Garden Court,
Or in New Square—its hues confer
Distinction on the Barrister.

How it recalls the silver tones
Of Artemus (once libelled) Jones,
The champion of the mildest folk
Who ever rioted in joke.

To any wise solicitor
It much commends a junior,
To note, from this, some silk has thought
He was not quite a fool in Court.

With heads bewigged we carry it
To every place where Judges sit,
And pray that finally our words
May soothe the slumbers of the Lords.

I should perhaps explain for the benefit of my non-legal readers, if I have any, that when a young man is called to the bar he is provided, as part of his outfit, with a blue cloth bag, in which his robes and wig box may be carried. If later on he is in a case with a K.C. as his leader, it is the privilege of the latter, if he thinks the junior has played his part well, to present him with a red bag. So that if a junior is seen carrying a red bag it is a sign that once at least he has acquitted himself well, in the opinion of a leader. I believe on some circuits a junior is only allowed to carry a red bag there if it was given to him by one of the circuit leaders, but not if he received it in London from a leader not of the circuit.

This is the present practice. I gather that it may not always have been so. Campbell, in his *Life* of Lord Ellenborough, says that on his first round of the Northern Circuit, in 1780, he was given a red bag by Wallace, one of the leaders. And he adds this foot-note: "Nowadays any young barrister buys a bag, and carries it as soon after he is called to the bar as he likes; but when I was called to the bar [in 1806], and long after, the privilege of carrying a bag was strictly confined to those who had received one from a King's Counsel.

The King's Counsel, then few in number, were considered officers of the Crown, and they not only had a salary of £40 a year, but an annual allowance of paper, pens, and purple bags. These they distributed among juniors who had made such progress as not to be able to carry their briefs conveniently in their hands. All these salaries and perquisites were ruthlessly swept away in 1830 by Lord Grey's reforming Government—and it was full time—as King's Counsel had become a mere grade in the profession, comprehending a very large number of its members."

This suggests that there was only a red, or purple bag, and that "nowadays" a junior bought one upon his call. But Lord Campbell is so frequently inaccurate that it may be, that then, as now, he bought a blue bag and waited to be presented with a red one. Of course, a leader who now gives a red bag buys it from the robe makers.

Cardiff is one of those places where, after the day's work is done, there is nowhere to walk, except in crowded or gloomy streets. But on this occasion we had leave from Lord Bute's agent to walk about the grounds of Cardiff Castle, and were grateful for the privilege. I cannot say I think they are beautiful, and the grime of the city is upon them. But they are very extensive, quiet, and secluded. We found we could get right through them, crossing the river by a wooden bridge, and emerge at Llandaff, which is much the pleasantest place near Cardiff.

One other diversion was to motor to Swansea on a Saturday afternoon, and see the Rugby match between Wales and France. It poured with rain all the morning, and when the match began, though the rain had stopped, the ground was soaked, and in places there were pools of water. In a very short time every player was plastered in wet mud from head to foot. France won a very notable victory.

✧ ✧ ✧

On 22 June 1927 I went to Durham with Mr Justice Talbot. Some time before we went North I realized that we should probably be at Durham on the night of 28 June, and so might see the total eclipse of the sun on the early morning of the 29th. It was easy to arrange that 29 June should be the "Commission Day", between Durham and Newcastle. And I wrote to the Dean of Durham to ask if he could let us go up the Cathedral tower: he promised very cordially that we should.

Later on, however, I realized that Durham was only just inside the northern edge of the belt of totality, and would not be as good a place for the spectacle as one nearer the central line. Just after I began considering this Mr Justice Talbot and I had each a delightful invitation from Lady Wrightson to go to her house, Neasham Hall, near Darlington, for the momentous night. Darlington was on the central line of totality, and, apart from the chances of cloud, as good a place for the spectacle as any in England. Lady Wrightson had her grandson from Eton, and his tutor, coming, and she added to her kindness to me by asking my son at Eton to come also. He was able to get leave: I suppose the Head Master thought it was not unreasonable to ask an *Exeat* for an event that would never recur in his lifetime.

So on Tuesday, 28 June, having finished the work at Durham, we motored from Durham to Neasham. There was a large house-party, and we were over twenty at dinner. We went to bed early. We were awakened about four, and went down to find a first breakfast. Then we all got into a variety of cars, and drove to a hill about three miles away. There were a good many people about there, but nothing of a crowd. The day before we had seen little or no traffic on the road.

It was a fine morning, but to the east there was an ominous bank of light clouds, and there was practically no wind: the clouds seemed barely to move. But they did move, and after a time the sun (which was higher in the heavens than I expected) became visible through a rift. We all had black glasses of some sort, and for a short time they were necessary. Then we realized that the astronomers had done their sums rightly. There was a circular black bite taken out of the sun, and we watched it for perhaps 6 minutes. Then the rift closed, and the sun was again behind the clouds. There was still 20 minutes or thereabouts before the great final moment, and we waited hopefully. But it was a flattering tale, and no more. We never saw the sun again.

It was a great misfortune. But I was not wholly disappointed. We did not see the corona, but we did see, and realize, the amazing phenomenon of the darkness of total eclipse. And it was one of the most wonderful experiences I ever had. It came at the last suddenly, the darkness for a few seconds was profound, the glare of a blast furnace at Middlesbrough shone red. And then as suddenly it was gone, and the light grew very quickly.

One thing I noticed. One had been told that birds and animals are strangely affected, and in particular that the birds fall silent. This was not true of the birds on our hill, or not of all of them. There was a lark singing as the darkness came sweeping over the land, and he went on singing all through it. Only when it was light again, because his flight was done and his song at its normal end, did he stop singing. Lord Cockburn, in his *Journal*,* records his similar experience on 16 May 1836: "There was an annular eclipse of the sun yesterday forenoon.... The day was warm and cloudless.... There was something very impressive in the obscuration.... The thermometer beside us fell eight degrees.... There were no stars visible... nor were animals (as was also predicted) amazed; at least the cows, horses, and sheep... never abated a munch of their young juicy grass. A bantam cock on the tower crowed frequently."

And then we went back to Neasham, I on foot, going briskly, for it had been chilly waiting on the hill. A second and more formal breakfast was very pleasant, and the party (enlarged by our two marshals who had motored over very early from Durham) seemed happy enough, though none had seen anything of the glories of the corona. We heard later that only a few miles away it had been seen perfectly. There was a long morning for a walk by the serpentine Tees, though we had lunch at noon. At one the Eton party left to take train at Darlington, and at two we left in our car for Newcastle. No living judge has ever had, or will have, such a diversion as this was when on circuit.

The work at Newcastle, where I tried the prisoners, was not heavy, and I had time for some sight-seeing, and for a day in the country. The Quayside, with its shipping, was very attractive. But far more delightful was the Trinity House, which I had not found before. You get to it by a narrow court, paradoxically called Broad Chare, off the Quay, and there, pent in by warehouses, you find a number of small courts, with charming eighteenth-century almshouses, a chapel with seventeenth-century panelling, a Court room, and plenty of fine old furniture. Mr Nicholson, who is "The Summoner", showed me everything, and so interested was I that I forgot about time, and suddenly found that I must run to the Mansion House if I was to be ready in time for the dinner to the Lord Mayor. To be late would have been ungrateful as well as discourteous; for after dinner the ancient ritual was followed, and he presented me with a beautiful Jacobus.

* Vol. I, p. 118.

The Holy Jesus Hospital, on the hill above Quayside, is picturesque. And All Saints' church, also on the hill, I liked very much. The woodwork inside must be about the most extensive display of fine mahogany anywhere. All the pews through its great circular space, the panelling, altar piece, pulpit—all are made of mahogany. Outside it was grim and desolate, with a great space cleared beside it for one end of the great new bridge that was beginning to reach out across the river.

On the day we were to go to York it poured incessantly. Newcastle's City Sheriff had offered to send his car to drive us there, and a big Renault appeared. The chauffeur drove like the devil, but with admirable care. We were held up for nearly ten minutes at a level crossing, and had to go very slowly for a mile or two through a flood on the road. But we did the distance of about 80 miles in a little under two and a half hours.

I was glad to find myself again in the fine old house in Lendal, and to dine in its magnificent dining-room. As the three Ridings of Yorkshire are practically separate counties, they have to combine specially for the provision of Judges' Lodgings, and the house at York is the concern of "The Commissioners of the Judges Lodgings". Yorkshire, of course, has a second Assize town in Leeds, but when that was established the City of Leeds undertook to provide the Judges' Lodgings. In the same way, in Warwickshire, the County provides the Lodgings at Warwick, but the City of Birmingham does so in Birmingham.

Next morning we went to breakfast with the Lord Mayor. He, or his Lady, had devised one pleasing variation from the old ceremonial. The bouquet for each judge was an awkward burden at breakfast, and as a febrifuge in Court is now happily unnecessary. But the tradition was continued; for we were each given a silver snuff-box filled with lavender.

I gather that the time for this breakfast has rather changed. In an account of the trial of Jonathan Martin, the lunatic who set fire to York Minster, in February 1829, Mr Justice Bayley opened the Commission at the Guildhall on Monday, 23 March. He sat at 8 a.m. and charged the Grand Jury. And "the Court then adjourned to the Mansion House, to breakfast with the Lord Mayor".

The business at York, and the time for an Assize there, are always too short: but if they were as long as at Leeds a judge, who was a sight-seer in his leisure time, could not exhaust the interests of York. Almost the only thing that is not worth seeing is the Municipal Art Gallery. There is too much of William Etty, R.A. He was not a great painter, and there is a monotony in his nudities. But he is more than adequately punished for any shortcomings by his statue outside the Gallery. He was at least enough of an artist for this to make him wish he had never been born in York. But if you turn your back on the Art Gallery, and on this deplorable statue, there is the King's Manor in front of you. It has suffered much in the past, and is now a school for the blind: but the managers of an excellent charity have done much to restore it.

We also saw St Wilfred's College, rescued in recent times and restored to be the Convocation House of the province of York. And we saw many of the innumerable churches. Perhaps the most pleasing was Trinity church in Goodramgate, because it was absolutely unrestored. Of course I spent long times in the Minster, and perhaps too much money at the excellent bookshop in Stonegate.

On our last day at York we had the afternoon free. We did a thing I have long wanted to do: for we drove over to see Beverley. One should see St Mary's church first and then the Minster. For though St Mary's is very fine, it or any church must be an anti-climax to the Minster. I even think the Minster is the finest Gothic building in Great Britain, and the Percy monument one of the best pieces of mediaeval art. I do not know what was the happy chance that in so small a town as Beverley preserved the Minster. If only there had been such good fortune elsewhere! If Reading had its great Abbey intact, that rather sordid town would be a pleasant place, and Bury St Edmunds an even more attractive town than it is. And what would not Oxford gain, if Osney Abbey had survived as its Cathedral, and St Frideswide's merely provided the chapel for Christ Church!

The Sheriff of Yorkshire at this Assize appeared after the first day in a brown uniform with trousers, as a change from his velvet court suit. He said he had got it because his Under-Sheriff told him to. I never saw any other Sheriff wear it, but I have been told by a colleague that he has met a Sheriff so attired in some other county.

Leeds kept us at work for 17 days, and was as tedious as usual. In one respect I found I had wronged the place. For it has one really fine ancient monument in St John's church. The woodwork, pews and screens, of the seventeenth century is very fine. It reminded me very much of Croscombe church near Wells, but it is much darker. On one of the screens I noticed what I thought was an error by the carver—"Fac cum sanctis munerari", etc. But later on I spoke of this to my friend the present Dean of York. And he, being a very learned theologian, told me that in all ancient MSS of the *Te Deum* the word is "munerari". It was altered to "numerari" in a breviary of 1491, and hence came our prayer-book version "Make me to be numbered" instead of "Let me be rewarded". He added that a clause was added by Gregory the Great to the Canon of the Mass—"in electorum tuorum jubeas grege numerari" and it is thought that the familiarity of these words caused the change of reading in the *Te Deum* to become current without difficulty.

This would suggest that the seventeenth-century carver in St John's, or those who directed him, were as learned as my friend the Dean. But on enquiry I found that this inscription was part of a modern restoration of the screen. I imagine that the ancient, and correct, "munerari" may have been instigated by one of the many learned persons who have been Vicars of Leeds.

In the churchyard of St John's I saw a stone with the inscription:

All cold beneath this narrow heap
The mortal charms of Frances sleep.

◇ ◇ ◇

In the autumn of 1927, when I had been on the bench for three years, I was for the first time able to spend a whole term in London, without going on circuit, and render my services to London litigants. Our system is based on the apparent theory that every Assize town, however unimportant, must have a judge come to it three times a year, and Liverpool, Manchester and Leeds four times a year. London litigants enjoy the labours of such judges as the provinces do not require. The result is that in London everyone has to wait far longer to have his case tried, than anyone in the country. If cases were to be tried with the same dispatch, when set down in London, as they would be in Bodmin or Beaumaris, there would have to be far more judges than there are.

The number of King's Bench Judges available in London—which is always too small except in the short Easter term—is apt to be further diminished by the necessity of one of them going to the Old Bailey. A judge's turn at the Old Bailey is very like an Assize. If he desires it, one of the Sheriffs will come to the Courts and conduct him to the Court in a gorgeous carriage. The first time I went I accepted this offer, since I had never been to that edifice and did not know my way in. The Judge does not, as on circuit, hear the reading of the Commission, nor does he charge the Grand Jury. These duties were discharged by the Recorder on the day before the Judge came.

When the Judge arrives he is conducted to a room where he is greeted by the Lord Mayor and Sheriffs, in all their splendour, and the whole party proceeds to the Court. In most Courts the entry of the Judge is heralded by a cry of "Silence" from an Usher. But at the Old Bailey the Usher knocks on the door with a wooden mallet, and the signal always reminded me of that for the rise of the curtain in a French theatre. On the bench the Lord Mayor sits on the left of the Judge. He usually departs before long, and an Alderman takes his place. At the Old Bailey, as on circuit, the Commission is "to you and any two of you, of whom one of our Judges of our Supreme Court of Judicature shall be one". The Lord Mayor and Aldermen are in the Commission, and one of them therefore sits alongside the Judge to make the quorum of two. On circuit the Circuit officers are named in the Commission, and the quorum is thus provided by the Judge and the Clerk of Assize, or the Associate. I don't know whether at the Old Bailey the Clerk of the Court is in the Commission: in fact the Lord Mayor, or an Alderman, is always on the bench, and there is a belief that he must be there to enable the Judge to do his work.

In the old days the Lord Mayor, or Alderman, did not merely sit on the bench as a κωφὸν πρόσωπον. When Elizabeth Canning was convicted of perjury at the Old Bailey in 1754, Chief Justice Willes proposed seven years' transportation as her proper sentence. An Alderman, Sir John Barnard, moved an amended sentence of six months' imprisonment. The Chief Justice's proposal was only carried by six judges (including the Recorder), the Lord Mayor, and two Aldermen, against eight Aldermen. I cannot conceive what would happen if the Lord Mayor and an Alderman tried nowadays to overrule the Judge as to a sentence. I suspect that he would ignore them.

Similarly, in the old days, lay peers used to vote on legal appeals in the House of Lords. When in January 1703 in the great case of *Ashby*

v. *White* the House of Lords overruled the judgment of the King's Bench the division was 50 peers to 16. And in the case of *Bishop of London* v. *Fytche* in 1783, the appeal was allowed by 19 votes to 18. Lord Thurlow was in the majority along with 13 Bishops and 5 lay peers, while the minority consisted of Lord Mansfield, Lord Loughborough, Lord Bathurst, and 15 lay peers.* So with four lawyers in the House the opinion of one prevailed. If an unlearned Peer attempted now to vote on the question being put at the end of the hearing of an appeal I believe the Lord Chancellor would ignore him, and refuse to take his vote into account.

In the summer months, at the Old Bailey, the Judge, as he enters the Court, is presented with a posy of flowers. And on his desk, and the floor of the bench, "sweet herbs" are strewn. Originally, of course, these were precautions against infection of gaol fever from the adjoining Newgate.† The "sweet herbs" are now the dried potpourri that you see in a bowl in a lady's drawing-room. I used to collect the herbs from my desk in an envelope, and take them home for that purpose. To carry the posy home made one conspicuous in the tube railway, so I used to take it next door to Amen House, leave it for Sir Humphrey Milford, and spend a few minutes in the show room of the Oxford Press.

When the Old Bailey is sitting there is a luncheon provided every day by the Sheriffs. One of them presides at the middle of the top table, with the Judge and the Common Serjeant on his right, and the Recorder and the Judge of the City of London Court on his left.

In the old days, before luncheon was invented, this used to be

* *Anecdotes of the Life of Richard Watson, Bishop of Llandaff* (1817), p. 122. For an occasion, in 1844, when Lord Lyndhurst successfully dissuaded lay peers from voting on an appeal, see Atlay, *Victorian Chancellors*, Vol. I, p. 145.

† Chief Justice Lee was "nearly cut off when attending the Old Bailey Sessions in May 1750. The gaol fever then raged in Newgate...and...it was communicated, by the prisoners brought into court for trial, to the judges, the jurymen, and the witnesses. He escaped, though exposed to the contagion; but Mr Justice Abney, and many others perished. He made a sharp remonstrance to the Lord Mayor and Aldermen...and preventives were introduced which are still kept up at the Old Bailey—such as fumigating the court several times a day by means of a hot iron plunged into a bucket of vinegar and sweet-smelling herbs." (Campbell, *Lives of the Chief Justices* (1874), Vol. III, p. 75.) "At the Lent Assizes 1730, in Taunton, some prisoners, brought from Ivelchester Gaol, infected the Court; and Lord Chief Baron Pengelley, Sir James Sheppard, Serjeant, John Pigot esq., Sheriff, and some hundreds besides, died of the distemper." (Howard, *State of the Prisons* (1780), p. 12.) At what came to be called "the black assize" at Oxford in 1577 "all who were present died within forty hours: the lord chief Baron, the sheriff, and about three hundred more". (Baker's *Chronicle*, quoted by Howard, *ibid.*)

a dinner. The Judges would leave the table, go into Court to receive a verdict, sentence a man to death, and return to the party. Dr Johnson was present at one of these dinners at the Old Bailey in April 1778. The Judges were Blackstone and Eyre. This is the only recorded occasion upon which Johnson met Blackstone, a fellow member of Pembroke College, Oxford.*

* Birkbeck Hill, *Johnson's Letters* (1892), Vol. II, p. 65.

1928

In January 1928 I went once again to South Wales. Just before Christmas I had to fix the Commission Days. I was not surprised to find that there was very little work in prospect at Haverfordwest, Lampeter, and Carmarthen, and I determined to do what I could to prevent the waste of time I remembered a year ago. There is a provision in an Act of 1925 that "if it appears to the Lord Chief Justice that there is no business, or no substantial amount of business, to be transacted at the assizes about to be held at any place on a circuit, he may, with the concurrence of the Lord Chancellor, order that the Assize shall not be held at that place".

This was an absurd enactment. The Lord Chief Justice could not possibly know the prospects of business on any circuit, except the one he might be going on himself. The only person who did was the Judge. And he only knew very shortly before he had to set out. The Act was a dead letter unless the Judge applied to the Lord Chief Justice, and he in turn invoked the concurrence of the Lord Chancellor. And it was very rarely that there was time for all this. In the result I believe very few orders were ever made under this section.*

On this occasion I was able to apply to the Lord Chief Justice, and stated the facts to him. Whereupon, with the concurrence of the Lord Chancellor, he made an order cancelling the Assizes at Haverfordwest and Lampeter, and transferring any of their business to Carmarthen.

This enabled me to start for Carmarthen on 25 January, and I saved at least a week, during which I sat in London and heard cases. Just before I left town I happened to hear a case that provided a striking example of the hardship that results from London litigants only having the services of Judges when they are not required by the pampered provincials, of which I spoke a little while back. A shopkeeper in a small way of business, in the autumn of 1926, did some upholstering work for some rascal in the suburbs. His bill of about £170 being

* In 1938, after I had ceased to go on circuit, this was at last altered by transferring this power from the Lord Chief Justice to the Judge going on the circuit, and dispensing with any concurrence by the Lord Chancellor. See *infra*, p. 189.

unpaid, he issued a writ in January 1927, and applied for summary judgment. The Defendant set up (1) that his wife had given the order and was liable, (2) that the work in various respects was badly done. He got leave to defend, and the case was put by the Master in the Non Jury list. It came on for trial just one year after the issue of the writ, though the Plaintiff had done all he could to expedite it. And then, of course, the Defendant did not appear, the Plaintiff in two minutes proved his claim, and got judgment for his debt about 14 months after it had accrued. If this Plaintiff had been living in Dolgelley, or Presteign, and done his work there, the 14 months would have been reduced to 3 or 4!

The three counties of Pembroke, Cardigan, and Carmarthen, and two county boroughs of Haverfordwest and Carmarthen, provided me with three prisoners altogether: one pleaded guilty, and two had to be tried. But there were two or three civil cases, and the four working days (including Saturday) that I had allowed for Carmarthen were fully occupied. My only diversion was to walk down to the sea at Llanstephan on Sunday, have tea there, and walk back. At Brecon there were two prisoners, both of whom pleaded guilty, and a hotly contested civil case: the two days I had given for Brecon were also fully occupied. I had no information as to Presteign, when I applied to the Lord Chief Justice. I might almost have assumed that its work would be not substantial, and asked him to transfer it to Brecon. In fact there was only one prisoner, and three hours on the Saturday, my only working day there, sufficed amply for his trial. The result was that when I arrived at Chester on the Monday, I had spent 35 hours in Court, and if I had been sitting in London I should only have been 45 hours in Court.

In the newspapers, while in these parts, I read two accounts of the proceedings of local authorities. At a meeting of the Pembrokeshire County Council there was a motion of protest against the suppression of the Assize at Haverfordwest. It occasioned much spirited declamation, and was carried unanimously. I believe it was forwarded to the Lord Chief Justice. A similar protest was made at a meeting of the Haverfordwest Corporation. The three prisoners that appeared before me at Carmarthen were all brought from Swansea prison. Only one was committed from Pembroke County, and not one from Haverfordwest. So the indignation of these worthy bodies appeared to be because

I did not go to Haverfordwest to spend two hours in trying this one man! I did not see in the papers any similar protest about the suppression of Lampeter Assizes: but the County of Cardigan had not produced a single prisoner.

Later on there was yet another motion of protest at the Pembrokeshire Quarter Sessions. I believe much was made there about the supposed grievance that a civil case from Milford Haven, with a fair number of witnesses, had to be tried at Carmarthen, and not at Haverfordwest. In fact I knew nothing of the existence of this case till I got to Carmarthen. It is one of the difficulties of arranging the times for a circuit, especially for these small counties, that a civil case can be entered for trial only seven days before Commission Day, whereas the duration of the Assize must be fixed much earlier. But there was little to be said for the grievance. It is true that Milford is only about 10 miles from Haverfordwest, and is 40 miles from Carmarthen. So the grievance was that, though the Milford litigant had his case tried perhaps 8 to 12 months sooner than a London litigant would have done, he actually had to travel 40 miles for it, as if he had been a resident in a county like Yorkshire or Devon, instead of 10.

The High Sheriff of Brecon lent me his car to drive to Presteign, and by his advice I stopped on the way to see the church of Llanvilo. It is a small church with a carved wooden rood loft, which is beautiful. I have a book in my library on *Screens and Galleries*, by Francis Bond. Of Welsh screens he says "they are found chiefly on or near the Welsh border, in Denbigh, Montgomery, Radnor and Brecon". He does not seem to mention Llanvilo, but he gives a picture of one at Patricio, which is very like it.

The Lodgings at Presteign, joined on to the curious little Court, looked rather less grim than when I spent one night in them three years ago. In the drawing-room there was a square Broadwood piano, rather more than a century old. It might be the very instrument that Frank Churchill procured for Jane Fairfax. Quite a number of the notes, when struck, would still produce a sound, but it had not been tuned for about a century.

From the bidding prayer at the church I discovered that Presteign is in the diocese of Hereford, and therefore belongs to the established English Church. And I found that a large part of the parish is over the border in Herefordshire. I believe there were some parishes in Wales, on the border, that were in an English diocese. At the disestablishment of the Welsh Church they were given an option whether to remain in the English Church or join fortunes with the Welsh. And I think Presteign (said to be the most valuable living in South Wales) was the only one that chose the former alternative.

Presteign, with 1172 inhabitants in 1931, is much the smallest Assize town in England and Wales. Appleby had 1786, Lampeter 1813, and Beaumaris 1839 inhabitants. Presteign boasts a railway station, which Beaumaris lacks, but it is at the end of a single line 8 miles long, which branches from a branch line. And Presteign is right at the end of its little shire; you can step into Herefordshire in a few minutes. If Radnor must keep an Assize town, it would be much better at Llandrindod Wells, with 4600 people, and a good railway service. Even Knighton, with 1710, is larger, and is more accessible.

There is a story in the guide-books that Rhayader, which now has 910 people, was once the Assize town, but that when the Judge of the Great Sessions was going to an Assize Service there in 1542 he was murdered by people described as "Cardiganshire banditti", whereupon the Assize was transferred to Presteign.

There may be some foundation for this story, but its details have gone wrong. Rhayader certainly was once the Assize town. For the Act of 1535, which created Radnor as one of the five new counties on the Welsh side of the border, provided that in Radnorshire the Assizes should be kept alternately at New Radnor and at Rather Gowey (i.e. Rhayader). The Act of 1542 which created the Great Sessions of Wales provided that the Court for Radnor should henceforth be held alternately at New Radnor and at Preston (Presteign), "and never from henceforth be holden at Rather Gowey". The attack of the banditti on a judge at Rhayader must therefore have been between 1535 and 1542. But the judge cannot have been a Judge of the Great Sessions.

At Chester I met Mr Justice Talbot, who had been in North Wales. We were lodged again in the very pleasant house, Heronbridge, on the road to Eccleston. We agreed that this house, and the one at Mold, were the best Lodgings possible. They had all the comforts of the big permanent "Lodgings" in places like Liverpool or Leeds, but they had also the added charm of being the homes of cultured people, a charm that an official house can never have.

I gathered from a guide-book of 1816, called *The Stranger in Chester*, that the Judges used to be lodged in the Castle. For in its description of it it said: "On a line with this tower are the orderly rooms, officers' apartments, the apartments of the Judges etc., which command uncommonly fine prospects. During the Assizes, the table of the Judges is furnished with wines etc. at the expense of the City; and they have the use of the Corporation plate." In 1816 the Judges at every Assize would be Robert Dallas, K.C., Chief Justice, and Francis Burton, K.C., M.P., Second Justice, of the Grand Sessions for Chester, Montgomery, Flint, and Denbigh.

◇ ◇ ◇

In the summer of 1928 I was again on the North-Eastern Circuit, and went to Durham on 21 June. It was a particularly fine summer, and I enjoyed this circuit very much. Durham Castle was slipping from its hill, and I was not allowed to use the usual quarters of the senior judge: they were thought to be in danger. Our usual dining-room was turned into a bedroom for my colleague, and we dined in the fine room next to it that is the Common Room of the dons of University College.

I have always found much hospitality on this circuit, and in the glorious weather I had many pleasant outings with old friends, and with some new ones. By one of the latter I was taken one Sunday to see Alnwick, Bamborough, and Chillingham Castles. At the last I walked in the park, and got fairly close to the wild cattle. They are not dangerous, at least not at this time of the year, but I was asked not to go too near them, lest they should stampede in fear of me, and in their rush the calves might be injured.

Otherwise the circuit was much as I had found it twice before. The Lord Mayor of Newcastle gave me a Rose Noble of Edward IV, and the Lady Mayoress of York another silver snuff-box. York I explored again incessantly, but left plenty of things unexplored for future visits. The Merchant Adventurers Hall I saw more thoroughly than I had before. And I found the Merchant Taylors Hall, now a Catholic Apostolic Church, and four minute alms-houses by it, in a court out of Aldwark.

An unfortunate incident at York was the illness of my marshal. Just after he had sworn two Grand Juries, at the Guildhall and the Castle, he complained of feeling unwell, and went back to the Lodgings.

I thought this was only the result of the unwonted dissipation of the Lord Mayor's breakfast. At luncheon time there did not seem much amiss with him, or when I saw him after the Court rose. Luckily I thought I would be cautious, and fetched a doctor. By further good luck I went to a very good surgeon. He came, and thought there was nothing seriously wrong, but said he would come later to make sure. All this was a tame prelude. For at 11.30 at night I was told the poor youth had acute appendicitis, and must have an operation at once. Much telephoning followed. I went with the patient in the Police Ambulance (they later sent me a modest bill—"To use of ambulance, 4*s*.") to the Purey Cust Nursing Home. There I waited, and talked to the Matron, till 2.30, when it was announced that all was over, and all was well. He made a good and speedy recovery. And if he was fated to have this trouble, he was lucky in the time and place. For the Purey Cust Nursing Home seemed to me quite the nicest I have ever seen—as a visitor, never as a patient. On one of my visits to see him I told the Matron, in all sincerity, that if ever such a thing happened to me I hoped it might be in York, so that I could come to her Home.

The most trying days at Leeds were those on which I had to deal with about eighty undefended divorce cases. This is the only form of judicial work that I have always detested. And I have resented having to do it. I do not know if the task of doing this work on circuit had already been imposed on Judges of the King's Bench by October 1924, when I accepted a judgeship. But I certainly did not realize that I was to be involved in so repulsive and degrading a duty.

Not only is it repulsive to have to sit and listen to repeated tales of adultery, but the actual work involved would be degrading to the meanest intellect. The text-books about divorce purport to set forth principles that are said to have been laid down, e.g. as to the exercise of judicial discretion in favour of a Petitioner who confesses to have himself, or herself, committed adultery. I have never been able to discover that there really are any principles at all: I believe you could find some authority for anything you thought fit to do. So I used to sit, in savage boredom, listening to the sordid stories, and occasionally interjecting—"That will do. Decree nisi, and custody. You can't have costs; you have not proved he knew she was married"—or to that effect. I cannot conceive why these cases cannot be heard in the County

Court, and by its Registrar. It would still be hard on that capable official; for in fact they would not tax the powers of the stupidest man who was ever an acting-deputy-Registrar of a County Court.

As for the evidence from hotels—the chambermaid of superhuman powers of observation and memory, who recalls that a man and woman spent a night in a bedroom a year or two ago, that she took morning tea to them in bed, that a blurred snapshot produced to her is a portrait of the man, and that the Petitioner-wife who has just left the box was not the woman—it was obviously incredible. But its production was part of the absurd ritual. I once shocked a regular Divorce Court practitioner very much by saying: "I am not sure if I can give you a decree. You have called the chambermaid to say her usual piece. She has said she saw them in bed. But she has not said she took them early morning tea. I thought that was a necessary incident in the depravity of adultery."

I can only remember a single occasion on which, among the many hundreds of these cases I have had to hear, I had any feeling of pleasure. Counsel for the Petitioner made the usual exordium—"This is a case for your Lordship's discretion". The Petitioner was a grey-haired working man of over sixty. Some thirty years ago his wife had deserted him, and gone off to live with another man. A year or two after he found a woman to keep house for him. For thirty years both spouses had been "living in adultery", but otherwise respectably. Not unnaturally I said to the counsel: "What is the meaning of this? Why, after all this time, does this old man want to get a divorce?" I was told the reason. His partner had recently been converted by the Salvation Army. They told her she was living in sin, and she left him. He was most anxious to get her back, and she was equally anxious to go back, if he could "make an honest woman" of her. I then realized the reason why two girls in Salvation Army bonnets had been sitting in Court: I was greatly puzzled why they should be listening to the sordid stories of a Divorce Court. And looking towards them I saw that they were guarding a respectable grey-haired woman. I need hardly say that I made no difficulty about exercising my discretion in the Petitioner's favour.

I cannot pretend to feel any scruples of conscience or belief as to divorce. I have said that I think Mr Justice Talbot was the greatest judge I have known. I am quite certain that he was the truest Christian, and firmest believer. To him it was not merely boredom and disgust to have to hear divorce cases: it was pain and grief as well. But he did the duty imposed on him, and he never made any public comment upon it. When Sir Walter Phillimore was Vacation Judge, he refused even to go through the formality of making decrees *nisi* absolute. There is a well-known story that Sir Gorell Barnes, having been, in consequence, called from the country to do it, emitted perhaps the only joke attributed to him, when he said that he hoped he would not find himself with a Unitarian colleague who refused to sit in Admiralty with the Trinity Masters.

The mention of Lord Gorell (as he became) tempts me to record a story that was told to me by Lord Mersey. The President of the Probate, Divorce and Admiralty Division wears, for full dress, the black and gold gown, like that of the Lord Chancellor and the Lords Justices. When as Sir John Bigham he was appointed to succeed Lord Gorell as President, he bought his gown from him for £50. In course of time he resigned, and Sir Samuel Evans was his successor. Bigham gave the gown to Evans. But meeting Lord Gorell, he said to him, with characteristic and impish humour: "I say, Gorell, I have done a stroke of business. You remember you sold me that gown for £50. Well, I have got £100 for it from Evans." Lord Gorell looked at him with grave solemnity, and said: "Really, Bigham, that's very interesting. You see, Jeune gave it to me."

◇ ◇ ◇

In the autumn of 1928 I was glad to go, for the first time, on the Midland Circuit, starting at Aylesbury. There I was very much at home. The Lodgings, which adjoin the Court, are used as a Magistrates Club, except during the Assizes. I became a county magistrate in 1916, and had often attended Quarter Sessions, when the magistrates lunch in an enormous room. The Judge uses a smaller dining-room.

A good many years ago a magistrate happened to be in Aylesbury, and was unaware that the Assizes were being held. He went into his club, and made his way into the drawing-room. There he found an elderly stranger. Supposing him to be a magistrate he had not met before, he politely said "Good-day", took up a newspaper and sat himself down. Alas, the elderly stranger was a judge now dead who always had ridiculous notions of his importance and dignity as Judge of Assize, but very little sense of humour. A painful scene ensued, and the unhappy magistrate very soon left the house, a chastened man. Since that dreadful episode a notice has always been exhibited at the front door, warning people that the Judge is in residence.

The Midland Circuit is an old name, but as at present constituted it is a comparatively new thing. Of the present six English circuits, only the Oxford and the Western comprise the counties they have always done. The old Northern Circuit is now split up into the present Northern and North-Eastern. There was also the Home Circuit, covering Hertford, Essex, Kent, Sussex and Surrey: this with the addition to it of Norfolk, Suffolk, Huntingdon, and Cambridge is now the South-Eastern, which is divided into two parts. The Norfolk Circuit covered Buckingham, Bedford, Huntingdon, Cambridge, Suffolk and Norfolk: this has disappeared, Buckingham and Bedford going into the modern Midland, and the others into the modern South-Eastern. The old Midland Circuit covered Northampton, Rutland, Lincoln, Nottingham, Derby, Leicester, and Warwick. In 1864 York (taken from the old Northern) and Leeds were added to the Midland Circuit. In 1876 the new North-Eastern was created, and York and Leeds transferred to it. The Midland, as now constituted, thus dates from 1876.

According to Dugdale, *Origines Juridiciales* (1671), when Edward I instituted the Circuit System he created Four Circuits, in which the counties were thus grouped: I. York, Northumberland, Westmoreland, Cumberland, Lancaster, Nottingham, Derby. II. Lincoln, Leicester, Warwick, Stafford, Salop, Northampton, Rutland, Gloucester, Hereford, Worcester. III. Cornwall, Devon, Somerset, Dorset, Wilts, Southampton, Oxon, Berks, Sussex, Surrey. IV. Kent, Essex, Hertford, Norfolk, Suffolk, Cambridge, Huntingdon, Bedford, Buckingham. It will be observed that the Counties Palatine, Durham, and Chester, are not included. Middlesex was, of course, provided for at Westminster.

I thought it would interest the Grand Jury at Aylesbury, when I spoke to them of "our County", to remind them that it has only been in comparatively recent times that a judge could use that pronoun. In 1385 it was enacted by 8 Rich. II, cap. 2, that no man of the law should from henceforth be a Justice of Assize in his own county. And in 1542 by 33 Hen. VIII, cap. 24, it was provided that no one should exercise the office of Justice of Assize within any county where he was born or inhabited, upon pain of forfeiting £100. The preamble of this Act refers to the earlier statute of Richard II, and recites that "some Jealousy of their Affection and Favour toward their Kinsmen, Alliance, and Friends, within the said Country where they were so born or inhabiting hath been conceived".

An Act of 1739 (12 Geo. II, cap. 27) recites the Acts of Richard II and Henry VIII, and "whereas a compliance with the aforesaid provisions has been attended with very great inconveniences", enacts that a judge may be Judge of Assize in any county, notwithstanding his birth or residence in it. But as this Act of 1739 only applied to Commissions of Oyer and Terminer and Gaol Delivery, but did not mention Commissions of *Nisi Prius*, it was found necessary to pass another Act in 1809 (49 Geo. III, cap. 91) "to empower the Judges to try civil causes in their own counties". It has the same preamble as the Act of 1739 about the "great inconveniences" of the old prohibitions.

Sir James Whitelock lived at Fawley Court, near Henley, now the splendid place of Major Roderick Mackenzie. In his *Liber Famelicus* (Camden Society, 1858) he says, at p. 105, in 1626: "Memorandum that all my ancients refused to go Norfolk Circuit, and then it falling to my torn, I could not, becaus I dwelled in Buckinghamshire, so of the two left I chose the Northe."

Mr Justice Rokeby, from whose *Diary* I have already quoted, between 1689 and 1699 went on the Western, Oxford, Norfolk, Home, and Midland Circuits. But he never went on the Northern, no doubt because he was born at York, and had a house there. In March 1690/91 he was on the Norfolk Circuit with Chief Justice Sir John Holt. I do not know how the latter could be there, without incurring a £100 fine under the Act of 1542. The Norfolk Circuit included Norfolk, Suffolk, Cambridge, Huntingdon, Bedford and Buckingham. And Sir John Holt had a house at Redgrave in Suffolk. He is buried in Redgrave church, with a magnificent and most interesting monument.

This prohibition, in existence for over 350 years, is in curious contrast to the inveterate principle that jurors must have a strictly local qualification. The Judge, who is to hold the ring, must apparently be a stranger to all local knowledge, prejudice, or interest. It is rather like the system by which, in an International football match, the referee is summoned from a third country.

Bedford

Perhaps unhappily for the occasion I was unable to congratulate the Grand Jury (most of whom I knew) on the lightness of the calendar, which occupied me four full days, and was the most serious, except that at Derby, on the whole circuit. I had no time for any sight-seeing, but I knew the region so well that I did not regret that. I would suggest to any of my successors, who do not, that the Museum of our Bucks Archaeological Society, close to the church, is well worth a visit.

They have preserved some old javelins at Aylesbury. They are now kept by the county police, and when the Sheriff's car conveys the Judge to the church, along the most picturesque street in the town, an escort of constables each bears one of the javelins.

In *A Tour of the Grand Junction Canal* (J. Hassell, London, 1819, p. 54) I find this: "At Aylesbury and its vicinity they are famous for rearing early ducks.... Let the Lent Assizes fall as early as may be, the Judges, who go this circuit, always have a supply of young ducks placed up their table, and who, with Counsel and Solicitors regularly going the Norfolk Circuit, are entertained at the expense of the high Sheriff of the County, a circumstance which renders the Shrieffalty somewhat expensive. This is the only county in England that has the honour of feasting the bar at the expense of the Sheriff, excepting the county of Cambridge, where the custom has prevailed from time immemorial: if it be an honour, I am inclined to think that gentlemen who have to hold the office, would willingly dispense with it."

At Bedford they housed the Judge in a villa hired for the occasion, and it was not a very good villa. The calendar there was as light as it could be, one prisoner, who pleaded guilty. Officially I had the company of the Sheriff for less than an hour, but on my way to Northampton by road I had tea with him, and the chance of seeing the fine Mordaunt tombs in Turvey church. By far the most difficult work I had to do at Bedford was to compose a reply to a Latin letter sent to me by the head boy of the School. "Si modo tu orabis ἀρχιδιδάσκαλον nostrum, ut, parte de solido die dempta, laboribus vacemus, gratias maximas feres", was the most important part of it from the boys' point of view. So I did my best for them. I hope I may be acquitted of improper pride if I add that the Head Master wrote to me: "I should like to add, if you will not think it presumptuous, a word in appreciation of the polished Latin in which you wrote to the head of the School."

Perhaps I should also say that my marshal (a recent graduate of Trinity College, Oxford, as my marshals almost always were) was, upon this occasion only, of no use at all: he had read Law.

At Northampton the Lodgings were a fine old house, next to the Court, with a passage from one to the other, as at Aylesbury. The Court, architecturally, is in my opinion the finest in England. It was begun soon after the great fire of 1675, which destroyed All Saints' church, and many houses. The date 1678 is on one of the leaden water-pipes on the front of it. The ceilings were made by a plasterer named Edward Goudge: the work took four years, and cost £150. The Crown Court remains as it was built, and its ceiling is magnificent. The *Nisi Prius* Court (now used for the County Court only) has been spoiled by having a wooden partition put across the middle of it to shut off one end, which is used as an entrance hall. It ruins the proportion of the chamber, and cuts across the ceiling, which is fine and dignified, but not so splendid as that of the Crown Court. The pictures of William and Mary were bought by the City in 1689, and there are later portraits of Anne, George II, and George III.

The Lodgings next door were bought by the County in 1819 for £3844. I cannot think that the present staircase is the original one. It is not worthy of the house, and the dignified panelled rooms it contains.

The Foreman of the Grand Jury, who was also Chairman of Quarter Sessions, must have been pleased to look on the ceiling of the Crown Court. For he was Mr J. A. Gotch, author of several admirable books on English Renaissance Architecture. On the strength of having read them with so much pleasure, I asked him to tea with me, and he told me many interesting things. I ventured to suggest that he should use his influence to get the *Nisi Prius* Court cleared of its disfigurement, and restored, so that it might be a dignified hall in the same way as the Shire Hall at Warwick, out of which the two octagonal courts there lead.

There were only two prisoners, and the work ended early on the second day. So I had the chance of a visit to one of the nicest High Sheriffs I ever met, and under his guidance saw some of the architectural treasures in which Northamptonshire is so rich. These were the works of Sir Thomas Tresham—the market house at Rothwell, Rushton Hall, and the extraordinary triangular lodge in its park.

I also saw the fine church at Rothwell, and the Jesus Hospital beside it. The worst thing in the church was to see the remnants of a fine Renaissance pulpit, used up as part of a screen to the vestry, and to observe the wretched stone modern pulpit that had taken its place.

The next place was Leicester. The Lodgings there are at the County Rooms, and are of an incredible spaciousness. There was a vast dining-room, and a drawing-room of the same size. In my enormous bedroom I found a second door, which looked as if it might lead into an adjoining dressing-room. I went through it—and found myself in a ball-room, about 80 feet long and 30 feet wide. "Sir, if a Judge has a mind to prance, let him stay at the Lodgings at Leicester."

These County Rooms were built as the Assembly Rooms in 1800: they included a Coffee Room and Tavern. The architect was John Johnson, a Leicester man, who in 1794 founded the Consanguinitarium, a sort of almshouse, primarily for his relatives: it still exists, after being rebuilt, in Earl Howe Street. The Assembly Rooms were bought by the County in 1825, and "the portion which was the hotel was handsomely fitted up for the lodging and accommodation of the Judges during the Assizes". The ball-room is a fine thing: it has painted panels done by Philip Reinagle, R.A. (1749–1833).

Whether he prances or not, a judge will find these Lodgings very comfortable. I was grateful for one thoughtful attention. Close behind is the clock-tower on the Town Hall, with a loud chime every quarter. I had a message, when I arrived, that, if I liked, they would stop the striking at night, while I was there. I gratefully accepted the offer. I remembered a bedroom in which I was supposed to sleep in a famous school. My host, *Magister Informator*, said he was afraid my slumbers might be disturbed by the adjacent clock. And he was right. The clock struck every quarter, and as I believed I never slept more than ten minutes consecutively all night. So they stopped the strike at Leicester, and I slept, and could have my window open.

For a place of such antiquity Leicester looks strangely modern. It has rebuilt itself very thoroughly. Of Roman Leicester I could find nothing except the small piece of wall in the Jewry. The Guildhall, or old Town Hall, with its great hall, and panelled Mayor's parlour, is charming, and has been admirably restored.

The Court, in the Castle, is part of the ancient Norman hall. In the Judge's retiring room there is a Norman moulding on the arch above the window, that window being in a thickness of wall that attests its Norman origin. As I sat in Court, I thought I could trace the outline of the old hall, with aisles at the side of wooden pillars supporting the roof. But it is all overlaid with modern partitions and plastering. In a Leicester Directory of 1845, that I found in the Lodgings, I read: "Within the memory of persons now living the interior of the hall was open from end to end, forming one apartment 78 feet by 51; the Court held at each end being divided merely by a curtain."

They had lately improved the river side very much, by pulling down buildings, and making a garden. I do not know if the old hall is beyond rescue and restoration. Seeing what has lately been done at Lincoln's Inn, perhaps not: but it would be a costly business.

If, within living memory from 1845, the Crown Court sat at one end of the great hall, and the *Nisi Prius* Court at the other end, that was a system that obtained elsewhere, and was all in the tradition of the greatest hall of all—Westminster Hall. The Courts of King's Bench and Chancery once occupied the two southern corners of Westminster Hall, and the Courts of Common Pleas and Exchequer were on each side of it farther north. At Taunton and at Winchester, until the nineteenth century, the Crown Court and the Civil Court sat at each end of the Castle halls. According to Robert Walton, *Random Recollections of the Midland Circuit* (1869, Vol. I, p. 10), at Northampton and at Derby the Civil Court used only to be divided from the Criminal Court by a green baize curtain: if this is correct, I think it can only have been before 1678 at Northampton. The only Castle hall that remains as an Assize Court is the wonderful hall at Oakham, adorned with the heraldic horse-shoes of visiting peers. Unfortunately Oakham has had no occasion for an Assize for many years. No Court could sit in finer or more interesting quarters.

From my point of view it was to Leicester's credit that I found quite a good bookshop, by which, of course, I mean a shop that is filled with old books. One thing I bought there was *The Trial of Sir Francis Burdett, for a Seditious Libel, at the Leicester Assizes on Thursday 23 March 1820 before Mr Justice Best and a Special Jury.* Burdett, on 22 August 1819, wrote from his house, Kirby Hall, an address to the Westminster Electors denouncing the Peterloo Massacre, which had taken place on 19 August. Members of Parliament nowadays use much more violent language about much less serious things. Mr Justice Best, who had been a Law Officer in a Tory Government, is reported as ending his summing-up with the words: "More poisonous ingredients never were condensed in one paper." The Special Jury, of Tory country gentlemen, in two minutes were agreed. "The Foreman then stepped into his place, and called out 'Guilty of Libel'." Sentence was postponed to the King's Bench in London.

For the sequel I had to look elsewhere. On 24 April 1820 Denman moved in the King's Bench for a new trial on the grounds, (1) no proof of publication in Leicestershire, (2) the matters in the letter were only fair comment on public events, and there could be no malice as no charge was made against individuals, (3) misdirection by the Judge in telling the jury that this was a libel; under the Act of 1792 this should have been left to the jury's discretion.

This motion was argued on 10 May, 17 June, 20 June, 16 November and 22 November. On 27 November the Court delivered judgment, dismissing the motion by a majority of three to one.

On 3 February 1821 the Attorney-General moved for judgment. Scarlett for Burdett spoke in mitigation of sentence. On 8 February Mr Justice Bailey delivered the judgment of the Court, viz. that the Defendant do pay the King a fine of £2000, and be imprisoned in the Marshalsea for three calendar months.

According to Lord Langdale, the four judges, in order to fix the amount of the fine, adopted a method which is believed to be sometimes used by a jury to assess damages, viz. for each to write down the figure he thinks right and then take the average. Mr Justice Best, as the junior judge, gave his figure first, and put down £20,000. The other three refused to accept this, as being outrageous. So he reduced it to £8000. The other three each wrote £0, and so the fine was fixed at £2000.

One experience, novel to me, was to attend a sale of hunters at the Leicester Repository. The crowd was very interesting, and I never saw so many men exhibiting the curious aspect that seems to be the result of lifelong association with the horse. As for the horses, they were beautiful, and paraded the narrow hall with all the conscious pride that 300 or 400 guineas apiece was being offered for them.

On Monday, 29 October, I went by train to Lincoln. The Lodgings are a gaunt house, between the Cathedral and the Castle, very grim of aspect, but comfortable enough inside. Naturally I spent the greater part of my leisure in the Cathedral. All the West front was still covered with scaffolding, but the end of the restoration was in sight, and, I believe, the money to complete it secured. That was due to the youthful ardour of Dean Fry, who, being only eighty-two, was frequently hauled up the scaffolding to a dizzy height, whence he ascended by ladders, in order to inspect the work, and be able to give an account of it, when he ran over to America to ask for some more money.

A thing that was new to me in Lincoln was the Usher Gallery. In the market-place at Aylesbury there is a statue of John Hampden. This was set up in 1912 at the expense of a Buckinghamshire farmer, John Griffin. Usher, of Lincoln, was an even more notable local patriot. He had a watchmaker's shop in the city, and spent much time and money in collecting beautiful things, including many watches. When he died he left his collection, and funds to build a gallery, to the city, and the funds seem to have been enough for the fine building by Sir Reginald Blomfield, R.A., on an excellent open site. Any city may envy Lincoln its Usher Gallery.

From Lincoln I drove to Nottingham, stopping on the way to see Newark church, and Southwell Minster. I had seen them both, years ago, and had forgotten how splendid they both are. Newark church I would put in the first class of parish churches, along with St Mary Redcliffe, St Mary Beverley, Wolverhampton, Terrington St Clement's, and a few more. As for Southwell, I suppose the Decorated work in and about its Chapter House is the high-water mark of English Gothic, and hardly to be surpassed in France.

I do not think I had been in Nottingham before, and I had not realized what a huge place it is. It has not rebuilt itself so thoroughly as Leicester, and there were some fine old houses surviving, especially in Low Pavement, and in Castlegate, and up by the Hospital near to the spot where Charles I raised his standard in 1642. Near there Collins's Almshouse is beautiful. One old house in Low Pavement was labelled "Willoughby House", and I suppose was the town house of the Wollaton family. St Mary's church, where I went for the Assize Service, is a fine big church, but, like so many town churches, has too much modern stained glass, and is very dark.

The Lodgings used to be an old house opposite the Court in High

Pavement. It was the scene of an unhappy judicial tragedy many years ago. Recently this house had been taken over for County offices, and since then the Judge had been housed in some furnished house hired for the occasion. I was in one in the Park, that prosperous suburb that, on a smaller scale, resembles Edgbaston at Birmingham. Such a house has some advantages. A house that is someone's home is usually more comfortable than one only occupied officially and occasionally. But there are drawbacks. One I sometimes have had to deplore is the habit of provincial ladies by which their drawing-rooms are crowded with photographs, nick-nacks, and other repulsive trifles, so that it is difficult to find a place on which to put a book down, and one is in constant fear of oversetting some worthless treasure.

On the Saturday afternoon I went out to see Wollaton Hall, lately bought by the Corporation, like Aston Hall, at Birmingham, and Temple Newsham at Leeds. Externally it is an astonishing and very interesting house. Internally I thought it was quite spoilt, partly because it lacks any furniture, and still more because it was crowded up with ugly cases of stuffed animals, and other items of a second-rate museum. I do not know that there was anything quite so incongruous as the early electro-plating machine that Birmingham had installed in Aston Hall. But generally the inside of Wollaton was as depressing as that of Aston. We walked on through the park, to Wollaton church, in the hope of finding Willoughby monuments to admire there. But the church was locked, which seemed a scandal on a Saturday afternoon.

Just outside the gates of Wollaton, over a small new shop, I saw the name Fettiplace. And that interested me very much. It was a very great name in Oxfordshire and Berkshire up to the seventeenth century. Their mansion at Swinbrook, near Burford (so utterly destroyed that I have tried in vain to find traces of it in the grass) was great and magnificent. Many of them were Sheriffs of Berkshire and Oxfordshire, five or six were knighted, and John Fettiplace, of Swinbrook, was made a baronet in 1661. Their monuments may be found in many churches, notably a set of six recumbent effigies at Swinbrook, and two great tombs at East Shefford in the Lambourn Valley.

I had supposed that the family was quite extinct. I have, indeed, a monograph,* *The Family of Fettiplace*, by J. Renton Dunlop. It contains pedigrees of Fettiplace of Denchworth, Berkshire (beginning

* Reprinted from *Miscellanea Genealogica et Heraldica* (1918).

in 1232 and ending in 1767), of Fettiplaces of Stokenchurch (1432–1627), of Fettiplaces of East Shefford and Besselsleigh (1327–1796), of Fettiplaces of Childrey and Swinbrook (1442 to the nineteenth century), of Fettiplaces of Swincombe (seventeenth and eighteenth centuries), and of three minor branches. Mr Dunlop, on p. 48, writes: "The first Fettiplace in England was Gentleman Usher to William the Conqueror, and came in with that monarch....The name is recorded in the Battle Abbey Roll....The latest mention of the name so far discovered is on a headstone in the churchyard of Holy Trinity, Gray's Inn Road—'Mrs Mary Fettiplace, who departed this life the 3 of August 1831, aged 82 years; also Mr John Fettiplace, husband of the above Mary Fettiplace, who died 12 June 1832, aged 75 years'."

I can supplement Mr Dunlop's information. The last Fettiplace did not die in 1832. He was selling tobacco, sweets, minerals, and newspapers, at a small shop outside Wollaton Park, close on a century later.

On this occasion the shop was shut. When I was at Nottingham again in the autumn of 1930, it was open. I found Mr Fettiplace, in his shirt-sleeves, and bought some tobacco from him. I told him I was interested in his name. "Well, Sir, you are not the first to say that." He said he was born in Nottingham, and so far as he knew his family had been there for a long time. He was quite ignorant of the old greatness of his ancestors, or his namesakes.

Oddly enough, the same morning in Court, my interest in surnames was roused. "John Sirdifield" was called as a witness: he was a Nottinghamshire labourer. At Bristol a few months later "Alice Sidsaph" gave evidence: she came from Lincolnshire. Soon after, at Winchester, there was "Alice Mynekyme", from Lancashire; and at Gloucester a policeman named "Eachus"; he said it was a Cheshire name. In London I have come across a "Footherape", and two petitioners in divorce were "Scardifield" and "Pettiford".

On Tuesday, 6 November, we drove to Derby, and came to another set of Lodgings attached to the Court, as at Aylesbury and Northampton. Again it was a fine old house, with some good furniture, and at least one fine picture. That was in the dining-room, a portrait of a Mundy, Sheriff in 1820, painted by R. Reinagle, R.A. In my bedroom was an admirable mezzotint of the same old gentleman and his charming young grandson, also after Reinagle, and probably a "private plate". Another thing that interested me in my bedroom was one of those old brass bolts on the door, from which a wire or a string could be carried round to the bed.

Derby has some fine old houses, e.g. in Friargate, especially one that is now a hotel. Near our Lodgings was a splendid old house, once obviously the town house of a county magnate (I believe of the Batemans) with his arms over the wrought-iron gates. The house had been gutted, and a Baptist chapel made out of its shell. There is just such another architectural degradation (even if it be a spiritual elevation) in the High Street at Burford.

Derby did most of its rebuilding a long while ago. Fire was the occasion for the rebuilding of All Saints' by Gibbs, but there was no such reason at St Werburgh's. All Saints', lately redecorated in bright colours, I liked very much, and its iron screens are almost as magnificent as its tomb of Bess of Hardwick.

To St Werburgh's I went to see where Samuel Johnson was married to Elizabeth Porter. When they knelt in its chancel—after the bride had been reduced to tears on the ride to Derby—they were in a small Palladian church, as remote from "Gothick" as St Clement Danes. Unhappily in 1893 there was a desire to make the church much larger, and it was said, and I dare say readily believed, that the old fabric was in a dangerous condition. So they pulled down all the old church except the chancel, and built a nice new Gothic church at right angles to that, running North and South. I am astonished that the Vandals who achieved this had heard of Johnson, and, because he was married there, refrained from pulling down the old chancel. The result is absurd. You enter a poor modern church by a southern "West" door, and find on your right the small east end of a cheerful Queen Anne church. I recalled what Johnson said of a project to melt down the leaden roofs of Lichfield Cathedral—"What they shall melt, it were just that they should swallow". When his book, *A Journey to the Western Isles*, was at the printers, he wrote to suppress this sentence. "In one of the pages there is a severe censure of the clergy of an English Cathedral, which I am afraid is just, but I have since recollected that from me it may be improper, for the Dean did me a kindness about forty years ago. He is now very old, and I am not young. Reproach can do him no good, and in myself I know not whether it is zeal or wantonness." So the page was cancelled, and only one copy is known to exist—of course in the possession of R. B. Adam, at Buffalo. I know no reason why it should be thought improper for me to wish that those who "dilapidated" St Werburgh's had been made to eat the stones they pulled apart—nor do I care whether in myself it is zeal or wantonness.

The ceremonial of this Assize at Derby was as splendid as any I ever saw. To begin with, the High Sheriff wore the full dress uniform of a regiment of the Guards. He was over six feet high, bareheaded, and about ten with his bearskin on. Then there was a swinging coach, with a fine pair, a bewigged coachman and groom on the box, and two footmen up behind. And twelve javelin men, in livery, with old javelins refurbished, marched beside. So far as I was concerned I played my humble part in the pageant only on the first day, when we went to the Cathedral: for on later days I had only to walk from the Lodgings into the adjoining Court. But Derby was not deprived of most of the splendour on other days. For the Sheriff used to come in every morning to the County Club in Friargate, there to induce his military glories: and the coach, flunkeys, and javelin men conveyed him and his chaplain (more gloriously than Cinderella to the ball) to my Lodgings.

In the past even splendours like these were outdone. John Evelyn, in his *Memoirs*, writes: "1633. 3rd November. This year my father was appointed Sheriff, the last, as I think, who served in that honourable office for Surrey and Sussex, before they were disjoined.* He had 116 servants in liveries, every one liveried in green satin doublets; divers gentlemen and persons of quality waited on him in the same garb and habit, which at that time (when thirty or forty was the usual retinue of the High Sheriff) was esteemed a great matter. Nor was this out of the least vanity that my father exceeded (who was one of the greatest decliners of it); but because he could not refuse the civility of his friends and relations, who voluntarily came in themselves or sent in their servants."

Brayley, the Surrey historian, adds that all these liveried men had "cloth coats guarded with silver galoon, as were their hatbands with white feathers in them". They had also new javelins, and were preceded by two trumpeters, with banners on which were blazoned the arms of Richard Evelyn.

* In fact he was not the last. Separate Sheriffs for Surrey and Sussex only began in 1637.

Sheriff's Profits

Sir John Reresby, in his *Memoirs*, gives an account of his doings as High Sheriff of York in 1667: "The Assizes were appointed this year in March. I took a house in the Minster Yard, where I entertained all comers for ten days together; my friends sent me twixt 200 and 300 liveries. I kept two coaches, one for myself, and one for my under-sheriff, had my own violins there all the Assizes, and gave a ball and entertainment to all the ladies of the town. The Assizes cost me three hundred and odd pounds."

To be Sheriff of Yorkshire now must involve an expense only to be surpassed by being Sheriff of Lancashire. But to do things on the scale of Sir John Reresby would be expensive indeed. In fact in his time, under the system then obtaining, his office was not burdensome, and despite this lavish display, he actually made money. For just before the above-quoted passage he writes: "The gaoler gave me £160 to have the custody of the gaol. I had the same sum presented to me for the County Court, and I made of the bailiwicks about £145, besides the profits of the seal, which made the whole near £1200; but the charges of both assizes, salaries to officers, liveries and equipages, took off so much that I cannot say that I saved clear £200, all charges considered." But £200 was a very considerable sum. A writer of 1696 says that the income of a country gentleman was £280, that of a dignified clergyman £72, and of an inferior clergyman £50. Pepys on 2 March 1661/62 writes: "Talking long in bed with my wife about our frugall life for the time to come, proposing to her what I could and would do, if I were worth £2000, that is, be a knight, and keep my coach, which pleased her."

It was no doubt because of such lavishness that in 1661 there was passed the Act 13–14 Car. II, cap. 21, which provided that no Sheriff should keep any table at the Assizes, except for his own family, or give any presents to the judges or their servants, or have more than forty men in livery: but, for the sake of safety and decency, he may not have less than twenty men in England, and twelve in Wales. This Act was in force until 1859, when by 22–23 Vict. cap. 32 it was provided that every Chief Constable should provide policemen to keep order at the Assizes, and it shall not be necessary for the High Sheriff to provide javelin men or other servants in livery, "anything contained in the Act of Charles II notwithstanding". So javelin men became a voluntary luxury in 1859.

There were twenty-eight prisoners at Derby, and I was so hard at work that I had no time to be abroad in daylight, except after breakfast. One thing I found to its credit was a large bookstall in the Market House. Among piles of rubbish there were some good things to find, and when found they were astonishingly cheap.

I worked so hard because I was very anxious to finish by the Friday evening, as I did. So I was able on the Saturday to go to Oxford, and "as in private duty bound" attend the opening of the War Memorial Library at Trinity College. I met many old friends, spent the week-end in College, and dined with the Law Club in Jesus on Saturday night.

On Monday, 12 November, I went to Warwick. The Lodgings there again are an official house adjoining the Courts. It is fairly comfortable. One of the things I have found to dislike at these official houses (I don't say it occurred on this occasion) is the system of lighting. In one's home one avoids glaring lights, high up, or at any rate supplements them with shaded reading lamps. In the official houses there are often only glaring lights on the ceiling or the walls. In the "Suggestions Book" that they leave in most Lodgings I have often pleaded for more wall-plugs and reading lamps.

The dining-room was very fine and large, with some interesting pictures bought out of "the plate fund", which I suppose is one to which newly appointed J.P.s make a contribution. For here, as at Aylesbury, and elsewhere, they use the Lodgings for luncheon at Quarter Sessions.

The County Hall, next door, is a fine and interesting building. The hall itself is a very well-proportioned room, and opening out of it on one side are two small octagonal Courts. The whole building was erected in 1756. The architect was an amateur. It was the age when Lord Burlington built his house in Piccadilly, and his villa at Chiswick, and when Dean Aldrich built All Saints' church in Oxford. Sanderson Miller (1717–1780), a country squire, of Radway Grange, Warwickshire, was the architect of the Warwick County Hall. He also built the tower at Radway, a well-known landmark. He also designed various ruined "Gothick" castles for his friends. Fortunately the Shire Hall is neither "Gothick" nor ruined, and is a very creditable performance. He also was the architect of Hagley Hall, for his friend Lord Lyttelton.

These facts I derived from *An Eighteenth Century Correspondence*

(1910), a book that I read, or looked through, at the Lodgings. For they were singular in that they contained quite a number of books. Hutton's *History of Birmingham* I looked at, but not through. I looked at it because I remembered that Malone described a visit to Samuel Johnson, and found him reading it by his fire, with some apples by it. And the great man said, "These are some of the solitary expedients to which we are driven by sickness. I have been confined this week past; and here you find me roasting apples and reading *The History of Birmingham.*" It is a melancholy picture, and looking at the book I found it did not lighten the gloom.

Another thing I read was *The Trial of John Donellan Esq. for the wilful murder of Sir Theophilus Boughton, Baronet, at the Assizes at Warwick, Friday* 30 *March* 1781. *Taken in shorthand by Joseph Gurney.* Donellan had married a sister of the Baronet, who was twenty when he died. At twenty-one he was to inherit £2000 a year, but if he died before that most of the money would come to his sister. Donellan poisoned him with a distillation of laurel leaves, putting the poison into his medicine. Lady Boughton, his mother, gave him the medicine, and almost at once he died in agony. The strongest evidence against Donellan was that when he was called into the room, he immediately rinsed out the medicine bottle and threw away the contents. The Judge was Mr Justice Buller (1746–1800), then of the King's Bench, but later of the Common Pleas. There were five counsel for the Crown, and three for the prisoner. "The indictment was shortly opened by Mr Digby", the junior of the five. Perhaps the most interesting thing is that the great John Hunter (1728–1793) was called as an expert witness for the defence. But he failed to convince the jury. The trial began at 7.30 in the morning. In those days luncheon did not exist, and there was no midday adjournment. At 6.24 in the afternoon the jury retired: at 6.34 they returned into Court, and found a verdict of "Guilty". Mr Justice Buller's sentence covers a whole quarto page. In its formal part are the words—"that you be taken from hence to the place from whence you came; that from thence on Monday next you be carried to the place of execution and there", etc. Donellan was accordingly hanged on Monday, 2 April 1781, three days after his trial.

Two variations from modern practice (in addition to the fact that the Court sat at 7.30 a.m., three hours earlier than it would now) may be noted. It was then the practice for the junior counsel for the Crown to "open the indictment", and for the junior for a Plaintiff to "open the pleadings", in a civil case, before their leaders addressed the jury. Opening the indictment in a criminal case has long been abandoned. I do not know when it was given up. As the Clerk of Assize, in giving the prisoner in charge to the jury, stated the nature of the accusation, and did this immediately before this opening by the junior, it was obviously an unnecessary formality, and it is not surprising that it disappeared. But in civil cases with a jury the junior still "opens the pleadings", i.e. states succinctly the issues raised by them, and ends—"and those are the issues you have to try". My readers will remember that on 14 February 1828, at the Guildhall, "The ushers again called Silence, and Mr Skimpin proceed to 'open the case'; and the case appeared to have very little inside it when he had opened it, for he kept such particulars as he knew completely to himself, and sat down, after the lapse of three minutes, leaving the jury in precisely the same advanced stage of wisdom as they were in before. Serjeant Buzfuz then rose...."

The other thing that is changed is that in 1781 the Judge fixed the day of execution in his sentence. This was pursuant to the Act of 1752, which provided that the death penalty must be carried out on the next day but one after sentence, and that after sentence the convict be fed on bread and water only.

Lastly it will be observed that in this trial the Court sat uninterruptedly for close upon 11 hours. The feats of endurance of judges, jurors, and counsel in the old days are almost incredible. Luncheon as a meal was only invented about 1820. And no Court ever adjourned at midday. It was true indeed that "Wretches hang that jurymen may dine". Lord Campbell when at the bar in August 1815 said: "We finished at Gloucester....I was nearly knocked up. One day we went into Court at 8 in the morning, and adjourned at half past two the next morning." In March 1819 he writes from Shrewsbury: "On Friday I was in court occupied from eight in the morning till half past one on Saturday morning. I had then to sit down to read a brief in a murder, attended with very complicated circumstances, which I had to state to the jury at eight the same morning. I was hardly in bed. But I am not at all knocked up." And in April 1832 he writes from Gloucester, "I am very wretched here from the slowness of the judges....All that I can do is to make them come into court at eight in the morning, and sit till midnight." In the Diary* of Sir John Taylor Coleridge (first, and best, of the three judges of his family) he records that in October 1823 the jury acquitted a prisoner at Quarter Sessions, after being locked up, without food or fire, for 17 hours. In August 1830 a trial at Salisbury ended at 2.30 a.m. In March 1845 he writes: "My Exeter work was very heavy. Last Monday I sat 12 hours, and Tuesday 19. I went in at 8 a.m. and sate till 3 a.m., summing up with as much freshness, and perhaps more perspicuity than I had done in any other case at the Assizes." I cannot help wondering whether the jurymen displayed perspicuity at 3 a.m.! This last was no unique occasion. In March 1832, for instance, Sir James Alan Park sat in a civil case at Winchester from 8 a.m. to 2 a.m. At the trial of Lord Cochrane before Lord Ellenborough on 8 June 1814 the Court sat from 9 a.m. until 3 a.m. next morning, and then adjourned for seven hours until 10 a.m. As late as 1850 Lord Denman speaks of leaving Court on a Saturday night at 10 p.m. "after a thirteen hours' trial".

In fact all these times are outdone by a famous Scottish trial. James Stewart was tried as an accomplice in the Appin murder, at Inverary, in September 1752, before the Duke of Argyll, as Lord Justice General, Lord Elchies, and Lord Kilkerran, with a jury of fifteen, of whom eleven were Campbells. The Court sat uninterruptedly from 6 a.m. on Friday, 22 September, until between 7 and 8 a.m. on Sunday, 24 September, that is for 49 or 50 hours.

Warwick is too well known a show place to need any comment of mine. Indeed it has the air, with the Castle, the Beauchamp Chapel, and Lord Leycester's Hospital, of being specially prepared for American tourists. A courtesy for which I was grateful is that before the Judge arrives a key is left for him at the Lodgings, which opens a postern gate into the Castle grounds.

On 15 November I returned to town, and on 3 December joined Mr Justice Talbot at Birmingham, to complete the circuit. The only thing of interest that I remember of that visit is that in the Art Gallery there were fourteen pictures from Hagley, deposited by Lord Cobham, while the house was rebuilding after the fire. Many of them were admirable.

* Printed by Bernard, Lord Coleridge, in *This for Remembrance* (1925), and as I think the most interesting part of his book.

1929

In January 1929 I went the "Long Western" Circuit. In the summer this is perhaps the pleasantest of all the circuits, but even in the winter it is nice. It is the only circuit about which a good book has been written, *Pie Powder* (1911), published anonymously, but well known to be the work of J. Alderson Foote, K.C. Most books of legal reminiscences are bad. I think *Pie Powder* and *As I went on my Way* (1924), by A. J. Ashton, K.C., are almost the only exceptions.

Mr Foote says: "The Western Circuit had one institution peculiar to itself. I refer to the Circuit Van, which was an enormous vehicle like those used for the removal of furniture, and was always conveyed by road or rail wherever the assizes were being held. Its primary and nominal use was to convey the book-boxes of those barristers who desired to take part of their library with them....The Circuit Van became gradually degraded into a mere receptacle of ordinary luggage, and there must be many occupants of the Temple even now, who can recollect seeing it standing in Brick Court for some days before the commencement of each assize. Eventually...it was sold to a travelling menagerie." He adds that one member of the circuit held the office of Baggage-Master. The resolution to abolish and sell the van was passed by the Mess in March 1893. R. G. Seton was the last Baggage-Master.

When I drove to Devizes on Saturday, 12 January, it was a time of hard frost, and the Kennet and Avon Canal, that comes into the town from the east, and then goes downstairs by a succession of locks, was frozen almost solid. At the Assize Service on Monday the civic authorities played a picturesque part. I need hardly add, for those who remember him, that the Recorder was present in his fullest attire. It is curious that, by a varying tradition, in some Assize towns the Mayor and Corporation do not wait upon the Judge. In Derby, for instance, I never met a Mayor. The Mayor of Devizes has one picturesque appendage. When he walks abroad in state he is preceded by the Town Crier, attired in a red uniform, and carrying an ancient silver-gilt cup.

There are some fine old Queen Anne houses in the town, one belonging to a dentist in the Market Place, and a still better one next to St Mary's church in New Park Street. The other things I remember are the astonishing record of the fate of the mendacious market woman in the market-place, and the aspect of The Bear Inn. In the eighteenth century the father of Sir Thomas Lawrence was its landlord; and he used to ask his guests: "Would you like my son to recite poetry to you, or to draw your portrait?" Fanny Burney was there with Mrs Thrale in April 1780, and wrote in her diary: "But though those pretty girls struck us so much, the wonder of the family was yet to be introduced. This was their brother, a most lovely boy of ten years of age, who seems to be not merely the wonder of their family, but of the times, for his astonishing skill in drawing."

There were only four prisoners, all of whom pleaded guilty, and a civil case collapsed at an early stage. So I had some leisure, which it was profitable to spend on the Downs to the north and east. My marshal and I had a walk, in hard frost and brilliant sunshine, to Coate, thence to Horton, over the canal to the top of St Ann's Hill, where there is a great view over the vale of Pewsey, and thence westward along the Wans Dyke, to the monument on Clerhill Down. It bore a notice-board: "This monument is dangerous." And so back to Devizes over Morgan Hill and Roundway Down.

On 17 January I drove to Westbury, and took the train to Dorchester. The Lodgings there are next to the Court, comfortable enough, but rather grim. At a later visit, in the summer, I found them very noisy from traffic in the street, and had to change to a bedroom at the back. I noticed that the table-napkins had the date 1867 upon them. Sixty-two years' use—by how many judges?—spoke well for their quality when new.

There were some books in the house. I wish there were in all Lodgings: for a book is a book "even if there is nothing in it". In one of the volumes* of *Proceedings of the Dorset Natural History and Antiquarian Field Club*, in an article on *Dorset Assizes in the Seventeenth Century*, by F. J. Pope, I read this: "Among the less frequent indictments may be included those for... Vagrancy. Vagrants received very stern treatment.... Some of these wanderers had travelled far from home. A family...had come from Derby, and another vagrant,

* Vol. XXXIV (1913), p. 22.

Dunkin MacKanon, was a Scottish highlander." The earliest direct ancestor of whom I know, was Duncan MacKinnon, who in the seventeenth century left Strath in Skye, and settled at Correchrevie in Arran. I can hardly hope that he was the vagrant of this record, and that he wandered to Dorchester on his way from Skye to Arran. But when, in the person of his great-grandson (my great-grandfather) we came to London, it was by as devious a route—via Naples and Buenos Ayres.

Dorchester is happy in its surroundings. The Walks, lined with sycamores, on the line of the ditch outside the Roman wall (of which one small piece remains) might be the envy of many a larger town. The only thing at all like them is the smaller walk at Shaftesbury, or "Shaston", as the milestones call it, from which there is a marvellous view. Then Dorchester has the very perfect Roman amphitheatre, where the gallows used to be until 1795. Above all there is Maiden Castle. This must be the biggest earthwork in Great Britain: I should not be surprised if it is the biggest in the world. In some parts of its circuit there are six concentric mounds and ditches; in places the mound, even after the wear of ages, must be 100 feet above the bottom of the ditch, and there are some 45 acres within these stupendous barriers. It is the most impressive of all works of early man.

As I walked there on 19 January I saw numbers of very big lambs. Round my home in Buckinghamshire the lambs were just being born at this time. I met a shepherd and asked him when these were born: he said about 1 November. Do these Dorset sheep have two families a year?

On the Sunday my marshal was not very well, so I walked by myself—about 28 miles as I reckoned. There was a sea-fog when I started, and Maiden Castle loomed mysteriously as I passed beside it. At noon the fog cleared, and the Hardy monument, at which I was aiming, shone out in sunshine close to me. So I went on to Abbotsbury, saw the great Abbey barn, and St Catherine's chapel, and got as near as I could to the swannery. The sun shone till it set, but it was dark long before I got back to Dorchester.

At Dorchester one meets with the first relics of Jeffreys and the Bloody Assize. An old house, now a tea-shop, claims to have been his lodgings. And in the Museum there is a chair, on which he is said to have sat in the old Court, removed when the present Court was built.

The Bloody Assize was in pursuance of a Special Commission, dated 8 July 1685, issued to Jeffreys, Chief Justice of the King's Bench, Sir William Montague, Lord Chief Baron, Sir Cresswell Levinz of the Common Pleas, Sir Francis Withens of the King's Bench, and Sir Robert Wright, Baron of the Exchequer. They opened the Commission at Winchester on 25 August. The trial and conviction of the unfortunate Mrs Lisle was the worst incident at Winchester. On 3 September they went from Winchester to Salisbury. And on 5 September the heaviest business of the Assize began at Dorchester. On that day 68 of the Sedgemoor refugees pleaded guilty, 29 were convicted, and one was acquitted. On Monday, 7 September 101 pleaded guilty, and 2 were acquitted. Next day 69 pleaded guilty. On 9 September 8 were convicted, and on the 10th 20 were convicted. So 298 prisoners were dealt with in six days. On Saturday, 12 September, the Judges went on to Exeter. In various Dorset towns 74 suffered the ghastly punishment of being hanged, drawn, and quartered, including 13 at Dorchester. The rest were transported to America or the West Indies.

The Museum is very like other county museums, a curious medley. The first qualification of a curator ought to be the faculty of politely declining undesirable acquisitions. A county museum should be strictly confined to local antiquities. Apart from the Roman relics, I thought the most interesting things were the two chairs that of old were used for chairing newly elected M.P.s for Dorchester, and two weights with "Mercy" stamped upon them. One Wilkins was hanged for arson in 1833. He was a small light man, and the Governor of the Gaol had these weights made to fix to his feet, and shorten his agony. In the parish church, next to the Museum, I admired the latinity of an epitaph to one who was "Sextae legionis equitum, scilicet Inniskilling, Signifer", the Jacobean pulpit, an Elizabethan monument behind the organ, and the great monument to Denzil Holles, Lord Ifield. At Fordington church the tympanum of the South door has figures of Norman knights, very like those in the Bayeux tapestry.

I heard of one curious survival at Dorchester. My old friend, J. C. Swinburne Hanham, Chairman of the Dorset Quarter Sessions, was Foreman of the Grand Jury, and came in to see me. He told me that it has always been the practice for the Chairman of Quarter Sessions to wear a top hat when presiding. I have since heard that this Dorchester custom also survives in part at Warwick. It is there the custom for the Chairman to enter the Court and take his seat wearing his hat, but he takes it off when the business begins, and sits uncovered.

I fancy these are survivals of what was once the usual custom. In the Records of our Buckinghamshire Quarter Sessions, there is an entry, 12 July 1682: "Forasmuch as Cavendish Weedon, esquire, Clerk of the Peace for this county, is a gentleman of the Long Robe, it is therefore ordered that for the tyme to come he sitt covered in Court."

When, upon the nomination of the Duke of Donkeytown, Lord-Lieutenant of the county, Mr John Jorrocks was appointed a Justice of the Peace, he attended Petty Sessions to be sworn in. "The Court was in full flower, when Mr Jorrocks entered. The Chairman, a red hot Tory, sat with his hat on, with three brother Tories on his right, and a solitary Whig on his left. This was Captain Bluster." After he has been sworn in, he is welcomed by Bluster as a recruit to the Whig interest, and Bluster says: "You had better put on your hat; there's no doing justice with your hat off."*

To wear a hat indoors was once quite usual. In the seventeenth century men wore their hats in church.† On 17 November 1661 Pepys writes in his diary: "To church...and heard a simple fellow upon the praise of church musique, and exclaiming against men wearing their hats in the church." And on 22 September 1664 he complains of "having got a strange cold in my head, by flinging off my hat at dinner, and sitting with the wind in my neck". When I first joined the Reform Club in 1901 I used to see some of the oldest members wearing their hats at luncheon.

For a long time the Lord Advocate was privileged to wear his hat in the Courts at the Parliament House. This is supposed to have had its origin from the fact that Sir Thomas Hope, who became Lord Advocate in 1626, had three sons who were Lords of Session. Before them he appeared covered, and so came to be allowed to do so before

* R. S. Surtees, *Hillingdon Hall* (1845), Chap. XIX.

† It was contrary to No. 18 of the Canons of 1604: "No man shall cover his head in the Church or Chapel in the time of divine service, except hee have some infirmitie. In which case let him weare a night-cap or coif."

the other Judges. On the other hand, Lewis Craig, Lord Wrightlands, was a Lord of Session when his father, Sir Thomas Craig, was still practising at the bar. When his father appeared before him Lord Wrightlands took his hat off.

The Lodgings at Taunton, annexed to the Courts, were a revelation to me. I really never imagined that anything so hideous could have been achieved in the age of Victoria. The style is of course "Gothic": it is a house beyond description, the furniture was ghastly, the artificial lighting detestable. The County Council were at the time taking steps to remove the seat of county government from Weston-super-Mare to Taunton. I wondered if it was possible that they might convert this awful house into offices, and house the Judge elsewhere. Clerks would be industrious in it, for they would shudder to let their gaze stray from their work, and be eager to hasten the time when they could escape from its horrors. I need hardly say there was not a book in the house, except those I brought there.

Next morning I went to the Assize Service at St Mary's church. It is a fine church, with one of the magnificent towers that look so well as one passes through Taunton by train. But just in front of me, where I sat, was a pulpit and a dwarf wall to the chancel of, I should think, about 1870. And I said to myself, "These are almost of a piece with the Lodgings. They must surely have been produced by that Mr Harry Hems, of Exeter, who disfigured so many churches in the West."

The work at Taunton was fairly heavy, including a strange charge of sheep stealing that created much local interest. There was also a civil case in which a hunting lady sought damages from a local authority because her horse had slipped and been injured on a tarred road. This was supposed to be a case of great importance. I was told that two local hunts had cancelled their meets, and the Masters and many of their followers were in Court. In fact the case was of very small importance. The Plaintiff's advisers did not venture to attack the whole modern system of making smooth roads, and only alleged negligence in a very small detail, the use of a particular sort of fine gravel to sprinkle on the tar. Eventually the jury disagreed hopelessly, and I had to discharge them. I do not know if the case was ever heard again.

There are again lively traditions of the Bloody Assize at Taunton. The Courts were then held in the great hall of the Castle, the Crown

Court sitting at one end of it, and the *Nisi Prius* Court at the other. This was still the arrangement in 1800, when Mrs Leigh Perrot, aunt of Jane Austen, was tried on a charge of shoplifting before Mr Justice Lawrence. I have told the story of this in my book *Grand Larceny* (1937).

Jeffreys and his colleagues only spent two working days at Taunton. On 18 September 382 pleaded guilty, and 3 were tried and convicted. On 19 September 117 pleaded guilty, and 3 were convicted. At Wells on 23 September 541 pleaded guilty. Of these Somerset convicts about 240 were executed.

The hall of the Castle, where these horrors took place, is now the Museum. The most interesting thing in it was, I thought, a very fine collection of the ornamental brass heads of staves carried by officers of various clubs and friendly societies; many of them are most decorative. I also saw a framed broadside, giving the calendar of the Somerset Lent Assizes in April 1827. There were two judges, and about 100 prisoners. Of course many must have been charged with offences which would now be dealt with at Petty Sessions or Quarter Sessions. But even allowing for this, and setting on the other side the enormous growth of the population, the contrast of this calendar and my own, of some ten prisoners, was striking. About six months later, in a northern county, I ventured to correct a Sheriff's Chaplain who, in his Assize sermon, deplored the modern increase of crime by comparison with "the good old days", and, I hope with adequate politeness, made it clear that nothing could be more inaccurate.

One thing I noticed which, so far as I know, is peculiar to Taunton. In the curbstone (or "the parapet" as they call it in Lancashire), outside various shops there are sockets in which the shopkeepers erect iron posts. I suppose they date from a time before there were curbstones, and were the temporary equivalent of the iron posts fixed everywhere in London to keep vehicles away from the houses. In Gay's *Trivia*, that charming picture of the London of 1716, there are many references to these posts, e.g.

> Though expedition bids, yet never stray
> Where no rang'd posts defend the rugged way,
> Here laden carts with thundring wagons meet,
> Wheels clash with wheels, and bar the narrow street.

Enough of them survived, in Johnson's time, to add to the eccentric appearance of his progress: for some instinct required him to touch each of them as he passed down the street. "Upon every post as he passed along, he deliberately laid his hand; but missing one of them, when he had got at some distance, he seemed suddenly to recollect himself, and immediately returning carefully performed the accustomed ceremony, and resumed his former course, not omitting one till he gained the crossing. This, Mr Sheridan assured me, was his constant practice."*

On 30 January we took the train to Bodmin. In the old days that was not Cornwall's Assize town. Roger North, in his *Life* of his brother, says that, when he was made Chief Justice of the Common Pleas, he chose the Western Circuit. This was apparently to be his regular circuit, though later, as I have recorded, he went at least once on the Northern. "There was no opportunity of penetrating into *Cornwal* yet, because the Judges, for compendium of Travel, took the first Town, upon the Borders, capable of receiving them, which is Launceston" (p. 120).

Bodmin, on the roof of Cornwall, is a chilly place in mid winter, though the frost had gone when we got there. In the gaunt Lodgings I found an unexpected note of welcome. "Major Buckley, and the Officers, The Depot, The Duke of Cornwall's Light Infantry hope that Mr Justice MacKinnon and his Marshal will consider themselves honorary members of their Mess during their stay at Bodmin." I was duly grateful for so charming a courtesy.

At the Assize Service the Mayor was dignified by having two maces carried before him. The High Sheriff had had the happy idea of inviting all the Mayors in Cornwall to serve on the Grand Jury, and eight of them attended. I had two working days at Bodmin. But four of the five prisoners pleaded guilty, and all was over by 3 o'clock on the first day. Then, in a downpour of rain, I went to call at the Depot. There were only four or five officers, training recruits, and I was surprised that they were so cheerful in this rather depressing place. Some of them came to dine with me next day, and were again cheerful and friendly.

On Saturday, 2 February, we went by train to Exeter, and Mr Justice Rowlatt joined me at the Lodgings. These are a modern house, comfortable but not beautiful, on the Topsham Road. There is a con-

* Boswell, *Life*, Vol. I, p. 485.

siderable garden round it, which has some big arbutus trees, and a great number of evergreen oaks. They shut out the gas-works on the other side of the Exe.

Exeter I knew well, but it was pleasant to be there again, and to admire its warm Georgian houses in Barnfield Crescent, Southernhaye, Bedford Circus, Melbourne Place, and the like. In the last-named the fan-lights over the front doors are admirable. Though I had been often in Exeter, I think I had never seen the Custom House on the quay, a very pleasant building, with a piece of the old city wall behind it. At the Cathedral Service on Sunday the Mayor had a Cap of Maintenance borne before him—that privilege of which they are so proud at York.

On the morning of the Assize two officers of the garrison called and presented my senior colleague with "the state". This informed us that there were 22 officers, and 457 "other ranks", including 74 recruits: also, 17 chargers, 53 riding horses, 123 other horses, 5 wagons, 4 limbers, 5 mess-carts, 4 field kitchens, 7 Lewis guns, and 15 quick-firing 4·5 guns. They also, according to the ancient ritual, requested permission for the troops to be let out of barracks. Mr Justice Rowlatt said "Certainly", and invited the officers to dine with us.

I was "in Commission", that is, taking the criminal work. (One small detail of the traditions of circuit is that it is the duty of the marshal of the Judge "in Commission" to say Grace at dinner.) There is in Exeter a separate Commission to the city as well as to the county. Unfortunately there were no city prisoners, and I was therefore deprived of the pleasure of charging a Grand Jury in the most picturesque Guildhall. The county only provided four prisoners. Its Court was built in 1774. In it there is a gigantic picture (by whom painted I did not discover) to illustrate the text "Thou shalt not bear false witness against thy neighbour".

After this easy first day I had a disturbed evening. For my marshal suddenly developed appendicitis. He was not the same young man who succumbed at York the summer before, but he was of the same college: and the whole affair, with the arrival of the ambulance, conveying him to a nursing home, and awaiting the operation, was almost an exact repetition of my experience at York. Happily he recovered equally well and speedily. In advertisements for servants in eighteenth-century newspapers you constantly see—"Must have had the small-pox". I began to think that in future, when inviting a prospective marshal, I should have to say—"Have you had your appendix out?"

There are two museums in Exeter. I liked best the one by the Castle, which is confined to local history. I saw there an old print—"John Cooke, Captain of the Sheriff's Troop during 74 Assizes at Exeter". That no doubt means leader of the javelin men. When there were only two Assizes a year that means thirty-seven years' service. This reminded me of a small print which hangs in the Judges' Lodgings at York, and is inscribed: "Harry Rowe, Born at York 1726, Trumpeter to the Duke of Kingston's Regiment at Culloden 1746, and 43 Years Trumpeter to the High Sheriffs of Yorkshire, 1796."

We had news at Exeter that the work at Bristol was so light that only one Judge would be needed there, and the question arose whether Mr Justice Rowlatt or I should go there. I had a particular reason for desiring to go, and my colleague, with his usual urbanity, let me do so, and went back to town, to rejoin me at Winchester. As my marshal was in the nursing home, I took his with me to Bristol. I wanted to go there because I had in hand the task of editing, and annotating, Fanny Burney's *Evelina*, and it was desirable to find out on the spot what I could about The Hotwells, and the social life there about 1775. This I did pretty thoroughly, and the result was an Appendix on *Bristol Hotwells and Clifton Hill* in my book published in 1929.

The Assize at Bristol is of a unique kind. Birmingham, Leeds, Manchester, and Liverpool all have Assizes in addition to those at the county towns, Warwick, York, and Lancaster. But the Commission at each of them is a County Commission, at which prisoners from the county as well as from the city are tried, and the High Sheriff of the county is concerned and is in attendance on the Judges. The Commission at Bristol is not a county Commission, like that to Taunton or Wells, but is a city Commission, like the separate city Commission at Exeter, York, or Norwich. But unlike them it is not joined to a county Commission, and stands by itself. So the High Sheriff of Somerset does not appear at Bristol, and the Judges deal only with the City Sheriff and the Lord Mayor. Moreover the Lord Mayor is named in the Commission, and sits, as a Commissioner of Assize, beside the Judge, as does the Lord Mayor, or an Alderman, at the Old Bailey. Indeed, the Old Bailey provides the nearest parallel to an Assize at Bristol. As a result at Bristol, as the Assize is so entirely a civic affair, the Judges are very properly lodged in the Mansion House. So they are at Newcastle and Cardiff, by the hospitality of those cities, at County Assizes. While at Birmingham, Leeds, Manchester, and Liverpool, the city in each case agreed to provide Judges' Lodgings when the Assizes were established in modern times, and as the price of that privilege.

This special Assize at Bristol arose in a curious way, though, in its present form, it only dates from 1865. Bristol is partly in Somerset and partly in Gloucestershire. To travel either to Taunton or Wells, or to Gloucester, was difficult. Edward III granted a special charter giving Bristol an Assize of its own. But the Commissioner of Assize was the Recorder, and not one of the Judges. The Recordership of Bristol was therefore one of special importance, and the Attorney-General very often held it. In 1831 Wetherell, formerly Attorney-General and a violent Tory,* was to hold the Assize, and the popular hatred of him, and of his opposition to Reform, was the direct cause of the great Bristol Riots. Much the best account of that disaster that I know is in Stanley Weyman's admirable story, *Chippinge*.

After the Riots Wetherell ceased to hold the Assize. And in 1835 the Corporation Reform Act abolished the special jurisdiction of the Recorder of Bristol. In 1836 Judges of the Western Circuit were holding Assizes at Bristol. In the summer of that year Baron Alderson records:† "The Mayor of Bristol declined to receive the Judge, as had hitherto been the custom, alleging as a reason for his conduct that there was in Bristol no Mansion House. Upon receiving this intimation Baron Alderson wrote to the Home Secretary to complain, and in the meantime demanded back his *fiat* for the Assizes, telling the municipal authorities that he saw no reason for holding any assize at Bristol at all, unless the Corporation received His Majesty's Commission in the usual manner; and that he was determined that with his consent the Commission should not be received with less than the usual respect." Whereupon the Corporation submitted. Later on, I think, the Assize was discontinued, and for a time prisoners from Bristol were sent to Gloucester. In 1865 the Assize at Bristol, to be

* He resigned the office of Attorney-General in 1829 rather than be a consenting party to the Roman Catholic Emancipation bill.

† *Memoir* (1858), p. 65.

held by the Judges of the Western Circuit, was restored. The first Commission was in March 1865. But by reason of the previous history the Assize was given the special quality I have described. Until the purchase of the present Mansion House the Judges used to be lodged at an hotel in Clifton.

The old Mansion House was in Queen Square, the scene of the hottest part of the 1831 riots. The Mansion House was looted and burnt. The modern Mansion House is up at Clifton, close to the Downs, Victorian and ugly, but comfortable enough. They keep there the Corporation plate, and the housekeeper used to put out selections of this on the dinner table every night for our benefit. The best pieces were a Standing Cup and Cover of 1597, and two silver gilt flagons, given by John Dodridge, Recorder of Bristol, dated 1658. I gathered that there might have been more of these ancient pieces: for the words "exchanged in 1709" were engraved on the bottom of (1) a Punch Bowl "the guift of Mr George Smythes", (2) a large tankard and cover "the guift of Mrs Martha Boucher", and (3) a large tazza, "the guift of Mrs Mary Jones". There was also a huge Punch Bowl, with an inscription recording that it was presented by the Company of Merchant Adventurers of Bristol to Captain Samuel Pitts for defending his ship, The Kirtlington Gally, against a Spanish Rover on 7 June 1628 on the voyage from Jamaica.

Finally there were two pieces that, but for a historic disaster, might have been the finest of the treasure, and, perhaps, because of it have the greatest interest. These were a Rosewater Dish and Ewer, the gift of Alderman Kitchen, with the hall-mark of 1595. When the Mansion House was sacked by the mob in 1831, the Dish was stolen by James Ives. He cut it up into 167 pieces, and took some of them to a local dealer to sell. This man's suspicions were roused, Ives was arrested, and the silver recovered. Ives was tried and was sentenced to transportation for fourteen years. Then they had a thin outer casing of silver made, and upon this the 167 pieces, some of them very small, are rivetted. Fortunately the rascal had used a fine saw for his dissection, and the lines between the pieces are small. But the Dish and Ewer were decorated with an incised floriated pattern, and the lines of this are of course everywhere intersected by the cutting. The story is engraved on the bottom of the silver lining. The man Ives served his sentence in Australia and returned home. Soon after his arrival he called on the Mayor and asked to be allowed to see the restored dish of which he had heard.

As a sequel to the Riots there was a Special Commission to Sir Nicholas Tindal, Chief Justice of the Common Pleas, Bosanquet J., and Taunton J., for the trial of the rioters. It opened at Bristol on 2 January 1832, at the Guildhall at 11 o'clock. The Commissions of Oyer and Terminer and General Gaol Delivery having been read, the Court adjourned till one o'clock. The Judges then went "to their lodgings in Park Street, from whence they were escorted with the usual state and ceremony to the Cathedral, where divine service was performed, and an admirable sermon was preached by the Reverend Professor Lee". The Court sat again at two, and the Lord Chief Justice charged the Grand Jury at great length.

The principal trial, before Tindal C.J. and Bosanquet J., was that of Christopher Davis as leader of the mob. Sir Thomas Denman A.G. (with him Serjeant Wilde, Wightman, Coleridge, and Follett) prosecuted. The Chief Justice began his summing up at 6, the Jury retired at 8, and they delivered a verdict of Guilty at 9.

Six men were charged with setting fire to the gaol. One was acquitted, and the rest found Guilty. Five were charged with burning the Bridewell: one was acquitted, and four found Guilty. Two were charged with burning the Bishop's Palace, and both found Guilty.

Of 102 prisoners, 81 were convicted and 21 acquitted. There were also 12 against whom the Grand Jury did not find a true bill, and 13 against whom the Crown offered no evidence. Five were hanged, and the rest of the convicted sentenced to varying terms of transportation or imprisonment.

There was also a trial, before Bosanquet J., of Capt. Lewis, committed on the Coroner's Inquisition for murder. The Grand Jury reduced the charge to manslaughter. Capt. Lewis, in charge of some soldiers during the riot, had shot a pistol and a youth was killed. He was acquitted, and the Judge said he was discharged without the least imputation upon him, and on the contrary he appeared to have done his duty in a manner which reflected great credit upon him.

The business of the Special Commission was ended on Saturday, 14 January.

While these trials were going on a Court Martial was opened at the Merchants' Hall on 9 January for the trial of Colonel Brereton. He had been in command of the troops in Bristol, and had behaved in an extraordinarily pusillanimous fashion. The proceedings went on for four days, and then came to an end because Brereton committed suicide by shooting himself through the heart with a pistol held in his left hand.

Another Court Martial began on 17 January upon Capt. Warrington, of the 3rd Dragoon Guards. This went on for eight days. He was found Guilty on some of the charges and sentenced to be cashiered. Whereupon "His Majesty was graciously pleased to authorise Capt. Warrington to dispose of his commission at the regulated value". Under the regulations issued by the War Office the full price of a Captain's commission in the Dragoon Guards was £3225.*

Every morning the Lord Mayor and the City Sheriff called for me in the Lord Mayor's State Coach. As the frost had returned, with more severity than ever, and there had been snow, it needed careful driving to descend the hill from Clifton to the city. The Assize Service was not at the Cathedral, or at the more magnificent St Mary Redcliffe, but in the Lord Mayor's chapel, a small Perpendicular church, opposite the Cathedral, with some good old glass. The Sword-Bearer had a Cap of Maintenance, as at Exeter. I began to think that York made too much of its Cap.

On the Sunday I had a young friend to breakfast from Clifton College, the buildings of which are close to the Mansion House. I asked him if he knew the Head of the School, and he said he did. So I told him to put him up to the practice of sending a Latin letter to the Judge with a view to a half-holiday. The suggestion was welcomed: but I had no letter. Perhaps the Head of the School was too industrious. Or possibly he consulted the Head Master, who thought it undesirable to import such a practice from Winchester, Shrewsbury, Bedford, and a few other schools.

For the rest of Sunday I went over to Bath. Who could resist a chance of another day in that noble city? And is there any spot that takes you more completely back into the eighteenth century than the Pump Room? Many of the great houses seemed to be divided up into flats, but, except for a few outrages like the Empire Hotel, Bath externally as the two Woods left it is not greatly changed. Except for one thing,

* This account of the Special Commission and the Courts Martial I summarize from *The Bristol Riots*, by a Citizen (Bristol, 1832).

of which, following on this visit, I wrote in my notes to *Evelina:* "If Evelina went to Bath to-day she would find not much change in The Parades, The Circus, and The Crescent, except for the pestilence of plate-glass, which spread all over Bath in the Victorian age, and is now endemic there. I believe there is no single thing that would do more for Bath to-day than the restoration of the small window-panes and cross-bars that were thus displaced."

The rest of my leisure was far too short for the things of interest in Bristol, when I had not been there for many years. I remembered St Mary Redcliffe as the finest parish church in England, but I had forgotten how magnificent—by how much the finest—it is. In St Stephen's there was a grandiose monument of Sir George Snygge ("Phoebus! What a name!") "Serviens at legem" and "Gazophylliae Baronus, 1617". A local barrister took me to see St Peter's Hospital, once an old merchant's house, later a workhouse, and now the office of the Guardians. The roof of the hall is good, and there are two fine Jacobean panelled rooms, with ornate plaster ceilings.

The Nails, outside the Corn Exchange, are curious. I do not believe that the phrase "on the nail" originated from them, as they are pleased to think in Bristol. Queen Square, and its surroundings, are a forlorn relic. A few of the fine old houses survived, e.g. No. 64, Excise Avenue. The old Theatre Royal, built in 1776, and still a "Patent" Theatre, seemed to be derelict: anyway it was degraded by an appalling modern front.

It was snowing all day, and freezing harder than ever, when, on Friday, 15 February, I went to Winchester, via Eastleigh, and there rejoined Mr Justice Rowlatt, coming from London. The Lodgings, a pleasant old Queen Anne house in the close, to the south of the Cathedral, were horribly cold for our first 24 hours. When a house has been unoccupied it needs more than a few hours to get warm, and the fires had not been started soon enough. Next morning the Mayor and Corporation called on us before the County Sheriff appeared. When he did so I observed that he was carrying a wand with a carved ivory top. This appears to be the local practice. It is common everywhere for the Under-Sheriff to carry a wand: at Warwick he has a fine malacca cane with a silver top, as long as an eighteenth-century footman's stick, and very likely that is its origin. A year later I found the High Sheriff at Gloucester carried a wand, but nowhere else have I seen a Sheriff so armed. It may once have been common, if not universal. Boswell, describing the reception of the judges, near Carlisle, in August 1778, says "the Sheriff with his white wand approached the carriage". Staves of office were common in the old days. The Vice-Chancellor at Oxford has an official gold-headed walking stick, now not often carried. "There are a number of these official walking-sticks in Oxford, their use being limited to heads of houses."* In the eighteenth century physicians carried gold-headed sticks. *The Gold-Headed Cane* (Macmichael, 1827) recounts the history of a famous one now preserved in the College of Physicians.

In due course the letter from the Prefect of Hall arrived. Mr Justice Rowlatt, the best scholar on the Bench, could have answered it much more easily than I, but he said it was the duty of the judge in Commission. I have read with amazement a sentence in Mr Foote's *Pie Powder*: "The Hon. George Denman...had been senior classic at Cambridge...and he is said to be the only judge who attempted to reply in the same language to a Latin petition for a half-holiday by the Winchester schoolboys." I am sure this is a gross libel on the Bench. Anyway I wrote to Magister Informator. At the end I said I hoped he would not cast too critical an eye on my Latinity. And I am glad to say that in his reply he said: "Quod extremum fuit in epistola illa gratissima ad id respondebo Latinitatis concinnitatem non modo venia nulla indigere sed admirationem potius ac delectationem summam movere."

So they had their half-holiday. But the only diversion possible must have been skating. Later in our stay, *antiquo more*, the Prefect of Hall and the Senior Commoner Prefect came to breakfast with us, and talked English very agreeably.

The Assize Service at the Cathedral on Sunday was very fine. As our Lodgings were so near we walked across the Close, instead of going absurdly about a hundred yards in a car. We then lunched with the Dean (Hutton), and after lunch spent some time in his delightful library. "When I lunched at the Deanery at Durham," I remarked, "the Dean showed us his kitchen. You, Mr Dean, show us your Library." "Ah well," said the Bishop, who was present, "you must remember their respective figures." Then I walked down to see St Cross. I saw it years ago and remembered it as ruined by Butter-

* *Oxford University Ceremonies* (Buxton and Gibson, 1935), p. 44.

field's so-called decorations. But its aspect now seemed to be strangely improved, and meeting the Master showing round some friends, I asked him if the kindness of time had effaced the horrors I remembered. "No," he said, "we scraped them off at great expense last year." About this time Merton was spending much money in demolishing part of another Butterfield monstrosity, St Alban Hall, solely in the interest of amenity. If only Balliol could do the same to mitigate Waterhouse!

But no outlay can well retrieve one outrage on Winchester. On the Sunday evening I went to the College chapel, and saw the mean Gothic woodwork put in there in 1875. And on the Monday afternoon we were taken by friends to Hursley Park, and saw the classical panelling that was ejected from the chapel to make way for this sorry stuff. And now it is one of the chief splendours of Sir George Cooper's great mansion. It was the ruffian Butterfield who was responsible for this wicked vandalism. The miserable story is told in Mr Avray Tipping's *Grinling Gibbons and the Woodwork of his Age* (1914) at pp. 230–237, with pictures of the magnificent woodwork as it now adorns Hursley Park.

If Butterfield is anathema, there is Sir Herbert Baker to restore the credit of the moderns. In the cloister, which is the College War Memorial, he has made one of the most beautiful buildings of this age—and, as I think, the most beautiful War Memorial anywhere. In a place of so many ancient traditions it might not be easy to create a new one. But the boys had already established one as sacredly observed as the most ancient: every boy bares his head as he enters the cloister.

And lastly—no, not lastly—the man of feeling will seek out the stone, in the north aisle of the Cathedral nave, beneath which Jane Austen lies. The house in which she died—alas, at the age of 41—is quite near the Lodgings on the way to the College gate.

The Western Circuit has one pleasant custom peculiar to itself. At the conclusion of the last case at the last Assize town (now always Winchester) the senior barrister in Court thanks the Judge for his courtesy during the circuit, and expresses a hope that it will not be long before he travels the circuit again. No other circuit displays any such politeness. I think it was Mr Blake Odgers who spoke on this occasion. I know I replied that I should come again on the first possible opportunity.

And so, on Friday, 22 February, I went home in the morning. The frost was nearly at an end, but I had the afternoon on my skates.

◇ ◇ ◇

On Thursday, 20 June 1929, I went once more to Durham, with Lord Finlay as my colleague. The Castle was still thought to be dangerous at its northern end, so I was debarred from my proper quarters in the Bishop's suite, and we had the same arrangements as a year ago. On the last day of my stay I went all over the works with Mr Jones, the architect, and a very interesting experience it was. He knew, and I think loved, every stone of the great building, and he knew, but did not love, every crack and flaw that threatened it. The work of boring holes through the walls and foundations right down to the rock, and then putting in long steel ties anchored to the rock was a slow business, but said to be sure. The only trouble seemed to be lack of money. I could not help thinking that those responsible had not gone the best way to get it. The Dean of Lincoln could have told them—"Go to America and make yourself pleasant." Durham could make at least as good a claim as Lincoln. And the Dean had collected far more for Lincoln than would have made Durham Castle safe for ever. I made some suggestion of this sort to one of the Durham dons, and proposed that they should send a pleasant-mannered emissary empowered to offer an honorary degree to any millionaire who would provide £50,000. His reply was not helpful. "I am afraid we could not prostitute our degrees in that way."

On the Grand Jury at Durham was my old friend, Alfred Chaytor, who stood next above me when about a dozen of us were sworn in as King's Counsel in October 1914. Soon after he went off to the war with his territorial battalion, and he never came back to the bar. I was quite sincere when I said in my charge to the Grand Jury that I thought there was no question of law involved in the bills to be brought before them, but if there was it would be unnecessary for me to say anything to help them: for I saw among them an old friend, one of His Majesty's Counsel, and I knew his capacity to advise them; indeed I had a strong conviction that if he had not retired from the bar and its competition, he would almost certainly have been sitting in my place on the Bench.

Newcastle at this time was notable for three things—the completion of the great bridge to Gateshead, the Exhibition, and the most competent and charming Lord Mayor I ever met. I believe the Exhibition was actually a financial success, and, though I do not much care for such things, I liked this one as much as any. The loan collection of pictures from all the great houses of the North was admirable. Lawrence's Master Lambton (in a very bad frame) was perhaps its prize piece. And one evening, after dining with the Lord Mayor at a very good restaurant in the grounds, I heard a first-class orchestral concert.

And so to York, where there seemed as much to see as ever. I always found it difficult to know what to say to a Grand Jury, and to vary the monotony of "charges". On this occasion I gave them some account of a small book I had lately bought, and read a very small part of it. This is its title-page. "Sergeant | Thorpe | Judge | of Assize | for the | Northern Circuit | His | Charge | As it was delivered to the *Grand* | *Jury* at Yorke Assizes the twentieth | of March, 1648 | Clearly epitomizing the Statutes belonging | to this Nation, which concerns (and as a golden | rule, ought to regulate) the severall | estates and conditions of men. | And (being duly observed) do really promote the | Peace and Plenty of this Commonwealth. | London | Printed by *T.W.* for *Matthew Walbanke,* and *Richard Best* | at Grayes-Inn Gate, 1649." The learned Commissoner was Francis Thorpe (1595–1665), of St John's College, Cambridge, and Gray's Inn, Recorder and M.P. for Beverley. He was a Colonel in the Parliamentary army and was pardoned at the Restoration.

"Gentlemen, Friends, and Countrymen," his charge begins, "I do not question but that the Stile and Title of our Commissions, under which we are now to act and execute the Authority and Power committed to our hands, being changed from *Carolus, Rex Angliae* to *Custodes Libertatis Angliae Authoritate Parliamenti,* workes divers effects upon the Tempers and Spirits of men, according as the spirits themselves are tempered and affected; and that some of those spirits (like the Sun upon Wax) it softens into Obedience and compliance, and others of them again (like the same Sun upon Clay) it hardens into stiffness and oppression."

"After this very decent preface, he spoke near three hours." So said the reporter, Sir James Burrow, of a judgment of Mr Justice Yates.* And so I might say of Serjeant Thorpe. For the print of his

* *Millar* v. *Taylor* (1768) 4 Burr. 2355.

Charge occupies thirty closely printed pages. It was partly to make known to my Grand Jury the modern clemency of Judges, not merely in sentences upon prisoners, but in their treatment of Grand Juries, that I gave them a short account of what their predecessors suffered from Serjeant Thorpe. The first nine pages argue the case of the Commonwealth against the late King. "And now I come to that which is our true business, our work of the first magnitude, *opus diei in die suo.*" There follows for twenty-one pages a complete summary of the criminal law, even descending to such particulars as that a *Tile-maker* commits an offence "if he do not dig his earth before the first of *November*, and turn it over before the first of *February*, and turn it again before the first of *March*, and then try and tue it from stones". And that there are among "*Common Nusances to be enquired after*"—"If any erect a Cottage, and do not lay to it foure acres of ground to it, to be occupyed with it"; and "If any keep an Inmate or Under-Sitter in a cottage"; and "If any keep a stoned horse in any common ground, not being fourteen hands high".

His final words I commended as being by no means obsolete: "And having said this much, I leave what remains to your diligence. All our Service begins in You; its your *Ignoramus*, or *Billa Vera*, which opens and shuts, which shuts and no man opens."

In the course of centuries charges to Grand Juries may have contained much wisdom: but I suspect they also produced a good deal of rubbish. In his account of the opening of the Assize at Carlisle, in August 1778, Boswell says: "Then the Grand Jury were called over. Sir James Lowther was their foreman.... He had travelled night and day from London to be present at the Assizes.... Judge Willes read a Charge to the Grand Jury, neat but commonplace, blaming neither Ministers nor Generals for our bad success in America, but the profligacy of the Nation, and recommending reformation."* This sounds more like an Assize sermon.

On a free afternoon, on our last day at York, Lord Finlay and I, by the invitation of the Dean (Ford), went to see the Cathedral workshops where they were cleaning and re-leading the ancient windows. It was most interesting work, and the men had had so much experience that they were obviously doing it very skilfully. The result has been amazing. The Five Sisters are many times as beautiful as they were

* *Boswell Papers.* Isham Collection. Vol. XIII, p. 138.

before the grime of centuries was removed. And the contrast between those windows in the chapter house and its approach which had been treated, and those which had not, was very striking. Happening to see some figures in a guide-book I said to my marshal, as we were looking at the great East window, "Do you realise that this window is exactly the size of a lawn tennis court?" He was rightly incredulous, for the fact is incredible as you stand in the choir. But the book said 78 feet by 36 feet.

Going up the narrow Stonegate to the Minster I had often stopped at an arched entry on the right, which leads to the courtyard of a house within, and gives a glimpse of greenery before it. Lord Finlay, and I, and our marshals had stopped, when the Doctor who lived there came along and asked us in to see more. And charming it was. I think he said it was once the town house of the Mowbray and Stourton peers.

Perhaps the finest old house in York is in Micklegate, now the warehouse of a firm of wholesale druggists. I asked permission to look inside, and was welcomed: the staircase is magnificent. The house next door to it, now a Y.M.C.A. hostel, also has a fine staircase. The best room is in the same street, on the first floor in the Queen's Hotel: the panelling is superb.

On Wednesday, 10 July, we drove to Leeds, rather sadly. For the prospect of perhaps three weeks in Leeds is apt to be depressing. But there were alleviations. On a Saturday my marshal and I walked on the moors from Ilkley, and so by Hawksworth to Guiseley. Archdeacon Howson, Rector of Guiseley, was the Sheriff's Chaplain. His church and house were delightful. The church was admirably adorned, and cared for. In it the Rev. Patrick Bronte was on 29 December 1812 married to Maria Branwell. In it also is the great seventeenth-century pew of the Calverleys. Addison is said to have stayed with his friend Sir Walter Calverley. That he took from him the idea of Sir Roger de Coverley is an obvious suggestion. That the pew at any rate prompted the episode of Sir Roger standing up to count the congregation is even more likely. Just beyond the church is the rectory, a beautiful seventeenth-century manor house of stone, admirably restored by the Archdeacon. And his garden was worthy of the house.

One evening Lord Finlay and I drove out to dine with friends of his at Grantley Hall. It is a fine place. I reflected that nowadays no fortune could be made at the bar which would provide such splendours. But it was built by Sir Fletcher Norton, Attorney-General 1763–1765, and Speaker 1770–1780. He was created Lord Grantley. He was, I think, unpopular. There is a story that, when arguing some point of copyhold law, he remarked: "May I cite my own experience? I happen to have two little manors." The presiding judge (who was he?) saw his chance, and interrupted: "We all know it, Sir Fletcher."

On another evening we dined with Lord and Lady Moynihan at Carr Manor. It was impossible to believe, looking out on the garden there, with no building in sight, that we were within about ten minutes' drive of Park Square, in the centre of Leeds. In one corner of that square there was a modest house. On its door were three brass plates. On the most worn you could just decipher "Mr Moynihan". The second, fairly worn, said "Sir Berkeley Moynihan". The third, new and sharp, said "Lord Moynihan". Unhappily this house was burned down in 1931, and the door perished.

Since I have had to give up going circuit, Judges at Leeds have the pleasure of finding their Lodgings at Carr Manor. And very pleasant that must be, especially in the summer. To move the Lodgings from the house near the hospital had been suggested before: I believe it was wanted for yet another nursing home. There was an occasion, I forget exactly when, on which the Lord Mayor wrote to the Lord Chief Justice saying that it was proposed to transfer the Lodgings to the house at Kirkstall Abbey, and asking if this would be approved. This was brought before a Judges meeting. And as I was going next to Leeds I was asked to inspect the house at Kirkstall, and report upon it. One afternoon I went there. The house was reasonably sufficient, or could be made so. But as I left it, something occurred to me, and I said to a policeman near it: "Am I right in thinking that I can smell the river, and that it does not smell very nice?" The policeman said: "Smell! Lord bless you, Sir, you come and smell it in the summer!" I reported this conversation to my colleagues. We did not approve the proposal. The Leeds policeman, all unwittingly, defeated the scheme of the Corporation. That the river does smell is rather hard on Leeds: for I believe it is Bradford, with its dye-works, that makes it smell.

And so on 30 July I finished my last civil case. "*Cras animarum,*

Mr Paley Scott", I said as I rose. Next morning I drove to Bradford and caught the convenient train that landed me at High Wycombe.

✧ ✧ ✧

In the autumn of 1929 I was again on the Midland Circuit, starting among my friends and neighbours at Aylesbury. I was able to congratulate them, when charging the Grand Jury, on the completion of the fine County Offices, close to the Court, in Walton Street.

Buckinghamshire, owing to its shape, is a difficult county in which to find a convenient centre. In the thirteenth and fourteenth centuries Assizes were usually held at Newport Pagnell for the northern hundreds of the county, and at High Wycombe, or occasionally Aylesbury, for the southern. From 1666 to 1717 there were 74 Assizes at Aylesbury, 19 at Buckingham, and 11 at High Wycombe. From 1720 to 1746 it was the regular practice to have the Summer Assize at Buckingham, and the Winter at Aylesbury. In 1747 both were held at Aylesbury. Thereupon in 1748 there was passed an Act (21 Geo. II, cap. 12) which recites that "for many years past it hath been usual in the administration of Justice to His Majesty's subjects residing at different Ends of the County of Buckingham, which is of great length, to appoint the Summer Assizes at the County Town of Buckingham, and the Winter Assizes at Alesbury" but "this usage was unnecessarily broken in upon in the last summer" [i.e. the Assize was held at Aylesbury]. It was therefore enacted "that from and after 1 June 1748" [the summer Assize] "shall be held and executed in each year...at the said town of Buckingham, and at no other Place within the said County....Provided always that if at any time the said Town of Buckingham shall be wholly unfit for holding the Assizes there by accident of Fire, or by means of any Contagious or Epidemical Distemper, or by any other unforeseen Cause or Exigency," [the Chief Justice may appoint] "another convenient place within the said County for the said Assizes."

I suspect that this Act, for the benefit of Buckingham at the expense of Aylesbury, was probably procured by the Magnate of Stowe, then Richard Temple, Lord Cobham. He died next year, and his sister married a Grenville. Her son was made Earl Temple, and her grandson, in 1822, Duke of Buckingham and Chandos. The cause of Aylesbury may have been supported by Lord Chesterfield, of Eythrope, near that town. If so Lord Cobham defeated him. These two magnates had another contest in 1812. Lord Chesterfield wanted to be Lord-Lieutenant of Buckinghamshire, and so did Lord Temple. Pitt gave the office to Temple, whereupon Chesterfield, in dudgeon, pulled down the great house at Eythrope, and left the county altogether.

Buckingham enjoyed the dignity of the Summer Assize for just over a century. In 1849 the Act 12 & 13 Vict. cap. 6 repealed the Act of 1748, and thenceforward fixed Aylesbury as the place for all Assizes.

I do not know what sort of Court there was at Buckingham, but I do not suppose it can have been as fine as the Crown Court at Aylesbury, which is now alone used at Assizes. The Shire Hall, in which it is, was built in 1724. The Court, with its dark panelling, is very picturesque. On one occasion my friend Mr de Laszlo, the painter (whose son happened to be my marshal), came and sat on the bench. He was greatly taken by the spectacle in the Court. He said he very much wished he could be allowed to sit in the front of the gallery, and make a sketch, with a view to a picture. I wish it could have been so, but even for an eminent artist that would hardly be possible.

The alternation of two Assize towns in a county was once much more common than it is now. There are now only five instances—Ipswich and Bury St Edmund's in Suffolk, Wells and Taunton in Somerset, Salisbury and Devizes in Wiltshire, Cardiff and Swansea in Glamorgan, and Welshpool and Newtown in Montgomery. In the old days there were Maidstone and Rochester in Kent, Croydon, Kingston and Guildford in Surrey, Launceston and Bodmin in Cornwall, Lewes, East Grinstead and Horsham in Sussex, Wells, Taunton, and Bridgewater in Somerset, Thetford and Norwich in Norfolk, and Abingdon and Reading in Berkshire. For the five cases that survive there is now no reason except local pride and vested interests. It involves the expense of keeping up two Court buildings instead of one. I think that Bury St Edmund's, Wells, Devizes, Swansea and Newtown should cease to be Assize towns. If I were still liable to go on circuit I should have hoped that the first two extinctions might be Ipswich and Taunton, since Bury and Wells are so very much the pleasanter towns to go to.

I was glad that the Assize was not held at Buckingham in October 1929. For on 14 October, being the first day of Michaelmas term, the Lord Chief Justice gave his annual dinner to his puisnes. I was able to attend this, and then travel to Aylesbury by a train that left Marylebone at 10.5 and got to Aylesbury in 52 minutes. But the last train by which one could get to Buckingham left Euston at 5.32, and after two changes one could arrive at Buckingham in just under two hours.

I suppose it is physically possible to go by train from Aylesbury to Bedford, but I do not know how you do it, since I have always driven. By road it is only about 30 miles through Leighton Buzzard and Woburn. One of the most impressive things by the way is the brick wall round the Duke of Bedford's park. I believe it is 14 miles long, and that till recently a small detachment of workmen spent their whole lives going round it, pointing, patching, and repairing. Another impressive sight as we neared Bedford was that of the great airship, R. 101, moored to its mast at Cardington, and glistening in the sun. My marshal and I had a much nearer view of it a day or two later, on our way to lunch with the High Sheriff near Luton. His place was partly in Bedfordshire and partly in Hertfordshire; either county might have claimed him as Sheriff, but apparently Bedfordshire got in first.

I mentioned in a foot-note (*supra*, p. 126) that until 1637 there was a High Sheriff for the combined counties of Surrey and Sussex. This was not unique. From 1125 to 1574 the counties of Buckingham and Bedford were similarly combined, and separate lines of Sheriffs for those two counties only date from 1575. In the same way until 1575 there was one Sheriff for the two counties of Norfolk and Suffolk: he was chosen one year from Norfolk, and the next year from Suffolk. The only example of such a union that now survives is that of Cambridge and Huntingdon. The list of High Sheriffs for those combined counties is complete from 1155 to 1939: for a long time it has been the custom to select the High Sheriff from each county alternately. So where a county has now two county councils, e.g. East and West Suffolk, it is the practice to select the Sheriff each year from each half of the county alternately. Yorkshire, with its three Ridings, has been so divided up for centuries. And each of the three Ridings has its own Lord-Lieutenant. But there has always been a single Sheriff for the whole county, and I do not know that there is, or has been, this alternation in his selection. Yorkshire, with its second lengthy Assize at Leeds, and a third one now proposed at Sheffield, must be the most burdensome Shrievalty for its occupant except Lancashire, with its triple Assize towns, and its eleven Assize sessions in a year. Such is the public spirit of country gentlemen that there has never been any

difficulty in finding people ready to fill the office of High Sheriff in any county, not even in Yorkshire and Lancashire. If as a result of the taxation and death duties, under which we groan, such difficulty does arise I think it might be well to make the Assizes at Liverpool, Manchester, Leeds, Sheffield, and Birmingham similar to the Assize at Bristol, city affairs for the City Sheriffs. Then the High Sheriffs of Lancashire, Yorkshire, and Warwick would only be concerned with the ancient County Assizes at Lancaster, York, and Warwick, as the High Sheriff of Somerset is only concerned with the County Assize at Taunton or Wells.

I have met so many kind and charming people as High Sheriffs (and made so many friends thereby) that I am tempted to add some words for the possible benefit of their successors. When a man is appointed High Sheriff I gather that he is given no instructions or guidance from the Privy Council or the Home Office. He is left unaided to make his own arrangements with his Under-Sheriff, and usually he can only apply to the gentleman who has filled that office before. Indeed I have found by enquiry that many a High Sheriff is under the belief that he must employ the Under-Sheriff of his predecessors and has no idea that he can appoint any one he likes. The man who has been Under-Sheriff for some time is obviously the best adviser, but he is in a very unfair position as a bargainer. I do not suggest for a moment that the position is abused. But I do know that in two counties of equal size and importance the tradition as to the remuneration of the Under-Sheriff varies extraordinarily, and the expenses of the Sheriff in one are vastly higher than in another. And I have known of cases in which a regular Under-Sheriff has insisted that totally unnecessary outlays by the Sheriff are an essential part of his duties.

Having regard to all this, and especially the helpless condition of a newly appointed High Sheriff, I think he ought to receive from the Privy Council or the Home Office, upon his appointment, a set of instructions and advice. And I think that one of those offices, or the Treasury, should control the scale of remuneration to which an Under-Sheriff is entitled. Of course the instructions or advice would point out that in such matters as the entertainment of county magistrates or the bar at luncheon, the banners on trumpets, or the provision of javelin men, the Sheriff is entirely his own master. All they would be concerned with would be his necessary and official duties, and outlays.

A Fund for Sheriffs

The traditional variation of a Sheriff's expenses in different counties is, I think, no new thing. In that pleasant book, *Passages from the Diaries of Mrs Philip Lybbe Powys* (1899), she writes, at Norwich, in 1781: "About one the Sheriff, Mr Doughty, came into the city in great state. That office is here attended with great expense, at least £300, whereas with us in Oxfordshire I have heard my father [in law] Powys say it cost him between one and two." The expense in Norfolk may have been partly because the Sheriff was expected to give an Assize ball, which she describes next day after "the procession of the Judges, Mayor, Corporation, Sheriff, and neighbouring gentlemen made a capital cavalcade as they came over Tombland". At the ball there was "a very numerous assembly, and numbers of the ladies profuse in jewellery....The High Sheriff's lady always stands the top couple...." The Rev. James Woodforde writes in his diary* on 6 August 1800: "Mrs Custance and eldest daughter &c. went to the Assize Ball at Norwich this Evening." As appears from his entry† on 8 October 1800, Norwich also had a ball in connexion with the Michaelmas Quarter Sessions.

Perhaps I may make a further suggestion for the benefit of future High Sheriffs. *The Purefoy Letters* (edited by Mr Eland, 1931) is a charming book, and gives a wonderful picture of country life in Buckinghamshire in the eighteenth century. Henry Purefoy, of Shalstone Manor, was High Sheriff of Buckinghamshire for 1748–1749.‡ They then had a system in the county under which all gentlemen of sufficient standing to be eligible as Sheriff belonged to an association to which they subscribed five guineas a year. When his year of office came, most of the Sheriff's expenses were paid out of this common fund. At p. 441 of Mr Eland's second volume is a "List of Subscribers to the Sheriff's Fund taken 27 July 1749". It contains sixty-five names, including that of John Wilkes, then living at The Prebendal, Aylesbury. Of the sixty-five names I think only nine now survive in the county—Drake of Amersham, Dashwood of West Wycombe, Knapp of Little Linford, Uthwatt of Great Linford, Chetwode of Chetwode, Purefoy of Shalstone, Palmer of Dorney, and Selby and Lowndes, now united as Selby-Lowndes. Among the better known

* *Diary of a Country Parson* (1931), Vol. v, p. 268. † *Ibid.* p. 277.

‡ As a Sheriff is one of the oldest officials in the land he not unnaturally holds office for the period of the old year. And the "year" in England, until 1752, was not from 1 January to 31 December, but from 25 March to the following 24 March.

names that have disappeared are Bowyer of Denham, Denton of Hillesden, Stanhope of Eythrope, Willis of Bletchley, Lee of Hartwell, Wright of Gayhurst, Grenville of Stowe, and Dayrell of Lillingstone Dayrell.

It is strange to find so practical and business-like a system in existence in the middle of the eighteenth century. I would suggest that it might be revived to-day in any county. A sub-committee of the Standing Joint Committee might organize it with little difficulty.

There were only two prisoners at Bedford, and the work was over in three hours. At Northampton there were four prisoners, all of whom pleaded guilty. So I was free before lunch. From Bedford to Northampton is 21 miles. If there had then been a proper system, leaving some discretion to the Judge of Assize, one or other of these Assizes might have been cancelled, and a great deal of time saved. But when such a simple and obvious course could only be taken by the Lord Chief Justice, and the Lord Chancellor, at a time before the facts could be known to them, it was impracticable. And the waste of judicial time, to the detriment only of litigants in London, was thus continued.

On the afternoon of my arrival at Lincoln I asked a verger in the Cathedral if the Dean was at home, for I knew he was about to start again for America to collect more money for his great work of restoration. I was told he was leaving on the morrow, so I ventured to make a brief call to wish him good-bye, and *bon voyage*. He was cheerful as ever, but he looked old, and said he was doubtful if he could survive another great journey. Unhappily this was true. He was taken ill, I think in South America, was brought home to Lincoln, and died soon after his return. But he had the satisfaction of knowing that the work he had so heroically planned, and carried on, was nearly finished.

Two witnesses from Grantham had the name Manderfield. As I walked in Lincoln I saw another curiosity in the way of words. A poster outside a Music Hall proclaimed as one of the "turns" that of "The World's Greatest Escapologist". I presume his display was to rid himself of knots and handcuffs. He may have been an Escapologist: he was not an Etymologist.

One diversion at Lincoln was a visit to Tattershall Castle. It is magnificent. I think it is the finest specimen of brick building in

England; and the only brickwork I ever saw to surpass it was the Cathedral of Albi near Toulouse. Perhaps even more magnificent was the patriotic generosity of Lord Curzon in restoring it. He was roused to action by the news that the great fireplaces had been torn out of it, to be shipped to America. He bought them back, and then restored the whole building very perfectly, and finally wrote an admirable book about it. There have been no greater acts of public spirit than what he did here and at Bodiam Castle in Sussex.

This great brick tower is so magnificent that one is apt to forget the church close by, also built in the fifteenth century by Ralph, third Lord Cromwell, and endowed by him as a collegiate church. It is a fine building, and in any village where it was not overshadowed by such a castle, would be very noteworthy.

We drove from Lincoln to Nottingham, seeing again Newark church and Southwell Minster by the way. Somewhere on the route I saw a public house with the sign "The Isaac Newton". He was born at Woolsthorpe, near Grantham, in 1642. The publican's tribute to his memory must be a good many miles from his birthplace.

At Derby I was faced with the most serious business on this circuit, with 44 prisoners. But many of them pleaded guilty: I disposed of 27 of them on the first day, and 11 on the second. The High Sheriff was surrounded with the same pomp as his predecessor of a year ago—coach, bewigged coachman, and javelin men all complete. Again I was rather sorry that I could only ride in that wonderful vehicle once, on the way to and from the Cathedral.

As it was a week-day we had no sermon at the Service. There was once an Assize sermon at Derby which had surprising consequences. On 15 August 1709 Dr Henry Sacheverell preached a sermon on "The Communication of Sin". On 5 November 1709 he preached another sermon, at St Paul's Cathedral, before the Lord Mayor and Aldermen, on "The Perils of False Brethren both in Church and State". It was resolved by the House of Commons that these sermons were malicious, scandalous, and seditious libels, and that he be impeached before the House of Lords. The hearing took ten days. In his Answer he admitted that he preached the first sermon at Derby "at the request of Henry Sacheverell, Esquire, High Sheriff of the County of Derby", and printed it at the request of the gentlemen of the Grand Jury for that county. His counsel must have enjoyed the proceedings very much. They spent many days in having sermons, and many passages of theology, read by the Clerk of the Court. On 23 March 1710 the Lords found him Guilty by 69 votes to 52. Of the 13 Bishops present 7 voted "Guilty" and 6 "Not Guilty". The sentence was that he should be enjoined not to preach for three years, and that the sermons be burned by the Common Hangman before the Royal Exchange. The House of Commons never made itself more ridiculous than by these proceedings. There were riots in favour of Sacheverell, and one sequel was the trial of Henry Dammaree for High Treason, "levying war against Her Majesty"—in fact for being one of a mob who burned a Meeting House in a drunken demonstration in favour of Sacheverell. He was found guilty, and was sentenced to the horrible form of death that was the penalty of High Treason: but he was reprieved and pardoned by the Queen. As for Sacheverell, he kept his enjoined silence for three years, and a month after their expiration Queen Anne presented him to the living of St Andrew's, Holborn.

I dined with the Circuit Mess at Derby, and spent a very pleasant evening. For its entertainment after dinner the Midland Circuit was then fortunate in having in one of its members the most accomplished mimic I ever knew. It was hard to say whether he was more perfect in his version of one of my judicial colleagues delivering a charge to a Grand Jury, or of another summing up to a common jury. I begged that I might have the salutary experience of hearing myself, but he declared, perhaps by way of polite pretence, that I had not sufficiently marked idiosyncrasies, and was useless as a model. He was a great artist. The circuit lost a great source of happiness by his untimely death a few years later.

On the Sunday my marshal and I were to lunch with my friend the Sheriff of a year ago. His place was near enough to Derby for us to walk there. The first part of the way, out by the race-course, was dismal enough. As we entered a depressing looking street of small houses, and of considerable length, I said: "Let us attempt a diversion. If you will give me a penny for every house in which there is an aspidistra in the parlour window, I will give you half a crown for every house in which there is none." The marshal agreed, and we tried it. Though I may not be believed—I won! The vogue of that deplorable vegetable was more than thirty to one.

As I was not so hard-worked at Derby as a year ago I had time to see the Municipal Art Gallery. Here, as elsewhere, a local artist provides the back-bone of the collection, and Wright of Derby was no mean artist—at any rate, I think, a better one than Etty of York. He took a special delight in chiaroscuro, and his two pictures, "The Air Pump" and "The Orrery" (which I think used to be in the National Gallery), are typical examples. But there is also a charming "Children playing at ball".

When we finished at Derby the High Sheriff offered to drive my marshal and me to Warwick. This meant going through Repton and Burton. I knew that the Sheriff was a director of Bass's great Brewery. So I asked whether he could let us see that by the way. He agreed with apparent alacrity. We stopped in Burton and lunched with him at the house attached to the Old Brewery. This was once the home of the Bass family, a fine, solid house, with some admirable panelling, and a good staircase. After lunch (not without some wonderful beer) we went over the Old Brewery itself: the company now has several more in the town. It was all very interesting and impressive. But I think I was more pleased with the cooperage than anything else. As the staves of a barrel (all made from Russian oak, entirely free of knots) may vary in width, the angle at the edge has to vary with that width so as to make an exact join with the stave next to it, and the planing machine which mechanically cut this angle in relation to the width of the stave it was dealing with was miraculous. Almost the whole process of making a barrel was mechanical. But the final stage, which involved hammering out the head of a heated rivet, with diamond-like facets, was done by a man with a hammer. And he was as miraculously skilful and exact as the planing machine itself.

My ignorance was illumined by the answer to a question that I think had never occurred to me before—"Why has Burton always been supreme in brewing?" For, when I asked it, I was told that it was because the town happened to have beneath it a bed of gypsum, and this gave a specially favourable quality to the water of the wells sunk through it. Naturally the next question was, "Is there a similar bed of gypsum anywhere else?" And I was told that there was at any rate one, at Tadcaster, in Yorkshire. So then I understood why Tadcaster, with a population about a fourteenth of that of Burton, seems relatively even more given over to brewing than Burton itself.

During this circuit I borrowed the early records of the Midland Circuit from the Junior. They are not quite so ancient as those of the old Northern Circuit. The records of the Northern begin in 1763, those of the Midland in 1773. In the old days, of course, the social life on circuit was much more flourishing than it is to-day. Railways and motor cars have annihilated distance. I suppose that in about half the Assize towns in England a barrister can appear in a case, having left London the same morning, and can return there at night. Another factor that has seriously diminished the social life of the Bar Mess is the growth of local bars. A man who has his home hard by only wants to dine occasionally with his circuit colleagues. The nominal members of a circuit to-day enormously outnumber those of the eighteenth century; but the percentage of them that really go the circuit and dine at the mess is equally diminished.

Here are some of the entries in the Records that I noted. My comments are in [brackets].

1773.

Mr White to be presented for saying all the Circuit were liquorish, & moreover undertaking to prove the same. Acquitted.

Mr Serj[t] Hill paid a Guinea for being made King's Serjeant.

Mr Dayrell to be presented for that most heinous sin of Huggery by dining with an Attorney when his brethren were assembled at the George. Guilty, a bottle free.

1774.

March 7. Mr Serj[t] Vaughan wagers Mr Dayrell one Bottle of Port that it is not "Audaces fortuna juvat" in Virgil. Mr Dayrell paid a bottle. [Dayrell rightly lost: The phrase is "Audentes fortuna juvat", Virg. *Aen.* x, 284.]

1783.

On the 17th March at three quarters after four o'clock p.m. by the Recorder's watch Mr Leigh Hill wagers a bottle with Burges that Lord Thurlow was at that moment Lord High Chancellor of Great Britain. Received 2/6 from Burges. [(1) The Recorder was the Junior of the Circuit, who kept the Records, not the Recorder of a borough. (2) The time is some indication of the dinner hour at that date, probably 4 p.m. (3) The question was not whether Lord Thurlow had been appointed Lord Chancellor, but whether he had lost office. He became Lord Chancellor 3 June 1778. Early in 1783, chiefly owing to the opposition to him of Fox, it was known that he was likely to be forced out of the ministry. In fact this happened on 7 April, when the Great Seal was handed over to Commissioners, of whom Lord Loughborough was the first. So Thurlow was still Chancellor on 17 March, and Burges lost the bet. (4) The payment of *2s. 6d.* by Burges seems to indicate the current price of a bottle, presumably of Port. In a price list at Vauxhall Gardens in 1762 Red Port and Sherry are each *2s.* a bottle, while Claret is *5s.* Burgundy *6s.*, and Champagne *8s.* a bottle.*]

Mr Gough presents Mr Newnham for going into a Barber's Shop at Coventry to be shaved. Fined a gallon but affeered to a Bottle—Recd. 2/6. [(1) The bar on circuit were expected to live in austere retirement. They slept in lodgings, and only resorted to the Inn for the Bar Mess. Probably Newnham ought to have had the barber come to his lodgings. (2) "Affeer" is an old English word from "Ad" and "forum", and means "to fix the market price". An "Affeeror" was one who fixed a price. Both words are old technical legal terms. Manwood, *Laws of the Forest* (1641), says: "They shal be amerced, and their amercement shall be affeared by affearers there." And *Termes de la Ley* (1641) has: "Affeerors are such as be appointed in Court Leets &c. to mulct such as have committed any fault which is arbitrably punishable, and for which no expresse penalty is prescribed by Statute." In the Court Roll of any manor the record of a Court Leet, or a Court Baron, begins by Jurors being sworn, and then "Affeerors", usually two or three. When the jury "amerced" someone, his fine is "affeered" at so much.]

1784.

Mr Isted presents Mr Willis for saying to Mr Barker, an Attorney, in the Court at Warwick, "My dear Sir". Paid 2/6.

Mr Clarke presents Mr (illegible) for dancing with an Attorney's daughter at Derby.

Mr Moody presented for giving a Supper to 3 Sisters of an Attorney (being his Sisters in law)—not guilty. [Under the old usage this may have meant his step-sisters. Cf. Sam Weller's use of "Mother-in-Law" for Stepmother.]

Mr Onslow presented by Mr Willis for bringing an Attorney in his chaise to Warwick—2/6.

1787.

Coventry, 24 March. Mr Rastall presented for dancing with an Attorney's wife at Derby. 2/6. [At this time the Assize towns on the Midland Circuit were Northampton, Oakham, Lincoln, Nottingham, Derby, Leicester, Coventry, and Warwick. The circuit began sometimes at Oakham and ended at Warwick, and sometimes began at Warwick and ended at either Northampton or Lincoln. Aylesbury and Bedford were then on the Norfolk Circuit.]

Warwick, 6 August. Mr Romilly moved that Mr Serjt Vaughan's distresses be taken into consideration upon which this Court voted twenty guineas to be paid out of the circuit fund. [The mover was later Sir Samuel Romilly.

* Warwick Wroth, *London Pleasure Gardens of the Eighteenth Century* (1896), p. 298.

He says in his *Autobiography*: "In the Spring of 1784 I first went upon the circuit. All circuits were indifferent to me, for I had no friends or connexions on any one of them; and my choice fell upon the Midland, because there appeared to be fewer men of considerable talents or of high character as advocates upon it than upon any other. It was, besides, shorter than some other circuits, and would therefore take me for a less time from the Court of Chancery; and, what was no unimportant consideration, my travelling expenses upon it would be less." It is perhaps significant of his personality that, a junior of three years standing on the circuit, he should be moving so important a resolution. The distressed Serjeant was not the later, and better known, Serjeant Vaughan, who was called at Lincoln's Inn 1791, and was eventually a Baron of the Exchequer, and Judge of the Common Pleas.]

1788.

Warwick. Mr Rastal is congratulated upon his marriage—£1—1—0.

Mr Newnham presented for dining with an Attorney at Leicester—paid 2/6.

Mr Shaw received the thanks of the Circuit for his attention to the Baggage Carriers' behaviour, & ordered to make what contract he thinks proper agst ye next Circuit, the present contract being thought extravagant. [I referred on an earlier page to J. Alderson Foote's *Pie Powder*, and his account of the Baggage Wagon on the Western Circuit. I presume the Midland may have had a similar institution.]

Mr Day to be presented for refusing to ring the Bell when required to do so by the Recorder.

1789.

Mr Brough presents himself for dancing with an Attorney's daughter—2/6.

1821.

Lincoln. Mr Adams presented Mr Goulburn for gross violation of the Circuit rules in clandestinely appropriating to himself a Bed at the Falcon at Uppingham out of his turn, and condoles with Mr Ellis on the injury done to his relation by taking the same bed from the great house dog. [I do not understand the end of this. The Falcon at Uppingham would be merely on the journey. It was never an Assize town.]

Mr Marriott is congratulated on having a bag presented to him—Guilty. £1—1—0. [A red bag given by a leader. See *supra*, p. 97.]

Mr Denman is congratulated on his appointment of Solicitor General to the Queen—Guilty—£1—1—0. [Denman was so appointed in 1820, and appeared for Queen Caroline in the Lords. He was still a junior, and was only given silk in 1828.]

1822.

Mr Adams presents Mr Ellis for playing the fool at a public theatre, and advertizing himself as a great actor. Also for degrading his species & acting the part of a spaniel. Guilty 5/-. [There is added a reference to the

Northampton play-bill: Ellis played the part of Fawnwell. The obscure reference to a spaniel may have something to do with the equally obscure reference to the great house dog above, and concern some circuit jest connecting Ellis with a dog.]

Mr Goulbourne and Mr Christie are condoled with on the breaking down of their Carriage. Guilty, 2/6 each.

Mr Williams condoles with Mr Finch on having his mare thrown down and her knees broken. Guilty, 2/6.

The Recorder is presented for degrading the Character of a Barrister by holding out a Sign of his profession (to wit a wig-block with a wig upon it) in the window of the house of one Ward, a Druggist, in Bridle Smith Gate, Nottingham. Teste L. C. Williams. Guilty, 2/6. [The Recorder no doubt had his lodgings at Mr Ward's.]

1858.

Derby, 15 March. Messrs Merewether, Wells, Manley Smith, and Bell are congratulated on having Red Bags presented to them by the Leader of the Circuit, and fined each 1 guinea.

Derby, 27 July. Mr Mellor moved a resolution that the rules resolved upon by a Meeting held at Mr Macauley's rooms in London to allow Members of the Circuit to go to Inns at the Assizes be rescinded. [Thirteen voted for the motion, and fifteen against it. Presumably this means that the permission given by the London meeting remained effective, and the old rule requiring the use of lodgings was henceforth abrogated.]

There is a dull book, *Bench and Bar, Reminiscences*, by Mr Serjeant Robinson (1889). He was not an eminent lawyer. He was called to the bar in 1840, and practised chiefly at the Old Bailey. When he was made a Serjeant his rings bore the motto "Ex Sese": a wag suggested the amendment "Ex C.C.C." He was made a Serjeant in 1865, being the last ordinary lawyer so appointed, though about nine were subsequently made Serjeants in order to qualify them as Judges.* The last of the latter was Lord Lindley in 1875. Shortly after, in the same year, the necessity of being a Serjeant for a common law judge was abolished. Dull though Robinson's book is, there are a few passages in it about circuit traditions that are interesting.

"There was an imperative rule, before railways were generally established, that no member of the bar could enter a circuit town by any public conveyance, and men used to club together and divide the

* When Lord Campbell was made Chief Justice of the King's Bench in 1850 he had to be made a Serjeant, and join Serjeants' Inn. He records that to do the latter cost him "near £700".

expenses of a post-chaise between them. A man who had gone the Northern Circuit for some time, without any profitable result, was told by a friend how he could increase his available income by £200 a year, and still be a member of the circuit. On enquiring how this was to be done, the answer was 'Stay away from it'."

"I chose the Home Circuit as being the most accessible and the least costly. It comprised the counties of Hertford, Essex, Kent, Sussex, and Surrey, which were visited twice a year, in the spring and in the summer. It was with great difficulty, and after much debate, that the rule against travelling by ordinary conveyance was relaxed, and permission given to journey by rail...."

"My circuit experience just began at the period of the alteration in question; although a very few railways had then been completed, and none that were altogether available to the members of the Home. It was only on one occasion that I shared in a post-chaise, and that was on part of the way to Hertford, to which there was no railway opened till a long time afterwards."

"Many have been the times when, after going by one of the 'Diamond' or 'Star' steamboats to Gravesend, I have walked on to Maidstone with a troop of companions, some of whom in after life would not care perhaps to be reminded of their then impecuniosity; for we walked, of course, in order to save expense and not transgress the settled rule. When the rail was only open as far as Woking, we used to have a merry walk to Guildford—from Broxbourne to Hertford, and from Hyde Park Corner to Kingston."

"The principle of the rule which prescribed exclusive travelling extended to lodgings at circuit towns, and we were precluded from taking up our quarters at any hotel. We must needs partake ourselves elsewhere, and most of the tradesmen in the locality—or rather their wives, for we understood that what we paid was treated universally as appropriated to their separate use—offered us the accommodation that we required. But this regulation has been for some time abrogated, owing probably to the vast increase in the Bar population, and, although the old stagers for convenience kept on their private rooms, it is not considered a breach of etiquette to put up at the Bar Hotel. Many of us kept on our lodgings from year to year, notwithstanding our absence from particular assizes. At Guildford, Chelmsford, and Maidstone I had the same rooms for upwards of thirty years."

Of this enforced aloofness of the bar there is a surviving echo in the existing Rules and Regulations of the Western Circuit. (I have been allowed to see them by the courtesy of the Treasurer of the Wine Committee.) One of them reads: "Members of the Mess are not allowed to use public rooms in any hotel in the Assize town during the Assizes. A mess room is provided at each Bar Hotel."

There is a well-known passage at the beginning of Chapter III of Trevelyan's *Life of Macaulay*. "Macaulay was called to the bar in 1826, and joined the Northern Circuit at Leeds. On the evening that he first appeared at mess, when the company were retiring for the night, he was observed to be carefully picking out the longest candle. An old King's Counsel, who noticed that he had a volume under his arm, remonstrated with him on the danger of reading in bed, upon which he rejoined with immense rapidity of utterance: 'I always read in bed at home, and if I am not afraid of committing parricide and matricide and fratricide I can hardly be expected to pay any special regard to the lives of the bagmen of Leeds.' And so saying, he left his hearers staring at one another, and marched off to his room."

This is a pleasant story, but there must be something wrong with it. For in 1826 Leeds was not an Assize town on any circuit. It was made an Assize town on the Midland Circuit in July 1864. And in 1876 it was transferred to the new North-Eastern Circuit upon its creation. Moreover, if Macaulay did join the Northern Circuit elsewhere, I am pretty sure that in 1826 members of the circuit would not sleep in the hotel where they dined, but in lodgings in the town.*

The name "T. B. Macauley" first appears in the list of counsel on the Northern Circuit in the Law List of 1827. It is repeated, with the same misspelling, every year until the volume for 1838, but disappears in later issues.

I have since, by the kindness of the Junior, been allowed to inspect the volume of the Circuit Records that covers 1826. I find that Macaulay did join the Northern Circuit on 8 March 1826 at Lancaster.

Trevelyan adds that "Under its social aspect Macaulay heartily enjoyed his legal career. He made an admirable literary use of the Saturnalia, which the Northern Circuit calls by the name of 'Grand Night', when personalities of the most pronounced description are

* The rule as to lodgings was only relaxed on the Midland Circuit thirty-two years later. See *supra*, p. 166.

welcomed by all except the object of them, and forgiven even by him.... He did not seriously look to the bar as a profession."

Lord Campbell, who was called to the bar in 1806, joined the Home Circuit in 1807 for the same reason as Robinson, "because it is the least expensive". In a letter to his brother of 30 June 1807 he says: "I went all round in a post-chaise with two other barristers. No public vehicle being permitted, this is far the cheapest mode of travelling. Upon an average the expense may be taken as five guineas a county. I was in four: Essex, Kent, Sussex, Surrey—twenty guineas. This is a mere trifle compared to the other circuits. The Western cannot be taken at less than £150 a year. But for this reason ours is more overstocked than any other. All married men too are urged to go the Home by their wives, as we are seldom more than four or five days out of town at a time.... We finished at Croydon, where we had a grand fête from fines imposed on Garrow, Best, &c., for going to other circuits on special retainers."

In another letter of 16 March 1808 he writes: "I don't know whether I ever attempted to convey to you any notion of our proceedings. We never go beyond a day's journey from London. The first day of the assizes at any place we travel down; some arriving before dinner, and the others in the evening. A few ride on horseback, or drive gigs, but the far greater number go in post-chaises. We must all live in lodgings, it being forbidden to sleep at the inns, on account of the attorneys being there; but at one inn in each town we all mess. The first night there is a general supper, to which every barrister at the assizes must contribute. We dine together next day, but none pay except those that are present; at least, absentees who give notice previously that they shall not attend by the existing regulation are excused, although it was formerly otherwise. The leader of the circuit sits at the head of the table, and Mr Junior at the bottom of it. This is the youngest barrister present, who has to fill a very arduous and disagreeable office. He orders the dinner, settles the bill, and next day (or when he can) duns every individual for his reckoning. But his principal duty is to take care of the wine. We have a stock at each place, and the *junior* is bound to see a proper quantity brought from the cellar, and to guard it from the depredation of the waiters. We sit down to table about five, and rise at seven. The men of business then retire to their briefs and their consultations, and cards are called for by the men of pleasure....The next day we dine with the judges (at least at three places on the circuit). This is a very formidable, uncomfortable, disagreeable meeting. The two judges sit at the head of the table, cheek by jowl. The barristers range themselves according to seniority....The dinner is always good and the wine execrable. At last 'Prosperity to the Home Circuit' comes to our relief. This toast is the signal for departure. In the course of the following day we generally get back to town."

Elsewhere* he writes of "the custom of the Judges, when the barristers dine with them, giving as a toast when the party is to break up, 'Prosperity to the —— Circuit', except that at the last place on the Spring Circuit they afterwards give '*Quinden-Pasch*', being the first return of Easter term; and on the summer circuit '*Cras Animarum*', being the first return of Michaelmas term; which is as much as to say 'To our next merry meeting in Westminster Hall'."

In October of the same year he writes: "In future I think I shall go the circuit on horseback, the most salubrious and most independent mode of travelling. The worst of it is that it is difficult to get your luggage along, and your wig and gown sometimes arrive in the assize town when the assizes are over."

In March 1810 he transferred himself to the Oxford Circuit, thinking that the prospects of getting work there were better, and the capacity of its members smaller. His first comment in a letter is: "Perfectly well received by the bar. The Oxford Circuiteers are accomplished gentlemen, but no lawyers." And a little later: "The expense may be reckoned about double the Home—to a man who joins at Worcester and leaves at Stafford by the mail, something more than £50 a circuit. The chief difference arises from the custom of carrying a servant on the Oxford, and having an entire post-chaise for him and yourself. On the Home the juniors travel three in a post-chaise, and carry no servant at all. Its cheapness and its convenience for family men render it crowded." By a servant he means his clerk. And the return from Stafford "by the mail" was permissible because the objection to public conveyances, with the possibility of the company of attorneys, was in journeying to Assize towns: Stafford was the last Assize town, and there was no objection to returning to London in the stage coach.

One incident of the Oxford Circuit he mentions in August 1814:

* *Lives of the Chancellors* (1857), Vol. VI, p. 166.

A Harmless Lunatic

"There is a mad man at Oxford of the name of Bickerton who has taken it into his head that he is a barrister-at-law. He has accordingly contrived to procure an old wig and gown, in which he travels about the country and walks into court, following us regularly from town to town. He is perfectly harmless, and people rather encourage his fantasy."

1930

For Hilary term 1930 I had the "Short Oxford" Circuit. He who has that goes only to Stafford and Birmingham, his colleague at the former place being the Judge who has gone all round the Oxford Circuit, and at the latter the Judge who has gone all round the Midland Circuit. It is an incident of this arrangement that at Birmingham the barristers of both circuits are entitled to practise.

I did not in fact go to Stafford, as Mr Justice Branson wrote to say that there was so little work there that he could easily do it without my help. I regretted the loss of his society, but I was glad to escape a visit to Stafford, which is as uninviting a city as any I know.

It is a curious thing that Stafford, always the county town of its shire, has no Recorder, while Burton-on-Trent, Lichfield, Newcastle-under-Lyme, Smethwick, Stoke-on-Trent, Walsall and Wolverhampton all possess such an officer and have Borough Quarter Sessions. Stafford had close on 30,000 inhabitants in 1931. By the chances of history some very small places have Recorders, e.g. Tenterden with 3500, Thetford (4000), Richmond, Yorkshire (4800), and Rye (4000). The smallest of all, I think, is South Molton, with less than 3000. Another curiosity is that there are five towns which have a Recorder, but he is an ornamental official only, since there are no borough sessions over which he can preside. These are Durham, Hartlepool, Kingston-on-Thames, Preston and High Wycombe. I believe the Recorder of High Wycombe is elected by the Corporation, instead of his being appointed by the Home Secretary, as happens with ordinary Recorderships. I do not know if the practice is the same in the other four places. The Recorder of London is also elected by the Corporation: there have been, in the past, occasions when his selection by the Home Secretary would have been preferable.

Before the Municipal Reform Act, which did not apply to London, I think every Recorder was elected by the Corporation. Boswell, on the recommendation of Lord Lonsdale, so became Recorder of Carlisle in 1788. His letter of 28 June 1790 resigning the office, and addressed "to the Mayor, Aldermen, Bailiffs, and Capital Citizens of Carlisle", is in the Adam collection at Buffalo.

The Recorder of London wears a red gown, of the same colour as that of a High Court Judge, but not the same cut. The Recorder of Exeter wears a blue gown: I have not been able to discover when, or how, this came about. All other Recorders wear the same black silk gown as a King's Counsel. It is said that this was first worn as a mourning gown on the death of Queen Anne and has been worn ever since, just as the black scarf worn by a seaman of the Royal Navy is the badge of mourning for Nelson that has never been laid aside. In the old days a Recorder wore a gown with tufts on the arms above the elbows, rather of the type of the gowns worn by the vergers in the Temple Church. There is in Narborough church near King's Lynn a standing effigy of Clement Spelman, who was Recorder of Nottingham, and died in 1679. This shows the robe I refer to.

I have said above that there are five boroughs which have a Recorder, but have no Borough Quarter Sessions over which he can preside. Oddly enough, and by way of contrast, there is one borough which has Quarter Sessions but has no Recorder. This is Haverfordwest. The borough magistrates can there hold Quarter Sessions under an elected Chairman.

I had only to spend eleven days at Birmingham in March. The week-end that was included my marshal and I spent pleasantly at "The George" at Lichfield. There is little to disfigure Lichfield except that horrible statue of Boswell. But if it comes to statues there are not many in the world worse than the four in the space behind the old Town Hall at Birmingham. Possibly two statues of deceased local magnates at Leeds (one with flowing side-whiskers in stone) and a Mr Palmer, holding his top hat, at Reading may successfully compete with them.

✧ ✧ ✧

In Easter term 1930 it was my lot to be one of the judges who had to go to Liverpool and Manchester, or to Leeds, which are the three cities which alone have four Assizes in the year. It is a lot that, by reason of an incomprehensible rota, seems to befall one at capricious intervals. I went with Mr Justice Acton to Liverpool on Sunday, 27 April, two days before the end of the Easter Vacation, and we spent a strenuous fortnight there, and an equally strenuous fortnight at Manchester. There were at each place about 60 prisoners, and about 50 civil suits, not to mention the detestable divorce cases. I think I worked harder during that month than I had since my busiest days at the bar.

I noticed one curious thing, for the first time, in St George's Hall at Liverpool. The two Courts are at each end of the great building, and the bench is against the outer wall. As I was sitting, with the doors on the other side of the Court opened, I could see Mr Justice Acton sitting facing me, an immense way off, and I could see nobody and nothing else! I suppose on my previous visits the two doors did not happen to be open, or I think I should have noticed this curious phenomenon.

An elderly London barrister with a practice has walked a good many times round the corridors out of which the Courts open. How many of them have observed that the pattern of the black and white pavement in the eastern corridor is different from the pattern in the western?

At Manchester, during the trial of a William Wagstaff, there was a witness called who was named William Shakeshaft: and in another trial a witness was named Etaugh. Near the Manchester Lodgings I went into Prestwich church. From a list of its Rectors I noted that there were seven successive Langleys who were incumbents from 1409 to 1632, the patron of each being also a Langley. I wonder if there is any church that can beat that curious record?

✧ ✧ ✧

One reason for the hard work put in by Mr Justice Acton and myself was that we were both due to start upon our Summer Circuits at an early date, and if we did not get done with Manchester we might find two circuits overlapping. As it was I got home from Manchester on Friday, 23 May, and left for Reading on Monday, 26 May. For in this summer, after trying for it in vain for five and a half years, I was glad to go upon the "Long Oxford" Circuit.

Berkshire is a pleasant county, but Reading is a very unattractive town. There were only six prisoners and two civil cases, and all the business was over in two and a half days. At the Assize Service at St Lawrence's church I found the front of my pew adorned with an old altar frontal of green velvet with the date 1632 embroidered upon it. Here, as at Bodmin, the officers of the barracks were polite and friendly: my marshal and I dined with them and spent a pleasant evening.

On Saturday, 31 May, I drove to Oxford. Ever since I was an undergraduate I had wanted to see the inside of the Judges' Lodgings, No. 16, St Giles's: for externally it is obviously the finest house in Oxford. It was built in 1702 for one Thomas Rowney. I believe it was once the town house of the Dukes of Marlborough. But it was not built by Vanbrugh: I think the only house he built in Oxford is one which I used to know very well as No. 17, New Inn Hall Street (now renamed St Michael's Street), opposite the garden gate of the Union; I had lodgings there in my fourth year.

I was not disappointed with the inside of the Judges' Lodgings. It is a magnificent house, with a beautiful panelled hall and staircase. There is a great dining-room that is not panelled, and a small one that is. There is also a very fine plaster ceiling on the half landing of the staircase. In the garden, facing the door from the house, is a fascinating little stone pavilion crowned with a miniature dome. The house belongs to St John's, and has long been let to tenants on the terms that they shall turn out three times a year for the Judge. The occupant in 1930 had done much for the house, in admirable taste, and with every modern comfort: no one in the world has a more excellent bathroom than the two he had created. He had also a wonderful collection of old china.

My son at Trinity was in his last term, and his sister was with me. We had a dinner-party of young people on Saturday evening, and, as a gramophone had been brought from home in the car, there was dancing in the great dining-room after dinner. This engagement prevented me, to my regret, from enjoying another. For after it had been arranged I had a letter from the Dean of Christ Church asking me to dine with him in hall on this evening. "Sir," said Johnson to Boswell, "it is a great thing to dine with the Canons of Christ Church." They also could not accept the invitation, as they were engaged to dine at University College. It was a great thing then in more senses than it is now: Birkbeck Hill, in a note on the passage, says (on the authority of Mark Pattison and Cardinal Newman) that they dined at three and sate regularly until chapel at nine.

On Sunday morning I went to the University Sermon at 10, was met at the door of St Mary's by the Vice-Chancellor (Dudden of Pembroke) and was conducted by him to his seat: I confess I felt an instinctive academic diffidence in ousting him from it. I told him afterwards that the first Assize Service I ever attended anywhere was as an undergraduate in 1894, when Archbishop Benson preached. He said he remembered very well the incident of which I have spoken on an earlier page: it made a considerable stir at the time.

It is ungrateful that I have forgotten who was the preacher on this Sunday, 1 June 1930. For it was an admirable discourse. I am afraid I do not always listen attentively throughout sermons: but I did throughout this one. I suspect that I might not have listened with so much interest to another Assize sermon close on a century before. This is a passage from Newman's *Apologia*: "On Sunday, July 14 [1833] Mr Keble preached the Assize Sermon in the University Pulpit. It was then published under the title of *National Apostasy*. I have ever considered and kept the day as the start of the religious movement of 1833."

I was interested to hear myself called, in the bidding prayer, "the reverend and learned judge of this Assize".

I see in Huddleston's *Circuit Notes*: "At Oxford there is no Sheriff's chaplain, as the Vice-Chancellor of the University officiates." There is a Sheriff's Chaplain now, if only for the reason that the Vice-Chancellor is rarely in orders. But Huddleston was not a University man. He may only have meant that at Oxford, and Cambridge, there seems never to be any question but that the University provides the preacher at an Assize Service, and the Sheriff's Chaplain is not given any duty. Some years later I had a letter from my friend the Dean of York, who said they had suffered from some pretty bad sermons from Sheriff's Chaplains at Assize Services at the Minster. He asked whether as prospective Judge of Assize I should feel any objection if he could arrange for a preacher of known capacity instead. I replied that I certainly would make no objection. If I had then known of it, I might have told him of a curious precedent, when objection was taken. Mr Justice Rokeby, of the Common Pleas, writes in his *Diary*: "Exeter, March 1693/4. Y^e^ D. & Chap. of Exeter refused to let Mr Hodder, ye Sheriff's chaplain, preach ye assize sermon at ye Cathedrall. They set up another. Both ye Judges excused ye Sheriff from comeing to ye church, & my brother Powell alone went there."

On the Sunday evening I dined with the Vice-Chancellor in hall at Pembroke. At official dinners, with Lord Mayors, a Judge wears his court suit, black silk gown, and tie-wig. I did the same when I dined in hall with the Master of Trinity, Cambridge; and I have done so when dining with the Bishop of Lincoln, with the Dean and Chapter of Exeter, and with the dons at the College of Lampeter. On this occasion I enquired beforehand of the Vice-Chancellor if he would prefer me to come in this guise, or like a gentleman. To my great relief, he said the latter; and I gathered that it was more in the Oxford tradition. I say "to my great relief", because a wig is a troublesome adornment for a pleasant evening.

In the eighteenth century judges (and bishops too) had to wear wigs everywhere, and at all times, in public. When Sir John Scott was made Chief Justice of the Common Pleas, his wife, who disliked a wig, persuaded him to ask George III if he might dispense with it except when performing official functions. The King would not consent, and it was only when he became Lord Chancellor, and Lord Eldon, in 1801 that "the wig of private life was discontinued".* The Bishops were allowed to give it up in 1832. Joseph Jekyll writes to Lady Gertrude Sloane Stanley, 9 January 1832: "The King has given the Bishops leave to abandon wigs except in the House of Lords or the pulpit. Bishop of London dined at General Phipps' on Sunday without one." And Copleston, Bishop of Llandaff, wrote in his diary on 22 February 1832: "On this day, following the example of almost all the bishops, left off my wig."

Though I went to Pembroke without a wig I was not unmindful of the Oxford etiquette which requires any member of the University to wear his gown at a dinner party at which the Vice-Chancellor is present: I believe an Oxford hostess giving a party at her own house does the right thing by putting "To meet the Vice-Chancellor" on her cards of invitation, if he is to be a guest. So I borrowed an M.A. gown from the ever youthful Gillam at the lodge at Trinity. He was my scout in 1892–1893, and was one of the salt of the earth.

On the Monday morning I was waited upon at 10 o'clock by the Vice-Chancellor, Proctors, and Heads of Houses. Subsequently I was waited upon by the Mayor of Oxford, with the Town Clerk, and some Aldermen. According to ancient usage the Vice-Chancellor presented me with a pair of white kid gloves, with small gauntlets of gold lace, and white silk ribbons. And the Mayor presented me with a second pair, only slightly less ornate, with a fringe of gold wire round the tops.

* Twiss, *Life of Lord Eldon* (1844), Vol. I, p. 339.

The Vice-Chancellor said that he believed his offering was in token of the fact that there was no member of the University to be tried at the Assize. But I ventured to doubt if this was correct. In the old days gloves were frequently presented on ceremonial occasions, especially in Oxford, where they were readily obtainable from Woodstock, an ancient place for their manufacture.

When Queen Elizabeth visited Oxford on 6 September 1566 she was presented with six pairs of gloves. One of these pairs is preserved in the Ashmolean Museum. They have an elaborately worked gauntlet in gold, and a fringe of gold lace very much like that on the gloves given me by the Mayor of Oxford.

According to Thomas Warton (who may, however, have invented the document) when Sir Thomas Pope visited his newly founded college of the Holy and Undivided Trinity on 15 July 1556, the Bursars presented to him "chirothecas aurifrigiatas".* Aurifrigiatae is exactly the epithet for the gloves given to me by the Vice-Chancellor and the Mayor. Warton only translates it as "embroidered".

"In the *computus* of the bursars of Trinity College, for the year 1631, the following article occurs: '*Solut pro fumigandis chirothecis.*' Gloves made a constant and considerable article of expence in the earlier accompt-books of the college here mentioned; and without doubt in those of many other societies. They were annually given (a custom still subsisting) to the college-tenants, and often presented to guests of distinction."†

"There used to be a Bodleian Dinner at the annual Bodleian Visitation. In the course of this the Yeoman Bedel in Arts went in *inter epulandum* and presented a pair of gloves and ten shillings to each of the Regius Professors and the two Proctors in consideration of their trouble in the visitation or inspection."‡

When Routh of Magdalen took the degree of B.D. in 1786 he had to pay £12. 17*s*. 4*d*. in fees. One of the items was £3. 8*s*. 4*d*. for *Chirothecae.*§ I do not know to whom they were presented.

"The Oxford City companies used to present the Proctors with gloves (to the value of 16/4, as a careful proctor, writing about 1840, notes)."||

* Warton, *Life of Sir Thomas Pope* (1772), p. 432. † *Oxoniana* (n.d.), Vol. II, p. 228.

‡ G. V. Cox, *Recollections of Oxford* (1868), p. 213.

§ Middleton, *Dr Routh* (1938), p. 47.

|| Buxton and Gibson, *Oxford University Ceremonies* (1935), p. 35.

As for the gold lace on the Oxford gloves I see that in the late Mr Arthur Denman's *Digest* he wrote in 1912 under "Maiden Assize": "When there are no prisoners for trial at an Assize town, by custom of great antiquity the Sheriff presents white gloves to the Commissioners of Assize. In the case of the judge these are ornamented round the wrists with gold lace, those given to the Clerk of Assize being plain." As "Maiden Assizes" are now a thing of the past, this may be worth recording: it may, however, only have been the practice on the South-Eastern Circuit, of which Mr Denman was Clerk of Assize. On the few occasions when I have received white gloves, e.g. at Haverfordwest, Carmarthen, and Lincoln, they have not had any gold lace on them.

By ancient custom the Judge of Assize entertains at dinner the Vice-Chancellor, Proctors, Heads of Houses, and the Preacher of the Assize sermon. At Cambridge there are added, as I discovered later on, the Esquire Bedels and the Public Orator. But as this is an ancient custom it only applies to the ancient Assizes in Hilary and Trinity terms, but not at the Autumn Assize, which is a modern invention. That is why I had no such party when I went to Cambridge in October 1926.

On this occasion at Oxford, on the Monday evening I had a party of twenty-four, including my marshal and myself. I had had a walk round Oxford in the afternoon, and had occasion to admire the public spirit (and fortunate opulence) of Merton in remodelling, and half destroying, that eyesore of Butterfield's, St Alban Hall, which had so long spoiled the aspect of Merton from the Long Walk. It is a rare and pleasant thing to find money spent solely on the amenities. I spoke of it to the Dean of Christchurch (White) at dinner, and said I wished his college could do the like with the Meadow Buildings with which Ruskin so infamously cursed them. The Dean sighed, and said he only wished they could do as Merton had done.

It is unfortunate for the Oxford Judge that the business of an Assize there is always so small that he cannot with decency allot more than two days to it. I hardly needed them, for the work was over by 3.30 on the second day. On that night we had another dinner party of young people at the Lodgings, and more dancing.

It was not without design, though happily the design fitted in with necessity, that I had made Wednesday, 4 June, the Worcester Commission Day. For I had received a pleasing invitation from the Provost of Eton to attend the Speeches, and luncheon in the College Hall, and it was obviously an easy thing to travel from Oxford to Worcester by way of Eton. We drove home after breakfast, and on to Eton, in time for the Speeches. As for the weather it was the most perfect 4 June ever known. My marshal (of Eton and Trinity) and I had to leave after tea, and catch a train at Slough by which we got to Worcester at 8.50. The sun set, as we travelled through the summer landscape, in a cloudless sky, and a glorious day ended gloriously.

The Lodgings at Worcester are an enormous house behind the Shire Hall. I can only remember the vastness of it, and that it was comfortable enough. There were sixteen prisoners, of whom not one came from the city itself. This gave me an opportunity, when charging the Grand Jury, of pointing out the appositeness of the motto, "Ever virtuous as ever faithful", to which the city lays claim on its Town Hall.

Somewhere about 1760 there was a strange affair at an Assize at Worcester. Sir Eardley Wilmot, then Judge of the King's Bench, and later Chief Justice of the Common Pleas, writes thus to his wife: "I send this by express, on purpose to prevent your being frightened, in consequence of a most terrible accident at this place. Between two and three, as we were trying causes, a stack of chimneys blew upon the top of that part of the hall where I was sitting, and beat the roof down upon us; but as I sat up close to the wall, I have escaped without the least hurt. When I saw it begin to yield and open, I despaired of my own life and the lives of all within the compass of the roof. Mr John Lawes is killed, and the attorney in the cause which was trying is killed, and I am afraid some others: there were many wounded and bruised. It was the most frightful scene I ever beheld. I was just beginning to sum up the evidence, to the jury, and intending to go immediately after I had finished. Most of the counsel were gone, and they who remained in court are very little hurt, though they seemed to be in the place of greatest danger.... Two of the jurymen who were trying the cause are killed, and they are carrying dead and wounded bodies out of the ruins still." In another letter he says, "It was an image of the last day, when there shall be no distinction of persons, for my robes did not make way for me. I believe an earthquake arose in the minds of most people, and there was an apprehension of the fall of the whole hall."*

* Campbell, *Lives of the Chief Justices*, Vol. III, p. 141.

Lord Campbell adds: "His safety is supposed to have been entirely owing to his presence of mind, which induced him to remain composedly in his place till the confusion was over—a circumstance which, with his usual modesty, he suppresses."

In the South aisle of the nave of Worcester Cathedral is a tomb that should be approached with reverence by an English lawyer, and especially by any Bencher of the Inner Temple. It is that of Sir Thomas Littleton (1402–1481), the renowned author of the treatise on Tenures, and traditionally the first known Reader of the Inner Temple. It is an altar tomb. On the top is the matrix of his effigy in brass, which was torn away during the civil war. The tomb is said to have been erected by him in his lifetime. It bears the inscription: "Hic jacet corpus Thome Littleton de Frankly, militis de Balneo, et unius Justiciariorum de Communi Banco qui obiit 23 Augusti An. Dom. 1481."

Not far away, in the same Cathedral, is a monument of another Sir Thomas Littleton (1593–1649), who was made a baronet in 1618. He was also a member of the Inner Temple, but I do not think he was ever called to the bar. Sir Edward Littleton (1589–1645), Treasurer of the Inner Temple from 1634 to 1638, was Solicitor-General from 1634 to 1640, Chief Justice of the Common Pleas 1640, and Lord Keeper in 1641. Foss, in his *Biographical Dictionary*, records that when he was Treasurer "he applied for a chamber then vacant over his own to be assigned to his kinsman, Thomas Littleton" [i.e. the above mentioned, Sir Thomas], whereupon "the whole company of the bench desired that the admittance should be freely without fine as a testimony of that great respect the whole Society doth owe and acknowledge to the name and family of Lyttelton".

My marshal and I saw a monument to another old Bencher of the Inner Temple when we had an afternoon off at Worcester. We drove to Kempsey and then (at the suggestion of Sir Reginald Coventry, K.C.) walked through Croome Park, and by Defford Common, Strensham, and Twining to Tewkesbury. The last few miles by the Avon were through hayfields with the most tremendous crop of upstanding hay that I ever saw. In the little church in Croome Park is the great monument of Thomas, first Lord Coventry (1578–1640), Lord Keeper 1625, and like his father, Sir Thomas Coventry (1547–1606), Judge of the Common Pleas, and his descendant Sir Reginald, a Bencher of the Inner Temple.

Lord Chancellors, and Chief Justices, in the old days made great fortunes, and were not the miserably paid beings they are now. So one is inclined to reflect on seeing such a great place as Croome, or Lord Kenyon's at Gredington, or Lord Harrowby's at Sandon, or Lord Mansfield's Ken Wood.

Yet another monument to an Inner Templar I saw a few days later in the lady chapel at Gloucester. This is the standing effigy, in his robes, of Sir John Powell (1645–1713), Baron of the Exchequer 1691, Judge of the Common Pleas 1695, and of the King's Bench 1702. Swift wrote to Stella, 5 July 1711: "In the evening I went to the Lord Treasurer, and among other company found a couple of judges with him. One of them, Judge Powel, an old fellow with grey hairs, was the merriest old gentleman I ever saw, spoke pleasant things, and laughed and chuckled till he cried again." Once he had to try a woman for witchcraft. She was said to be able to fly. He said to her: "Hark ye, if you can fly, then fly away. There is no law against flying."

I think one of the most interesting forms of art in this country is the sepulchral monument. Certainly there is none of which good examples are more numerous and more widespread. One can rarely go into a church without finding at least one monument of interest, even if it be only as an example of the admirable lettering which should be, but so rarely is, an inspiration and a model to an age miserably addicted to "Block Letters".

Having this interest I was struck by the contrast between Worcester Cathedral and Gloucester Cathedral in one matter. All the monuments at Worcester are kept beautifully clean. The Dean (Moore Ede) had written an admirable little book giving an account of them. I can remember when the effigy of King John was gilded all over, and a tin crown placed about his head: this was done by the Office of Works, as responsible for royal tombs, about 1875. Recently the Dean had had this gilding removed, with advantage. Whether the effigy would look better if the original colours, which no doubt adorned it, could be restored, may be a question. The two gaily coloured tombs in the nave, of Beauchamps and Wyldes, suggest that it would. Flaxman's monument to Mrs Digby is fine. And so is that to Bishop Hough, by Roubiliac, with the interesting bas-relief of the expulsion of the dons from Magdalen. But the finest work of art, to my thinking, is the bust of Bishop Johnson by Nollekens. Of the smaller wall tablets two of the best are those to Izaak Walton's wife, and to Bishop Fleetwood. The epitaphs of Mrs Izaak Walton and of Mrs Rae are delightful.

In contrast with this cleanly care at Worcester, the monuments at Gloucester were dirty and neglected. In the nave I saw a memorial to Dr Adams, the Master of Pembroke, who was the friend of Johnson's later years. His wig was encrusted with dirt. I touched the top of it with a finger and the dirt came off in a black smear, as when one touches the top of a book in the Law Courts or the Temple.

Fortunately the interest in English Monumental Sculpture has been very much awakened in recent years, largely owing to the writings of Mrs Esdaile. When on almost every subject far too many books have been written, she had the cleverness to discover one on which little, if anything, had been said; and everyone should be grateful to her for that discovery and for using it to such good purpose. I think the Dean of Worcester's care for his monuments began before she wrote, and not from her inspiration. When I write (in 1939) a like care has extended to many cathedrals. The cleaning process has been carried round Westminster Abbey almost to a conclusion. And at Canterbury the mere washing of the effigy of the Black Prince, changing it from a dingy blackness to a lovely hue of old gold, was almost a miraculous operation!

On Whit-Monday we were due to move on to Gloucester. My marshal and I took the train to Tewkesbury, and then walked by the Severn to Gloucester. This took us past Deerhurst, and we turned off the towpath to see the church there, with its Saxon details, and the small Saxon chapel near it. I had seen them nearly forty years ago. I had a recollection that perhaps the most interesting thing in the church was that there was a communion table set to the East and West, after the fashion of the Commonwealth, with fixed seats around it, and also the old fashion of houseling clothes. This was gone in 1930. On enquiry of the verger he said that a Vicar in 1893 (two or three years after I was there) had done away with the old arrangement from a desire for ecclesiastical uniformity. I thought I detected a hint of disapproval in the man's guarded statement. If it were so, he may have gathered that I sympathized with his attitude. To destroy such an historical fragment is a pity. If the Chairman at Dorset Quarter Sessions gave up his top hat, or the Royal Assent in the House of

Lords were changed from "Le Roy le veult" to "The King agrees", it would be even worse.

There is (or was in 1930) one surviving example of this puritan arrangement of the table, at the small church of Dale Abbey, in Derbyshire. I saw it in November of that year when I was walking from Nottingham to Derby. I suppose at one time there were a good many similar survivals. In the *Diary of Thomas Cartwright Bishop of Chester* (Camden Society, 1843) he writes on 21 September 1687: "I went... to Liverpool, where the mayor and aldermen met me in the church, and I commanded the churchwarden to set the communion table altar-wise against the wall." The Rev. William Cole did the same at Waterbeche in Cambridgeshire in 1767. On Christmas Day he writes* in his diary: "I ordered the table to be set under the middle East Window, it being before in the middle of the Chancel."

The Lodgings at Gloucester were a big house (though nothing like as big as at Worcester), looking on to the public gardens, comfortable enough but not beautiful. When the High Sheriff, Mr Huntley of Boxwell Court, appeared I noticed that he was carrying a wand, like my friend at Winchester. I also noticed that he was wearing an old-fashioned looking sword, quite unlike the bodkin that is usual with a velvet court suit. He told me that this sword usually hung on the wall in his drawing-room. It had been worn by the last of his ancestors who was High Sheriff of Gloucester, and with it that High Sheriff had been knighted by his Sovereign. When one was told that this previous Huntley was Sheriff in 1574, and that the Sovereign was Queen Elizabeth, what could be more romantic than to have his descendant wearing it in 1930! If King George V had been there, and not merely his Judge of Assize, I feel sure he would have had the sword handed to him and performed the accolade there and then.

One further thing of interest in the story was that, though there had been many Huntleys of Boxwell Court between 1574 and 1930, not one of them had been High Sheriff. The reason for this was that every one of them, down to my friend's father, had been in Orders, Rector as well as Squire of Boxwell.

We had the Assize Service at the Cathedral on the first day of the Assize. I had the pleasure there of bowing with proper gravity to a Canon and an Archdeacon, both of whom were fellow undergraduates

* *The Blecheley Diary of the Rev. William Cole* (1931), p. 304.

with me at Trinity College, Oxford. The Canon remained as thin as he was at twenty. The Archdeacon had attained a majestic Archidiaconal rotundity. Of course they both came to dinner with me.

The work at Gloucester finished on the last day in time for me to drive out to lunch at Boxwell Court. It is not a very large house, and only parts of it are ancient. Originally it was a country lodge of the Abbots of Gloucester, and the Huntleys lived there as tenants of the Abbot. After the Dissolution it was granted by Queen Elizabeth to Sir Walter Raleigh. He had his own home, and did not want to live in this one, so the Huntley of the day bought it from him, and they have been there ever since. In the house is a picture of Prince Rupert, and a pair of spurs which he left behind when he stayed a night. The little church, of which so many Huntleys have been Rectors, is close to the house.

After lunch we went to see the famous arboretum at Westonbirt, and to tea with the Rector of Westonbirt, who was the Sheriff's Chaplain. As a Chaplain in the great war he had won the D.S.O. But I noticed in the Gloucestershire Directory that the printer had thought fit to put after his name, not D.S.O., but D.Sc. Clearly a parson might be a Doctor of Science, but only a soldier a D.S.O.

In February 1896 there was an epidemic of small-pox in Gloucester, and accordingly the Assizes were held at Cheltenham. So, because of plague in London, the Benchers of the Inner Temple met at Hertford, and at St Albans, in November 1592, and at Reading in November 1625. In the great plague year 1665 they had no meeting at all after 11 June.

On Saturday, 14 June, I motored to the Speech House in the Forest of Dean, in order to walk from there to Monmouth. I was alone, for my second change of marshals on this circuit was taking place, and the new one was coming by train from Oxford to Monmouth—and a fearful journey he found it. I heard that the Bar amused itself with a story that I had disabled the two predecessors by making them walk too far. On the way to the Speech House, at Westbury, I saw a wonderful formal garden by the road, with a glimpse at the far end of what appeared to be a perfect William and Mary, or Queen Anne, house. I stopped the car to admire, and wished I had some excuse for asking to go inside the gates. Indeed I often wish for the easier ways of little more than a century ago. When Mr and Mrs Gardiner, and Elizabeth Bennet, on their way from Bakewell to Lambton, were minded to see Pemberley they drove up to the front door. "On applying to see the place they were admitted into the hall"—and were then taken over the house by the housekeeper, and about the grounds by the gardener.

My walk through the forest was very pleasant. I came down to Newland, and saw its fine church, with Wyndham and Probyn monuments, and a Chief Baron of the Exchequer among the latter. Finally I came into Monmouth along the grass-grown track of a disused railway.

On the Sunday my new marshal and I walked up the bank of the Monnow, past Llanrosal church, and to the bridge at Skenfrith. There was an inn there, very convenient for lunch. Unhappily it was built on the west side of the river, where Welsh licensing law was in operation. So beer was unobtainable. If it had been at the other end of the bridge it would have been otherwise. We came back to Monmouth over the hill, by a path through the park of Hillstone House, and by St Maugham's—a very good walk.

The Lodgings at Monmouth were a pleasant house belonging to a Doctor, who had turned out for the period of the Assize. It was not a bad house, but to call it spick and span would have been inaccurate. There was not very much work, but one case in which a man was convicted of trying to swindle bookmakers by sending telegrams with a false time of dispatch upon them was lengthy, though not without its humours. The weather was fearfully hot. It was on Wednesday, 18 June, the hottest day of all, that a thunderstorm ruined so many expensive dresses at Ascot. With us there was no rain, but it was so hot that it would have been almost a relief to be soaked to the skin.

The Lodgings at Hereford were again a private house, and a very pleasant one. Not so admirable as the one at Mold, nor so stately as the Oxford house, and perhaps not so comfortable as the one on the Eccleston Road at Chester. But it stood on a remarkable site on the hill to the north of the city. In the garden the trees had been cut away so that from the windows you looked down at the Cathedral set in a leafy frame. On a smaller scale the effect was like that remarkable view of Windsor Castle from a spot near Queen Victoria's Oak to the west of High Standing Hill.

On the Monday morning the Sheriff came in a coach, and not the car which is now almost universal. Norwich, Bristol, Newcastle, Derby, Chester once, Cardiff once, and now Hereford—these were the coaches I had known. The music was good at the service in the Cathedral; but what a ghastly thing is Scott's metal screen.

Huddleston, in his *Circuit Notes*, says that it is always the custom for the Dean of Hereford to present the judges with two bottles of sherry. I had no such pleasing offering.

There were only eight prisoners, and they were all dealt with on the first day. I told the Grand Jury that I should like to think that this absence of crime was due to a general rise in the standard of morality. But I added that I had travelled towards Hereford the day before, from Oxford, in a first-class carriage of the Great Western Railway. I found that in the lavatory the towels were chained to the wall. And if the Company found it necessary to adopt that precaution in a first-class carriage I was led to doubt if one could think there was a very widespread raising of moral standards.

Though there was little crime, there were a good many civil cases, including a hotly contested one about a right of way, so that the three days allotted to Hereford were fully occupied. But I found time to walk about the city. One of the most remarkable things is the bowling green behind All Saints' church—a perfect piece of turf. A day or two before a team of bowlers from Australia, on tour in England, had played there against the local side. Hereford had won, and the captain of the team, whom I chanced to meet on the lawn, was rightly proud of the victory. There were some good eighteenth-century shop-fronts (alas! how few have survived the attack of plate-glass), e.g. an ironmonger's in Widemarsh Street. Of smaller things in the Cathedral I liked best the charming windows in the chantry of Bishop Stansbury, first Provost of Eton.

And so, on the afternoon of 27 June, to Shrewsbury, and to its admirable Lodgings in Belmont. I again thought Shrewsbury as pleasant a town as any in England, and I saw some things I had missed before. The Assembly Room behind the Lion Hotel is by the Adam brothers, and a beautiful and well-preserved room it is. I had often noticed the great lion, on its circular end, from the windows of the Lodgings.

On the Saturday afternoon we walked by the canal to Uffington, and so to the ruins of Haughmond Abbey. Near by Sundorne Castle, a vast red-brick Georgian house looked attractive, and I wished we could get nearer to it. On Sunday we walked out by the English Bridge to Sutton, with a minute abandoned church, Berrington, Mascot Eaton, and Pitchford. The black and white house at Pitchford is a great and beautiful place. Thence to Acton Burnell, with its famous castle in ruins. In the church the best thing was the tomb of Richard Lee (d. 1591). And so to Cross Houses, Atcham, and home by the river.

If I thought as I had before of Shrewsbury, I did the same of Stafford. Lord Campbell was right when, in 1819, he called it "the dullest and vilest town in all England", if he was speaking only of Assize towns.

✧ ✧ ✧

In the autumn of 1930 I went on the Midland Circuit. In the early part of it I had again experience of the waste of judicial time that must continue to occur until a more elastic system, with some discretion entrusted to the Judge of Assize, is introduced. At Aylesbury there were four prisoners, and the work took one day. At Bedford there were four prisoners, of whom three pleaded guilty, and three hours sufficed for the fourth. At Northampton there were three prisoners, all of whom pleaded guilty, and the entire business of the Assize was finished in about an hour. From Aylesbury to Bedford is about 30 miles, from Bedford to Northampton is 21 miles.

These were, no doubt, unusually light calendars. And at the Autumn Assize no civil cases are taken at these towns. But at Bedford I have only once known the work to last beyond the first day at any Assize. Considering how small a county Bedford is, and how short the distance from any part of it to Northampton, and how easy are modern means of travel, I would certainly unite the two counties for Assizes. The Sheriff could be chosen alternately from each. The Assizes might be held alternately at Bedford and Northampton, if it be thought that Bedford's pride must not be hurt. If efficiency be alone considered I would have all the Assizes at Northampton.

Throughout this circuit the work was unusually light. Even at Derby there were only 15 prisoners, by way of contrast to the 44 exactly a year before. As it happened Mr Justice Talbot was on the Midland Circuit in the next term in January 1931. His experience was just the reverse of mine, except at Bedford. He had a sensational murder trial at Northampton, which took a long time, and a very lengthy trial at Nottingham. And after finishing at Warwick he had to go back to Nottingham and Lincoln to hear some civil cases that he had had to postpone.

I said just now that a more elastic system, by which some discretion was given to the Judge of Assize, ought to be introduced. After I had been removed to the Court of Appeal this was done. During my time, as I have mentioned before, under the Act of 1925, it was only the Lord Chief Justice, with the concurrence of the Lord Chancellor, who could cancel forthcoming Assizes "if it appears that there is no business, or no substantial amount of business, to be transacted" at them. But by sect. 5 of the Administration of Justice Act, 1938 it is provided that the power exercisable under that Act by the Lord Chief Justice, with the concurrence of the Lord Chancellor, shall for the future be exercised, in his sole discretion, by the Judge going the circuit, or, if the place is a place at which two Judges will be on circuit together, by the senior of them. It is a mystery to me why an amendment so obviously desirable should have been delayed so long, and my only regret is that it was delayed until I had been deprived of the task of going on circuit.

When we moved from Northampton to Leicester my marshal and I started by driving to Brixworth. I had long known of its church by repute and greatly wished to see it. Nor was I disappointed. I fancy it must be the largest piece of Roman building extant in Great Britain. Of course the great wall in Northumberland, and the walls at Silchester are greater in bulk. But they are mere ruins. Brixworth church, however greatly altered, began, I feel sure, as a basilica and has perhaps been a roofed building from Roman times.

From Brixworth we walked by Cottesbrooke, Haselbeech, over the battlefield of Naseby, Sibbertoft, and Marston Trussell to Market Harborough, and there took the train to Leicester. Cottesbrooke interested me very much, because I became satisfied that it is the Mansfield of *Mansfield Park*. A number of passages in the novel fix Mansfield Park as about 4 miles north of Northampton. Cottesbrooke is 9 miles. But in every other respect Cottesbrooke is exactly Mansfield. The great red-brick house would do admirably for Sir Thomas Bertram's. It is just the proper distance from the village, in which there are several houses that would do for Mrs Norris: perhaps the most likely is the first house on the right as you enter the village from the south. There is a Rectory spacious enough to be the home of Dr Grant, who later became a Canon of Westminster. Lastly one remembers that Henry Crawford was at Mansfield for the hunting: it was when he was out hunting that he came on Thornton Lacey, where Edmund was to have the living. Of course Cottesbrooke is in a great hunting country: the Pytchley kennels are at Brixworth.

Cottesbrooke in 1812, when Jane Austen was writing *Mansfield Park*, belonged to Sir James Langham, Bt. When I was at Leicester I wrote to my friend Mr R. W. Chapman telling him how exactly Cottesbrooke fitted in as Mansfield, and said: "I suppose there is no reference in Jane Austen's letters [which Mr Chapman was then editing] to any acquaintance with the Langhams?" A year later Mr Chapman discovered that Jane Austen had some acquaintance, probably through her brother Henry, with Sir James Langham. For in her record of "Opinions of *Mansfield Park*", and "Opinions of *Emma*", the estimates given by Sir James Langham are quoted. With this corroboration I am satisfied that Cottesbrooke was the original of *Mansfield Park*, and so, I believe, is Mr Chapman.*

Cottesbrooke interested me in other ways. One hears talk of the break-up of estates, and the supersession of old landed families, as if it were a modern phenomenon. In truth it has been going on all through our history. Cottesbrooke anciently belonged to the Redes. Behind the squire's pew in the church there is a sixteenth-century tomb of the last Redes, father and son. I suppose they stayed at home and did nothing, and so, without the modern spur of death duties, came to mortgages and embarrassment. So they were supplanted by one who would now be called a *nouveau riche*. For close by their tomb is a very magnificent seventeenth-century tomb of the first Langham—Sir James Langham, Knight and Baronet, Alderman of the City of London. His effigy is clad in his alderman's robes. The Langhams reigned for 200 or 300 years, and got to a 12th or 13th baronet. One of them rebuilt the house magnificently in the eighteenth century. Then they sold the place to a Brassey, one of a comparatively new family. This regime will perhaps be shorter. In February 1931 I saw an advertisement in *The Times* of Cottesbrooke Hall, with 1340 acres, being for sale. Nothing came of this, but I saw it advertised again in 1935.

* Anyone who is interested in this may like to refer to letters in *The Times Literary Supplement* of 15 April 1920, 10 December 1931, and 31 December 1931.

The church is delightful. There are square pews, and a three-decker pulpit, and many pleasant Langham monuments. The squire's pew is in a sort of gallery in a transept, with charming turned balusters along its front and up the staircase leading to it. In the gallery there are a set of chairs for the family, and a fireplace. Curtains make the occupants invisible to people in the church below. A few days later I was dining with a friend in this neighbourhood, and spoke of this church and this pew. And I was told a local story. About eighty years ago one Sunday the Rector chanced to make a pause in his sermon. And in the moment of quiet the squire's voice was heard to say—"Damn it, George! Why did you lead trumps?"

That would not do for the stately Sir Thomas Bertram. But it may have been Tom after he succeeded to his father.

At Lincoln there was a very beautiful Assize Service in the Cathedral on Sunday. Two of the senior choir boys wear copes: this is an ancient tradition at Lincoln, and I believe there alone in England. I thought it might have some connexion with the election of a boy-bishop, but I was told it was not so.

At Nottingham the Foreman of the Grand Jury was, as usual, that remarkable man, Sir Lancelot Rolleston, who had played so many parts with distinction. He won the D.S.O. in the South African War, he was Master of Hounds for many years, he was at this time a most efficient Chairman of the County Council and Chairman of Quarter Sessions, and he was High Sheriff of the county in 1877—when I was six years old!

We were lodged at Nottingham in the same villa in the Park. I was not there much, as I spent several nights at a hospitable and delightful house with a former High Sheriff. Collins's almshouses, that pleasant old building in the street leading from the market-place to the Castle, had been repainted, but three words on it in Greek had been too much for the painter, and apparently no one had put him right. Ἀποθανὼν ἔτι λαλεῖ was the text, in capitals. But the third word was strangely disguised as AAAEI. I wonder if two dabs of paint to delete the cross bar in two of the A's have ever been applied.

The Castle Museum I have always found interesting. Of the permanent exhibits I think the old Baskerville carriages are the most remarkable. At this time, as Clumber was shut up, eighty-three of the pictures from that great house were on loan, and very fine they were. It is an ill wind that blows no one any good, and the citizens of Nottingham profited by the death duties that had temporarily eclipsed the Dukedom of Newcastle. Vandyck, Rubens, Rembrandt, Quentin Matsys, Teniers, Correggio, Canaletto, Holbein, Lely, Hogarth, Reynolds, Gainsborough, and Romney—all these great ones were in the collection, and many lesser ones. I think the three pictures I most coveted were Holbein's portrait of a cleric, "The Return from Shooting", by Francis Wheatley, R.A., and a charming little picture of Mr Hope of Amsterdam playing cricket.

It is only 16 miles from Nottingham to Derby, and all prisoners for trial at Derby, if not on bail, are brought there from Nottingham prison. If it were not for county pride (in its way as troublesome as nationalism) these two counties might have a joint Assize, to be held alternately at one or the other. The immediate result of the nearness of the two cities was that my marshal and I did the journey on foot—through Wollaton Park, avoiding Stanton and its hideous ironworks, by Dale Abbey, Morley, and Breadsall.

It was on this occasion that I found the last of the Fettiplaces in his shop, and had a talk with him. Wollaton church was open this time: there are some Willoughby monuments, but not very good ones. The ruins of Dale Abbey are not remarkable, but the minute church is extraordinary. It is said to have been the chapel of the Infirmary, and it is strangely mixed up with a small house, of which the upper storey is partly above it. There is curious woodwork, with some old pews, and the communion table is set with the narrow ends to East and West in the old puritan fashion. I have rarely seen so strange a little church. Farther on we came to Morley: the north aisle of the church had some beautiful glass that was said to have been brought from Dale Abbey. And the same aisle is full of monuments of Sacheverells and Sitwells. There were traces of the vanished house of one of these families in the grass to the west of the church.

The lightness of the calendar at Derby provided me with a holiday, on which I made an expedition to Ashbourne. It has a noble church and the Cokayne and Boothby monuments are very fine. A little east of the church is the fine Georgian house where the great Dr Taylor used to live in opulence, and Johnson used to stay. It now belongs to Dr Sadler, and I have been told he is as good a Johnsonian as he is hospitable to other Johnsonians. If I had known that, I might have been tempted to knock at his door, and hope to find excuse in the facts that I was President of the Johnson Club of London in 1925, President of the Johnson Society of Lichfield in 1933, and am a Trustee of the Johnson House in Gough Square. As it was I did not think I could intrude on a stranger at ten in the morning. Through the side windows of the front door, and from the back, I could see the great circular room, of which Boswell records the lighting up on one occasion. Nearly opposite is the grammar school where the Rev. William Langley played so scandalous a part as Head Master, and was such a trouble to the Rev. Dr Taylor.*

The High Sheriff of Derbyshire was Mr H. S. Bagshawe of Ford Hall near Chapel-en-le-Frith. The Bagshawes have been there for centuries. We went to lunch with him on Sunday. One of the oldest things in his ancient house was a horn, and by virtue of its possession the Bagshawes have been privileged to appoint the Coroner for a surrounding Liberty. Jervis, *On Coroners* (7th ed. p. 17), says: "An unusual tenure of the office of Coroner was by virtue of the possession of a horn. For instance, the family of Achard formerly held by inheritance, as owners of a horn, the offices of Feodary or Bailiff in fee [i.e. hereditary Steward] of the two royal Manors of East and West Leake in Nottinghamshire, Escheator, Coroner, and Clerk of the Market of the Honour of Tutbury. The horn...was an instrument of summons similar to that in use at the present day at the Middle Temple for summoning to the Hall. The 'Cornicularius', or Sergeant of the Horn, calls the Moots and public assemblies at the Cinque Ports, and a similar use is still made at Canterbury for summoning the Burgmote Court."

Horns as symbols of tenure (Cornage) occur elsewhere. The famous one at Pusey in Berkshire was the subject-matter of the action *Pusey* v. *Pusey* (1684) 1 Vern. 273. There is a similar horn at Dorton House in Buckinghamshire. At Hungerford the town has an ancient horn, which is used in the festivities of Hocktide (which means the Second Monday and Tuesday after Easter day), and is supposed to have been the gift of John of Gaunt.

Unfortunately Mr Bagshawe will not be able to appoint another Coroner. For sect. 4 of the Coroners Amendment Act 1926 provides:

* See Boswell's *Life* (Powell's 2nd ed. of Birkbeck Hill, 1934), Vol. III, p. 494. I regret to say that Langley was a member of Trinity College, Oxford.

"The right of any person having power to appoint a franchise coroner shall cease on the next vacancy in the office which occurs after the passing of this Act."

I walked out to Markeaton Hall, the old home of the Mundys, one afternoon. In the previous year the Corporation of Derby had bought it for a public park, and it was being laid out for that. The fine red-brick Georgian house had evidently been empty for a long time, and had a woeful look: the ivy was forcing its way through the windows. When I looked into the Derby Picture Gallery there were other relics of the Mundys, in the shape of pictures from Markeaton. A set of six fox hunters, portraits by Wright of Derby, were charming: they included the Sir Lancelot Rolleston of that day, and Sir Francis Burdett.

Judges' Lodgings in a county town are the concern of the Standing Joint Committee of Quarter Sessions and the County Council. I have sometimes wished that that august body might be assisted by a sub-committee with some pretensions to taste, and with some lady members. When there is a question of redecorating the Lodgings, or buying some furniture, I can only imagine, judging by the results, that the Committee instruct a builder to do the work, and leave all questions of style and colour to him, or tell a furniture shop to send round a piece of furniture of his own selection. The Derby house had been repainted, but with the most appalling colours. As for pictures, there was in the dining-room the fine Reinagle portrait of a Mundy, and in my bedroom the charming mezzotint I mentioned earlier. In the sitting-room, this year and last, there was a ghastly display of so-called water-colours and chromo-lithographs. But I noticed that this year these egregious adornments were not the same as last year, though equally bad. I asked the Under-Sheriff about this, and, with some shamefacedness, he said that normally there were no pictures on the walls. But they had an arrangement with a local shop that, when the Judge was coming, it should send round and hang some "pictures", being paid 15*s.* a time! This does not seem to me a satisfactory plan. Let the Chairmen of other Standing Joint Committees go to Stafford, and there observe, and envy, the magnificent collections of Staffordshire prints, both views and portraits, collected for the Lodgings, and the adjacent County Council offices, by Mr Joy.

Another illustration of the same lack of judgment in matters of taste

I noticed at the Derby Lodgings. In my bedroom was a dreadful "suite" of bedroom furniture, not cheap, I expect, but certainly nasty. Out in the passage, near the bathroom, was a really fine eighteenth-century wardrobe, that might have been made by Chippendale himself. I spoke of this admiringly to the housekeeper. She said it was hers. It used to be in the Judge's bedroom, but was turned out when the abominable "suite" was purchased. Someone in authority said they must get rid of this old thing, and the housekeeper could have it if she liked.

Another thing the arbiters of taste might do would be to check the well-meant, but often misguided, ideas of the Housekeeper. At Warwick, on my earlier visits, on the top of the stairs in the passage to the drawing-room, there used to be ranged on either side a row of aspidistras in flower pots draped in crinkly green paper. I think they disappeared because I wrote something in the Visitors' Book about this "Aspidistra Avenue" that was not exactly complimentary. The most bucolic member of the Standing Joint Committee would hardly stand this sort of thing in his own home, or the hired "pictures", or even the Nottingham lace curtains, that adorned the Derby Lodgings. And it is rather hard that the Judge should have to endure them.

I finished at Warwick on 20 November, and went home. To complete the circuit I ought to have gone to Birmingham in December. But there were some cases in the Railway and Canal Commission Court, in which I was Ex-officio Commissioner. It is provided by sect. 5(5) of the Railway and Canal Traffic Act 1888 that "the judge... assigned to hold the office of Ex-officio Commissioner... shall be required to perform any of the other duties of a judge... only when his attendance on the Commission is not required". I have heard that one of my predecessors in the office, who disliked going on circuit, was able to avoid doing so by a judicious arrangement of the times for Railway Court cases. As I liked going on circuit it was only rarely that I was constrained to stay in, or return to, town for them. On this occasion it was necessary, and accordingly the Lord Chancellor appointed the late Mr Mitchell Innes, K.C., to be Commissioner of Assize at Birmingham, and I stayed in town.

The Midland Circuit is, I think, the only one about which a book has been expressly written. This is *Random Recollections of the Midland Circuit* (2 vols. 1869 and 1873). The author, Robert Walton, was not a barrister but a newspaper reporter who was specially attached to the circuit to report cases. He began his attendance in 1833. It is a poor book, with the usual sort of stories about trials, judges, and barristers. I have managed to read through the two volumes but without much entertainment, and certainly with no profit.

1931

In January 1931 I was booked to go on the North Wales Circuit. Ordinarily this means going to Welshpool, Dolgelley, Carnarvon, Beaumaris, Ruthin, Mold, Chester, and Cardiff. Enquiry shortly before I was to start for Welshpool elicited that there were no prisoners committed for trial, and no civil cases entered for hearing, at either Welshpool, Dolgelley, Beaumaris, Ruthin, or Mold. Under my own limited powers, by Act of Parliament, I could only cancel each of these Assizes if the same state of things existed five days before the commission day for each of them. This might involve my starting off for Wales, and then having periods of enforced idleness which were not long enough to make it feasible to return for work in London. So I informed the Lord Chief Justice of the facts, as above, with a view to his making an order, with the concurrence of the Lord Chancellor, under sect. 77 of the Supreme Court of Judicature Consolidation Act 1925. It was no part of my duty, or of the duty of any Circuit official, so to inform him; and if I had not done so, of course he would have known nothing about it.

As I did inform him he very properly, with the concurrence of the Lord Chancellor, made an order suppressing the Assizes at these five towns. It was a necessary formality in that order to provide that if any business should turn up at any of them it should be transferred elsewhere. And accordingly the order provided that any business at Dolgelley or Beaumaris should be transferred to Carnarvon, and any business at Welshpool, Ruthin, or Mold should be transferred to Chester.

This order caused a tremendous fuss in Wales. All sorts of public bodies passed indignant resolutions of protest about the suppression of Welsh Assizes, and much fervid rhetoric was emitted. The part of the order transferring Welsh trials, or cases, to Chester was seized upon as the crowning outrage, and harrowing pictures were drawn of unhappy monoglot Welshmen being at the mercy of English juries! In fact, of course, nothing of the sort happened: there was no business transferred to Chester. But the affair gave a great opportunity for heated declamation.

The result of the order thus wisely made was that I was able to stay a fortnight doing serious work in London, instead of idling about in Wales, while London litigants had to wait for a judge to try their cases. At Carnarvon there were four prisoners for trial, and three civil cases. So I allotted four working days at Carnarvon, and travelled there on Monday, 26 January. Next morning three of the four prisoners pleaded guilty, and one was tried and acquitted. It was also announced that one of the civil cases was settled, and in another an application was made, to which I had to accede, to postpone it, as the defendant was in hospital. So my work on the Tuesday was 2½ hours before lunch. Next morning they settled the remaining case before the jury was sworn, and in a quarter of an hour I was back in the Lodgings. In this week, therefore, I did less than 3 hours judicial work, while any of my colleagues remaining in London did 25 hours.

As I was due to go to Chester on the Saturday it was, of course, useless to go back to London, and I had the Thursday and Friday as complete holidays. On the Thursday my marshal and I drove to Llanberis for a walk on Snowdon. There were clouds all above about 1500 feet, and we could not safely try to find one of the paths. So we walked up the track of the rack and pinion railway, a track you could not miss. We got to the top, and lunched in the shelter of the crazy wooden inn, which was almost buried in snow. It was very cold up there. Every post and notice board had horizontal icicles, up to 18 inches long, standing out at right angles and pointing to the north-east, the creation of gales from the south-west. There was no view above about 1700 feet, but only rolling cloud. There was never any danger of losing the railway track, though in places the snow was very deep upon it.

The Friday was a glorious day of frost and sunshine, and the clouds were gone. So we thought we would try Snowdon again, and this time from the south by the ordinary path. We drove to Pen-y-pass, and started up to the lake, where the disused mining works are. I had not seen before the pipes from that lake for some generating station in the valley—just like those I had so often seen in the Pyrenees. Whether the level of the lake has been raised in connexion with these works, or it was merely the result of winter floods, I do not know, but the causeway across the lake was submerged, and we had to go all round the edge of the lake to the east. We did not get to the top of the mountain. There was such a thick coating of ice on the rocks above about 2500 feet that we thought it too risky to go on, especially as we had not proper climbing boots. But the sunshine was glorious, and we lunched in it on the snow, with a magnificent view to the south.

When we got out of the car in the morning at Pen-y-pass a rough-haired sheep-dog, lying in the sun outside the inn, greeted us with effusion. He had lost one of his hind legs. But he went with us the whole day, and left us only when we came down again to the inn. I hope he enjoyed the outing as much as I did.

At Chester, where I joined Mr Justice Humphreys, we were lodged again in that pleasant house, Heronbridge, on the Eccleston road. The work at Chester, and also at Cardiff, was light, and I got back to London on Ash Wednesday, 18 February. My total working hours on the whole of this circuit were just under 50, while a judge who had remained in town would have done about 90.

◇ ◇ ◇

In the summer of 1931 I went again on the North-Eastern Circuit, and travelled to York with Lord Finlay on 17 June. This was a variation from the usual procedure, which was made necessary by the date of the Newcastle races. We went to York, Durham, Newcastle, Leeds, instead of Durham, Newcastle, York, Leeds, as is usual in the summer.

York was as pleasant as ever, and as hospitable. The Lord Mayor's breakfast provided for the other guests that spectacle which can be seen nowhere else in the world—two elderly gentlemen, in scarlet robes and full-bottomed wigs, eating bacon and eggs to the strains of a string band!

We lunched with the Archbishop and Mrs Temple at Bishopsthorpe on the Sunday, and we had tea one day at the Deanery. After tea the Dean (Ford) took me into his study. I looked up at the wall, and said: "How do you come to have portraits of Gray and Mason here?" The aspect of Gray is unmistakeable, while the Mason appeared to be a copy of the well-known Reynolds' portrait that is, I think, at Pembroke College, Cambridge. The Dean said these pictures were official heirlooms of the Deanery, and were supposed to have been given by Mason, who was made a Canon of York in 1762.

My friend, Dr Paget Toynbee, who lived near me in Buckinghamshire, knew more about Gray than anyone, and was at this time at work on an edition of Gray's Letters, afterwards completed by Mr Leonard Whibley. When I got home I asked Dr Toynbee if he knew about this portrait at York, and found that he did not. So the Dean had the picture photographed and sent a copy to Toynbee. He found it very interesting. For it is one of the portraits of Gray which Mason engaged Benjamin Wilson to paint after Gray's death. It is similar to the Pembroke portrait, but shows Gray with his profile to the right. Mason was a versatile person: he was not a bad artist, a good deal of his poetry is still readable, he composed music, and he invented a musical instrument called the Celestina.

When we went on to Durham I found that it was still thought improper to allow me, as senior judge, to use the two charming rooms at the north end of the Castle, because of the possibility of that part slipping down the hill. I had no fear of that, and happening to meet Canon Ellershaw, Master of University College, which occupies other parts of the Castle, I asked him whether I might not occupy the rooms at my own risk. He consented, and I went there, and of course nothing happened. About a fortnight before, at 1.20 a.m. on Sunday, 7 June, there was an earthquake felt all over England. It woke some of my family, but not me, in Buckinghamshire. I think the greatest disturbance was in the North. I was told that when it happened at Durham it caused great alarm for the Castle. But when they came to examine the pieces of glass that were cemented everywhere across cracks in the stonework, not a single one of them was found to be broken.

And so to Newcastle. The Lord Mayor's dinner, or (if it may be so called) our dinner to the Lord Mayor, was as pleasant as usual, and I was enriched by a fine Jacobus. On another evening we dined at the Officers' Mess of the joint depot of the Northumberland Fusiliers and the Durham Light Infantry.

I ought to have gone on to Leeds. But again there happened to be some cases in the Railway and Canal Commission Court for which I was wanted in London. So the Lord Chancellor appointed Mr Rayner Goddard, K.C. to be Special Commissioner at Leeds. He was made a Judge of the King's Bench Division about nine months later. I was not sorry to escape going to Leeds. My only regrets were the loss of another fortnight of Lord Finlay's companionship, and of the possibility that Lord and Lady Moynihan might have asked me to dinner again at Carr Manor.

◇ ◇ ◇

In the autumn of 1931 I was again on the Midland Circuit, and went to Aylesbury on 12 October. Quarter Sessions had been held there on that day, but the work was not finished. Lord Cottesloe, the Chairman, had written to me beforehand, asking what should be done if this happened. I said I should be glad if they would sit in the second Court on the opening day of the Assize. This they did, and there was the unusual occurrence of Assizes and Quarter Sessions being held simultaneously in the same building. As it happened I was qualified to sit in either Court.

The High Sheriff of Buckinghamshire was Major Coningsby Disraeli, of Hughenden. He was a very picturesque figure, as he wore the old full-dress uniform of the Bucks Yeomanry, resplendent with silver lace. In the course of my 12½ years in the King's Bench Division I reckon that I have had to do with 174 High Sheriffs. The majority of them, of course, wore black velvet court suits. But I have seen a great and pleasing variety of uniforms. Some were magnificent as Deputy-Lieutenants. How many different regimental uniforms there were I have no idea, but they were very numerous. One, being a retired Ambassador, wore diplomatic uniform, and one the uniform of the Royal Household. One was a Rear-Admiral, another a Captain R.N., and one a Captain R.N.R. The last mentioned appeared in a small rural county, and he puzzled me very much. He was a charming man, and I soon found that he had been for years in the service of a great steamship line. He knew that, at the bar, I had had much to do with shipping; I think he even claimed that I had once cross-examined him in the Commercial Court. Except on the supposition that he had inherited a fortune, I could not think how he came to be playing, very admirably, the part of a prosperous country gentleman. When I lunched with some friends in the neighbourhood I asked them about him. And they told me that a few years before he had won the Calcutta Sweep! I cannot believe that anyone who had that stroke of luck used the winnings so well.

I find an old precedent for this nautical Sheriff. Mr Justice Rokeby writes in his *Diary* at Stowmarket, March 1694/5: "The High Sheriff had been an old Master of a Ship, and bought a good estate in this county, and was very rich."

I have never known a High Sheriff appear otherwise than in uniform or in court dress. In Huddleston's *Circuit Notes* he frequently records, with asperity, that the Sheriff was "not in uniform" or "in morning dress". I gather that he always protested, and he sometimes records a promise of amendment. His time as a judge was 1875 to 1890.

I had two days' work at Aylesbury, and then drove to Bedford through Olney. On the way I stopped to look at Willen church. It is a pleasant little Palladian building, that would look very much at home in the City, and would be attributed to Wren. In fact it was designed by Robert Hooke (1635–1703), who was a Fellow, and Secretary, of the Royal Society, and a considerable scientist (see the *Dictionary of National Biography*). He was educated at Westminster, under the great Doctor Busby, and at Christchurch. Busby owned a considerable property at Willen (which is now owned by the Busby Trustees) and he was minded to rebuild the church. So in 1680 he employed his former pupil Hooke as his architect. All the fittings in the church, panelling, pews, small organ case, communion rails, and doors, are of the admirable woodwork that one finds in Wren's churches. From the western tower a straight avenue of limes leads to the Rectory, built at the same time. On one side of the tower is a room in which a library of some 600 books, given by Busby, was once kept: they are said to be now in the Rectory.

Tempora mutantur. The Rev. William Cole, Rector of Bletchley, and friend of Horace Walpole, wrote in his journal on 4 November 1767: "Mr Lord told me that as he was out with Mr Ja. Cartwright a-Coursing to Day they met with some Newport people, and brought them to dinner to Mr Cartwright's, & that they were now pretty drunk, among whom the Rr of Willen, Mr Shipton, was so bad that he was forced to be put to Bed."

Bedford provided me with an agreeable surprise. On previous occasions there I had been lodged in an unattractive villa. This time we went to a country house, about a mile to the east of the town, which had been lent to the county by its owner. He was as fortunate as he was public spirited. For it was a delightful Queen Anne house in a miniature park. I was never in pleasanter quarters except at Mold. The gentleman's final politeness was to leave for me a brace of partridges, with a note hoping, very unnecessarily, that I should be comfortable. I was, indeed, and my only regret was that I could only stay there for two nights. For the work, light as usual at Bedford, was finished easily in two days.

For Northampton, in consultation with the Clerk of Assize as to its probable needs, I had allowed two working days. When the Commission was opened, there were only three prisoners. Two of them pleaded guilty. The third was tried and the whole business was finished by 4 o'clock on the first day. After this experience at Bedford and Northampton I confess I thought again, as I did a year ago, that, in the autumn, if not at all times, a joint Assize for the two counties might be arranged with public advantage.

The Assize Service in the parish church at Northampton was a striking contrast to that at Bedford. Here there was a choir, that sang admirably, and even a congregation. At Bedford there was no choir, and no one in the church except our official selves. And we were called upon to sing a hymn, which of course was a farce.

I looked again into the second court at Northampton. It was really lamentable to see it so degraded. A coarse wooden partition ran across the noble room, and cut through the middle of its splendid plaster ceiling. The outer half seemed to be used to house bicycles; the inner half was used as a police court. If they cleared away the partition, restored the ceiling, and cleaned up the whole chamber, they might have just such a noble hall, as an ante-room to the Assize Court, as they have at Warwick.

I sighed as a judge, but as a man I rejoiced, at my enforced idle day at Northampton. I had in that county a good friend who was High Sheriff on my first visit there. Then, and on each subsequent visit, he took trouble to give me the opportunity of seeing the places of interest with which Northamptonshire abounds. On a previous occasion he had taken me to see Boughton, and on this he took me to Drayton House. I do not know which was the more interesting. Boughton, the vast mansion of the Duke of Buccleugh, near Kettering, was built about 1690 by Ralph Montagu, who was eventually created Duke of Montagu in 1706. He had been ambassador in France, and Versailles inspired him to rebuild his family seat on a gigantic scale. So he did, but it was too gigantic even for him: one of the huge wings on the north front is a vast open space, with a roof and windows, but no floors or partitions. He, and his son, the second Duke, adorned the house and its surroundings magnificently. The gardens have disappeared, but immense avenues, running for miles across the park and the country beyond, with the house as their focus, mostly survive. The Montagu line ended with an heiress who married the Duke of Buccleugh in 1767. As the fortunes of three dukedoms came to be united in that of Buccleugh, they had many houses to live in, and Boughton has not been much occupied. This had the result that its furniture, pictures, tapestries, painted ceilings, and other treasures remain very much as they were in 1700. To be taken all over it, as I was, was a rare privilege.

Drayton was different, but equally interesting. It has one of the best formal gardens surviving in England, and the Tijou iron-work on the garden stairways is as fine as that at Hampton Court. The house is wonderfully picturesque, and is filled with beautiful things. There was once a time when the Duke of Dorset owned both Drayton and Knole: for one human being to own two such houses was surely tempting the vengeance of Fate.

When we went on to Leicester I repeated the walk from Brixworth to Market Harborough, going through Cottesbrooke, and then by a grass-grown road through Maidwell and Arthingworth. It was fitting that, in the Pytchley country, as we neared Maidwell a great fox got up from the grass just ahead of us and trotted away down the lane, turning at intervals to look at us.

For Leicester I had allotted nine working days, and there was work that kept me busy throughout them. There was a strange charge of murder against a hospital nurse, who, never having shown the least sign of abnormality before, had suddenly poured boiling water over her unfortunate lady patient. She was rightly found "Guilty but Insane", that illogical verdict that is said to be due to the *amour propre* of Queen Victoria. But the longest case of all (one of the longest criminal cases I ever tried) was that of a Leicester stockbroker, who for years had been well known to everyone who received his incessant circulars. And every one did receive them: I believe that for many years he paid about £1000 a week to the Post Office.

This was October 1931, when a desperate financial crisis had just overcome the nation. After the Grand Jury had been discharged their foreman, Sir Arthur Hazlerigg, came to see me, and brought me this letter:

23 Oct. 1931.

My Lord

We, sitting as the Grand Jury for the County of Leicester, beg to submit to you a resolution that in these times of financial crisis, when every possible economy should be exercised, we should support the suspension of the calling of Grand Juries, both for Assizes and Quarter Sessions, for one or two years, if His Majesty's Judges so advise.

ARTHUR HAZLERIGG, *Chairman.*

As the Grand Jury had dispersed I could only tell Sir Arthur that I would forward the resolution to the Lord Chancellor and the Lord Chief Justice. He told me that this resolution was passed with only two dissentients. But he also told me that another resolution was passed unanimously, viz. that the Grand Jury desired to intimate to the High Sheriff that for the rest of his year of office they hoped he would not put himself to the expense of giving them luncheon.

Sir Arthur Hazlerigg, in Leicestershire, was perhaps even more of a pluralist than Sir Lancelot Rolleston in Nottinghamshire. For besides being Lord-Lieutenant, Chairman of the County Council, and Chairman of Quarter Sessions, he had also been for years captain of the county cricket team. Sir Arthur is the 13th Baronet. One of the treasures of his house, Noseley Hall, is a portrait of Cromwell given by him to Sir Arthur Hesilrige (as the more usual spelling then was), who was one of the five members in 1642, and fought at Edgehill later in that year. He was spared at the Restoration, but died in the Tower in 1661. I believe the Hazleriggs are really a Durham family, and came into Leicestershire by marriage with an heiress of Noseley. But that was at the end of the fourteenth century. In a few more centuries, with heads of the family serving as chairmen and cricketers, they will doubtless be recognized as really and truly Leicestershire people.

On my last day at Leicester I had a free afternoon. There is so little left of antiquity or picturesqueness in the city that I was glad to find two good houses out by Belgrave church, one, dated 1713 on its excellent lead water-spouts, with a fine iron gateway; and a Georgian house on the other side of the road. All around is a waste of dinginess.

And so to Lincoln. We had service in the Cathedral on the first day of the Assize. When it finished and we got to the West door, rain was falling in torrents. A car cannot drive close up to the door, and in this downpour we should have been soaked in the short walk to it. The Mayor and City Sheriff were in attendance to conduct me to the city Court. But there were no City prisoners, so the Commission was not to be opened, and I was only going to the Court to be informed officially of this fact, express my congratulations to the city, and receive a pair of white gloves. As we waited for the rain to abate a little, someone happily suggested that we might transact this piece of ceremonial in the Consistory Court at the south-west end of the nave. I asked the Dean if he could allow this, and he said he would be glad for us to do so. So we proceeded to the Consistory Court, I took my seat on the bench, the Sheriff spoke his piece and gave me the gloves, and I made a few remarks. When we had finished, the rain was over, and I went off to the Castle.

That is the only occasion on which I have ever sat in a Consistory Court! When I was at the bar I used sometimes to regret that no one ever regarded me as in the least qualified to be a Chancellor of a Diocese. I should have been very much interested in the duty of controlling the issue of faculties for restorations or adornments of ancient churches.

This may not have been the first occasion on which a Judge of Assize sat in part of the Cathedral. Walton, *Random Recollections of the Midland Circuit* (1869, Vol. I, p. 31) says that the present courts in the Castle at Lincoln were opened in 1826, and that while they were building the *nisi prius* cases were heard in the Chapter House.

It is a pleasant tradition at Lincoln that the Bishop and the Dean take it in turns to entertain the Judge at dinner at successive Assizes. On this occasion it was the Bishop's turn. By his permission, and that of Mrs Swayne, I went without a wig, gown, and knee-breeches, and a pleasant evening was thereby made all the pleasanter for me.

For the week-end my marshal and I stayed with the High Sheriff near Newark. On the Sunday, which was 8 November, we all drove to the Armistice Day service at the Air Force camp at Cranwell. Their church was made out of an enormous hangar, that would hold some 2000 people, and it was filled. Music was provided by a wonderful band. The Archbishop of York preached a fine sermon. At the end of the service came one of the most impressive things I ever heard. The band had a vast number of kettledrums. As we all stood in silence, one drum began a faint tap, growing louder—and louder still as others joined in, until there was a thunderous noise: then *diminuendo* until it came back to the single faint tap—and then silence. Three times this was done, quite perfectly. But at the third time there was a sudden and instantaneous silence at the middle of the central thunder. And then, in that silence, there was heard a single bugle, some distance away outside the church, playing the Last Post, faintly but clearly. And then final silence.

And so to Nottingham. The house in the Park, that I had been to before, was no longer available, and we were lodged in another house in the same region. It was Victorian in architecture and furnishing, inconceivably ugly, and rather depressing.

I used always to be rather at a loss to know what to say to a Grand Jury. But as they were being called I was glad to see a familiar figure in the gallery, and I thought of, at any rate, an exordium. My clerk, according to the ritual, said: "Gentlemen, are you all sworn? My Lords the King's Justices do strictly charge and command all persons to keep silence whilst the charge is given to this Grand Jury upon pain of fine and imprisonment." Then I said: "Gentlemen of the Grand Jury. I am glad to greet you as the representatives of this County of Nottingham. The rest of you will, I am sure, forgive me, if I say that I am particularly pleased to see your distinguished Foreman, I might almost say your perpetual Foreman, looking as vigorous as ever, and with a straighter back than the youngest of you."

My impertinence was forgiven. Lady Maud Rolleston asked me to dinner.

There were only six prisoners at Nottingham, and they were all convicted or acquitted by lunch-time on the Saturday. In the afternoon my son, who was with me as marshal, and I went for a walk along the banks of the Trent. Somewhere near the river a very friendly dog, of doubtful pedigree, joined us and intimated very clearly that he was coming with us. He paid no attention to our orders to him to go home, and as the highway is as free to dogs as to men, we had to let him come. By a big lock, where we watched a barge coming up, he invited a canine friend to join the party, but after a time this one did obey us and turned back. Eventually we arrived at Radcliffe-on-Trent, whence we proposed to return by train. I bought two tickets, and said to the man, "There is a dog here who, I think, wants to go to Nottingham, so you had better give me a ticket for him". Not being desirous of being suspected of dog-stealing, we made no effort to keep him with us. But he understood the position thoroughly, and led the way for us into an open carriage. When we got back to Nottingham we began to wonder if he would insist on accompanying us for the rest of the circuit. So we played a trick on him. My son engaged his attention, while I walked away to the Lodgings, and then he walked with the dog down to Bridge Street, where he had first joined us: and there he managed to lose him in the crowd. I believe he enjoyed his afternoon; of course he shared our tea at Radcliffe.

On the Monday we had to go to Derby. That is only 16 miles from Nottingham, but it is hard to find a rural way by which to walk. We tried a new one with some success, starting out over Widford Bridge, by Clifton Grove to Clifton and so to Barton-in-Fabis. In the church there were some interesting Sacheverell tombs. And so by the fields to Thrumpton, Ratcliffe on Soar, and Kegworth, where we had luncheon and then took a train to Derby via Trent Junction.

At Derby I was faced with 39 prisoners. The proneness of Derbyshire to indictable offences is remarkable. Nottingham in 1931 had a population of 641,134 and Derbyshire 714,539. Derbyshire may console itself by a belief in the greater efficiency of its police force, but the fact remains that there seemed always to be far more prisoners at Derby than at Nottingham. On this Assize Nottingham had 6 and Derby 39.

As I had only five working days for Derby, I was glad on the second day to enlist Maurice Healy, K.C., who was in the Commission as a Circuit Leader, to join me at the Lodgings and sit in a second Court. He did so for four days, so that we finished all the work by five o'clock on the Saturday afternoon. It was only fair to let him have in his Court the only amusing case. A miner was charged with obtaining money by false pretences. Living in a four-roomed cottage he called it "—— Hall", with a board bearing that name fixed over the door. He then advertised to this effect—"Lieut.-Col. Farquharson has a few pedigree Airedales for sale. Healthy dog puppies, 5 guineas. Apply Head-Gamekeeper, —— Hall." Guineas were sent, and dogs were sent in return, but their connexion with Airedale was said to be unrecognizable. I believe, however, they were charming mongrels, whom their purchasers came to love, though they deplored their price. Several of the dogs were produced in Court, and enlivened the proceedings. The man defended himself, not without ability, and with some sense of humour. "There was nothing to prevent his calling his house '—— Hall', if he liked. There was nothing illegal in his carrying on business as 'Lieut.-Col. Farquharson'; in fact he had registered the name under the Business Names Act." And so forth. I think he was convicted, but I believe the learned Commissioner thought that his dogs were so engaging that he gave him only a light sentence.

With all this work to do there was not much time for diversions. But I dined with the bar, and rejoiced again after dinner at the performance of their famous mimic.

When I was due to go to Warwick it occurred to me that I had never been to Coventry, and that I might repair that omission on the way. And so, by changing at Birmingham, I did, and had five or six hours there. It was well worth a tiresome journey. St Michael's is magnificent, and Trinity church very fine. I suppose as a parish church St Michael's was the biggest in England except Great Yarmouth: architecturally it is much finer than Yarmouth, though not as fine as St Mary Redcliffe. No church, I think, can have so large a proportion of window space in its walls. The scale of enrichment of this church—in what is said to have been, after London, Norwich, and Bristol, the fourth city in the kingdom—is shown by its possession of fourteen bells in its great tower. I believe they can only be chimed, but not rung, for fear of the vibration. Trinity church has eight bells, in a wooden belfry in the churchyard. What a place Coventry might have been, if the great Priory church had survived alongside them! Lastly, St Mary's Hall is full of interest. I had that sense of the middle ages that one gets so often in France, but in England only in a few cities like Norwich, Exeter, Bristol, and Coventry. Oxford has it differently: the borough there counts for little; in these it is insistent.

At Warwick there were only five prisoners, and one day disposed of them. Next morning I went to see the Beauchamp Chapel once again after breakfast, and then drove home.

The usual interlude followed until I went to Birmingham. There were there only 10 prisoners from Warwickshire, so that Warwick and Birmingham together had only 15 as against the 39 at Derby. But there were also 3 prisoners committed to the Birmingham Assizes from Spalding in Lincolnshire, on a charge of forging cheques and thereby swindling a local bank. This was under the modern act which enables prisoners to be committed for trial to any convenient Assize, if the proper county Assize is not available for some time. This very sensible legislation has of course entirely abandoned the old strict rule* that a man must be tried "by God and my country", i.e. by a jury of the county in which his offence was committed. And the abandonment of that principle, I think, lends force to the suggestions I have ventured to make that efficiency would be secured, and the waste of judicial time avoided, if counties were grouped together for a joint Assize, e.g. Northampton and Bedford, possibly Nottingham and Derby, and, undoubtedly and above all, among the little counties in Wales.

* It was because of this rule that in 1745 there was passed a special Act (19 Geo. II, cap. 9), empowering the King to issue commissions for trying the Scottish rebels in any county of the Kingdom, "in the same manner as if the Treasons had been committed in that county". After Culloden, pursuant to this Act, a Commission of Oyer and Terminer, and Gaol Delivery for the County of Surrey passed the Great Seal in June 1746. It was addressed to every Privy Councillor by name, to all the Judges, and to some others, and empowered them, or any three of them, to execute it. Sir William Lee presided at the Court in Southwark, and Lord Kilmarnock, Lord Cromartie, Lord Balmerino, Colonel Towneley, and many others were tried. (See Michael Foster's *Report*, Oxford, 1742.) I think the Commission at Carlisle to which I referred, *supra*, p. 4, must have been issued under this Act: for prisoners at Carlisle were tried for acts none of which were done in Cumberland.

1932

In 1932 I remained in London for Hilary and Easter terms, and only on Monday, 30 May, went to Newtown, Montgomery, on the North Wales Circuit. I had not been there before, but I had not missed much. It is an ugly little town: the parish church, to which I went for the Assize Service, must have been built about 1850. In a competition for the most hideous church in Great Britain it would stand a good chance of a prize, or at the least very honourable mention.

There were only three prisoners, and one civil case with a special jury. The whole business was over on the first day. Dolgelley had provided no work at all, so after spending two nights at Newtown I went back to London, as I was not due at Carnarvon till the following Sunday. The uninstructed might ask me why, when I cancelled the Dolgelley Assize, I did not postpone that at Newtown, so as to go on from there to Carnarvon. The answer is that the provisions made by the wisdom of Parliament made this impracticable. By Act of Parliament a judge was only authorized to cancel an Assize if five days before its Commission Day there was no work in prospect there. This fifth day before Dolgelley's Commission Day was Saturday, 28 May. If I had then telegraphed to the Under-Sheriff of Montgomery that his Assize was postponed, I should have put him to enormous trouble. For he had, of course, made all the arrangements for the opening of the Assize at Newtown on the Tuesday. Letters, or even telegrams, would have had to go to Grand Jurors, special jurors, and common jurors, probably about sixty-five in all. And a great many other things would have had to be rearranged as well. In this legislation I cannot think that Parliament, for all its wisdom, remembered that there is a chronic lack of judges to try cases in London with reasonable dispatch, and that consequently every effort should be made to prevent judges wasting their time in attendance upon pampered provincials.

So I sat in London on the Thursday and Friday. But two isolated days like this are not of much use. For one can only take short cases, that are sure to finish in the limited time available: probably, though I do not remember, I had only a short day's work on the Friday.

As the Saturday was George III's birthday, I spent it at Eton, and on the Sunday went to Carnarvon. I always resent having to go into London, and come out again, and avoid it if I can. I managed this by taking a morning train from Beaconsfield to Rugby on the old Great Central Line, and there driving across to the L.M.S. station. I had never been in Rugby before. I lunched near the School and had a look at its buildings. And that was a shock. I had conceived a pretty mean opinion of Butterfield before, but not even Keble had made me realize what he could do if he tried!

At Carnarvon I was attended by the most youthful High Sheriff I ever met. He was just twenty-five. Sir Lancelot Rolleston was thirty, when he was High Sheriff of Nottinghamshire. My young friend discharged his duties with charm and dignity, and I dined with him at the most magnificent place (except Powis Castle) in Wales, of which he was the fortunate owner. There were five prisoners, and one civil case, and I had finished by luncheon on the second day. In the afternoon we drove to Glynnog Fawr in order to see the church. It was, excepting St David's, Llandaff, and Brecon, the most interesting church I had seen in Wales. The chapel of St Beuno, oddly and irregularly set to the south of its western tower, with a curious passage to it, is unique. The church, of late Perpendicular, is admirable, and the stalls (for it was a collegiate church) are good. Among its possessions are a fifteenth-century mazer of maple wood and silver, and a pair of tongs for the ejection of dogs from the church.

On the Wednesday I was to go to Beaumaris, but an hour would suffice for that in the evening. So my marshal and I walked up Snowdon, going this time by the path from South Snowdon station on the west of the mountain, and coming down to Llanberis. There were clouds on the top, as usual, but we had a very good walk.

At Beaumaris the old Lodgings in the terrace had been given up, and we were housed in a pleasant villa out at Penmon, with that view of the Snowdon range, across the straits, which is one of the best in Great Britain. Next day Beaumaris provided its usual sort of Assize—two prisoners, both of whom pleaded guilty, and one trumpery suit for slander. Everything was finished by 3 o'clock.

Next day I had a holiday. We walked up the east coast of the island to Red Wharf Bay, and back inland by Llandoona and Llangoed. The flowers were abundant, but the most beautiful display was the great sheets of *Scilla Verna* in many places on the cliff. There must be fewer opportunities of getting a drink in Anglesey than in any part of the civilized world. We took our sandwiches, but counted on a public house to wash them down. At last, when very thirsty, we got some nasty lemonade in a shop at Llandoona. I asked the man where one had to go to get a glass of beer, and he said the nearest bottle or barrel was in Beaumaris.

We went by train from Bangor to Rhyl, and thence drove to Ruthin. In the afternoon we went to the Castle (now a nursing home), and got leave to walk in the park. Upon the hill, inside the wall of the old deer park, were many beautiful views, and some magnificent trees. On the Sunday we drove over the hills, by the very romantic road, to Llangollen, on our way to lunch with friends beyond. I reckon Llangollen to be the most hideous little town, set in beautiful natural surroundings, that exists. Its inhabitants appear to desire to further this pre-eminence by a welter of notice boards and advertisements. The most notable effort in this way we saw about half a mile out of the town—a huge board by the road-side, with the legend, in horrible lettering, "You are approaching Llangollen, the World's Beauty Spot". It would have been an extravagant claim before man appeared there at all: now that he has created and adorned Llangollen as it is, I do not know what I would substitute for the inscription on the board.

It was a perfect day (15 June) when we were to move on to Mold. We walked over the top of Moel Famman, lunched by the ruined monument, and then made a bonfire. It was primarily to burn the paper that had covered our sandwiches, but we added a vast quantity of paper and cardboard that had been concerned with other people's provisions, sweets, and cigarettes. The result was a really notable blaze, and when we departed from the memorial of George III it was much tidier than it had been for a long time. We came down the hill to Cilcain, which has a good Perpendicular church. Its wooden roof, with hammer beams and winged angels, is very notable. I know some finer roofs of similar type in Norfolk and Suffolk, but I never saw anything so good in Wales. Another thing of interest in the church was the survival of some brass name-plates, taken from the old square pews that have been destroyed. They were fixed on a panel and kept polished. I never saw the like before, but in the following autumn I saw some specimens in the museum at Shrewsbury that had come from St Julian's church there.

A little beyond Cilcain we at last found an inn. Of course the opening time had elapsed—it always has—but we asked the good woman to give us a non-alcoholic drink. She suggested several that did not sound attractive. Then she added cider, being apparently under the belief that this was in the innocent category. We did not dispute the point with her. If we had asked for port I have no doubt she would readily have produced some decoction bearing that name. Among what used to be called the lower orders, there is an almost universal belief that port is a temperance drink. I remember somewhere a witness being asked, "When you and your friend went to the inn what drinks did you have?" And the answer was, "He had a pint of bitter. I am teetotal, so I had a glass of port."

Not only do none of us ever speak of the lower orders, but refinement is carried much further. No one in any court nowadays, except perhaps an unrefined judge, ever speaks of a man or a woman. Everyone is a gentleman or a lady. I remember a woman (I beg pardon, a lady) giving evidence in a bad case of rape. She said: "I was walking by the footpath through the fields. A lady met me. Just after, a gentleman passed me. Then I heard a scream. I turned and looked back. And I saw the gentleman pulling the lady down on to the ground." And so forth. From the same growth of refinement no one ever speaks of a woman taking in lodgers; the lady receives paying guests.

And so to Rhuol, the delightful house that, by a lady's courtesy, provided the best Judges' Lodgings in England or Wales. Previously I had only been there in the winter, when it was pleasant enough: in the summer it was perfect. Mold had only two prisoners, and its Assize took four hours. With Ruthin 8 miles away to the west, and Chester 12 miles to the east, it is, of course, preposterous that there should be an Assize at Mold at all. But personally I was glad of the absurdity, when it compelled me to spend two days of perfect summer weather at Rhuol, and on the second day walk over to luncheon with Sir John Eldon Bankes at Soughton Hall. On the way we saw a seventeenth-century walled baptistery in a field. I never saw anything like it elsewhere: the spring that feeds it is the most copious fount of clear, cool water.

I should be very much interested to know the correct answer to the question—"Which family in which county has provided the greatest number of High Sheriffs?" The High Sheriff of Flint, on this occasion, was Sir Edward Hanmer of Bettisfield Park in the parish of Hanmer. He told me that he was the nineteenth of his surname to be High Sheriff of Flint since the reign of Henry VIII. He had only seen a list of Sheriffs as far back as that, and did not know how many he could add before. But I am not sure if there were any High Sheriffs in Wales, or even counties, before Henry VIII. And if there were, perhaps the Hanmers, despite the advantage of being in a small county with few eligible residents, would not win the prize. There must, for instance, have been many Plowdens, Eytons, and Corbets in Shropshire: I don't think I had a Grand Jury in Shropshire without one or more of these names on it. If Durham had been a normal county Surtees might have been a constantly recurring name. I have met two Surtees Sheriffs there, and the author of Jorrocks was Sheriff in his day. But as I said elsewhere, the Bishop used to appoint Hedworth Williamsons alone for a long time; so Durham, like Westmorland, is not a normal county.

Since writing that I have found a note in Grantham's *Circuit Diary*, in which he says he had a Corbet as High Sheriff of Salop at Shrewsbury in March 1893, and he said he was the thirty-second member of his family to fill that office.

When I lunched with Sir Edward and Lady Hanmer they took me to tea with the dowager Lady Kenyon at Gredington Hall. Lloyd Kenyon was born at a humbler Gredington in 1732. He was sent to Ruthin grammar school, and then articled to an attorney at Nantwich. In 1750 he became a student of the Middle Temple, and in 1756 he was called to the bar. In 1782 he was made Attorney-General, in 1784 Master of the Rolls, and in 1788 he succeeded Lord Mansfield as Lord Chief Justice. He filled that office for fourteen years, till his death in 1802. According to Lord Campbell he was parsimonious. But a Chief Justice in the eighteenth century did not need that quality to amass a fortune. And a great fortune Kenyon must have made, to judge by Gredington as he rebuilt it, with its enormous walled gardens. There are three pictures of him in the house, a beautiful Romney as a junior barrister, another Romney as a judge, and an Opie in later life. They are all fine, but the earlier Romney is delightful.

And so to Chester, where I joined Mr Justice Talbot, coming from South Wales. We were again lodged in the pleasant house on the Eccleston road. I had kept my usual record of working hours in Wales. From leaving London until I had arrived at Chester I had spent 31 hours in Court, and any colleague remaining in town had spent 65 hours in Court. I did not forget to omit Friday, 3 June, when the London Courts were closed in honour of the King's birthday. As to gaol delivery I found that, if not on bail, prisoners were brought to Newtown and Ruthin from Shrewsbury prison, and to Carnarvon, Beaumaris, and Mold from Liverpool prison.

I was "in Commission" at Chester, and had to deal with 31 prisoners. But 20 of them pleaded guilty on the first day. This is the most trying sort of day that a Judge of Assize has. It is not repulsive, like a day of undefended divorce cases, though that puts no strain upon the meanest intellect. But to have, at frequent intervals, to determine the fitting sentence for an admitted offence, is as troublesome as it is responsible. There is not merely the problem of the particular case, there is also the natural desire to apply some standard of uniformity in the relative sentences for all the cases. An excess of severity can be corrected later, but too light a sentence has to stand. The excess can be corrected for the reason that a prisoner's ultimate sentence depends not upon the words of the Judge uttered in Court, but upon the written list of the various sentences which the Judge signs at the end of the Assize: it is this signed list which gives authority to the Governors of gaols to keep the convict in custody. Mr Justice Day, before whom I appeared as a very junior barrister, had a reputation for passing very severe sentences. And so he did, orally, in Court. But I have been told that it was his constant practice to mitigate this severity in the subsequent Gaoler's list, and therein greatly reduce the length of the sentences he had pronounced in Court.

We dined one evening with the bar at the Queen's Hotel. It was their Grand Court, and three postulants were admitted as members of the circuit. I was interested in the proceedings, as I never belonged to a circuit, or shared its social amenities. The senior man present delivered an allocution to the novices, and added to the affected solemnity of it by adorning his head with a table-napkin in the manner of the black cap. This appears to be an ancient circuit jest. Lord Campbell, in a letter of 1807, describes his admission to the Home

Circuit. "I was tried for some mock offence, and being found Guilty, the judge, putting a doyley on his head for a black cap, sentenced me to be carried back to the place from whence I came."

Grantham, in his *Circuit Notes*, says: "At the bar dinner at Chester the health of the Prince and Princess of Wales is given as that of The Earl and Countess of Chester." There was no Princess of Wales in the summer of 1932, and I do not remember if we toasted The Earl of Chester.

Though I had been five times to a Glamorganshire Assize, I had always been to Cardiff, and never to Swansea, where we went this time. The Lodgings are in the Mansion House, which is an extremely ugly Victorian edifice half-way up the hill. It has grounds of some four acres, and they are so planted with trees that on the terrace in front of the house you can see nothing of the town, or of any buildings, and might be in the depths of the country. The house might be called a first-class example of the pitch-pine period, with Gothic windows, those in the hall being filled with awful stained glass. The garden had a tennis court, but owing to the steepness of the hill it was a difficult thing to provide, and in fact it was the worst court I ever played on. We had no rackets with us, and did not want to buy expensive ones. I commissioned my marshal to see what he could do economically. He amazed me by returning with two new rackets, and eight balls, for a total outlay of 19*s.* 6*d.* They were about worthy of the court. It was a poor sort of game, but it gave us some exercise on several evenings.

At our procession to the Assize Service, there were twelve policemen carrying javelins, as they do at Aylesbury. I noticed that the heads of them were inscribed "Swansea 1760", and various other dates up to about 1785.

The Courts, down near the river, were poor and inconvenient. But Swansea was spending an enormous amount of money in erecting a great new municipal building, which was to include two Courts. I confess this seemed to me an example of the waste of public money that arises from the rivalry of provincial cities. For Swansea is as jealous of Cardiff, as Manchester is of Liverpool. And I have no doubt that Swansea wanted to have better Courts because they had such magnificent ones at Cardiff. It is, of course, necessary for Manchester and Liverpool each to have Courts, for at each of them the lengthiest

Assizes in the kingdom take place. It is wholly unnecessary for Courts to exist both at Swansea and Cardiff, except as a concession to the pride of Swansea. Cardiff is 45 miles from Swansea, and there must be plenty of trains that do the journey in under an hour. I do not know exactly what control can be exercised in Whitehall over such expenditure. If there is any power, I think Swansea should have been prevented from spending a huge amount of public money over new Courts, by Swansea ceasing to be an Assize town, and the Assizes for Glamorgan all being held in the splendid Courts at Cardiff.

On the Saturday we all drove to Rhosili, at the end of the Gower Peninsula, and walked along the coast to Llangeneth and back. Mr Justice Talbot was the most learned botanist I ever met, except Claridge Druce. It was a gloriously fine day. The flowers, especially on the marsh and dunes at Llangeneth, were wonderful. Perhaps the most beautiful sight was the great sheets of the Marsh Pimpernel, *Anagallis tenella.* I am used to finding it as a small shy plant on the edge of a pond. Here it was in places in sheets of 30 to 40 square feet, a blaze of delicate colour.

My colleague being "in Commission" I tried the civil cases at Swansea. I spent most of my time trying cases about motor cars and motor cycles, which was becoming the staple industry in civil litigation. The only thing I remember of any of them is that one witness was asked where the motor cycle came to rest after the collision. He replied: "Against one of them posts with an advertisement of Bass on it." On enquiry it appeared that he seriously thought that the motor warning signs, topped with a red triangle, were all erected in honour of that generous liquid.

◇ ◇ ◇

In the autumn of 1932 I was upon the Oxford Circuit, and on the first day of Michaelmas term went to Reading. The only thing I noted in my diary at Reading was that in the churchyard of St Lawrence I saw a tombstone to a man who in 1840, at the age of 24, was "killed by a whirlwind at the Railway Station". The only other thing I remember is that after the finish of a very horrible murder trial I walked westwards along the towpath towards a beautiful sunset. On my way back there was a full moon making the scene beautiful again. And my walk was a blessed relief from my day's work.

I was faced at Reading with the sad news that there was no work of any kind at Oxford, so that I must cancel its Assize. This was rather awkward, as my wife and daughter had come with me for a time, our home was shut up, and our servants on holiday. Moreover, I had made a number of engagements in Oxford. So we went and stayed in the beautiful house in St Giles's. As the Assize was cancelled I said, in answer to an enquiry from the Senior Proctor, that I could not expect the Vice-Chancellor, Proctors, and Heads of Houses to wait upon me, though I should be delighted to see them if they chose to come. As it happened, it would have been very inconvenient for the Vice-Chancellor to come, so he took advantage of my suggestion. Unhappily for me this meant that I did not get my pair of *Chirothecae Aurifrigiatae*; and as I had been carrying about on all ceremonial occasions the pair I got in June 1930, they were getting rather soiled, and I wanted a new pair.

This being the autumn circuit, it was not proper for me to entertain the Vice-Chancellor, Proctors, and Heads of Houses at dinner. On the Sunday evening I dined with the Dean in hall at Christchurch, on the Monday I dined in Trinity, and on the Tuesday we had a party at the Lodgings. Meanwhile on the Monday and Tuesday I went to London by train for the day, and sat in the Law Courts.

Next day we went on to the rather gaunt Lodgings behind the Shire Hall at Worcester. Scattered about various Lodgings on the Oxford Circuit there were a number of photographs of Baron Huddleston, a Victorian judge, who died in 1890. Each of them was elaborately framed, and inscribed "Soli Deo Honor et Gloria". Whether that was his heraldic motto, or is meant as thanking the Deity for having produced so good and great a man I do not know. In some of the photographs his wife, a Lady Diana, stood beside him in very Victorian attire. The Worcester Lodgings were profusely blessed with these photographs. When I left, my entry in the Visitors' Book included something like this: "I do not know if Worcester has a special devotion to Baron Huddleston and his wife. But I venture to think that six photographs of him in this house, including two in my bedroom, are an excessive tribute. If I am at all representative of the judges of to-day I fancy that they take little interest in this their predecessor."

When I went to the City Court (where I was received by a Lady Mayor), to open the City Assize, I was staggered by being confronted in the Court by a colossal photograph of Baron Huddleston—somewhere near life size! Someone then told me that he had begun life as an assistant master at the Worcester Grammar School. Perhaps some of the photographs at the Lodgings might be taken round to the School—unless they have a dozen or so already.

Huddleston appears to have been one of those judges who have been appointed as a reward for their service in the House of Commons. Atlay, *Victorian Chancellors* (Vol. II, pp. 121, 122), records the pressure put on Lord Chelmsford by Disraeli in 1868 to have him so appointed, Chelmsford's refusal on the ground that "fitness and not politics ought to govern me in the choice of a judge", and Chelmsford's personal note that Huddleston was "utterly unfit to be a judge". He was appointed in 1875 by Lord Cairns, who may have had a higher estimate of his fitness. If all Lord Chancellors had followed Lord Chelmsford's maxim that "fitness and not politics ought to govern me in the choice of a judge" Courts of first instance might sometimes have been better manned: but Prime Ministers appoint to all higher judicial posts, and it is perhaps too much to expect them to look only for fitness and disregard politics.

Foote, in his delightful book, *Pie Powder*, wrote: "The custom of wearing a powdered wig was cherished on the Oxford Circuit long after it had been abandoned elsewhere. Huddleston, Henry James, and Henry Matthews were all wont to appear with this effective but troublesome adjunct to forensic dignity, and I think I remember that Mr Justice Darling once followed their example. I doubt not that the archives of the Oxford Circuit contain some explanation of this peculiarity, and it is perhaps to be regretted that so picturesque an adornment has fallen into disuse." It has not completely fallen into disuse. There is still in 1939 one barrister who adds to the picturesqueness of his appearance by wearing a powdered wig in Court. He is Mr George Bancroft, Clerk of Assize on the Midland Circuit.

The Shire Hall at Worcester was built in 1834. I took the opportunity one day of going in at the front door to see the great hall. It is a fine room, and in recent times has had its windows adorned with heraldic achievements of Lords-Lieutenant, High Sheriffs, and Chairmen of Quarter Sessions. I was told that until recently the hall was wont to be used to store pockets of hops, between which those attending the Courts had to pick their way: but it was all empty when I saw it.

This account of the Shire Hall as a hop store put me in mind of a passage in Boswell's *Life of Johnson*:* "A learned gentleman who in the course of conversation wished to inform us of this simple fact, that the counsel upon the circuit at Shrewsbury were much bitten by fleas, took, I suppose, seven or eight minutes in relating it circumstantially. He in a plenitude of phrase told us, that large bales of woollen cloth were lodged in the town-hall;—that by reason of this, fleas nestled there in prodigious numbers;—that the lodgings of the Counsel were near to the town-hall;—and that those little animals moved from place to place with wonderful agility. Johnson sat in great impatience till the gentleman had finished his tedious narrative, and then burst out (playfully however), 'It is a pity, Sir, that you have not seen a lion; for a flea has taken you such a time, that a lion must have served you a twelvemonth'."

At Gloucester I was again struck by the unkempt condition of the monuments in the Cathedral by comparison with those of Worcester. Another thing that I think is unfortunate at Gloucester is the treatment of the cloister. In itself it is perhaps the finest in England, and the lavatory is especially perfect. Many years ago they glazed the arches towards the garth. I do not object to the glazing: indeed in our climate it is almost a necessity. It has always seemed to me extraordinary that this sort of living-room for monks, copied from warm and sunny climes, was universally introduced in England. The rigours endured by mediaeval monks, say at Durham, must have been awful. Glazing is almost necessary now. But this glazing at Gloucester was done with that horrible opaque stuff called "Cathedral glass", that was once thought essential to piety. The result is that you cannot look out, and see a trim lawn, and the beauty of the other side of the cloisters. Why this abomination has been endured so long I cannot imagine.

On the Sunday, after the Assize Service, I was asked to go to the Guildhall to meet the city fathers. It is a modern building, but they had some pictures, and some good pieces of silver. In wandering about the city I found some admirable old houses—the Police Station and the District Telephone Office in Long Smith Street, Lady Belle House, and the New Inn were perhaps the best.

The Bell seemed to have sadly rebuilt itself, since the days when it was kept by the father, and then by the brother, of the Rev. George

* Vol. II, p. 194.

Whitefield, and was the scene of stirring incidents in *Tom Jones*. I was rather surprised, in these days of advertisement (or should I say "publicity"?), to find no reference to *Tom Jones* on the Bell Inn, and my marshal, whom I sent in to look, said he could see none within it. The Hop Pole at Tewkesbury, and the Great White Horse at Ipswich, are plastered with references to *Pickwick*; and so, I expect, are the Bull at Rochester, the Angel at Bury St Edmund's, and the Saracen's Head at Towcester. Perhaps American visitors are not expected to have read *Tom Jones*, or perhaps the landlord of the Bell has never heard of it. In any case the contrast is a measure of the relative popularity of *Pickwick* and *Tom Jones*.

In fact the way in which Fielding wrote of the Bell and of the Whitefields, and Dickens wrote of the Great White Horse would be very strange, if not perilous, nowadays. Fielding, describing the advent of Tom Jones and Partridge to the Bell, says that "the master of it is brother to the great preacher Whitefield", and goes on to describe his wife in condescending terms. Later on he says that when Tom Jones desired the favour of Mrs Whitefield's company to drink tea with him, she refused. "And now he soon perceived her behaviour totally changed; for instead of that natural affability which we have before celebrated, she wore a constrained severity on her countenance which was so disagreeable to Mr Jones that he resolved, however late, to quit the house that evening."

That was printed in 1749. In 1773 in *The Spiritual Quixote* the Rev. Richard Graves also indulged in personalities about Mrs Whitefield. Wildgoose and Tugwell come to the Bell on foot, and ask for a lodging. On which "Mrs Whitefield...rose up with some reluctance, and came to the window of the bar; where, spying two such dusty figures, her usual politeness to strangers forsook her—'Heyday', quoth she, 'lodgings indeed! yes, to be sure; because Squire Fielding, forsooth, in that romancing book of his, pretends that Tom Jones was harboured here, we shall be pestered with all the trampers that pass the road'". And they are driven away.

As for the Great White Horse, Dickens does not indulge in personalities about the landlord or his wife. But of the inn he says: "It is famous...for its enormous size. Never were such labyrinths of uncarpeted passages, such clusters of mouldy, badly lighted rooms, such huge numbers of small dens for eating and sleeping in, beneath any one roof, as are collected together within the four walls of the Great White Horse at Ipswich." The waiter is described as "a corpulent man, with a fortnight's napkin under his arm, and coeval stockings on his legs", who "ushered them into a large, badly furnished apartment, with a dirty grate, in which a small fire was making a wretched attempt to be cheerful, but was fast sinking beneath the dispiriting influence of the place". Later Mr Pickwick and Mr Magnus "ordered a bottle of the worst possible port wine, at the highest possible price, for the good of the house, and drank brandy and water for their own".

Let some novelist write such things of a named hotel to-day, and I fancy he will receive a writ for libel! That the landlord of the Great White Horse in 1837 took it so meekly can hardly have been because he foresaw that the day would come when this book would provide for his house the most glorious advertisement that any landlord could desire.

On Friday, 28 October, my marshal and I drove to the Speech House and thence walked to Monmouth. But on the way we stopped at Westbury. I had been encouraged by a lady, whom I met when dining with the Bishop at Gloucester, to go in and look at the wonderful garden I had admired from the outside in June 1930. It was indeed admirable, with its formal canals, and wonderful yew hedges. From the road you see a piece of Queen Anne work on the house, and I had thought the whole house was like it. Unfortunately it was not, having been poorly rebuilt, I think after a fire. But the small piece of the old work is happily the only part visible from the road and ends the vista of the garden perfectly.

There are a few good old houses in Monmouth. As I was peering at one, called Ivy Bank, its occupant politely asked me in, and showed me some finely proportioned rooms, with rounded ends, and doors set in the round. Up in the Castle (now disused barracks) is a big stone house with 1613 on its pediment. I was told it had some fine plaster ceilings, and was once a dower house of the Dukes of Beaufort, who had their greater house at Troy.

Going to Hereford we took the train to Ross, saw the fine church there and admired the Rudhall tombs, and then walked by Bristow, Hoarwithy, and Alconbury. The Assize at Hereford was a farce. There were only two cases. One was a charge against an imbecile, who was at once proved to be unfit to plead. In the other two boys pleaded guilty to breaking into a "lock-up" shop, and stealing some packets of chocolate. I suggested to the Grand Jury that as Hereford is 31 miles from Worcester, and the same distance from Gloucester, and Worcester is 26 miles from Gloucester, the three counties might well be united (as they are for the Three Choirs Festival) so as to have a joint Assize at each of the three cities once a year. I need hardly say that this provoked indignant protests in the local papers.

There is an interesting piece of furniture in the Court at Hereford. The Clerk of Assize in every Court has a box in which he puts the cards, or slips of paper, on which are written the names of jurymen, and draws them out one by one when calling a jury. The box at Hereford is a finely made one of mahogany, with brass fittings, and a brass plate on which an inscription records that it was presented to the county by Edward Harley, Esq., Member of Parliament for the County, in the year 1730. In the Court at Monmouth there is a similar box "presented by Mr Auditor Harley, 1730". (He was "Auditor of the Imprest". See the *Dictionary of National Biography*.)

These handsome boxes were provided by Harley to fulfil a requirement of an Act of Parliament, 3 Geo. II, cap. 25. That enacts that the Sheriff shall retain one panel of jurors for all the causes to be tried at an Assize, containing not less than forty-eight nor more than seventy-two names: these names being written on tickets shall be put into a box or a glass: and when each cause is called on, twelve of these persons, whose names shall be first drawn out of the box or glass shall be sworn upon the jury, unless absent, challenged, or excused. This is an Act, says Blackstone, which is "well calculated to restrain any suspicion of partiality in the Sheriff, or any tampering with the Jurors when returned".

These boxes, of 1730, are rather early examples of the use of mahogany. The first mention of "mohogeny" cited in the Oxford Dictionary is of 1671, and its first reference to furniture made of mahogany is of 1733. I think the earliest use of the wood I ever came across is a chest in the tower of Radclive church, in North Buckinghamshire, which is described in the *Report of the Commission on Ancient Monuments* (Buckinghamshire, Vol. II, p. 249) as "large chest, of mahogany, with two drawers, fine brass handles, escutcheons, and strapping, probably late 17th century".

Almost the only anachronism that Jane Austen ever permitted herself was when, in *Mansfield Park*, she describes the chapel at Sotherton as having a "profusion of mahogany", and makes Mrs Rushworth say of it—"This chapel was fitted up as you see it in James the Second's time. Before that period, as I understand, the pews were only wainscot."

The High Sheriff of Hereford, resplendent in the uniform of the Herefordshire Yeomanry, came for me again in the old coach and pair. As the business took less than an hour, I had a holiday for the rest of the day, and another on the morrow. I wanted to see Holme Lacey, the great house of the Scudamores. The clerk of the County Council kindly took me there. When it was sold by Lord Chesterfield, about 1910, to Sir Lucas Tooth, much of the famous Grinling Gibbons carving was removed to Benningbrough in Yorkshire. But Sir Lucas Tooth modernized the house very splendidly, and added a great ball-room to the already enormous house. The modern woodwork and panelling put in by him are very fine, and when age has added its glamour will be as good as any seventeenth or eighteenth century work. When the Tooth regime ended, the place was bought by the late Mr Noel Wills, for the sake of its miles of salmon fishing in the Wye. On his untimely death, his executors sold the fishing separately, and presented the house and park to the County Council. When I saw it the Council were still uncertain how to use it, but I gathered that it was likely to become a lunatic asylum. Such was the fate of one of the most magnificent of houses! Unhappily the day when I went there was one of the wettest I ever saw, and it was impossible to see the gardens. So I did not see the great clipped yew hedges of which I knew the pictures in the books.

When next day we were to go on to Shrewsbury it was fine. My marshal and I took the train to Ludlow, and I saw again the great church, and the greater castle. But a thing I had not seen before was the delightful Guildhall in a street full of charming old houses. The Court in it is very picturesque, and the Recorder of Ludlow sits in delightful surroundings. Perhaps it was in gratitude for this that the late H. D. Greene, K.C. presented a very fine clock which adorns the Guildhall. When Ludlow has this, and many other charming buildings, it is deplorable that its citizens should have allowed the erection in 1887 of a hideous market hall. I daresay it took the place of one that was beautiful; it remains a ghastly blot on the otherwise charming town.

The eighteenth century created Bath. The nineteenth century created —Bournemouth!

And so to Shrewsbury. On the Sunday we went to lunch with the High Sheriff at Apley Park, near Bridgnorth. The park was beautiful, with the Severn winding through it. The house interested me very much. It is Gothic, and good Gothic, of about 1820. I never saw a house that so nearly realized my conception of Northanger Abbey. I could picture General Tilney beneath its carriage porch.

Next day the Grand Jury included a Plowden, a Corbet, and an Eyton. That is common form in Salop. Until a century ago there was usually a Mytton as well.

There were only eight prisoners in the calendar, and when I congratulated the Grand Jury on that fact, I happened to say that I felt sure that a century ago the number must have been enormously greater. For the moment I forgot that this was an autumn Assize, which is a modern invention.

Because of my remark the Clerk of the Peace kindly sent up to the Lodgings two volumes of Calendars from 1786 to 1834, and I looked through them with much interest. Against the name of any prisoner who could "read and write" was set R.W., against any who could "read only" was set R., and the illiterate were left blank. At the Lent Assize 1832 the Judges were Mr Justice Littledale and Mr Justice Taunton. There were 47 prisoners, of whom 15 could read and write, 9 could read only, and 25 could do neither. Two were sentenced to death for stack burning, 13 were transported for life—for, *inter alia*, "stealing one sheep", and "entering a dwelling house and stealing four shirts". And a man who stole four pigs was transported for 14 years.

At the Summer Assize 1832 the Judges were Mr Justice Bosanquet and Baron Gurney. There were 37 prisoners, of whom 10 could read and write, 8 could read only, and 19 could do neither. There was no death sentence, but 13 were transported for life, for, *inter alia*, "stealing one ram", and "stealing a bay mare".

I was glad of one day's holiday in the delightful town of Shrewsbury. I managed to get inside the fine house, once Lord Bradford's mansion, and now the Guildhall, which has a very good staircase. In the Castle I saw the circular room, restored by Telford as the Pulteneys' dining-room. This effort of Telford, the self-taught engineer, is a very creditable piece of architecture. In the Castle grounds a small turret at the top of the mound is a good example of the earliest efforts of revived "Gothick". And at the east end of the Abbey I saw what I could of a fine Queen Anne house, now degraded to be the offices of the District Valuer and of the Inland Revenue: the panelled hall and staircase were very good. In the afternoon we walked by the Severn, and the canal, and came to Battlefield. Its most interesting church is, I suppose, the earliest "War Memorial" in the land.

I left Shrewsbury reluctantly, and came to Stafford still more reluctantly. But Sunday was a very pleasant day. My marshal and I drove to Lichfield, went to service at the Cathedral, and had luncheon with one of the Canons. They have a pleasant tradition in the Cathedral by which the choir and clergy bow to the Dean at the beginning of the service. In the afternoon we were taken all over the Cathedral by the Dean, who knew the building as a Dean should. In some ways the most remarkable thing was the sixteenth-century glass in the seven windows of the lady chapel. It was once in the Belgian Abbey of Herckenrode. This was suppressed by Napoleon, and the glass was bought about 1801 on the continent for £200 by Sir Brook Boothby of Ashbourne. He handed it on to the Chapter for the same very moderate price. Another version of the story is that the glass was shipped for South America, but captured by a British privateer, and that Sir Brook Boothby bought it from the captors or the Prize Court. The glass is magnificent, much finer than the similar examples in the chapel of Peterhouse, Cambridge.

Two other windows in the lady chapel are filled with Flemish glass of a later date. The story about these is that they were bought at the end of the eighteenth century by a Marquess of Ely, that in 1845 they were sent for sale to Christie's, and that they remained unsold in their cellars for fifty years! They were then bought by the Chapter for £2000, ten times the price of the seven finer Herckenrode windows.

After Stafford I had twelve days at home before joining Mr Justice Humphreys at Birmingham. He of course came from Warwick. That pleasant town retains its ancient status as an Assize town. Birmingham was given an Assize in 1884, thus gaining what Coventry once enjoyed but had long lost. I am bound to confess that there is no justification for having an Assize at Warwick and another at Birmingham which is only 21 miles distant. Personally I shall be sorry when Warwick becomes a town, like Croydon, Thetford, Buckingham, Horsham, East Grinstead, and Guildford, that once had an Assize. If I were still qualified to go on circuit, I should be still more sorry. For Warwick is delightful, and its Shire Hall an admirable building. Anyone would prefer to go there than to Birmingham.

1933

In February 1933 I went again on the North-Eastern Circuit with Lord Finlay. We were to start at Newcastle, and I was to take the civil work. We heard in London that there was one very lengthy criminal trial, but very few causes. So, as I had some work that needed to be done in London, Lord Finlay went up first, and I joined him a few days later.

The High Sheriff, Capt. Charlton of Hesleyside, near Bellingham, asked me to spend the first week-end at his house. My marshal and I drove out there with him along roads piled with snow on each side. As chance had it I had been within a few hundred yards of Hesleyside in the previous September, when I had a wonderful walk across the moors from Haltwhistle to Bellingham.

The Charltons have been at Hesleyside for centuries, and their eponymous village of Charlton is just across the river. The house shows not much outward sign of antiquity, but some of the walls are of enormous thickness, refashioned in the eighteenth century. I had heard the legend of the Charlton spur, and as we went down to dinner I asked Mrs Charlton if it was going to appear at table. She said, "No, but I will show it to you in the drawing-room after dinner". And so she did.

The legend is that in the old days, when cattle raiding on the border was the staple industry of that part of the world, if the Hesleyside larder ran low, the mistress of the house would serve up a dish at breakfast, which, when the cover was removed, displayed the spur. This was the signal that the men must take horse, and be off to collect some cattle.

One lady visitor played very charmingly on the old Northumbrian bagpipes, accompanied by her sister on the violin. I had heard the Brittany bagpipes, but never the Northumbrian.

On the Tuesday we had the Lord Mayor's dinner at the Mansion House, and I was given dagger money, in the shape of a particularly beautiful "broad-piece", a Jacobus. The Charltons, like so many of the oldest northern families, have always belonged to the ancient church, and the High Sheriff was attended in Court by a Roman Catholic chaplain. So Lord Finlay and I thought that, in addition to the usual guests, we would invite the Roman Catholic Bishop of Hexham and Newcastle to the dinner. The Anglican Bishop of Newcastle was also with us, and he and the Bishop of Hexham were evidently very good friends. All this, and the harmony of the whole party, made me think how things, and manners, have changed in about eighty years. For I remembered a passage in the *Life* of Lord Campbell. He wrote in his journal on 14 April 1852 thus: "I have gone another circuit.... At Aylesbury, my first assize town, I had a brush with a Roman Catholic Sheriff which has been much discussed in the newspapers. He had written to me that he did not intend to appoint any chaplain, and I had told him I wished him to do nothing which should be at all disagreeable to him on the score of religion. When I first met him, and we entered his carriage while the trumpeters were blowing, I was surprised to see a person jump in after us in the costume of a Roman Catholic priest. Before I had any time to collect my thoughts, the door was shut and the horses moved on. At the judges' lodgings I found that this was a *perverted* clergyman of the Church of England, who had gone over to Rome. I intimated to the sheriff that, although he was not bound to appoint a Protestant chaplain for us, and he was at liberty to appoint a Roman Catholic priest to minister to himself, I could not recognize this priest as the person who was to officiate as chaplain to the judges of the assize, and therefore I must decline his presence in the carriage, and he must not sit by me in his canonicals in court. I explained the matter to the grand jury, who unanimously thanked me for what I had done. The proceeding was fully reported in the newspapers, and was the subject of innumerable commentaries, generally taking part with the Chief Justice. Thereupon a Roman Catholic conclave was held, and Cardinal Wiseman wrote a long letter to me in the name of the sheriff, which I answered, to the great amusement of the public."

I saw again some of the pleasant things in Newcastle—the Guildhall, with the Merchant Adventurers' Hall, and the Mayors' Room, and the Trinity House. But a place I saw for the first time was the Old Assembly Rooms. Fortunately when I went there I happened to meet Mr Ford, who was chairman of the committee, and he showed me all over it.

The Old Assembly Rooms were built in 1776, at a cost of about £7000. Nearly all the county magnates took shares—Clavering, Trevelyan, Blackett, White, Ridley, Allgood, Charlton, Clennel, Collingwood, Delaval, Fenwick, Hedley, Liddell, and Silvertop were among the names of the original subscribers. The architect was William Newton of Newcastle. The great ball-room is a magnificent room, 92 feet long and 37 feet wide, and is adorned with seven splendid glass chandeliers. The biggest of them in the centre is said to have cost £700. There are other fine rooms, and in one of them a picture by George Downman, A.R.A., presented by himself.

Mr Ford and his associates had recently spent £25,000 in renovating and redecorating this excellent building. The result is most successful. Newcastle has a much finer ball-room than York, Leicester, or Shrewsbury, and is only surpassed by Bath, where the Upper Rooms have now been happily restored and made most beautiful.

On Monday, 27 February, I went to Durham. Lord Finlay was still immersed in his great criminal trial, and had to stay in Newcastle to finish it. But he came on next day, in time to join me in dining in the Castle Hall with the Master of University College and the other dons. This was pleasant and friendly. I confess that on previous visits to Durham I thought that the University kept aloof from the Judges, and I was glad that Dr How, the new Master, had introduced a more genial attitude. I think the majority at the High Table were Oxford men, including Dr How, who was at Wadham when I was at Trinity. Down in the body of the hall were the undergraduates of University College and of Hatfield Hall. They sat separately, and the Master told me that each set used its own door of the two at the end of the hall: if a man was rash enough to go out by the door that did not belong to his party there was trouble.

The Castle, thanks to the Pilgrim Trust, was now safe, though the works were far from finished. This allowed me to have the pleasure of being in the Bishop's rooms on the great staircase.

As Bishop Welldon had resigned the Deanery, and was to leave at Easter, there was much speculation in Durham as to his possible successor. On the Friday morning the papers announced the appointment of my old friend, and fellow undergraduate, the Head Master of Eton. Before the day was out I heard that he and his wife were arriving that night to stay the week-end at the Deanery: "long leave" provided the opportunity. So on the Saturday afternoon I walked about with them as they inspected their prospective domain. Welldon's furniture was deplorable, and I am afraid they found the house rather depressing. I have since come to know how pleasantly it could be reformed and beautified under their regime. In the course of our walk I saw yet one more of the many amazing views of the Cathedral and Castle. This was from the hill, by the chapel of Durham School, across the river. It is a fine view, but I still think that the finest view of all is that which you get from the up platform of the railway station.

On the Sunday we had a very fine Assize Service, and then lunched with the old Dean, the new Dean and his wife being of the party. Welldon's old butler had died, but apparently he had bequeathed his art of table decoration to some successor, and there was another elaborate, and hideous, display.

While we were at Newcastle there had been a tremendous snow-storm. It had prevented my spending my second week-end with friends high up the Coquet: they were entirely cut off for three weeks. The snow on the hills to the west of Durham was still very deep. The High Sheriff, who lived near Tow Law, had only managed to get in to the opening of the Assize after a heroic battle with the drifts. When we drove out to dine with him there were still enormous banks of snow by the road side. When we went on to York there was no snow, but tremendous floods. All the path along the Ouse by St Mary's Gardens was deep under water, which extended beyond the railings into the gardens themselves. When we went out to tea with Mrs Temple at Bishopsthorpe the water had just begun to subside from the terrace before her drawing-room windows: if it had risen less than a foot farther it would have been over the sill into the room.

At the Lord Mayor's breakfast one of the first guests I met was the new Dean of York, who had also been a fellow undergraduate with me at Trinity. The College was rather specializing in Deans at this time, providing those of Durham, York, Peterborough, and Westminster. There were also three Trinity High Court Judges, Mr Justice Bateson, Mr Justice Goddard, and myself. (When Mr Justice Bateson died, his successor was, very properly, another Trinity man, Mr Justice Bucknill.) A few years earlier there had been three, one in each of the three Divisions—Mr Justice Astbury in the Chancery Division, Mr Justice Bateson in the Probate Divorce and Admiralty, and myself in the King's Bench: I doubt if this concatenation is likely to recur.

I saw a few more of the beautiful things in York. The Queen's Hotel has a very fine staircase, and a magnificent panelled room on the first floor. St George's House in Castlegate, once the home of the Lord Fairfax, now degraded to a dance hall, had a fine staircase, with a modelled plaster ceiling, and some good rooms. Cumberland House on the quay had one beautifully panelled room, with two charming alcoves at the sides of the chimney breast.

The Assembly Rooms, built by the Earl of Burlington in 1730, is an interesting building, and the passages along its colonnaded sides an ingenious piece of planning. It had some chandeliers, but not as fine as those at Newcastle. And it was very much vulgarized. York would do well to rescue and restore it, as Newcastle and Bath have so happily done with theirs.

I also tried to see the inside of the Old Prison, which is next to the Assize Courts in the Castle. This is a magnificent building, and externally looks more like a palace than a prison. It was built about 1700, and I believe the architect is unknown. Unfortunately I got there when the caretaker was away at his dinner, and I could not wait for his return. While I was wandering round I noticed on the front wall of the building this inscription:

This Prison is a House of Care,
A Grave for Man Alive,
A Touchstone to try a Friend,
No Place for Man to thrive.
1820.

Somehow the lines seemed familiar. A few months later I was re-reading *Guy Mannering*, and as the motto at the head of chapter XLIV I found this:

A Prison is a house of care,
A place where none can thrive,
A touchstone true to try a friend,
A grave for one alive.
Sometimes a place of right,
Sometimes a place of wrong,
Sometimes a place of rogues and thieves
And honest men among.

Inscription on Edinburgh Tolbooth.

On Monday, 13 March, we drove to Leeds through Tadcaster. On the way there was much evidence of the storm of Friday, 24 February. Dozens, if not hundreds, of the telegraph posts, especially to the east of Tadcaster, were blown down, and many snapped off, while the wires for miles were a tangle of confusion. My friends at Tadcaster were deprived of their telephone for nearly a month.

Leeds, as usual, was a sad contrast to York. I was glad to see that St John's church, almost its only building of interest, had been improved by clearing away houses to the north of it, and making a garden on their site.

For one week-end I went to Scarborough and stopped at the Crown. The Saturday was a day of cloudless sunshine, and I walked along the cliffs northwards. Scarborough seemed a well-governed town. Its gardens along the front were admirably kept, and there was no sign of the vulgarity that disfigures so many popular sea-side resorts.

On the last day of March I drove to Bradford, and there caught the convenient train that landed me at Aylesbury, near my home.

✧ ✧ ✧

In the summer of this year I did not go on circuit. But I did not sit continuously in London. In 1930 Parliament passed one of the few Acts for which I have ever found reason to be grateful. This provided new bodies of commissioners, both in England and Scotland, to assess the rateable value of railways. Appeals from their decisions, on questions of principle, were to be to the Railway and Canal Commission Court. And appeals as to a matter affecting a railway running both in England and Scotland were to be to the Ex-officio Commissioners for England and Scotland, sitting together, along with one of the appointed Commissioners. Two appeals of this sort arose. Accordingly in May 1933 Lord Blackburn, my Scots colleague, came to London, and sat with me and Sir Francis Dunnell in the Law Courts. In a preliminary correspondence I told Lord Blackburn that I very much hoped that, for the benefit of London lawyers, he would bring with him the picturesque robes of a Lord of Session: I said that if he did I would undertake, by way of return, or reprisal, to bring the robes of the King's Bench with me when I paid my visit to the Parliament House. He consulted the Lord President (Clyde) as to this, and, to my regret, he did not approve of the suggestion. I think it was a great pity.

So Lord Blackburn sat on the bench at the Law Courts without robes. He was my senior, but at his request I presided. Mr Tyldesley Jones, K.C., who opened the appeal, was able to welcome our visitor to the English Courts as the nephew and namesake of the Lord Blackburn of an earlier and an English fame. For my part I said to Mr Tyldesley Jones: "Lord Blackburn is accustomed to a very high standard of advocacy in Edinburgh. You and Mr Wilfrid Greene must do your best to prevent him from feeling any want of it in London." And of course they did.

The second case concerned the rating of the Forth Bridge, and was obviously one to be heard in Edinburgh. So on Monday, 9 June, I travelled to Edinburgh with Sir Francis Taylor. Thanks to Lord Blackburn I was made a temporary member of the New Club, where I had a magnificent bedroom: its furnishings included a very large bible. The New Club (which, like New College, is very old) is one of the best and most comfortable clubs I was ever in. One thing that struck me during my stay there was that, though I heard many of the members talking, I hardly heard one who had a trace of a Scottish accent. Indeed, I thought I heard more of it in the Reform Club in Pall Mall. Very likely the majority at the New Club were people who had been at school and university in England. Lord Dunedin, who was at Harrow and Trinity, Cambridge, would never be taken for a Scot from his speech; nor would the Archbishop of Canterbury, or his predecessor, Lord Davidson.

It is true that Lord Mansfield left Scotland in 1718 when he was fourteen, and was at Westminster and Christ Church, and in England for the rest of his life. And he is said always to have shown signs of his birthplace in his speech. But the Scottish dialect was then far more pronounced. When Alexander Wedderburn changed in 1757 from the Scots bar to the English, he found it desirable to receive lengthy instruction from old Sheridan (father of R. B. Sheridan) and Macklin, to mitigate his Scottish speech. Boswell also had recourse to old Sheridan for the same purpose. Lord Campbell could "never overcome the broad Fifeshire speech of his childhood. 'I would surrender a considerable portion of my legal acquirements to have a pure English accent', he once wrote in a splenetic mood."*

Owing to a misunderstanding on my part our case was not in the

* Atlay, *Victorian Chancellors*, Vol. II, p. 141.

list on the Tuesday. To have a holiday was all in keeping with being on a quasi-circuit, and I was glad to spend the morning in the Parliament House as a spectator. I had, of course, been there before, more than once, but only in vacation. And it was very interesting to see the Scottish Courts at work. The Vice-Dean of Faculty, Mr Leadbitter, was a kindly and learned guide, and I spent a delightful morning. In the afternoon I went to the Castle, to the National Gallery—that admirable collection—and to certain bookshops. At night I had a remarkable experience. I had been to dine with the Lord President and Lady Clyde in Moray Place. When I came away it was a gloriously fine, warm, night, I strolled along George Street, and turned to go down Castle Street. And suddenly I was aware that all the upper part of the Castle was flood-lighted! I thought it was one of the most beautiful spectacles I ever saw. I wandered up and down Princes Street, gazing at the sight, turned in very late to the New Club, and found that by pulling up the blind in my bedroom I could still watch it, lying in bed, until I fell asleep.

Next morning Lord Blackburn took me up to the Parliament House, and to the Judges' Common room. The Lords of Session all share one large room, as I believe the English Judges used to do at Westminster Hall. In the Law Courts we each have a separate room. I was glad to examine at close quarters, and admire, the Judges' robes, and renewed my regret that Lord Blackburn had not been able to display them for the benefit of the bar in London. I think their robes are more picturesque than ours. And they seemed obviously to me to have a civil origin, rather than an ecclesiastical one, as ours have. The English Judge's robe is like a cassock, with an added hood, or cope, for full dress. The Scottish robe is a robe, or gown, hung upon the shoulders and not fastened down the front, or girt with a cincture. The Lord Justice Clerk has a special robe of his own, with a different sort of decoration in the ermine, and without the broad crosses of the Lord President and all the other Lords of Session. The Lord President, who is also Lord Justice General, has a large silver-gilt mace borne before him into Court, except during the week of the General Assembly, when he lends it to be borne before the Lord High Commissioner. The Lord Justice Clerk has a small mace. In England of course the Lord Chancellor has a great mace precede him into the House of Lords, much bigger than the Lord President's. The only other such symbol appurtenant to an English Judge is the silver oar carried into Court by the Admiralty Marshal.

I had not realized before that all the Scottish Judges wear in Court the wig, with three rows of curls, that is worn by barristers in England, and advocates in Edinburgh. In England, of course, wigs are not really part of the legal uniform, as robes are. Wigs are simply a fashion in headdress that was once universal for gentlemen, and was given up by all of them except Bishops, Judges, and barristers towards the end of the eighteenth century. Bishops, with the permission of William IV, gave them up in 1832: Judges and barristers retain them still.

It is probably only chance that has brought about in England a difference between the Judge's wig and the barrister's. In full dress, of course, Judges, King's Counsel, and Recorders wear the same full-bottom wig. There is a print of a portrait of Sir Soulden Lawrence, a Judge from 1794 to 1812, in judicial robes. But he is wearing what would now be a barrister's wig, as a Scottish Judge does now.

For advocates to wear wigs in Scotland is really a revival, copied from England, and not a survival. For there was a time when, like other gentlemen, many of them gave them up. Lord Campbell, speaking of Lord Loughborough's admission to the Scottish bar in 1754, writes:* "He was accordingly in due form presented to the Fifteen as worthy to be made a member of the Faculty, and he was invested with the long robe, wearing a cocked hat over his powdered hair—for barristers' wigs were not yet known beyond the Tweed." I am well aware that Lord Campbell was one of the most inaccurate men who ever tried to write history.† But his statement is partly true. No doubt at one time barristers in Edinburgh wore wigs like other gentlemen. And when other gentlemen gave them up some of the advocates did so. But I do not think they all did, and I do not think the Lords of Session ever did.

* *Lives of the Chancellors* (4th ed.), Vol. VII, p. 346.

† For example, he writes of "Old Baron Maseres, who used to say that he was born on the day when Lord Holt tried Tutchin, the libeller, and whom I remember walking about at the age of ninety, in the costume of the reign of George I. (*Lives of the Chancellors*, Vol. VII, p. 303.) Maseres, who was a great mathematician, cannot have said anything so absurd. He was born 15 December 1731. Lord Holt tried Tutchin 4 November 1704, and he died more than twenty years before Maseres was born. Atlay, *Victorian Chancellors*, Vol. I, p. 232, calls attention to an even more amazing inaccuracy. Brougham was made Attorney-General to the Queen in 1820. Campbell says he was present when, by virtue of that promotion, he was called within the bar by Lord Ellenborough. And he says he remembers Ellenborough's "sarcastic smile" when doing so. Lord Ellenborough had died in December 1818. See also *ibid*. Vol. II, pp. 185–189.

Barristers' Uniform

Not long ago I wrote to my friend Lord Normand, the Lord President, to ask if he could give me any information as to the universal legal resumption of wigs, and whether it was voluntary or by reason of some resolution of the Faculty. I may quote from his reply: "I think that the portraits of the Judges in the Parliament House are all bewigged. There is a prim, ladylike statue of Cockburn in a gown without a wig: I am not sure if the gown is a judicial robe.... In Kay's *Portraits,** No. CL, you will find 'Twelve Advocates who plead with wigs on', with a note that the wearing of wigs is a matter of choice. No. CLVI is a picture of 'Twelve Advocates who plead without wigs'.... All the portraits of Judges in Kay's book have wigs, and they are the wigs with curls (e.g. Nos. CXXX and CXLII).... In 1908 the Bar gave a dinner to Innes, the then father of the bar, and of great age. I believe that he spoke of advocates pleading without wigs in his youth....I have some recollection of an anecdote of an advocate appearing without a wig before Lord President McNeill in the Eighteen sixties....I think that our Judges always wore wigs from the Restoration onwards, and that members of the Faculty did so until the fashion for gentlemen changed: then for a time it was optional, and did not become universal again until 1860–1870.... Your specific question whether the resumption of the wig by the advocates was by voluntary changes or under an Act of Sederunt or resolution of the Faculty will need investigation. My impression is that it was a voluntary change....It is, I think, true that Sir Walter Scott never wore a wig. There are many portraits of him with gown and without wig, and he figures in Kay's twelve non-wig-wearing Advocates."

The advocates in Edinburgh wear the same uniform as barristers in England, with the exception of one permanent difference for a King's Counsel, and one permanent and one temporary one for a junior. Instead of the bands worn by an English Silk, the Scottish leader wears a fall—a broad cravat of white linen—which is much more decorative than bands. The Scottish junior also eschews "bands": he wears a white dress-tie, like an Eton boy. On the back of an English junior's gown, in the region of the left shoulder-blade, there is a curious

* *A Series of Original Portraits and Caricature Etchings*, by John Kay, 2 vols. Edinburgh, 1838. There is a copy in the library of The Athenaeum. The two pictures of the advocates who do, and do not, wear wigs are dated 1810 and 1811.

pleated appendage. This was once a purse, slung by a string over the left shoulder. The Proctors at Oxford have the same appendage on their gowns. And there is one, of an enormous size, on the back of the statue of the Founder in the School Yard at Eton. A newly fledged advocate in Edinburgh does not have this appendage on the back of his gown: but he is allowed to assume it when he appears as counsel in an appeal to the House of Lords, and thereafter to wear it. So for a junior to have the purse on his gown in Edinburgh is a distinction rather better than carrying a red bag in England.

When Lord Blackburn was in London I happened to say to him that I regarded the trial of Madeleine Smith as the most interesting criminal case I ever read. Remembering this, Lord Blackburn took the trouble to arrange that our railway rating case should be heard in the Justiciary Court, which was in July 1857 the stage for that momentous drama. There was no excitement in our case, only a solid argument about figures and sections of Acts of Parliament.* And there was no scope for oratory like that of Inglis. Has any speech for the defence ever been opened more effectively?—"Gentlemen of the jury, the charge against the prisoner is murder, and the punishment of murder is death; and that simple statement is sufficient to suggest to us the awful solemnity of the occasion which brings you and me face to face."

There was no scope for oratory, but there was very able argument: and I felt that I was right in the words I had used in London. Mr Graham Robertson, K.C., who opened the appeal, graciously welcomed me, and said that no English Judge could be sent to Edinburgh with a more appropriate name. Before either of our cases were heard, after consultation, Lord Blackburn had announced in Edinburgh, and I in London, that we should be glad to hear members of either the English or the Scottish bar, in London or in Edinburgh. In fact we had English counsel in London, and Scottish in Edinburgh. When I said a few words of thanks to Mr Graham Robertson for his greeting, I alluded to our announcement. I added that I had no desire to promote any rivalry—any forensic Bannockburn or Flodden—but I thought it would be interesting if in some later cases it were so arranged that the Scots should argue in London, and the Englishmen in Edinburgh. In fact there have been no more such cases up to now, and I can continue to

* The case is reported, *Fife County Council* v. *L.N.E.R.* (1933), Sc. L.T. Rep. 472.

pride myself on being the only English Judge who has ever sat on the bench in the Parliament House.

Our case finished by noon on the Thursday. Then I spent some time wandering by myself into various Courts as a spectator. As it happened I had the chance of seeing seven Judges of the Inner House all sitting together, which I believe is a rare event. The case involved some question on legislation affecting both England and Scotland, and there had been some difference of opinion between English and Scottish Courts of first instance. I also listened for a time to a case before Lord Fleming concerning the Trust Deed of a Presbyterian church, that involved nice questions of doctrine: I felt grateful that such a task had never come my way. By comparison I seemed on familiar ground when I turned into Lord Pitman's Court, and found him trying a motor collision case with a jury: for that is the staple of our civil business on circuit.

In the afternoon I saw a little more of the Courts at work. And then happily it occurred to me that I had not been to Holyrood for a very long time. From that long ago I retained a general impression of a rather gaunt, ill-kept place, with such cheap pseudo-antiquities as the blood of Rizzio on the floor. But when I went this time all was changed. It is now a magnificent palace, clean, well kept, with admirable furniture, and with magnificent modern panelling in some of its greatest rooms. The levees and soirées of the Lord High Commissioner must be very splendid. My friend, Lord Tweedsmuir, had held his court about a fortnight before.

And so, after dining with Lord Hunter at the University Club, I went back to London by the night train. As it happened my wife and I had been invited for the week-end to stay with a friend near Bath; and on the Saturday morning I found myself in that city. Happy is he whom fate permits to be within 48 hours in two of the noblest cities of Great Britain—in Edinburgh and in Bath.

◇ ◇ ◇

In the autumn of 1933 I was upon the conjoined North and South Wales Circuit. Upon that one goes alone to Carnarvon, Ruthin, Chester, Carmarthen, and Brecon, and is then joined at Cardiff or Swansea by a second judge. Even this programme I was able to curtail: for the work at Brecon was negligible, and I got the Lord Chief Justice and the Lord Chancellor to cancel its Assize and transfer its one prisoner for trial at Cardiff.

In this autumn the Courts opened in London on 2 October, the earliest day, I fancy, on which the Courts have ever sat at Westminster or in the Strand. I went to Carnarvon on Wednesday, 16 October. My friend the Rector had lately been promoted to be Rector of Llandudno. (In less than a year Llandudno lost him; for he was made Bishop of Swansea and Brecon, and a very good Bishop he will make.) His successor was not yet in residence, so the rectory was not available as Judges' Lodgings. We were housed some way out of the town on the road to Pwllheli. It was not a very satisfactory house.

I had made it a rule to go to the top of Snowdon whenever I was at Carnarvon. So on the Saturday my marshal and I drove to Quellen Lake, and walked up from there. It was wet and very cold at the top, and there was no view: we came down to Llanberis.

At Chester, unhappily, the Lodgings were also changed, and in place of the very pleasant house on the Eccleston road we were in a huge place of rather forbidding aspect at Upton Heath, a long way out of the city to the north. We had the Assize Service at the Cathedral on the Sunday, with an unusual display of colour. For there was the High Sheriff, in the uniform of a Deputy-Lieutenant, the General of the Western Command, and the Mayor, all adding their scarlet to that of my robes.

After the service my wife drove me out to luncheon with friends who are the present owners of Halston. That was a place I was very interested to see, as I had often read with amazement the life of John Mytton by "Nimrod". I possess that curious work in the form of a bound set of *The New Sporting Magazine* for October to December 1834. Taking down the volume just now I find on the fly-leaf (or "end-paper" as it is the fashion now to call it) a note—"Cambridge, Autumn Assize, 1926, bought at David's stall in the market place."

Halston is a fine, square, red-brick house, dating from 1695. Beyond the lake in the park is a small chapel, full of Mytton hatchments and achievements. That poor lunatic, who died of *delirium tremens*, at the age of 38, in the King's Bench Prison, after doing everything in his power to ruin his ancient family, was buried in this chapel in March 1834. He was High Sheriff of Salop in 1823, following in that office any number of his ancient name since Thomas Mytton, High Sheriff in 1480.

I had another interesting experience at Chester, by the kindness of the High Sheriff. For he took me to the annual dinner of the Tarporley Hunt Club at the Swan Inn at Tarporley. There is no Tarporley Hunt as a pack. In the Swan the Club has a big room upstairs. Round the walls are panels with the names of the Presidents since 1762—Cheshire names recurring over and over again. In this year, 1933, the President was Mr Leicester Warren of Tabley. All the members wore a picturesque uniform, knee-breeches, and a coat with green facings. There were some fine old chairs, and the glasses were engraved with the Club crest, and its motto "Quaesitum meritis". There seemed to be some difference of opinion as to the meaning of those words; and I do not feel certain that Cicero would have understood them; but that really does not matter. I saw a new member admitted, by the ritual of "drinking his Quaesitum"—one of the engraved goblets full of port. Among the toasts was that of the Masters of the two neighbouring packs, but by the tradition of the Club they were referred to not as "Masters" but as "Managers". Altogether it was to me a most interesting evening. I had to reply for the Visitors and was able to be genuinely grateful. I think I added that though I never rode a horse, still less ever hunted a fox, I constantly read the accounts in *The Times* of the doings of various packs. And I do so because of the music of the country names which echoes throughout them.

In the same way, though I never play golf, I always read the articles in *The Times* "by our Golf Correspondent", because he is so entertaining a writer. I wish he would write about things other than golf.

As it was dark I could not see much of the Swan, but it must be an unusually fine country inn. Joseph Farington, R.A., in his *Diary*, writes on 18 September 1808: "At Tarperly, where we stopped to change our Chaise and Horses we found a large and commodious Inn, built to accommodate those gentlemen of the County who form the Tarperly Hunt." He has another mention of Tarporley on 6 August 1807. "Mr Hallet spoke of several persons who from a low beginning had made great fortunes. He mentioned a Leather Breeches maker, of the name of White, who formerly resided at *Tarperley* in *Cheshire* & made Leather Breeches for the gentlemen of that *Hunt*. Being recommended by them He came to London & settled in St Albans St. & now resides in Bond Street, & is said to be worth £150,000."

On the Saturday I went over to Wrexham, as I wanted to see its fine church again, and the very interesting monuments in it. That to

Owen Bold is by William Stanton, who was a considerable artist: he also made the great effigy of the second Lord Coventry at Elmley Castle, and a Salisbury monument at Whitchurch, near Denbigh, that I saw a few days earlier. There is also the remarkable Roubiliac monument to Miss Mary Myddelton, a white figure emerging from a breaking sarcophagus, while a pyramid topples up above. It is the same fancy as his Hargrave monument in Westminster Abbey. That one is too high up to be easily seen: the Wrexham one is on a happier level.

On the magnificent iron gates of the churchyard I saw one thing with regret. Over the centre of the design is an open book for a painted inscription. This, with all the rest of the ironwork, had been recently repainted. But the painter had been allowed to use that ghastly form of type which is commonly called "block lettering". There is nothing which is more significant of the good taste of the eighteenth century, and of the degradation of to-day, than the pattern of lettering used for public notices, inscriptions, tombstones, and the like.

The journey from Chester to Carmarthen, via Newport, was a tedious business. There was less than two days' work there, and I wished it could have been treated as "no substantial amount of business" so as to have transferred it to Cardiff. On the way to Cardiff my marshal and I broke the journey at Kidwelly, and saw the Castle, which had been well restored by the Office of Works. I doubt if there is better value to be got in modern books than the three little volumes (costing 1*s.* each) by Lord Harlech on the Ancient Monuments in the care of the Office of Works. But they deal with Northern England, Southern England, and the Midlands. Lord Harlech should surely add a fourth volume for Wales, and I hope he will. Welsh Castles—Carnarvon, Harlech, Beaumaris, and Kidwelly—are the real things in castles.

At Cardiff I had 58 prisoners to try, and that took twelve working days. I see on one day, in my diary—"Trial for Sedition!" I have absolutely no recollection of the case, or its result. But a charge in these days so unusual justified my note of exclamation.

There were some diversions. The High Sheriff took me to see St Donat's Castle, the property of an American of apparently boundless opulence. Much rebuilding had been done, and the whole place was like a museum. It is, or was, a remarkable place: there can be nothing in Britain like its terraced gardens down to the sea. I also walked along the coast, past Dunraven Castle, and quite near it saw a fox leisurely running across the field.

Lord Bute, who was at Cardiff Castle, took me to see Caerphilly Castle, which he had been restoring for five years. There are few owners of ruined castles who can compete with, and even outdo, the Office of Works in such pious restoration. On the way back he showed me over Castle Goch, that his father had even more magnificently restored.

When I got away from Cardiff I found I had not done with circuit for 1933. About a fortnight later Mr Justice Charles wrote to the Lord Chief Justice from Lewes to say that there was so much work there that without help he could not finish before Christmas. So on 13 December I went down to Lewes. This was the first time I had ever been on any part of the "Second South-Eastern", and I only went all round it once, in 1936. There were some fine old houses in Lewes. But I thought the very best thing in the town was an admirable shop front, with small panes in its windows, just opposite the Town Hall. I think it was the most picturesque shop I ever saw—and, alas, how few have survived! More than once I went to it, to buy a knife, or scissors, that I did not really want, but just for the satisfaction of entering an almost perfect eighteenth-century shop. There was a sequel—but I shall come to that in 1936.

As Lewes is so near town I could go home for the week-end. And on 21 December Mr Justice Charles and I had both finished our tasks, and went home for good.

Lewes has only been the regular Assize town for Sussex since 1831. From 1734 to 1799 the Lent Assize used to be at East Grinstead, and the Summer Assize alternately at Lewes and Horsham. From 1800 to 1830 the Lent Assize was at Horsham and the Summer Assize at Lewes. Since 1831 they have all been at Lewes.

1934

In January 1934 I was to go on the "Long Western" Circuit, and to begin its work at Devizes on Monday, 15 January. The Assizes at Aylesbury began on the previous Saturday. The High Sheriff of Buckinghamshire, who was an old friend of mine, had invited me to his Sheriff's luncheon. If Grand Juries had not been abolished I believe I might have had the privilege of being Foreman of the Grand Jury, and listening with all due deference to the charge of my brother Humphreys. As it was I went over to Aylesbury and sat on the bench, and for the first time (except in a Divisional Court) watched a brother judge doing his work. The luncheon, held, as usual by the Judge's permission, in the great dining-room of the Lodgings, was a very pleasant function. I had the congenial task of proposing the health of our host. I took occasion to thank him for thus continuing the opportunity for county justices to attend the Assizes notwithstanding the recent abolition of the Grand Jury. And I said I hoped, and I was sure my brother justices hoped, that future Sheriffs would follow the precedent he had thus established. Later in the afternoon Mr Justice and Lady Humphreys drove over to tea at my home.

On the next evening I went to Devizes by a very slow train from Maidenhead, and on the Monday morning was attended at church by the Mayor preceded by his scarlet-clad Ganymede. There was but one prisoner, and one civil case, and all was over on this first day. Next day my marshal and I walked through Roundway Park, and over the downs through Colstone to Calne. I wondered if Charles Lamb would still call it "Sweet Calne" if he could see the vast bacon factory that now dominates and crushes the town. We came back a different way, through Heddington.

The Devizes Town Hall, which I had not been in before, has a fine room in the style of the Adams, with three good glass chandeliers. Brownston House, next to St Mary's church, is charming.

Next day we went by train to Dorchester, with changes at Trowbridge and Westbury. Here there was a novelty in the ritual of an

Assize. The High Sheriff had apparently been taking counsel with the officer commanding the Depot. So when I arrived at the Courts from the church I found a guard of honour of the Dorset Regiment drawn up in the street. Rather reluctantly, at their urgent request, I "inspected" the guard. My only military experience had been as a private, over thirty years before, in the Devil's Own. And I had only a vague idea that I must walk slowly along the ranks, observing with an approving eye the cleanliness of buttons.

If there had been a Grand Jury to address I should have been tempted to remind them that it was within a few days of a century ago that a notable trial took place at Dorchester. At the Lent Assizes in 1834 the Judge in the Crown Court was Baron Williams. It was his first Assize, for he had only been raised to the Bench on 28 February of that year. On 19 March there appeared in the dock six farm labourers, George Loveless, James Loveless, James Hammett, Thomas Standfield, John Standfield, and James Brine. They are now better known as the Tolpuddle Martyrs. Their offence was that in December 1833 they organized a primitive Trades Union, the Grand Lodge of Tolpuddle of the Agricultural Labourers' Friendly Society. The immediate aim of the Grand Lodge was to try to get the wages of farm hands raised from 7*s*. a week to 10*s*. After the manner of such early friendly societies, or trades unions, members were admitted with a short religious service, and, being blindfolded, took an oath to be loyal to the union and its objects.

The farmers and local landowners were alarmed at the successful increase of the Agricultural Labourers' Friendly Society. Mr James Frampton, one of the latter, and a Justice of the Peace, was most active. Lord Melbourne, the Whig Home Secretary, was applied to, and he suggested that "in cases of this description suitable provisions relative to the administration of secret oaths had been frequently resorted to with advantage". This was a reference to the Mutiny or Unlawful Oaths Act of 1797 (37 Geo. III, cap. 123), which was passed to deal with the trouble of the Mutiny of the Nore. On 24 February 1834 the six men, all of whom were very respectable and keen Methodists, were arrested at Tolpuddle and committed to Dorchester gaol by Mr James Frampton. A few days later a full bench of magistrates committed them for trial at the Assizes. And so on 19 March they stood in the dock before Baron Williams. That they had taken and administered oaths (as the Oddfellows, Freemasons, and others notoriously did) could not be gainsaid: the jury found them Guilty.

Baron Williams had for years been a Whig Member of Parliament. He had been made a judge for that reason; the worst defect of our legal system has always been such a possibility. Two days after the verdict he passed the appalling sentence of seven years' transportation on all the six convicts.

They were taken away in chains to Portsmouth, kept for six weeks in the hulks, and then shipped in a convict ship to Australia. She was the *George Metcalf*, and she took 14 weeks upon the voyage. George Loveless was landed at Hobart; the other five were taken on to Sydney.

Meanwhile an immense agitation spread all over England in protest against this trial and sentence. One of the most prominent leaders was Dr Thomas Wakley, M.P. for Finsbury. Eventually the Government had to give way, and in March 1836 Lord John Russell announced that the King's pardon had been granted to the Tolpuddle Martyrs. James Loveless, John Standfield, and James Brine got back to Plymouth in March 1838. James Hammett only arrived in August 1838, and George Loveless and Thomas Standfield were even later. They came back to Tolpuddle, but only James Hammett spent the rest of his life there. The other five went to Essex for two years, and then emigrated to Canada.

In St Peter's church at Dorchester there is a fine monument to Denzil Holles, Lord Ifield, now at the West end of the North aisle. In front of it there stood on the ground two charming amorini in alabaster, which seemed oddly placed. And then in the vestry I found an old print of the church, in which this tomb appeared at the East end of the South aisle, with the two little figures standing, as part of the design, on each side of it. The place to which it was moved being narrower, there was no room for them, so they were left forlorn and incongruous in front. Thus is Art sacrificed by the zealous cleric!

At Taunton they had heard of the military honours that Dorchester had paid to me, and they were not to be outdone. So there was again a guard of honour at the Courts from the depot of the Somerset Light Infantry. There was a troublesome and lengthy case from Bath, in which an offence was alleged to have been committed in Westgate Buildings. I gathered from the evidence that it was now rather a sordid street. But even when Anne Elliot went to visit Mrs Smith there Westgate Buildings was not exactly fashionable. For I remembered how Sir Walter exclaimed—"And who is Miss Anne Elliot to be visiting in Westgate Buildings! Westgate Buildings must have been rather surprised by the appearance of a carriage drawn up near its pavement! Sir Henry Russell's widow, indeed, has no honours to distinguish her arms; but still it is a handsome equipage, and no doubt is well known to convey a Miss Elliot."

On my last day at Taunton I found I could get a train to Bodmin in the afternoon. So in the morning I drove over to Montacute, which I had long desired to see. In 1931 it was given to the National Trust by an anonymous benefactor. I suppose visitors in January were few. The lodge-keeper happily appeared to think that I was respectable. So he gave me the key of the front door, and I was left to wander as I liked all over the house and gardens. It is a wonderful place, built at the end of the sixteenth century for Edward Phelips, of the Middle Temple, from the designs of John Thorpe, who also built Wollaton. Edward Phelips became Master of the Rolls in 1608. His descendants showed less energy, and followed all too readily the unhappy tradition that a country gentleman should stay at home and do little or nothing. So the race came to its inevitable end, and the last Phelips had exhausted the family fortunes. Lord Curzon was tenant for a time and did some of that work of careful restoration of which he did so much more at Tattershall and Bodiam.

It is a wonderful building, but it could not really be made a habitable residence, and it is best left as a museum piece. One capital defect of the Elizabethan plan, however, was strangely rectified in the eighteenth century. Originally all the rooms opened one into another, on each floor, an awkward arrangement for more civilized days. In 1786 the then Edward Phelips bought an old house—older than Montacute, and built in Henry VIII's time—at Clifton Maybank, 6 miles away in Dorset. He pulled it down, and used its front to build a new West front to Montacute, so forming on the ground and first floors long corridors. This Henry VIII work fits in admirably with the Elizabethan to which it was added. And Montacute was thus given the practical advantage of having passages of connexion outside its living rooms.

I was alone at Montacute because my marshal had gone back to town that morning, and only rejoined me three days later. On the Sunday morning at Bodmin there was a sharp white frost, a cloudless sky, and, as the day went on, brilliant sunshine. I drove down to Fowey, and then walked back by lanes parallel to the main road through Lostwithiel, Restormel, Fairy Cross, and through the great park of Llanhydrock. After my marshal rejoined me I had one free day, so we repeated my Sunday walk, with a slight variation. In the street at Lostwithiel was a man playing the penny whistle, by way of begging, and he played it amazingly well. At my request he played "Cherry Ripe", though he did not appear to recognize the quotation (nor, I regret to say, did my marshal), when I remarked that "it was originally composed for this instrument". But he was a great *and* a fine performer—better than Sergeant Brand: he did not lack the bird-like richness, and he extracted all the honey out of "Cherry Ripe". I think I gave him half a crown. He may have thought me a trifle crazy; for he was clearly puzzled by my parting admonition that whenever he got the chance he should read *The Wrong Box*.

There was, rather to my relief, no guard of honour at Bodmin, but we dined very pleasantly with the officers of the depot.

And so, on Friday, 2 February, to Exeter, where I was joined by Mr Justice Talbot. I was very glad to be in Exeter again; but there was a good deal of work, and as darkness set in so early there was not much chance of diversion. One afternoon we all took the train out to Christow, and walked to Doddiscombleigh, where there is a set of fine ancient painted windows. We walked on to Higher Ashton, which has a painted screen and parclose. One of the figures on it was St Appolonia, duly figured with a pair of forceps grasping a tooth. And so back to Exeter past the Haldon Tower and through Ide. It was dark long before we got back.

I do not think I had ever before noticed Parliament Street in Exeter. One might well overlook it. It must be the narrowest "street" in the world: at one end I doubt if it is three feet wide, and at no part more than four. By comparison Taylor's Buildings, the alley that goes from Chandos Street, at the bottom of Bedfordbury, into St Martin's Lane, is a wide thoroughfare.

On 10 February we went on to Bristol, and spent the afternoon in visiting St Mary Redcliffe. Since I was here last that had been nobly restored by one of the Wills family. What would Bristol be without tobacco, and the Wills family? The church, I again avow, is the finest parish church in England. It has but one defect, the Victorian reredos of, I suppose, about 1870.

Next morning, being Sunday, my marshal and I heard most of the service in the Cathedral, and then took the train to Bath. I always go to Bath if I am near enough. And being in Bath I always go to the Pump Room. There you can get back more thoroughly to the eighteenth century than anywhere else that I know.

On Monday morning Mr Justice Talbot and I drove in the State Coach, with the Lord Mayor and the Sword Bearer, to the Mayor's chapel. The Sword-Bearer wears a fur hat; the sword has to go sticking out of the window of the coach. At the chapel were eight large policemen, each carrying a small silver mace. On the wall of the Crown Court, in which I sat, an even greater sword—"the Sword of Justice"—was suspended on the wall. But we saw more of the municipal treasures. A selection of the plate was set out each evening on our dinner table at the Mansion House. And one night, after dinner, the Housekeeper showed us the whole collection in the strong-room.

One afternoon I had some leisure. I walked down to Dowry Square, and admired its fine Queen Anne houses, now sadly degraded. In my annotated edition of Fanny Burney's *Evelina* (1930) I wrote: "In Paradise Row, between Dowry Parade and The Parade were two Assembly Rooms....The *Lower* or *New Long Room*, or at any rate its large room, still survives, a dilapidated relic, as 'The Dowry National School for Girls'. I went twice to its doors in February 1929 in the hope of seeing the interior, but on each occasion the murmur of children at their lessons within warned me away." On this occasion I saw grown-up people standing about the entrance of the school, and found that some sort of a tea party was taking place. I asked someone if I might look inside, and was permitted. So I saw the old Assembly Room of the Hotwells. But every trace of ancient splendours was gone: the only thing that survived was one fireplace.

On Saturday, 17 February, I travelled to Winchester, via Devizes and Newbury, and so by that line (once called The Didcot, Newbury, and Southampton Railway) that was sadly allowed to intrude its ugliness round the east side of Winchester. Mr Justice Talbot who, as Sub-Warden, had to attend a meeting of the Governing Body of the School, went by car, starting very early in the morning. The Lodgings in the Close had been newly decorated, and were very spick and span. But the furniture, for a fine old house, was deplorably Victorian.

We had two masters to dinner, and four boys to breakfast. The Latin letter from one of them, the Prefect of Hall, had been duly answered by Mr Justice Talbot, in an epistle that Tully might have been proud to have written. So they had their "rem." The Prefect of Hall told me that on such a holiday custom required that he should wear, at least for part of the time, an old ring—the Rem ring—which was given out to him by the Head Master, and returned in the evening. Thereupon Mr Justice Talbot told us that when, on the Saturday before, as Sub-Warden, it was his duty to admit Mr Gavin Symonds, K.C., as a newly elected Fellow, he had to wear the Founder's Ring, which is always assumed by the Warden or Sub-Warden on such an occasion. Such are the enviable antiquities of Winchester! And as Mr Justice Talbot was the most loyal and enthusiastic Wykehamist who ever lived, one could have no happier companion in Winchester.

Mr Gavin Symonds has, of course, since become a judge. Of recent times it has been difficult for anyone to attain that promotion unless he was educated at Winchester. When I wrote to congratulate yet another of them, Mr Cyril Asquith, I told him that my first instinct was to write to congratulate the Lord Chancellor on so admirable an appointment. "How gratified he must have been", I added, "when he received an affirmative answer to the essential question, 'Is he a Wykehamist'?"

As Winchester College was founded by a Lord Chancellor it is fitting that she should be the nursing mother of judges. Atlay's *Victorian Chancellors* contains the lives of ten. Only four of them were at an English public school. Lord Cottenham was at Harrow; but the other three, Cranworth, Hatherley, and Selborne, were all at Winchester.

And so, on 26 February, the work was finished. My clerk, in the ancient formula, bade those in Court to "depart hence and give their attendance at my Lord's lodgings". And, in the happy practice of the Western Circuit, and of that alone, the senior barrister bade me farewell, and hoped that I should come again soon on the circuit. To which I replied, in all sincerity, "Thank you very much. I shall come again on the earliest possible opportunity". For there is no circuit so pleasant as the Western.

◇ ◇ ◇

In the summer of 1934 I went on the Oxford Circuit, and on Sunday, 27 May, drove over to Reading from my home. The Lodgings were in a new place, a villa off the Basingstoke Road, fairly comfortable but entirely hideous. But I should not look for amenity in Reading, which has less in it of beauty than any town of its size in the South of England. If only its great Abbey church had survived, and there had been a Bishop of Reading instead of a Bishop of Oxford!

Next day the whole business of the Assize was finished by luncheon. I could not foresee this. There was only one prisoner, who pleaded guilty. But there were three civil cases entered for trial. Two were settled before they were called on, and the third was settled after I had heard about an hour of it. If I could have foreseen this I might have got the Lord Chief Justice to cancel the Reading Assize, and transfer its one prisoner for trial at Oxford. As it was, I had sacrificed the last day of my Whitsun Vacation for this business at Reading, so I had no compunction in taking the Tuesday and Wednesday as holidays at home.

At Oxford there was more work than usual. The Thursday was Commission Day, and the criminal work was to begin on Friday morning. But for the convenience of counsel I drove up early on Thursday morning, and tried a civil case. In the afternoon I was taken by the High Sheriff to a garden party given by Mrs Morrell at Headington Hall: it was in connexion with the Royal Agricultural Show, which was being held in the park. I suppose I must have driven a hundred times down Headington Hill to St Clements between the two parts of the park that are joined by a bridge across the road, but I had never been inside its gates. And I had no conception of the spacious seclusion, the magnificent trees, and the views of Oxford, that the place affords. Happily the trees shut out the results of Lord Nuffield's astonishing career.

When I was an undergraduate bicycling was coming in. None of us owned bicycles, but occasionally we hired them. We did so at a small shop in Holywell. The tyres usually wanted blowing up before we started. And the tyres were blown up by a boy, who seemed to run the whole of the small establishment. That boy is now my Lord Nuffield.

On the Thursday evening I dined with a friend in the hall at Magdalen. On Friday the Vice-Chancellor, Proctors, and Heads of Houses dined with me at the Lodgings, a party of twenty. On the Sunday I dined in hall at Christ Church, on the Monday at Brasenose, and on Tuesday in my own Trinity. The Assize sermon on Sunday was a Bampton Lecture, a learned and interesting discourse. I had not before seen the new seating at St Mary's. It could hardly fail to be an improvement on the ghastliness of the old woodwork, though I did not feel very enthusiastic about it. But the opening out of the choir, and of Adam de Brome's chapel, was a great improvement.

After the service we drove out with the High Sheriff, Colonel Rhys Wingfield, to luncheon at his fine place, Great Barrington. One of his treasures, in a glass case in the hall, is the Lord Chancellor's purse of Lord Talbot, an ancestor. How it came to Colonel Wingfield rather than to Mr Justice Talbot, a direct descendant of the Lord Chancellor, I was told but I have forgotten.

On this, as on my previous visit to Oxford, I had asked the High Sheriff to direct that places in Court should be reserved for undergraduate law students wearing cap and gown: he did so, and got his Under-Sheriff to intimate this to the various law tutors.

James Woodforde, when an undergraduate at New College, wrote in his diary on 6 March 1761: "Went up into the Hall [the Court at the Castle] this afternoon after the Judge was in, and I could not get a tolerable Place some time, but at last I jumped from two men's shoulders and leaped upon the Heads of several men and then scrambled into the Prisoners Place where the Judge said I must not stay, so one of the Counsellors desired me not to make a noise, and he would let me have his Place, which was immediately under the Prisoners and opposite the Judge, where I sat and heard three or four tryalls, and likewise condemnation passed on Dumas, alias Darking, alias Hamilton, alias Harris.* Was up there from 5 till 9, and then the Judge had finished everything. 1 condemned to die, 4 transported for seven years, 1 burnt in the hand and acquitted."

On this occasion my young friends, who came in some number, behaved more properly. And I was glad that they had the opportunity of listening to an interesting and amusing case. Several men had planned to rob the mail between Paddington and Reading. There arrived at Paddington, just before an express for South Wales started,

* On 2 February he had written, "Went and saw Dumas, alias Darking, a famous Highwayman, in the Castle. Gave a girl there, in for stealing a Shift, 2*d*."

two men with a large and heavy hamper, and a light and seemingly empty trunk, both labelled to Reading. On the top of the hamper was tied a cardboard box, marked "Fragile". The hamper and the trunk were put in the van just before the train started. There is no doubt (though no witness saw it) that soon after it left a man emerged from the hamper, stole some registered mail-bags, put them into the trunk, got back into the hamper, and closed it from within. At Reading the two passengers got their hamper and trunk loaded upon a lorry, and departed sitting beside the driver. There is again no doubt (though no one could give evidence of it) that soon after the man got out of the hamper, and he and the two accomplices transferred themselves to a motor car driven by a fourth man. Into the car they also put the registered mail-bags: in addition to registered letters these also contained many packets of Postal Order forms which were on their way to Welsh Post Offices. The car thus loaded set off hell-for-leather towards London.

And then Providence intervened! Somewhere near Hare Hatch a spinster lady was learning to drive a car. She emerged, nervously and unskilfully, from a side road out on the Bath Road, right into the path of the robbers' car. There was a tremendous smash. We never heard what happened to the poor emissary of Providence. But the bad men's car was wrecked in a ditch. Spectators were amazed to observe that out of this wrecked car there crawled four badly wounded men, who at once took to their heels and ran away. The spectators, and the police who soon arrived, were further surprised to find that the inside of the car was littered with registered letters, postal-order forms, and mail-bags. Telephones got to work, and four men, blood-stained and considerably damaged, were arrested without difficulty. Next day the lorry that had come to Reading station was found in a garage in Maidenhead, with the hamper and trunk in it, and inside the hamper the cushions that had made its occupant's journey more comfortable.

This made a very pretty case. The men made a fight of it, and pleaded "Not Guilty". Their defence was that they had nothing to do with the robbery in the train. They were innocent people, out for a drive in the car, which one of them was proposing to sell to another. In a side road they saw a suspicious-looking car drive off, and then found the letters and bags at the side of the road where it had been standing.

Like good citizens they thought they ought to take these to the police, and so put them in their car for that purpose. And then unhappily the accident happened.

It was an ingenious story. But one obvious question was "Why had they run away?" And another—"Why had they told a pack of lies to explain their injuries when arrested?" For two had been in a fight, and another in a motor-cycle accident. And why had one of them a ticket to Reading in his pocket, and another a label of a registered mail-bag? Of course the jury convicted them.

It came out in the evidence that the scheme had been tried about a fortnight before. On that occasion the two men arrived in good time for the train at Paddington. The result was that the hamper was put in the van and a heavy piece of luggage was put on the top of it: so the man could not get out. There was even a suggestion that he was loaded in the van head downwards, and so had a most uncomfortable journey. Hence it was that, when they tried again, they arrived only just before the train started, and had the cardboard box tied to the top of the hamper, and labelled "Fragile".

This case, of course, ought to have been tried at Reading. But it was still being heard at the Police Court, when the Reading Assizes began. Under the modern Act to which I before referred, the magistrates were able to commit them for trial at Oxford, instead of to the Autumn Assize at Reading. Providence again intervened in this—for the benefit of the undergraduate spectators.

In the course of my summing up I told the jury that if they believed the men's story, they would of course acquit them. But I added that they might think that if that story were told to the Marines not one member of that traditionally credulous corps could be found to give it credit. As a result of this remark I received, a few weeks later, a copy of "The Globe and Laurel", the magazine of the Marines, with a polite note from the editor, a Major who had been called to the bar. In his paper he quoted my remark, and recorded that the Berkshire police constable, who arrested two of the men at Maidenhead, had previously served in the Marines—and he did not believe their explanation. I wrote to thank the editor, and asked him if he had any views as to the origin of "Tell that to the Marines". He replied that he had heard two suggestions, but neither seemed plausible or satisfactory. I have forgotten what they were, but I know I agreed with him.

This case about the mail-bags lasted two days, and there was another long criminal trial at Oxford. So I had to be at work there all the day on which I should have opened the Assize at Worcester. I arranged with Sir Reginald Coventry, K.C., who as a leader on the circuit was "in the Commission", that he should go on ahead of me, open the Commission, and try some cases at Worcester, while I was still at Oxford. I went on to Worcester in the evening.

For the week-end between Worcester and Gloucester I went to stay with an old Trinity friend at his most beautiful place. On the Sunday he drove me into Gloucester for the Assize Service, and at the Cathedral another Trinity contemporary received me as Sub-Dean. It was 10 June, and so there came in the Psalms the 51st, of which the first verse was of old "the neck verse" for convicted felons who claimed Benefit of Clergy. "Have mercy upon me, O God, according to thy loving kindness : according to the multitude of thy tender mercies blot out my transgressions." As I heard it sung, I wondered how many there were in the Cathedral who knew what a close connexion that verse once had with an Assize.

After the service, and before driving back for luncheon, we went to the Guildhall to meet the Mayor and Corporation. And happily there was at the time a collection of pictures on exhibition, that were lent from houses in the county. There were some delightful pictures. This is a thing that might well be done from time to time in every county town. If it were, we might realize, despite all the acquisitive rapacity of America, when she was rich, what a wealth of beautiful things still remains in English country houses.

As I finished by luncheon on the last day at Gloucester, my marshal and I went out to Painswick in the afternoon. The churchyard is notable for its collection of tombs and yew-trees. The tombs are of great variety in design, but they are all of local stone. Not a single piece of that horrible Italian marble that ruins most English churchyards could be seen. The church is a fine one, and the little town contains many charming Cotswold houses.

Next day we went to Monmouth in my usual way—a drive to the Speech House, stopping to have a look at the garden at Westbury, and then a walk through the Forest of Dean. It was a hot day, and at the end of our walk the climb over the Kymin was very hot indeed.

The Assize Service on Sunday was so crowded that I believe

numbers of people could not get into the church at all. This was not from their desire to see the Judge of Assize, but because the British Legion, all wearing their medals, was present. The Mayor of Monmouth was attended by two Mace Bearers.

I had several times, when in Monmouth, walked into the Castle, and admired the outside of the old house there, dated 1613 upon its front. It was the Headquarters of the local territorial artillery. At this time the K Battery of the R.H.A. from Newport happened to be there for some sort of exercises, and the officers hospitably invited my marshal and me to dine at their Mess. We spent a very pleasant evening, and I had the chance of seeing the inside of the house. The plaster ceiling of the great room on the first floor, with massive pendants, is very remarkable; and there is some good panelling.

As I write (in December 1939) Monmouth has ceased to be the Assize town for its county. They have been allowed, at great expense no doubt, to build a new Court at Newport, and last autumn the Assizes were for the first time held at Newport. This is one of the few things that console me for having lost the privilege of being a Judge of Assize. Monmouth is a very pleasant town: Newport is not. I do not know what the new Court at Newport is like, but I am sure it cannot have so picturesque a façade as the old Court at Monmouth, with its statue of Henry V looking down on his birthplace.

If any change were needed, and Monmouth was to be deserted, I think the proper plan would have been to unite Monmouthshire with Glamorganshire for a joint Assize at Cardiff. From Newport to Cardiff is a little over 10 miles, and there are dozens of trains every day. To have an Assize at Newport and an Assize 10 miles away at Cardiff is only surpassed by the case of Ruthin and Mold, which are even nearer to one another. But here again, as at Swansea, Newport was allowed to swell its local pride, by becoming, at great expense, an Assize town, without regard to national interests and national economy.

And so to Hereford, stopping on the way at Ross, that very pleasant town. At Hereford my best new experience was to spend a long time in the Cathedral library, with its enthusiastic and learned custodian. I knew the book of Canon Streeter, afterwards Provost of Queen's, and what he had accomplished in the way of restoration. But on previous visits I had only had a fleeting look at the library. Its rescue and rehabilitation was a wonderful feat.

Shrewsbury was the charming town I have always found it, and the Judges' Lodgings in Belmont (so used since 1821) as pleasant as ever. I spent a good deal of time each evening, after the Court rose, in watching cricket on the School field. And I dined with the bar at "The Raven". On the last day my case ended at three. My marshal and I drove to Wroxeter. All the excavations were interesting. But the bases of the great peristyle of the Forum, lately uncovered, were magnificent—the finest Roman remains in England, as I think. In the church were four tombs with recumbent effigies. One of them is that of Sir Thomas Bromley and his wife. He was Chief Justice of the Common Pleas from 1553 to 1555, and a Bencher of the Inner Temple. He is not to be confounded with his kinsman, and namesake, Sir Thomas Bromley, Lord Chancellor in 1579, and also of the Inner Temple: his tomb is in St Paul's chapel in Westminster Abbey.

I was anxious to be able to get to London for Saturday, 30 June. For I had an invitation to a performance of *Twelfth Night* in the Middle Temple Hall. That play was first performed in that hall on 2 February 1601/2, and it seemed a desirable thing to see it there again 332 years later. It was a delightful performance, with practically no scenery, but gorgeous costumes, and I enjoyed it immensely.

Next day I drove from home to Watford in the afternoon and got a train to Stafford. There were alleviations even of the dullness of Stafford. To the east we found almost a country lane, leading to a footpath through the park of Ingestre, and to its interesting church, built by Walter Chetwynd in 1676. And one evening, on our way to dine with the High Sheriff, we made a small detour in order to see the great church at Wolverhampton. Of that I had read, but had never seen it. It is magnificent. Perhaps the strangest part of its history is that for centuries (in fact until 1846) the Dean of this collegiate church was also always Dean of Windsor.

Perhaps the most interesting thing to me in this great church was the wonderful leaden statue of Admiral Leveson by Le Sueur, in a chapel. Unfortunately, it is now set on a pedestal that is modern, and is too small. In the vestry they showed me two charming amorini that once adorned the pedestal that Le Sueur designed. These I was told had been removed because it was thought that their nakedness might be a stumbling-block to Sunday-school children! Another monument, more curious than beautiful, but of great interest, is that of

Colonel Lane, whose sister was of such service to Charles II after Worcester Fight. The Boscobel Oak is figured upon it. And the stone pulpit, of the fifteenth century, against one of the pillars of the nave is very remarkable.

I was also shown the entry in the parish register of the marriage of Button Gwinnett. Americans grow very excited over this. I must confess I had never heard of him before. He was a Wolverhampton man who signed the Declaration of Independence in 1776, and was killed in a duel a year later. I believe the Wolverhampton Grammar School made (very properly) a large sum of money by selling a page of their records containing his signature, keeping a photographic copy. I daresay the money may have bought a cricket field, or founded a scholarship. And when a country is so poor in its inheritance from the past, it is as well to let them have, at a price, so valueless a thing as the signature of Button Gwinnett. I would like to sell them the page of the marriage register, and use part of the proceeds to restore Le Sueur's masterpiece.

Lastly we went to dine with Lord and Lady Harrowby, he being Lord-Lieutenant, at Sandon Park. It is a magnificent place, and it contains many wonderful pictures, including as fine a Holbein portrait as exists. I could not help reflecting that the founder of this family, and of its great estate, was a Chief Justice of the King's Bench. Sir Dudley Ryder (1691–1756) was the son of a nonconformist London shopkeeper. He was called to the bar at the Middle Temple in 1725, became Solicitor-General in 1733, Attorney-General in 1737, and Chief Justice in 1754. He was about to be made a peer when he died in 1756. His son was made Lord Harrowby in 1776, and his grandson was advanced to the Earldom in 1809.

There was published in 1939 *The Diary of Dudley Ryder* 1715–1716. It is a curious and interesting document. If one had merely been told that it was the diary of a young man of 24 to 25, I am sure no one would fancy the writer was likely to end as a Lord Chief Justice and a peer.

On Friday, 6 July, I finished my work at Stafford at 4.15, and caught the 4.28 train to town. It was a very hot day, and so was the next day, which I spent at Henley Regatta.

In the autumn of 1934 I had no circuit, and stayed in London.

1935

For January 1935 I had been fortunate in being able to choose the first South-Eastern Circuit, i.e. Huntingdon, Cambridge, Ipswich, Norwich, and Chelmsford. I was looking forward to this very much. But unhappily I had to begin, in December, the hearing of a case of appalling complexity in the Railway and Canal Commission Court. This was about the assessment for rating purposes of the whole of the Southern Railway. By Christmas we had had ten days of it, and we had only heard one side. It was bad enough to have the vacation intervene: during that I could forget much. But if I had then gone away for five or six weeks on circuit, at the beginning of the next term, I should have forgotten everything. Moreover, by the Act under which I was "Ex-officio Railway Commissioner" (an ugly title), I was required to give precedence to the work of that Court. So, to my great regret, I had to ask the Lord Chief Justice to relieve me of this circuit. My regret was increased by the receipt, just before I should have started, of an invitation from the Master of Trinity to dine with him in hall on the Sunday evening at Cambridge.

Mr Hilbery, K.C., was appointed Commissioner of Assize in my place, and I had to stay in town and resume the estimation of the possessions of the Southern Railway. It was, I think, while he was still on this circuit as Commissioner that Mr Hilbery was appointed a Judge of the King's Bench Division.

✧ ✧ ✧

In the summer of 1935 I was on the South Wales Circuit, and on Thursday, 6 June, I went to Haverfordwest. This was the Thursday before Whitsunday, that is to say the day before the end of the Easter term. This meant that I was at work all through the Whitsun Vacation. That sometimes happens on circuit, and one is entitled to take an equivalent holiday in term, before or after. In fact a Welsh circuit is so much of a holiday that I did not suffer much, and I forgot all about my right to a substituted holiday later.

I had not been at Haverfordwest since January 1925, and I had memories of the house there as almost the worst I ever had to stay in. So it was a great relief to find that it had been given up, and a very pleasant house, Glenafon, a little way outside the town, had been substituted. It was as good a house as one could wish, and the garden was very pleasant.

Haverfordwest managed to provide two prisoners, both of whom pleaded guilty. And there was one very trumpery civil case. The whole business of the Assize was finished in 2½ hours.

On the night 16–17 May, just three weeks before I went to Wales, there was the worst frost ever known for that time of the year. The effect round my home in Buckinghamshire was disastrous. I wondered how far west I should see signs of it. They were very manifest almost everywhere in South Wales, especially in the valleys: trees on the hills had been much less injured. Almost the only place where I saw no trace of the frost at all was at Dale, on the north shore of Milford Haven.

On the Saturday my marshal and I spent the day at St David's, and next day we lunched with Mr Wilfrid Lewis, the Attorney-General's "Devil". Only a week later he was appointed a Judge of the King's Bench Division, in succession to Mr Justice Avory.

On Whit-Monday the Pembroke Sheriff's car took us to Carmarthen, and there we changed to the Cardigan Sheriff's car which carried us to Lampeter. I suppose this may be the modern equivalent of the ancient practice by which the Sheriff of a county escorted the Judges to the county boundary and there handed them over to the cavalcade of the neighbouring Sheriff. In the evening we dined with the dons at the College.

Cardiganshire had one prisoner, who was tried, and one simple civil case. The whole business took less than four hours. Next morning Lampeter appeared to be in an excited condition over its Whitsuntide Fair. We were to go on to Carmarthen. We went by a rather round-about journey, for we had been invited to attend a luncheon of the West Wales Law Society at Aberystwyth. That was a place I had never been to. I expected to find it much larger than it was. It seemed an odd thing to have the National Library for Wales in a great building up behind the town, and I could not help wondering whether a big library in such a spot could be much used. I wondered whether it was put there by way of compromise, because no one dared resolve the conflicting claims of Cardiff and Swansea. If the Scottish National Library had not been evolved from the Advocates Library, a like decision between Edinburgh and Glasgow might have planted it at Oban. Under sect. 15 of the Copyright Act 1911 the Library at Aberystwyth is entitled to claim a copy of every book published in Great Britain, subject to the exclusion of such books as may be specified in regulations made by the Board of Trade. If what I am writing is ever published, I wonder if a copy will slumber on a shelf at Aberystwyth!

On the roadsides, on the way to and from Aberystwyth, I noticed great numbers of acacias in the hedgerows: the frost seemed to have done little harm to them.

At Carmarthen I had been advised to provide four working days. There were three prisoners (including one who was rightly found to be insane), two civil cases, and five undefended divorce cases. The whole business took 10 hours, so that two days would have sufficed. As it was, seeing that this was in the middle of what should have been my Whitsun Vacation, I had no scruple in adjourning the Court on the first day soon after noon, and taking the 1.4 train to London. In the evening I went to the Jubilee State Ball at Buckingham Palace, where I enjoyed the magnificent spectacle. I slept at the Paddington Hotel, caught the 8.55 train next morning, breakfasting in the train, and sat in Court after lunch.

On the Saturday Carmarthen was crammed with people, mostly children. There was a gathering, or "Rally", of a Welsh children's organization, which I think they called an Urdd. I was told that at midday the children were to march past the Town Hall, and I was invited by the High Sheriff and the Mayor to join them on the balcony. As they assured me it would please the young people I agreed: but except to please them, I am afraid I was not enthusiastic. For I gathered that this was a manifestation of that parochial nationalism of which I am suspicious. The children were dressed up like Boy Scouts and Girl Guides. I was told that they were not part of Lord Baden Powell's great family. For the promoters desired to have a really Welsh organization, with Welsh words of command and Welsh cries, or "slogans".

In the autumn of this year I was asked to take the chair at an annual dinner in London of the English Association. My health was proposed, and in reply I said something to this effect. "It has been for me a privilege and a pleasure to preside at this meeting of the English Association. I have been recalling that in all probability, though I do not know it for a fact, my great-great-grandfather could not talk a word of English. Happily, even at the latter part of the eighteenth century Scotland enjoyed great educational advantages, as she has ever since. And if my great-grandfather as a child talked Gaelic, he was enabled to get a sound education in English, he came away from the poor country of his birth, and here, in the course of time, am I, completely English, except for my name. I am, as I have said, proud and pleased to be allowed this evening to preside over a meeting of the English Association. But I cannot help reflecting that, if I had belonged by origin to a branch of the so-called Celtic race less endowed than the Scottish with a sense of humour, I might, instead of being here, have been attending the meeting of some organization whose aim was the dissemination and glorification of an uncouth tongue that is rightly dying."

On the Sunday my marshal and I walked southwards by lanes to the mouth of the Taf river opposite Langharne. There was a marsh of which many acres were covered with Thrift. The blaze of pink flowers was magnificent. The ways of flowers are a great mystery. Thrift (*Armeria vulgaris*) grows wild all round our sea shores, *and* on the tops of some Scottish mountains. But if you dig up a root and transplant it, it will grow and flower quite happily in an inland garden, even in a London suburb. Why then does it not spread inland naturally? We turned left to Llanstephan, had tea there, and walked back, about 20 miles altogether.

We also went to the museum at Carmarthen. The most notable thing in it was its enthusiastic and learned custodian. He showed us many things of interest, and I was sorry that he had so small and overcrowded a building.

For Brecon, as for Lampeter, I had provided one working day. There was one prisoner, and one civil case. The prisoner pleaded guilty: he had broken a pane of glass, put his hand through the hole, and stolen some chocolates! The civil case was settled. So the business of the Assize was finished in a quarter of an hour.

Presteign had no business at all, so I cancelled its Assize. This meant that I had two idle days before I was to join the North Wales

Judge at Chester. Lord Trevethin, who came to dinner with us at Brecon, asked us all—my wife, my daughter, her spaniel, my marshal and me—to come and stay with him at Abernant. So we gladly went, and spent two delightful days with that best of men. When we arrived I was told he was down at the river, and I found him wading and fishing. A few weeks before, so wading, he had hooked, played, and landed a 36-pound salmon. And he was then ninety-one.

One afternoon he drove us round the country, and took us to tea with Mr Ralph Harley at Brampton Bryan: I found he knew all about the mahogany boxes in the Courts at Hereford and Monmouth, the gifts of his ancestor. On the way we passed an inn, "The Baskerville Arms" at Eardisley. I think it was from the big house there that the old carriages in the Nottingham Museum came.

On Saturday, 22 June, a fearfully hot day, my ladies and the dog drove home, and my marshal and I went by train from Builth Road to Chester, via Shrewsbury. There I joined Mr Justice Talbot, who came from Mold. We were housed again in the house at Upton. When I got to Chester I had spent 16½ hours in the Courts in South Wales. If I had been sitting in London, and it had not been vacation, I should have spent 60 hours at work in the same period, that is 12 working days.

On the Sunday, after the Assize Service at the Cathedral, my marshal and I drove out to Erthig, close to Wrexham, where we had been invited to luncheon by Mrs Yorke.* There were many beautiful things in her house, but in particular I was interested in a portrait of Lord Jeffreys, the Lord Chancellor. It was, indeed, because I had mentioned my wish that I could see this to a friend of Mrs Yorke, and he spoke of it to her, that she very kindly invited me to come.

George Jeffreys was born at Acton, near Wrexham, in 1648. He was called to the bar at the Inner Temple on 22 November 1668. He was elected Common Serjeant in 1671, and Recorder of London in 1678. On 27 January 1677/78 he was made a Bencher of the Inner Temple. In 1680 he became Chief Justice of Chester, King's Serjeant, and a Baronet: he would then, under the old practice, cease to be a Bencher of the Inner Temple, and transfer himself to Serjeants' Inn. In 1682 he became Lord Chief Justice, and in 1685 (after the conclusion

* An uncle of Lord Chancellor Hardwicke (his father's younger brother) married the heiress of Erthig.

of the Bloody Assize) he was made Lord Chancellor, having been created Lord Jeffreys of Wem earlier in that year. If he was born, as is commonly said, in 1648, he became Lord Chancellor when only thirty-seven. But there is some ground* for thinking that he may have been born in 1644.

In 1687 Jeffreys, despite his doings on the Bloody Assize and elsewhere, was still sufficiently popular in the Inner Temple for the Benchers to commission Sir Godfrey Kneller to paint his portrait at a cost of £50, and it was hung in the Hall. It is said that this was the first occasion on which the Benchers ever had a portrait of an Inner Templar provided out of the funds of the Inn.

After the Revolution Whig enthusiasm seems to have prevailed. The picture of Lord Jeffreys was removed from the Hall to the chambers of Mr Holloway, a Bencher, where it remained until 1693. Jeffreys's eldest son John had been "specially admitted" a member of the Inn, at the age of eight, in 1679. In 1693 he made a request to the Benchers to have his father's picture. As a result there was a Bench Table Order on 9 February 1693/94 "that the Treasurer do declare to Lord Jeffreyes that, at his Lordship's desire, the House do make a present to his lordship of his father's picture, now in Mr Holloway's chamber, who is desired to deliver the same to his lordship or his order, by direction of Mr Treasurer".

This was the picture I saw in Mrs Yorke's house. It was presumably taken to Acton Park by the second Lord Jeffreys in 1694. He died in 1702, and the peerage became extinct, as he had no male issue. I believe he was in financial straits, and his possessions were sold. The picture appears to have been bought by his neighbour, the Mr Yorke of Erthig of that day.

The Whig dogs have had all the best of it about Jeffreys. I have no desire to whitewash him, but I am sure he was not the unmitigated ruffian of tradition. That he was a good-looking man this, and other pictures, manifest. And he had some redeeming graces. The vexed question whether the organ of Bernard Smith or that of Renatus Harris should be acquired for the Temple Church raged from 1682 to 1685. The story that Jeffreys was called in to settle this early in 1686, when he decided in favour of Smith, is probably true. The Harris organ went to the great church at Wolverhampton.

* See a letter in *The Times Literary Supplement*, 1 August 1929, p. 607.

After a week at Chester, which was as pleasant as usual, we went down to Swansea on a very hot day. It was a Saturday, and after tea I walked down to the sea front beyond the new Law Courts. I doubt if I ever saw any space so crowded with human beings as that beach on that afternoon—except, possibly, the Piazza of St Peter's on a fine Easter Day.

On the Sunday afternoon we drove out to the Gower peninsula in quest of flowers. That I was so often during my time on the Welsh circuits was, I think, indirectly due to the botanical enthusiasm of Mr Justice Talbot.

On the following Saturday I escaped to Oxford, for a dinner in Trinity. Next day one of my friends, a don, was going down to Wales to inspect a house he had taken for a long vacation reading party, and he offered to drive me back to Swansea. We left Oxford at 10, and we lunched at Carmarthen at 1.15. Since that means about 156 miles in 3¼ hours, it was pretty good going. But the way, by Witney, Gloucester, Ross, Abergavenny, and Brecon is comparatively free of "built-up areas", and there was not much traffic. The house we went to inspect was near Amroth, so we passed the great Pendine Sands. On this Sunday afternoon they were an extraordinary spectacle. The herd instinct that seems to prevail among the owners of Sunday-driven cars is one of the strangest things I know. At Runnymede, for example, on a Sunday afternoon, you find hundreds of cars parked close together, with their owners (or hire-purchasers) sitting inside, reading Sunday newspapers. At Pendine there were hundreds of cars, mostly small, driving about on the sands. It must be very bad for the cars to have sand and salt water flying about beneath them.

At the Mansion House at Swansea the Housekeeper had a springer spaniel named Podger, whom I remember with affection. He was as amiable as all spaniels are. And he had one simple and unending pleasure—to have a tennis ball thrown, after which he ran, brought it back, put it down, and wagged "Please again". I never went into the garden but in a second he had deposited the ball at my feet, and stood expectant. He never tired, but I always did. My marshal one day determined to outlast him: but the dog won easily. I hope Podger is well, and is still enjoying this simple diversion.

◇ ◇ ◇

In the autumn of 1935 I went on the North-Eastern Circuit. My friend, the Dean of Durham, when I met him in the summer, reproached me with not having been there since he became Dean. So I said I would choose this, if I could, as my next circuit.

On the autumn circuit only one judge goes to Newcastle, Durham, and York, and a second one joins him at Leeds. On 30 October I went to Newcastle, and was well content to find myself again in that pleasant city. When the Lord Mayor, and the other notables, came to dine with me at the Mansion House I received a Rose Noble of Edward III as dagger money.

On Saturday, 9 November, I drove to Durham, and my wife arrived to stay at the Deanery, where I dined in the evening. Next morning we had the Assize Service in the Cathedral, as impressive as it has always been, and, as I thought, with the music even better than it used to be. As soon as I had time to wander about the Cathedral I found many notable improvements. When Bishop Welldon retired he took credit to himself that he was leaving the Cathedral in the same state as he had first found it: which seemed a curious boast. Now the Galilee, forlorn and neglected in his day, had been swept, beautified, and adorned. Under Cosin's great font canopy there was now Cosin's font. This, because it was not Gothic, was ignominiously cast out by the Dean and Chapter early in the nineteenth century, and a substitute after a Norman design substituted, which was itself hideous, and was utterly out of keeping with the canopy. They gave Cosin's font to the church at Pittington. In 1935 the new Dean and his Chapter were happily able to induce these people to give the font back, so that after about eighty years' banishment it was restored to its old place of honour in the Cathedral.

The nineteenth century insulted the memory of Cosin in another way. He erected a magnificent carved oak organ screen of Renaissance design. In 1847 this was ruthlessly destroyed on the ground that it was "after designs wholly unsuitable to a place of worship". But many pieces of the woodwork were put in the Castle, against the wall of the long passage, and at the sides of Cosin's noble staircase. The Dean collected many of these, and against the South wall of the nave re-erected a large part of Cosin's screen and organ case. It is only a part, for there are still pieces left on the staircase in the Castle, including an enormous carved mitre. But the effect of the reconstruction in the nave is admirable.

Of yet another scheme of "restoration", in the true sense, I saw the beginnings. There used to be at the South side of the South transept an ancient clock in a most picturesque wooden case of great size and elaboration. This was destroyed in the nineteenth century, but the fragments survived in the great dormitory. They were being collected and fitted together. I saw them under the instructed guidance of Mr Vereker, who was especially interested in this pious work. On later visits I have seen the clock and its case completed: it is a charming and curious thing.

If one deplores the destructions of the past, it is perhaps rash to desire the removal of anything in a cathedral. So transitory and uncertain seem the canons of taste. But I cannot bring myself to believe that the day will ever come when Sir Gilbert Scott will be again regarded as a great artist, or the Albert Memorial as a thing to be reverentially admired. Scott cursed Durham Cathedral with the horrible metal screen at the entrance to the choir, and the atrocious metal lectern near by. I wish that the Dean and Chapter may be emboldened to cast these out as "wholly unsuitable to a place of worship". If any church can be found anywhere to accept them as gifts, let them be given: but I doubt if anyone will want them.

There is another improvement I should like to see effected at Durham, but it does not concern the Dean and Chapter. The Norman crypt chapel in the Castle is one of the most delicate pieces of Norman architecture that exists. I always found it in a condition of squalor and neglect. To illumine it there was hung one unshaded electric light bulb. There is an undergraduates' common room close by, to which this beautiful little chapel forms a passage of access: on several occasions I have found bicycles propped against the walls, and rubbish on the floor. It deserves better treatment.

One thing I saw in Durham for the first time—its Town Hall. I had not realized that behind its uninteresting front there was a fair hall, with some pictures, and one very charming old panelled room. In this, the Mayor's room, there was one picture labelled "Judge Jeffreys". It is a ludicrous error. The man depicted is in fact some fat seventeenth-century parson. He was as much like Napoleon or the Duke of Wellington as Lord Jeffreys of Wem!

On Tuesday, 19 November, I was to go to York. I arranged to go by an afternoon train, and in the morning my marshal and I drove out to Barnard Castle to see the Bowes Museum. When motoring I had before passed that astonishing building, but I had never been within it. I went this time because during the summer a friend of mine said he had been there, and "Do you know that they have got there some of the woodwork from the Temple Church?"

If my friend had been in error about this, I should still have been glad that I made this expedition. For the Bowes Museum is a very interesting place. There cannot be anything quite like it anywhere else in the world. It is sufficiently surprising to find a vast French Château, out in the wilds near a small market town. John Bowes, the founder, was married to a French wife. They began this great building in 1869, with a French architect, M. Jules Pellechet, of Paris. The lady died in 1874, and her husband in 1885. The building, which cost £100,000, was not finished at his death. He and his wife left all their treasures to be housed in it, and he left an endowment fund of £125,000. Only in 1892 was it opened to the public. By reason of its remote situation I am afraid fewer people see it than its contents deserve. To see the tapestries alone would be worth a journey from London. Then there are vast collections of china, glass, French furniture, ironwork, and other things. Of the 900 pictures many are poor things: but there are some very good ones. Altogether it is a very remarkable place.

The chief object of my visit, relics from the Temple Church, would have repaid me by itself. The joint action of the Inner Temple and the Middle Temple in the so-called "restoration" of the Temple Church in 1842 is the most discreditable thing in their history. The story of these horrible proceedings may be read, with indignation, in the pages of Mrs Esdaile's *Temple Church Monuments* (1933). St Anne's Chapel had been ruthlessly destroyed in 1827 by Sir Robert Smirke, R.A. Even worse was achieved in 1842. It was not altogether the fault of the Benchers. They had resort to what was supposed to be the best expert and artistic advice—to Smirke, Savage, Cottingham, and Willement, whose names are now sunk in deserved oblivion. The Benchers even struggled successfully against some of that advice, and Mrs Esdaile records that, but for the refusal of the Benchers, these experts might have played even more devastating havoc than they did.

The principle on which these vandals acted is stated, with glowing approval, in a little book, *The Restoration of the Temple Church* (1843), by William Burge, Q.C., F.R.S., F.S.A., and a Bencher of the Inner

Temple. "It was scarcely possible they could err in the manner of restoring the Temple Church. Fidelity in replacing that which was originally part of the edifice, and in removing that which never was, and never could have been part of it, must constitute their great merit." It was on this principle that the whole of the magnificent series of monuments were cast out of the church: the experts and artists would have destroyed them altogether; it was only upon the insistence of the Benchers that they huddled them into the triforium, more or less in fragments.

The greatest architect this country ever produced was Sir Christopher Wren. He was employed by the Benchers of a happier age to do work in the church in 1682. One thing he did was to lay a floor of black and white marble squares. But as this "never could have formed part of the original edifice" it was torn up, and hideous encaustic tiles, designed by Willement in imitation of rude old ones in the Westminster Chapter House, and made by Messrs Minton, were substituted.

Of course Wren's magnificent Renaissance woodwork never could have been part of the original edifice: and to Mr Burge Wren's work was "pagan" and "unchristian". Three pieces of this woodwork, which survive, were the screen or reredos, parts of the organ loft, and the pulpit. The screen, and two columns of the organ loft are in the Bowes Museum. The pulpit is in Christ church, Newgate Street, to which it was given by the Benchers.

The reredos is a beautiful piece of work. It was carved by William Emmett, who did much fine work for Wren at Hampton Court, Chelsea Hospital, and elsewhere. One of the two pillars from the organ loft was carved by Emmett and the other by Thomas Lowe. All these are in perfect condition. On the back of the reredos is pasted a "Lot No. —", significant of the auction of discarded lumber at which the judicious Mr Bowes bought it.

I had a long talk with Mr Harrison, the learned curator, and he gave me a copy of a monograph he had written, *The Wren Screen, from the Temple Church, London, re-erected in the Bowes Museum, Barnard Castle, with some account of William Emmett's work.* I told him that I thought the screen ought to be restored to the church for which Wren designed it. He said that personally he agreed with me.

Later on, by judicious enquiries, I gathered that if the Trustees of the Museum were approached by the Temple authorities it was possible that they might agree to this return. The affairs of the Temple Church are managed by the Choir Committee, which is composed of representatives of both the two Inns. I believe its traditional policy is conservative. I have even heard that a former Master of the Temple, on hearing the complaint of a clerical friend about dry rot in his church, dared to remark, "I have not any trouble with dry rot. But I have the Choir Committee."

I have never been a member of this Committee. I put forward my suggestion to my Inner Temple colleagues who were upon it, and they seemed to favour the idea. But it was rejected by the Middle Temple party.

Rebuffed as to this, I tried again, a few years later, to do something to undo the wickedness of 1842, and pay a repentant tribute to the great Wren. I defy anyone to deny that the "Gothic" pulpit, put into the church by the Smirkes and Willements, is absolutely hideous and repulsive. And I think few would deny that the pulpit now in Christ church, Newgate Street, is a magnificent thing. Christ church had a fine pulpit, when they acquired our finer one, but they cut theirs up, and used the panels to make choir stalls and a litany desk. When the wicked scheme to destroy All Hallows, Lombard Street, was being pushed forward, it occurred to me that we might perhaps buy the All Hallows' pulpit (a very fine one), give it to Christ church, and get back our own. I made enquiries in the proper quarters, and found that this scheme might be feasible. So through my Inner Temple colleagues, all of whom seemed to favour the idea, I again approached the Choir Committee. Again the Middle Temple refused to participate.

I have some great friends who are Benchers of the Middle Temple. I hope I may be acquitted of any improper asperity, if I say that I have not an enthusiastic regard for the Middle Temple Bench in its corporate capacity.

On our drive back to Durham we stopped to see Staindrop church, and that too repaid us. It is a fine church, and the monuments of the Nevills, Earls of Westmorland, including two effigies in wood, are admirable.

The first thing that pleased me at York was when I went into the splendid dining-room at the Judges' Lodgings. The panelling used to be covered with brown varnish, and there was an ugly brass pole across the middle of it to carry a red baize curtain. The room on this occasion had been immensely improved. The pole and curtain were gone. And all the woodwork had been pickled and scraped, so that it had that delicate hue of old pinewood, and the carving of the capitals was sharp and fine. The effect was admirable. When I congratulated the Housekeeper upon this notable improvement, he astonished and puzzled me very much by saying: "It is all due to your Lordship." By way of explanation he brought me the Visitors' Book, which is always provided in Judges' Lodgings. And I found that at the end of my last visit to the house, in March 1933, I had put in the book a suggestion that, if it would not cost too much, it would be a great thing to treat the room in this way, and that so noble a room deserved it. And I had forgotten all about it. As there are three County Councils in Yorkshire, the Judges' Lodgings at York are looked after not by the "Standing Joint Committee", as in most counties, but by the Commissioners of the Judges' Lodgings, as I think they are called. I was very grateful to the authorities, whatever their precise title, and I hope they agreed with me that the money involved by the improvement was very well spent.

I showed my marshal one other thing of interest in that room and its panelling. The sanitary arrangements of the eighteenth century were strangely primitive. In many old sideboards you find at the side a small cupboard with a utensil that nowadays is only found in a bedroom. There is one in the sideboard in the dining-room at the Judges' Lodgings at Derby. More rarely this convenience is in the panelling. If in the dining-room at York you go to the westernmost window, and pull out the shutters from their recess on the western side, you will find a recess and the utensil still inside it.

These simple methods were in vogue elsewhere. In the first edition of Campbell's *Lives of the Chief Justices* (1857) there is this passage at p. 85: "The following anecdote I have heard related of Lord Kenyon by and before very decent people, and it ought not to be lost, as it illustrates his character and the manners of the age in which he flourished. In those days retiring rooms for the use of the Judges were unknown, and a porcelain vase, with a handle to it, was placed in a corner of the Court at the extremity of the Bench. In the King's Bench at Guildhall the students' box [in which I myself have often sat] was very near this corner. One day a student, who was taking notes, finding the ink in his little ink bottle very thick, used the freedom secretly to discharge the whole of it into my Lord's porcelain vase. His Lordship soon after having occasion to come to this corner, he was observed in a few moments to become much disconcerted and distressed. In truth discovering the liquid with which he was filling the vase to be of a jet black colour, he thought the secretion indicated the sudden attack of some mortal disorder. In great confusion and anguish of mind he returned to his seat, and attempted to resume the trial of the cause, but finding his hand to shake so much that he could not write, he said that on account of indisposition he was obliged to adjourn the Court. As he was led to his carriage by his servants, the luckless student came up to him and said, 'My Lord, I hope your Lordship will excuse me, as I suspect that I am unfortunately the cause of your Lordship's apprehension'. He then described what he had done, expressing deep contrition for his thoughtlessness and impertinence, and saying that he thought it his duty to relieve his Lordship's mind by this confession. *Lord Kenyon:* 'Sir, you are a man of sense and a gentleman—dine with me on Sunday.' Lord Ellenborough pursued the same practice. I myself have often heard his large seals dangling from his watch-chain rattle against the vase, as he took it in his hand *coram populo,* decorously turning his back upon them."

In his subsequent editions Lord Campbell omitted this passage, in the interests of propriety. But I agree with his earlier view that an incident so illustrative of the manners of the age ought not to be forgotten. In the old House of Commons the Speaker was provided with a similar utensil, made, I believe, of silver, beneath his chair. When he desired to use it the Clerk at the table in front of him stood up and raised his elbows, so that his gown might provide a screen.

I had not much time at York, and there was one very heavy criminal case. So I wrote to Mr Justice Porter, who was to join me at Leeds, and asked him to start a few days earlier and join me at York. This proved very necessary. The long case kept him busy all his time, and I was equally busy with the rest of the calendar. There was one change at York. The enormous wall all round the Castle and the old prisons was being pulled down. We drove to the Courts by a new way, through a breach in the wall, and not through the old Gateway. A writer in the local paper said that we were the first judges to come thus to the Courts. He added that there had been a proposal to name the new road after the first judge who made use of it, but as, unexpectedly, two judges had come on this occasion, it had spoiled the plan. I think Portergate would be a better name than MacKinnon Avenue.

Just after we began work at York there came the sad news of the death of Charles Bernard Johnson, whom I had known as the Associate on all my visits to the North-Eastern Circuit. He was called to the bar in 1913. He went off to the War in 1914. There he was horribly wounded, and lost an arm. Soon after the war ended, a shattered wreck as he was, he accepted the office of Associate. It was not worthy of his abilities, and its duties he of course discharged admirably. But it was as a man that I lamented his loss. For I can say in all sincerity that he was one of the most lovable men I ever knew. I believe he was often in pain, but he was always cheerful and courageous; and he had a rare smile. The circuit lost a very great deal by his death.

My friend, the Dean of York, wrote to me when I was at Durham to say that there was to be a dinner of the Oxford Society at York during the Assizes, at which he was to preside, and asked me to come to it. That I did, and took with me my marshal, who had been President of the O.U.B.C. the year before, and belonged, like the Dean and myself, to Trinity. We had a pleasant evening, with a large gathering of Oxford men, including the President of St John's.

On the Saturday my marshal and I walked up the towpath by the Ouse. There had been much rain recently, and the river was very full, but we managed to get along the path, sometimes having to avoid wet places. I was interested, when we got to the railway bridge that crosses the river, to see a notice board stating that no one was allowed to use the bridge to cross except members of the York and Ainsty Hunt. When we came to the junction of the Nidd we shouted for the ferry, though not very hopeful that at this time of the year, and with the river running as it was, anyone would respond. But the boatman came almost at once and put us across to Nun Monkton. We saw the church, and I admired it again. And we very much admired the delightful William and Mary house, close to the ferry. I said to my marshal, "What a pity it is that we cannot be bold and call on the people who live here. Probably they are very nice, and would like to give us lunch." The very next day we were lunching at Bishopsthorpe. And the first fellow guests to whom Mrs Temple introduced me were the very nice people who did live in this house. I told them the story, and we exchanged regrets that we had not met 24 hours earlier.

As it was we went to an inn on the village green, which is adorned by a maypole, and had bread and cheese. This inn was oddly named "The Alice Hawthorn". The landlady said this was the name of a famous race-horse that was bred in the neighbourhood.

I think I mentioned on an earlier page the small portrait print in the Lodgings at York of "Harry Rowe, Born at York 1726, Trumpeter to the Duke of Kingston's Regiment at Culloden 1746, and 43 years Trumpeter to the High Sheriffs of Yorkshire 1796". I always spend some time at York in a bookshop in Stonegate. This time, I found there a curious little book of 144 pages, of which that print was the frontispiece. The title-page is "Memoirs of Harry Rowe: constructed from materials found in an old box after his decease; by Mr John Croft, Wine Merchant. For the Benefit of the York Dispensary. York, printed by Wilson and Spence. Sold by all the Booksellers in the City and County of York. Price *5s.*" The opening sentence is: "Harry Rowe was born in the year 1728, in the town of Nottingham, where his father kept a school and his mother followed the business of a mantua-maker." After being tried as an assistant in his father's school, where he was a failure, and bound apprentice to a stocking-weaver, with a like result, "he entered as a volunteer in the Duke of Kingston's Light Horse, and in a short time he was raised to the rank of a Trumpeter. Being the year of the rebellion, the regiment was ordered down into Scotland, and at the battle of Culloden he behaved with great gallantry. On the suppression of the rebellion, the regiment was ordered to return to England, soon after which it was reduced." He then went to London, and for a time was employed by Orator Henley "in the double capacity of door-keeper and 'groaner', for which last office he was admirably calculated". He was then assistant to a sham physician "to represent persons labouring under various diseases, a service for which he was well qualified. In the course of six months he had been nine times cured of a dropsy, and before the expiration of his year he had been the faithful representative of every disease incident to the human body."

He next went back to Nottingham "as an outside passenger on the Nottingham Fly", and was for a time again employed as an assistant in his father's school. Having married "a genteel looking woman, who then kept a milliner's shop", he went with her to Coventry, "with cash amounting to forty pounds, arising from the sale of his wife's stock in trade". There they assumed the name of Tack, and set up a matrimonial agency, with advertisements in the Coventry *Mercury*. Thirty-three of Mr Croft's most tedious pages are then filled with supposed letters received by Mr Tack from aspirant brides and bridegrooms.

Mrs Tack having died, Rowe "embraced the favourable opportunity that offered of a new engagement with the widow of a puppet showman, who died about a fortnight before. The bargain was soon struck, and Harry was put in possession of a well-appointed puppet show, for the management of which he was admirably calculated. Fortunately, he came, in the course of his travels, to York, which place he made his headquarters; and from that centre he branched out to every market town and village in the kingdom. During his stay at York the office of Trumpeter to the High Sheriffs became vacant, when he was chosen into that employment, in which he continued for the space of forty years, returning from his country excursions twice a year, to be present at the Assizes."

"Grown old and infirm he found himself under the necessity of disposing of his Puppets, and his wife dying at this time, he retired from his public office, oppressed with poverty and sickness; and in the 74th year of his age, he died in the Parish workhouse....The remains of this most extraordinary man were deposited in the burial ground belonging to the parish workhouse of St Olave's."

There follows "The Sham Doctor, a Musical Farce, by Harry Rowe", said to have been left in MS. in an old box at the workhouse. Worse rubbish was never printed. And the little book ends with "Subscribers' Names", a list containing all the Yorkshire quality. This was no doubt the contemporary equivalent of a "Flag Day" for the York Dispensary. W. Wilberforce, esq., M.P., is down for two copies. He was Member for Yorkshire. Even in that day apparently a county member had to subscribe to anything in his constituency.

At intervals at home I have to go through my bookshelves to clear out what I do not really want, so as to make room for more desired additions. Rowe's *Life* came under the ban of expulsion after a time, and I sent it to the Clerk of the Commissioners of the Judges'

Lodgings, with a suggestion that it might find decent burial in that house. I think perhaps Serjeant Thorpe's *Charge* (1649) might have been of more interest to my successors. But that is a very slim volume, and I have room for it still.

Leeds, whither we drove on 25 November, kept us at work for not quite three weeks, until 14 December. I had hoped to get away rather earlier. For on Thursday, 12 December, there was the trial of Lord de Clifford before the Lord Steward and the Peers, and if I had been in London I might have been one of the Judges in attendance. I cannot believe there will ever again be such a proceeding. And I should dearly have liked to play a humble part in the last of such historic scenes.

The city of Leeds had been changed a good deal in the short time since I was there last. The great new Municipal Building, to the north of the Town Hall, was completed. I do not admire its elevation. But when we dined there with the Lord Mayor it was in a noble room, much better than the narrow, passage-like, room, where such dinners used to take place in the old Town Hall. The Head Row had been widened out of all recognition. And north of St John's church (the one building in Leeds of real interest) they had made a pleasant open space and a garden.

One Sunday I drove out to Tadcaster. The road thither crosses the Great North Road at a spot that has probably seen more accidents in recent years than any in the world. I was told that in the last twelve years there had been on an average eight collisions every month. They had lately set up automatic red and green lights: I fancy that a "roundabout" would be more effective, and as these cross-roads are right in the country, with no houses, I was surprised that this had not been made.

The mention of automatic red and green lights reminds me that I first saw this device in operation in Leeds. I think that was on my first visit in May 1925, or in July of the same year.

1936

In January 1936 I went on the First South-Eastern Circuit, and was thus consoled for my disappointment of a year ago. That meant, at this time of the year, starting at Huntingdon, which is a very pleasant little town. The Lodgings were the house of Lord Sandwich's agent inside Hinchingbroke Park. And Huntingdon is a nice clean town. It is a pity that the bricks made in this part of the world appear to have become white in modern times. Huntingdon, and Godmanchester, and much of modern Cambridge would look much better if the bricks were of the old colour, as at St John's or Queens' College.

I dined at Hinchingbroke with Lord Sandwich, on the evening of my arrival, and saw the many treasures of that beautiful house. And there I met the High Sheriff of the two counties of Huntingdon and Cambridge, Mr Granville Proby, of Elton Hall. That he was of Trinity College, Oxford (long after my day) was a bond between us at once: my marshal, as usual, came from that college, though long after Mr Proby's day.

I had only given one working day to Huntingdon, but it was more than enough. For the whole business was over by one o'clock. The Sheriff then told me that he was giving a luncheon to the magistrates at the Bridge Inn, and asked me if I would come to it. As the Assize was finished I was, of course, free to go, and did so very gladly. It was a pleasant meeting, and I had the privilege of proposing the health of the High Sheriff. Then he drove me out to his place, Elton Hall, near Peterborough, and I spent the afternoon in its great picture galleries. It is a fine collection, of old and new masters, from early Italians and Germans down to Poynter and Alma Tadema. There are many fine family portraits by Reynolds, Romney, and Hoppner. The great Catalogue, with an Introduction by Tancred Borenius, includes 135 pictures.

The High Sheriff's Chaplain was Mr Hodgson, the Rector of Elton: he was also an Oxford man, of Christchurch. Later in the year Mr Proby revived an ancient custom by printing two of the Chaplain's

Assize sermons, including the brief, but excellent, discourse preached before me on 13 January 1936. Mr Proby added a very interesting Introduction, and appended at the end a complete list of the Sheriffs of Cambridge and Huntingdon from 1155 to 1936. The little book, beautifully printed at the Cambridge University Press, is charming.

Mr Proby's father, Col. D. J. Proby, was Sheriff in 1923, and Sir Heneage Proby in 1651. The absence of more Probys of Elton from the list is due to the fact that many were exempt as being Members of Parliament, and from 1752 to 1909 they were Peers (Lord Carysfort). They had another property near Amersham in Buckinghamshire, and some of them were Sheriffs in that county.

Mr Proby notes in his Introduction that, on the death of the Sovereign, it is the High Sheriff's duty to proclaim his successor. And he adds, "This duty it fell to my lot to perform at Huntingdon, Cambridge, March, and Ely on the 22nd January 1936. I am informed that I was the only Sheriff who read the Proclamation of H.M. King Edward VIII in four different places."

Next day we were to drive to Cambridge in the afternoon. So in the morning my marshal and I walked out to Brampton, where I had often been mentally with Samuel Pepys. His house there is not greatly changed. And in the church there is the tombstone of his tiresome sister, Pall Jackson.

And so to Cambridge, to be greeted in the middle of the Great Court of Trinity by the Master, and conducted to his Lodge. The mulled port then appeared, and on a cold January day it was a very pleasant drink.

This being one of the old Assizes, it was my privilege to entertain the Heads of Houses to dinner. Shortly before I came to Cambridge I wrote to the Vice-Chancellor and asked him to select a day that would be convenient to him. I added that at Oxford the Vice-Chancellor's secretary kindly circulated my invitation to the guests, and it would be a convenience if this was the practice at Cambridge. But I was a stickler for precedent, and if he said I ought to send separate invitations myself, I would gladly do so. The Vice-Chancellor replied that his secretary would certainly do as I had suggested. He also told me that in addition to the Heads, the Proctors, and the Preacher of the Assize sermon (whom I had named in accordance with the Oxford practice) it was usual at Cambridge for the Judge to invite the Public Orator and the Esquire Bedells. I replied that I very much hoped they would be included, and I should be particularly interested to see an Esquire Bedell. For at Oxford, with our traditional devotion to reform, we had abolished Esquire Bedells about eighty years ago.

I found later on that I was unwittingly breaking precedents in all this. For soon after I arrived at Trinity my clerk told me that he had been approached by a college butler who said that it was customary for him to go round to the Heads, Proctors, etc., convey the Judge's invitation, and bring back a reply. For this there was also a customary fee to himself. I desired my clerk to say that, being an Oxford man, I hoped I might be excused for following the Oxford practice, and that the officer would accept the customary fee without being further troubled in the business. So I hope all was well. In fact, several of my guests told me that my method of invitation was much more convenient, as it gave them a decently long warning of the day, instead of their being invited only at the last moment.

In the result I had a very pleasant party—the Vice-Chancellor, nine Heads, the two Proctors, the Preacher, the Public Orator, and an Esquire Bedell, making, with my marshal and myself, seventeen in all.

On another evening I had a smaller party. Six Cambridge friends came and met six Oxford men—the High Sheriff, his chaplain, Judge Farrant, my son who happened to be passing through Cambridge, my marshal, and myself.

For these entertainments the half dozen of wonderful port, which the College magnificently presents to the Judge, was very useful.

Cambridge is the best place in which to see and admire the works of the greatest sculptor who has worked in England—Roubiliac, who was a Huguenot born at Lyons in 1702. The busts in Trinity Library are very fine. But the statue of Newton in the ante-chapel is the real masterpiece:

> Newton, with his prism, and silent face,
> The marble index of a mind for ever
> Voyaging through strange seas of thought alone.

I found some interest in the problem whether I should recognize Newton, if by a miraculous resurrection I saw him before me. The bust in the library seems to me not precisely like the statue in the chapel: and the various portraits in the Lodge and elsewhere in the College seemed to differ from these, and from one another.

My stay pleasantly ended with dinner in hall with the Master on Sunday evening, and the stirrup cup of mulled port next morning, when I departed for Ipswich. I did not want to arrive there till the afternoon, so my marshal and I spent the day at Bury St Edmund's. And we wished that the Assize was there and not at Ipswich. For I always think Bury is one of the pleasantest market towns there is, and I do not like Ipswich.

We had heard, of course, at Cambridge of the King's illness. When we got to Ipswich, and found a wireless set at the Lodgings, the bulletins grew graver. At 9.30 came the words—"The King's life is drawing to its close"—and we heard them at intervals through the evening. Finally, at 12.15, I heard the voice of Sir John Reith (who is my nearest neighbour at home), saying that the end had come, and King George V was no more.

Next morning I had a telegram from the Lord Chancellor's secretary: "You may like to know that the Lord Chief Justice has decided not to hold his court at Oxford today." This was for me the opening day of the Assize. There were several prisoners, and jurymen and witnesses had all assembled. I thought that I ought to sit. When I came into Court I said that we were met under the shadow of a great sorrow, and that I had debated with myself whether it would be right to go on with the business or to adjourn. But that I had decided that, considering the inconvenience and expense that would be occasioned by an adjournment, we ought to go on. And I added that I felt sure that his late Majesty would have wished it to be so.

In the old days I should have had no such problem to decide. For until 1760 a Judge's appointment lapsed on the demise of the Crown, and he had no authority to act unless, and until, he was re-appointed. Nor was he necessarily re-appointed in the new reign. To remedy this inconvenience, on the accession of George III, an Act was passed providing that every Judge's Patent or Commission should continue in force notwithstanding the death of the Sovereign.

King's Counsel used to be appointed by Letters Patent under the Great Seal.* A King's Counsel's appointment, like a Judge's, used to lapse on the demise of the Crown. Roger North, in his *Autobiography*

* I was, in 1914, one of the last batch, which included Lord Caldecote and Lord Finlay, who were so appointed. In 1917 four, who included Lord Hailsham and Lord Wright, were appointed by a document bearing a wafer seal, and this has been since then the practice.

(p. 139), makes a note that on 26 October 1682 he had "The first patent to be of the King's Council", and on 9 February 1685 "The second patent of King's Council under Jac. II".

Next morning at 11 I went with the High Sheriff to the Town Hall, and stood by the Mayor when he read the Proclamation of King Edward VIII. It was a fine piece to read, but the Mayor was nervous, and perhaps moved, and he did not read it well. I should have liked to have heard it read by Mr Barber, the Clerk of Assize on the North-Eastern Circuit, or by Sir William Jowitt, to whom Nature has been so kind in her gift of a voice.

And so, on Saturday, 25 January, to Norwich, and to the pleasant house in the Close that was the Judges' Lodgings. Since I was there last there had been a new Dean, and under his regime the Cathedral was already greatly improved. That has since continued. In particular, the achievement of Dean Cranage in cleaning and colouring the marvellous series of roof bosses in the Cloisters is a blessing indeed. We had a fine Assize Service on Sunday. And on the following Tuesday, the day of the King's funeral, I did not sit, but went to another great service in the Cathedral.

I also dined with Mr Russell Colman, the Lord-Lieutenant. He postponed a large party whom he had invited, but let me come quietly with my marshal. This was all the better because it gave us more opportunity of seeing his amazing collection of the Norwich School. The Cotman drawings, in perfect condition, are magnificent.

The end at Norwich, on the Saturday afternoon, was a wretched business. Over a very simple issue a special jury disagreed hopelessly. They retired at 2. They remained, as I imagine in fierce debate, until 4.30, having had no lunch. They then avowed that it was hopeless to expect that they could ever agree. So I had to discharge them, and leave the parties to try the case again at the next Assizes, or to compromise it. This delay meant that I had lost all the decent trains to Chelmsford, and had to go by one that involved change and delay both at Ipswich and Colchester. Each of the three trains stopped everywhere, none of them had any heating, though it was 1st February, and the whole journey of 83 miles took nearly four hours. Such an experience is only possible on the descendant of the old Eastern Counties Railway. The result for me was a very bad cold. I am not an enthusiast for Trial by Jury.

I thought I had this cold coming on next day, but I also thought I might stave it off by walking. So my marshal and I walked by Chignal, Smealey, Pleshey, Great Waltham, Little Waltham, and Springfield—about 20 miles. The remains of the Castle at Pleshey, with a wonderful brick bridge over the moat, are remarkable. I had never heard of the place before.

✧ ✧ ✧

In the summer of 1936, at the end of my twelfth year on the Bench, I got for the first time the opportunity to go upon the long Western Circuit, and so to visit Salisbury and Wells as Judge of Assize. On 20 May I arrived at Mompesson House in the Close at Salisbury. That is as beautiful a house as any in England, and of town houses I am sure it enjoys the most beautiful surroundings of any. It was built in 1704, about as good a date for English house-building as one could select. At that time the Dean and Chapter were encouraging county families to build their town houses in the Close.

About 1830 Mompesson House was leased by Mr George Bernard Townsend. His eldest daughter, Miss Barbara Townsend, was born in the house in 1843. She continued to live in it until she died, aged 96, in 1939. The Summer Assize for Wiltshire is always at Salisbury, and the Autumn Assize is there alternately with Devizes: so once or twice a year Miss Townsend left her house for the Judge's use. So it was when I was there in May 1936. In the year following, owing to her great age, she could not be turned out, and the Judges began to go to another house in the Close, which I knew as the home of Archdeacon Carpenter.

When the Dean met me at the door of the Cathedral for the Assize Service he said, "I wish you good luck in the name of the Lord". I imagined that this must be an ancient and traditional Sarum use. But when I asked him about it later, he said it was his own invention.

I missed the spectacle of one very ancient Sarum use by a few days. Salisbury's newly appointed Bishop had been enthroned the week before. By a practice coeval with the founding of the Cathedral in 1220 the Bishop, on the morning of the ceremony, starts from an ancient house outside the Close. There he is robed, walks to the Gate of the Close, and knocks for entrance. This ancient house, called Mitre House, was, in May 1936, let as a women's hairdressing establishment. I believe the Bishop put on his vestments amid some of those sprightly figures that Willlam Dent Pitman essayed to imitate in his Empress Eugénie. Such is the mixture of ancient and modern.

Lord Campbell records* one more Sarum use, in his *Life* of Sir Matthew Hale. "According to a custom which prevailed 'from time whereof the memory of man runneth not to the contrary', the Dean and Chapter of Salisbury had presented to the Judges of Assize six sugar-loaves. Lord Chief Baron Hale, when upon the Western Circuit, having received the usual donation, discovered that the Dean and Chapter had a cause coming on before him for trial, and he sent his servant to pay for the sugar-loaves before he would allow it to be entered. Those venerable litigants, instead of firing up at the notion of their becoming grocers, or taunting the Judge, as they might have done, with making them violate the statute of Henry 8 against clerical trading, received the money, tried their cause, and obtained a verdict."

I do not know when this practice came to an end. A judge now might find it embarrassing to be given three sugar-loaves. It is a pity that a token payment has not survived, in memory of the ancient tribute, e.g. a pound of lump sugar.

For some reason sugar-loaves were frequently offered as presents of dignity. My friend the Attorney-General has lately been elected by the Corporation to the sinecure office of Recorder of Kingston-on-Thames. I believe the only remuneration attached to that post is one sugar-loaf annually.

Close to the North Gate, at which the Bishop knocked for admittance, is the Almshouse of Bishop Seth Ward. I always admire it as one of the most perfect pieces of its admirable time. And Seth Ward was President of Trinity College, Oxford, 1659–1660. I was to find another very notable piece of building by a President of Trinity a little later at Wells.

Of course I spent much of my time in the Cathedral. One of the most surprising things is to find Lord Radnor's pew, created out of the Hungerford Chantry, with a row of dignified Chippendale chairs.

On this circuit I had an unusually good experience of the opportunities that befall a Judge of Assize of seeing great country houses and their treasures. For I was shown very thoroughly over Wilton, Longford Castle, Sherborne Castle, and Kingston Lacey. There are not many great English collections that can rival those four. And for

* *Lives of the Chief Justices*, Vol. II, p. 205.

the week-end between Salisbury and Dorchester I stayed at Ven House, Milborne Port, then tenanted by friends of mine: it is one of the most beautiful houses I know.

On my first day at Dorchester I finished by three in the afternoon. So my marshal and I walked out by Maumbury Rings to Maiden Castle. It was an afternoon of perfect sunshine with a strong wind. We walked all round the top rampart of that amazing place. I doubt if there is in all the world a more impressive monument of human industry. Then we came down to Winterbourne St Martin, and so back to Dorchester. Outside that delectable town, on the Roman road to Bridport, there had lately sprung up some of the most hideous little villas in the world. And close by, opposite the Barracks, was a Baptist Chapel, with the date 1914 upon it: it would stand a very good chance of pre-eminence in ugliness even among Baptist Chapels.

For the next three and a half days I had only hard and repulsive work, and no relief from it. For there was a particularly sordid murder trial. It ended on the Saturday. I had to spend all the morning from 10.30 to 1.30 summing up, and the jury brought in their verdict of Guilty an hour later. It was very hot weather, and the Court was packed every day with ghoulish spectators. It was indeed a relief on the Saturday afternoon to be taken for the week-end by the High Sheriff to his delightful house near Cranborne. On the way we had a look at Cranborne Manor, that very perfect Jacobean specimen. And on the Sunday I was taken to tea at Creech Manor, which had wonderful gardens, and to Kingston Lacey. I realized that there are pleasures on circuit that compensate a judge even for such horrors as the murder trial that had been my wretched occupation all the week!

On the Monday morning I went back to Dorchester to try a civil case. It was over by three, so I had time to go to the Museum, which is close to the Court. There was one thing there that was new, and was indeed worth seeing. On 16 May 1936 men were at work excavating the foundations for a new shop. Suddenly they came upon a vast hoard of Roman silver coins. The pile of them was removed to the Museum, and was there on show, almost exactly as it had been found. Only a few had been cleaned to display their beauty. Then we walked by a path alongside the river Frome to Bockhampton. On the way there was a pleasant sight—a swan with a baby cygnet upon her back. And so back to Dorchester, through the park of Stinsford House, with a sight of its dignified façade.

Next day we drove to Wells, by Sherborne, Castle Cary, and Shepton Mallet. And this road brought us through Croscombe. I stopped the car at the church, and we all went in, including the chauffeur. The Jacobean woodwork, screens, pulpit, and pews, is magnificent—rather like that at St John's church in Leeds, but finer: and there is the great advantage that the church is much lighter.

And so into Wells, and to the very pleasant house that is provided as the Judges' Lodgings. In that capacity it is a unique institution. Some benefactor left it to Trustees (the Dean of Wells told me that he was one of them) to serve as the Judges' Lodgings. For that purpose it is only needed once or twice a year. The Trustees let the house to a tenant (who at this time was Mr Basil Johnson, formerly Precentor at Eton), who turns out when the Judge comes. Any profit on the rent goes to charity. It is a good house, with a pleasant garden.

One strange and novel duty I found awaiting me at Wells. There had been sent to the Lodgings an ancient-looking MS. book. I found that it contained the Bye-Laws of the Bath Hospital. In 1739 there was passed an Act of Parliament (12 Geo. II, cap. 31): "An Act for establishing and well governing an Hospital or Infirmary in the City of Bath." A section of this provides that the President and Governors may make bye-laws, provided that they be approved by the Bishop of Bath and Wells and by the Justices of Assize for the County of Somerset, for which approval no fee shall be taken. The book first contained "Bye-Laws approved and ratified by a General Court, 12 June 1793". These were signed by ten Governors, among whom were Daniel Lysons and Thomas Fothergill. And at the end of these was

> August 3rd, 1793. The foregoing Bye-Laws made by the President and Governours of ye general Hospital or Infirmary in the City of Bath have been examined and approved by us—
>
> Charles Bath and Wells.
>
> R. Perryn } Justices of Assize for the County of
J. Heath } Somerset, Summer Assizes, 1793.

The second set of Bye-laws were dated 1 May 1843, and were signed

> Wm Wightman } Justices of Assize for the County of
C. Cresswell } Somerset, Lent Assizes, 1844.

There were judicial signatures to further Bye-laws in 1904, 1912, and 1932. In each of these cases they were signed by two Judges at Bristol. Now this was wrong. As I explained on an earlier page the Judges at Bristol are not Judges of Assize for the County of Somerset, but only for the City and County of Bristol. In 1739 when the Act was passed, and in 1793 and 1844, there would always be two Judges of Assize for the County of Somerset, at either Wells, or Taunton, or Bridgewater. As the Act of 1739 spoke of "Justices of Assize", and as by 1904 it had become the practice for only one Judge to go to Wells or Taunton, but for two to go to Bristol, I suppose it came about that in 1904, 1912 and 1932 the Bath Hospital book was, by a venial error, submitted to the two Judges at Bristol: one of them, on each occasion, had been Judge of Assize for the County of Somerset shortly before.

On this occasion I signed the book, adding to my name "Justice of Assize for the County of Somerset, Summer Assizes, 1936". A space was left for the Bishop to sign, as I suppose he did later. Being mindful of the terms of the Act of 1739, I did not ask for any fee.

Wells I knew well, though this was my first judicial visit. It is one of the most charming places in England. But it suffers for its charms. The combination of Wells Cathedral, the Cheddar Gorge, Wookey Hole, and Glastonbury, attracts a greater number of motor charabancs, and their contents, than almost any place in the world. Wells must sometimes sigh for the time when it was, by railway, one of the most inaccessible spots. But the charabancs fill it to overflowing every day. And the crowd seems to be mostly devoted to two things—the old clock in the Cathedral, and the swans on the Bishop's moat.

The business of the Assize was all finished by luncheon on Friday, and I was not due to go to Bodmin till the following Monday. One afternoon we walked by the fields to Dinder. The church provided a timely refuge from a thunderstorm. There was at least one terrific clap of thunder. Next day we heard that the wonderful church at Croscombe had been struck and seriously damaged. I believe the Cathedral, and St Cuthbert's, were also struck but without much injury.

On the Saturday morning my marshal and I walked by a lane and footpaths to Priddy. On the way some memory made me say to him "I wonder how I know the names of 'Priddy and Hale'. I think they must be Solicitors in London." In fact, as I found later in the London

Telephone Directory, it is the style of a firm of London timber merchants: I must have remembered them as litigants, and perhaps as clients. The odd thing was that when we had inspected the church at Priddy my marshal, in the porch, said "Look at that". *That* was a notice signed by the Rector. And the Rector's name was Hale.

One afternoon we had tea at the Deanery with the Dean and Mrs Malden. We were in the magnificent room on the first floor with its wonderful carving and panelling. This was created by Ralph Bathurst, who was Dean from 1670 to 1704. But he was also President of Trinity College, Oxford, from 1664 to 1704. And there he was responsible for the panelled interior of the Old Bursary, one of the most beautiful rooms in Oxford, and for the Chapel. The Old Bursary was thus beautified in 1681, and is very similar to the room in the Deanery, though smaller. The Chapel was finished in 1691, and contains, of course, some of the finest work of Grinling Gibbons. A man who created three such interiors as the Old Bursary and the Chapel at Trinity, and this great room in the Deanery, is indeed to be remembered with praise.

On Monday, 8 June, we left Wells at 9.43 by a train that took us to Yatton. There our coach was shunted on to a train going to Plymouth. At Plymouth we had a considerable wait, happily sufficient to let us take a walk on the Hoe. Then another train took us on and landed us at Bodmin Road at 4.15. Everywhere along the line there was in every rocky cutting a blaze of red valerian, and in flatter parts yellow iris by every pool and ditch.

I do not admire Bodmin, or the country round it. Indeed, except for its margin by the sea, I do not much admire Cornwall at all. But on the Saturday we got to the sea. We drove to Padstow, where I had never been before. Prideaux Place is a pleasant-looking house, and the church has good monuments of Prideauxs and Prideaux-Brunes. Then we walked out to Stopper Point, and along the cliffs westward. Everywhere thrift made a beautiful pink carpet; and it was a day of brilliant sunshine. We had, of course, too many sandwiches for lunch—has anyone ever eaten all the sandwiches provided for him? We put the surplus in pieces on a stone wall, and stood close by. In a few seconds a gull descended; in a few more there was a shrieking crowd of gulls, and no food left. We came round to Padstow, had tea in a room overlooking the harbour, and drove back to Bodmin. The sun was still shining in a cloudless sky: but the evening papers told us that all over England all cricket matches had been abandoned owing to a deluge of rain.

On the Sunday we went to the sea on the other side, driving to Fowey. Thence by lanes to Lostwithiel and Restormel, and home through Lord Clifden's beautiful park. The rain began as we entered Bodmin, and it poured all night.

There is in Bodmin church a monument to one Durrant, who was Mayor of the town and died in 1636. He married twice: he had fourteen children by his first wife, and six by the second.

In the usual course one goes from Bodmin to Exeter, and there joins the second judge. But before the circuit began we had been approached by the Lord Mayor of Bristol. The Royal Agricultural Show was to be held there, and the Duke of York was to come to open it. Following our usual route we should be holding the Assizes at Bristol at this crowded hour. So we agreed to go to Bristol before Exeter, and on 16 June I travelled from Bodmin to Bristol, and was joined at the Mansion House in Clifton by Mr Justice Rayner Goddard.

Next day was the usual Assize Service in the Mayor's chapel. Six policemen carrying the small silver maces, and the Sword Bearer with the great Sword of State dignified the ceremony. Then I took my seat in the newly built Civil Court. Its predecessor had been recently burned down, and I do not remember that there was any reason to regret it. The new one was convenient, and well planned: I believe I was the first Judge to use it.

I saw one thing in Bristol that was new to me. Mr F. A. Wilshire, of the local bar, took me to see Wesley's Chapel, with its attached rooms, in the Horse Fair. It had been beautifully restored and adorned by Mr Edmund Lamplough. And it is an extraordinarily curious and interesting place.

On Wednesday, 24 June, a very hot day, Mr Justice Goddard took me in his car, with our two marshals, to Exeter, by Bridgewater, Milverton, Bampton, and Tiverton—93 miles. The Lodgings at Exeter have always been a rather gloomy house, and my colleague and I were so depressed by their shortcomings that we called the attention of the Standing Joint Committee to the necessity of some reform. Nothing seemed to have been done for many years, and we pointed out threadbare carpets, worn upholstery, and decaying wall papers. I believe the Committee soon after made an inspection, and were very much of our opinion.

If reform in that house were drastic, perhaps it would involve the banishment of the sideboard in the dining-room. But I think that would be a pity. It vies with the Albert Memorial as a monstrous triumph of Victorian taste, and is probably the largest and most hideous sideboard in the whole world. I believe it was an exhibit at the Great Exhibition of 1851, and I expect it was there awarded a Gold Medal.

We were invited by the Dean and Chapter to dine at the Deanery, and after dinner there was a large addition of further guests. I presume this is an incident of the Summer Assize. It was a very pleasant function, but I should have found it even more pleasant if I had not been under the necessity of wearing knee breeches, my silk gown, and a wig. The Dean was our friend who until the year before had been Master of the Temple.

I do not think I had seen before the Exeter Workhouse in the Heavitree Road. It is an admirable Queen Anne, or early Georgian, building, and is much the most attractive looking Workhouse I ever saw. But I forget: there are no Workhouses now; we call them Poor Law Institutions.

On 2 July we went to Winchester by train, via Salisbury, Romsey, and St Denys. Winchester was as pleasant as ever. One afternoon when the Court rose I walked out to see a cricket match between the Hampshire Police and the Bar. It was a melancholy spectacle. Soon after I arrived the Police declared, with their score at 228 for eight wickets. I had to come away without knowing the result, but I cannot suppose that the Bar won.

We had five boys to breakfast, and we had the Bar to dinner. As my colleague was an old member of the Western Circuit he kept me in order as to the proper traditional toasts. They were

The King,
The Western Circuit,
The Judges of the Western Circuit,
Cras Animarum.

And so on Saturday, 11 July I finished my last case, and was addressed by Mr Scott Henderson with the valediction that is the special incident of the Western Circuit, and of it alone.

◇ ◇ ◇

Wimpole

In the autumn of 1936 I went for the first time on the Second South-Eastern Circuit, that is to Hertford, Maidstone, Kingston, and Lewes. I was to go to Hertford on 11 November. I could drive there from my home in an hour. But Sir Joseph Priestley, K.C., had asked me to come to luncheon at his house near Hitchin, and arranged to take me in the afternoon to see Wimpole, once the seat of Lord Chancellor Hardwicke, but now the property of Lord Clifden. It was a very interesting experience. And the splendours of Wimpole emphasized what I have said before—that a Lord Chancellor in the old days was a really well paid official. Philip Yorke, born in 1690, was the son of a small attorney at Dover. He was called to the bar in 1715. In 1720, when only 29, he became Solicitor-General, and in 1723 he was Attorney-General. In 1733 he became Chief Justice of the King's Bench, and a peer. In 1737, at the age of 46, he became Lord Chancellor, and sat on the woolsack for twenty years. Wimpole Hall, formerly the seat of the Chicheleys, he enlarged and adorned on a magnificent scale. The church, rebuilt by Lord Hardwicke in 1749, is still close to the house: in it is his immense monument. The village was rebuilt to the east, as was done at Houghton by Sir Robert Walpole. From the vast front of the house a great double avenue of elms runs southward for three miles. Apparently Lord Clifden had bought the place lock, stock, and barrel. The Library was full of Lord Hardwicke's books, with his bookplate. I saw four Great Seals, two of which adorned Lord Hardwicke's bedstead. Lord Campbell, in his *Life* of Hardwicke, says that his wife had one of the rooms adorned with velvet curtains in which twenty of the ornate purses of the Great Seal were incorporated. We did not see these. Among the pictures was a portrait, on panel, of Sir Edward Coke, but not a very good one.

In less than 200 years apparently the vast fortune of the Lord Chancellor had so diminished that the whole place had to be sold. When Peter Thelluson died in 1797, leaving the extraordinary will under which his vast fortune was to accumulate during the lives of his sons and grandsons, it was calculated that in about eighty years his designated heir would come into some £140,000,000. In fact Rendlesham Hall, the family place in Suffolk, has for some years been a home for the treatment of inebriates!

My day ended rather miserably. I went back to tea with Sir Joseph Priestley, and then drove myself to Hertford. Just before I started it began to rain, and it rained in torrents. I never like driving at night very much, but to do so on a black night in a deluge of rain is a wretched business. It was so wet that the streets were almost empty, and I had much ado to find my way to the Lodgings at Bengeo. The rain continued all the next day, and when we went to dine in the evening with the High Sheriff we had to drive through a flood that nearly came over the floor of the car.

One of the prisoners I had to try at Hertford was a man who had broken into the house of the Lord Chief Justice during the Long Vacation. He was an impudent thief. He took some things, and he noticed a typewriter. He enquired of a dealer if he would buy a typewriter, and was told that he would. So he went and broke into the house a second time, and brought it away. This, however, was his undoing; for the machine had a number on it by which it could be traced, and so he came to be arrested.

I suppose the most remarkable case that was ever known at Hertford was the trial of Spencer Cowper in July 1699 for the alleged murder of Sarah Stout. He was the younger brother of Lord Chancellor Cowper, and he himself became a Judge of the Common Pleas in 1727. Sarah Stout, a Quakeress, was apparently in love with him. In March 1699 he was at the Lent Assizes at Hertford, and one morning she was found drowned in a stream. The only ground of suspicion against Cowper was that he had been in her company the night before. The Cowpers were Whigs, and the local Tories promoted an agitation against him. He was committed for trial apparently on very flimsy evidence, and remained in prison until the Summer Assize. The Judge was Baron Hatsel, and the record of the trial suggests that he was one of the feeblest judges who ever existed. Much was made of the fact that the body was floating. It was said that this showed she had been suffocated before being thrown into the water, and that if she had drowned herself she would not have floated. Cowper of course had to defend himself, which he did with firmness and ability. After a ridiculous summing up Baron Hatsel said: "I am sensible I have omitted many things, but I am a little faint, and cannot repeat any more of the evidence." Fortunately the jury said "Not Guilty".

In the manner of the time a considerable war of pamphlets ensued. I possess two of them: "The Hertford Letter: containing several brief observations on a late printed Tryal, concerning the Murder of

Mrs Sarah Stout; London, 1699"; and "Some Observations on the Trial of Spencer Cowper &c.; London 1702".

The Tory faction tried to bring an Appeal of Murder, and various proceedings took place upon this.* It was eventually defeated on technical grounds.

In Hertingfordbury church, a little way to the west of Hertford, there is a monument to Spencer Cowper. It is by Roubiliac, and is a beautiful thing. He died only a year after he became a judge.

Maidstone is a pleasant enough town, and the Lodgings in Stone Street are in a fine roomy house. One of the advantages of all the places on this circuit is the nearness to London. On more than one occasion I went up by train to dine in London, and got back in quite good time. My longest dinner expedition was to drive to Mr Justice Luxmoore's house, Bilsington Priory. And when I was due to go to Kingston I was able to be at our Inner Temple Grand Night on the way.

That there should be an Assize at Kingston for the County of Surrey is a ridiculous absurdity. Surrey is just as suburban as Middlesex. Middlesex has always been satisfied with Westminster Hall or the Law Courts for civil cases, and the Old Bailey for criminal trials: there is no reason why Surrey should not be served in the same way.

The Lodgings at Kingston were in fact at Esher, in a very spacious house belonging to Miss Talbot. This means a drive of 4 miles to and from the Court, four times a day. But it would probably be hard to find a satisfactory house in Kingston. At the Assize Service I was greeted by the Rector of Kingston, eldest son of Lord Justice Scrutton, whom I first knew as a small boy.

In the hall at Miss Talbot's house there was an old-fashioned letter box, divided into two compartments. One was labelled "General Post", and the other "Twopenny Post".

Esher was fast losing its amenities. Esher Place and Claremont were both being cut up as building sites. The old parish church is very quaint, with an enormous Claremont pew in the gallery.

And so to Lewes. I took a walk down to the town after I arrived. I was puzzled because I could not find the beautiful old shop that I used to admire. I was fairly sure of the spot, but upon it was nothing but an atrocious modern façade with two immense sheets of plate glass. I stopped a man who was passing, and asked him where the old shop

* See *Stout* v. *Towler* (1701) 12 Modern Rep. 372.

used to be. "Oh, that old place," he said, "it was there"—pointing to the plate glass abomination. I am afraid righteous indignation moved me to rudeness: "Do you live in Lewes." "Oh, yes, I have lived here all my life." "Well, you Lewes people ought to be ashamed of yourselves for allowing such an outrage." He was quite unmoved, and explained that, when the old proprietors gave up business, no one would take the shop unless it was "brought up to date".

In London to possess an old-fashioned shop appears to be a cherished asset, e.g. Fribourg and Treyer in the Haymarket, or Lock the hatter, and Berry the wine merchant, in St James's Street. Vulgarity no doubt spreads to Lewes from Brighton, and they care nothing for a thing of beauty if it is not "up to date".

I was told afterwards that someone had the good sense to buy this old shop front, and that it had been re-erected in a museum of similar pieces at Hull. It was the best shop I ever saw. As it is now one must console oneself with a good one in Abbeygate Street, Bury St Edmunds (Oliver's the grocers), and another admirable one in Kingsgate Street, Winchester, which bears the inscription "Tailor to the Gentlemen of Winchester College".

One of the prisoners at Lewes was named Hogsflesh. I had thought that Charles Lamb invented that surname for his unlucky play.

There is a milestone in the High Street with the pleasing inscription: "50 miles to the Standard in Cornhill, 49 miles to Westminster Bridge, 9 miles to Brighthelmstone."

On 10 December the abdication of Edward VIII was announced. On 15 December at noon I adjourned the Court for ten minutes, and stood by the High Sheriff in the street as he read the proclamation of King George VI. It was on 22 January previously that I stood by the Mayor of Ipswich when he read the proclamation of Edward VIII.

There was a great deal of work at Lewes, including one peculiarly repulsive murder trial. The man was convicted, but subsequently, to my surprise, I was told that the doctors had declared him insane, and he was sent to Broadmoor. It would have been quite impossible on the evidence to have got a verdict of "Guilty but Insane".

There were also forty-two undefended divorce cases. I believe I established something like a record by disposing of them in just over three hours.

All this kept me at Lewes for sixteen days. On Saturday, 19 December, I went home.

1937

In February 1937 I went on my last circuit. It was a short outing, for I only went to Stafford and Birmingham. The only matter of interest was that at Stafford for the last time I had Mr Justice Talbot as my colleague. He was his old, kindly self, but he was obviously ill and failing. He resigned less than two months later. I believe he would have resigned sooner, but he stayed on to have the delight of taking part in the reception "Ad portas" at Winchester, when seven Wykehamist Judges were ceremoniously greeted. Winchester was the greatest enthusiasm of his life, and to be at this function must have given him great happiness.

✧ ✧ ✧

On 22 April I had a letter from the Prime Minister to say that he desired to recommend my name to His Majesty for the Court of Appeal. It was with mixed feelings that I accepted the offer. And obviously my chief reason for regret was that I should have no more of these pleasant circuit journeys.

There are 61 Assize towns in England and Wales. I have been to 58 of them, that is to all except Appleby, Oakham, and Bury St Edmunds. I have been 8 times to Chester; 7 times to Durham, Newcastle, York, Leeds and Birmingham; 6 times to Cardiff; 5 times to Carnarvon and Stafford; 4 times to Aylesbury, Bedford, Northampton, Leicester, Lincoln, Nottingham, Derby, Warwick, Shrewsbury, Carmarthen and Ruthin; 3 times to Liverpool, Manchester, Dorchester, Bodmin, Exeter, Bristol, Winchester, Reading, Oxford, Worcester, Gloucester, Monmouth, Hereford, Brecon, Beaumaris and Mold; twice to Cambridge, Norwich, Ipswich, Chelmsford, Devizes, Taunton, Lewes, Swansea, Haverfordwest, Lampeter, Presteign, Welshpool and Dolgelley; and once to Carlisle, Lancaster, Huntingdon, Salisbury, Wells, Hertford, Maidstone, Kingston and Newtown. This means that I have attended, or awaited, the "opening of the Commission" 186 times.

To Marshals and Sheriffs—Thanks

It will be manifest from various passages in these discursive recollections that I think the Circuit System is capable of reform and improvement, chiefly to the end that the London litigant may be better treated than he is at present. As to the merits and pleasures of the Circuit System from the point of view of the travelling judge I have no grievances. Circuit life, if one has some curiosity, and a zest for life, is uniformly delightful. For my own happiness I feel gratitude to two sets of friends, my marshals, and the many kindly people whom I met as High Sheriffs. I have said little of the endless hospitality of the High Sheriffs, for I have left out on purpose the more personal part of my journals. To my marshals, and to the High Sheriffs, I owe a great deal of happiness.

Appendix A

[Modern form of Judges' Precept to the High Sheriff of a County.]

CHESHIRE to wit } We the Honourable Sir Frank Douglas MacKinnon, Knight, and the Honourable Sir Hugh Fraser, Knight, two of His Majesty's Justices of the High Court of Justice, and others our fellow Justices of our said Sovereign Lord the King, assigned by Letters Patent of our said Sovereign Lord the King under the Great Seal of the United Kingdom of Great Britain and Ireland, to Us, and others, and to any two of us made to enquire more fully the Truth by the Oath of good and lawful Persons of the County of Chester and by other Ways Means and Methods by which we shall or may better know (as well within the Liberties as without) by whom the truth of the matter may be better known and enquired into of all Treasons Misprisions of Treasons Insurrections Rebellions Counterfeitings Clippings Washings False Coinage and other Falsities of the Money of the United Kingdom of Great Britain and Ireland and other Kingdoms and Dominions whatsoever and of all Murders Felonies Manslaughters Killings Burglaries Rapes of Women Unlawful Meetings and Conventicles Unlawful Utterings of Words Assemblies Misprisions Confederacies False Allegations Trespasses Riots Routs Retentions Escapes Contempts Falsities Negligences Concealments Maintenances Oppressions Champerties Deceits and all other evil doings offences and injuries whatsoever and also the accessories of them within the County of Chester aforesaid (as well within the Liberties as without) by whomsoever and in what matter soever done committed or perpetrated and by whom and to whom when how and after what manner And of all other Articles and Circumstances concerning the Premises and every of them or any of them in any manner whatsoever And the said Treasons and other the Premises according to the Laws and Customs of England for this time to hear and determine TO THE SHERIFF of the said County of Chester GREETING. On the behalf of our said Sovereign Lord the King we command you that you omit not for any Liberty within your Bailiwick but that you cause to come before us and others our Fellow Justices aforesaid or any two or more of us at Chester on Tuesday the 2nd day of February 1926 a competent number of good and lawful Persons of the body of your said County qualified according to law to do and receive all those things which on behalf of our said Sovereign Lord the King shall be then and there enjoined to them And that you yourself and your Under Sheriff be then and there in your own Persons together with your Bailiffs and other your Ministers to do those things which to your and their offices appertain in this behalf to be done And that you have then and there the names of the Jurors and this Precept. *Dated* under our hands and seals at Westminster this twenty first day of December in the sixteenth year of the reign of our Sovereign Lord George V by the grace of God of the United Kingdom of Great Britain and Ireland King Defender of the Faith.

F. D. MacKinnon (L S)

Hugh Fraser (L S)

When at the opening of the Assize the High Sheriff was invited by my clerk "to return the several precepts and writs to you directed", the above Precept was included in the roll of papers that he handed to me. And upon the back of it there was this indorsement, signed and sealed by the Sheriff:

"By virtue of this Precept to me directed and delivered I have caused to come before the Justices within named and their Fellow Justices within mentioned twenty-four as well Knights as other good and lawful men of my Bailiwick to do and receive all things which on behalf of our Sovereign Lord the King shall be then and there enjoined them as within I am commanded. The residue of the execution of this Precept appears in a certain panel to the same annexed."

Appendix B

Modern form of Precept issued by the Clerk of Assize, and sent to each Sheriff along with the foregoing Judges' Precept. The Clerk of Assize signs it with his surname only, without initials.

CHESHIRE to wit } The Honourable Sir Frank Douglas MacKinnon, Knight, and the Honourable Sir Hugh Fraser, Knight, two of His Majesty's Justices of the High Court of Justice and others their Fellow Justices of our said Lord the King assigned to take all the Assizes Juries and Certificates before whatsoever Justices arraigned as well by divers writs of the Lord George the Third first of Great Britain and afterwards of the United Kingdom of Great Britain and Ireland late King of the Lord George the Fourth and of the Lord William the Fourth of the said United Kingdom late Kings as by divers writs of our now Lord the King in the County of Chester TO THE SHERIFF of the said County of Chester GREETING On behalf of our said Lord the King we command you that you omit not for any Liberty of your Bailiwick but that you cause to come before Us at Chester on Tuesday the 2nd day of February 1926 All Writs of Assize Juries and Certificates before whatsoever Justices arraigned as well by divers writs of the Lord George the Third [as before]...as by divers Writs of our said Lord the King in your said County together with the Panels Attachments Reattachments Summons and Resummons and all other Muniments whatsoever any ways concerning those Assizes Juries and Certifices *Provided always* that the Attachments Reattachments Summons and Resummons therefore be made fifteen days before the said date *And also* that you cause to come before the said the Honourable Sir Frank Douglas MacKinnon, Knight, and the Honourable Sir Hugh Fraser, Knight two of his Majesty's Justices of the High Court of Justice and others their Fellow Justices of our said Lord the King assigned to deliver His Gaol of the County aforesaid of the Prisoners therein being at the day and place aforesaid all the Prisoners being in the said Gaol with their Attachments Indictments and all other Muniments any ways concerning those Prisoners and a competent number of good and lawful Persons of the body of your said County qualified according to Law to try all issues whether civil or criminal which may then and there come on for trial also a sufficient number of Special Jurors to try the Special Jury Cases to be tried at the said Assizes PUBLICKLY also cause to be proclaimed throughout your Bailiwick that all who will prosecute against those Prisoners be then and there to prosecute against them as shall be just GIVE NOTICE also to all Justices of the Peace Mayors Coroners Escheators Stewards and also to all Chief Constables and Bailiffs of every Hundred and Liberty within your said County that they be then and there in their own Persons with their Rolls Records Indictments and other Remembrances to do those things which to your and their offices in this behalf appertain to be done. And that you yourself and your Under-Sheriff together with your Bailiffs and other your Ministers be then and there in your own Persons to do those things which to you and their offices in this behalf appertain to be done And have you there and then the names of the Jurors Justices of the Peace Mayors Coroners Escheators Stewards Bailiffs Chief Constables and of all them whom you shall so cause to come before whom and by whom you shall so cause them to come. And that you shall then and there have this Precept. Dated at Westminster this twenty-first day of December in the Sixteenth year of the Reign of our Sovereign Lord George V by the Grace of God of the United Kingdom of Great Britain and Ireland King, Defender of the Faith.

STUBBS (LS)
Clerk of Assize

When the High Sheriff handed to me his roll of documents the above Precept was included in it, and on the back of it was this indorsement, signed and sealed by the Sheriff.

"I have caused to be publickly proclaimed throughout my whole Bailiwick that all those who shall prosecute against those prisoners be then and there to prosecute against them as shall be just. I have also given notice to all Justices of the Peace Mayors Coroners Escheators Stewards and also to all Chief Constables and Bailiffs of every Hundred and Liberty within my County that they shall be then and there in their own persons with their rolls records indictments and other remembrances to do those things which to their offices in this behalf appertain to be done as is within commanded me. The residue of the execution of this Precept appears in certain Schedules to the same annexed."

Appendix C

The modern form of the single document constituting the Commission of Assize. As appears from its terms, this applies to the whole Circuit and all the Counties upon it. Indeed this particular one applies to Cheshire and all the Welsh counties, upon both the Welsh Circuits. In the same way, I believe, a single Commission is issued for all the eight or nine counties upon both parts of the South-Eastern Circuit. The document does not now have the Great Seal attached to it, but only a wafer seal.

GEORGE THE FIFTH, by the Grace of God of the United Kingdom of Great Britain and Ireland, and of the British Dominions beyond the Seas, King, Defender of the Faith. To our most dear Cousin and Counsellor, George, Viscount Cave, Lord High Chancellor of Great Britain, Our most dear Cousin and Counsellor Arthur James, Earl of Balfour, Lord President of our Council, Our most dear Cousin and Counsellor James Edward Hubert, Marquess of Salisbury, Lord Keeper of our Privy Seal, Our most dear Cousins Ivor Miles, Earl of Plymouth, Ernest Edmund Henry Malet, Earl of Lisburne, Our most dear Cousin and Counsellor John Wynford, Viscount St David's, Our well-beloved and faithful Lloyd, Lord Kenyon, Joseph Henry Russell, Lord Glanusk, Owen Cosby, Lord Kylsant, Our beloved and faithful Sir Richard Henry Williams-Bulkeley, Sir Herbert Lloyd Watkin-Williams-Wynn, Sir Arthur Osmond Williams, Baronets, Sir William Bromley Davenport, Knight Commander of our most excellent Order of the British Empire, John Ernest Greaves, Henry Neville Gladstone, John Hinds, Charles Coltman Coltman-Rogers Esquires [the preceding 14 names are those of the Lords Lieutenant of the various counties]; our well-beloved and faithful Counsellor Gordon, Lord Hewart, Lord Chief Justice of England; Our Judges for the time being of our Supreme Court of Judicature; Such of our Counsel learned in the Law as are for the time being authorised by our Royal Warrant or by the Warrant of our Lord High Chancellor to be of the Commission; and the Clerk of Assize and Circuit officers of the Wales and Chester Circuit. GREETING. KNOW YE that we have assigned you and any two of you, of whom one of our Judges of our Supreme Court of Judicature, or one of our said Counsel learned in the Law shall be one, OUR JUSTICES to enquire more fully the truth by the oath of good and lawful men of our Counties of Anglesey, Brecknock, Cardigan, Carmarthen, Carnarvon, Denbigh, Flint, Glamorgan,

Merioneth, Montgomery, Pembroke, Radnor, and Chester, and also in the County of the Borough of Carmarthen, and Town and County of Haverfordwest, of all offences and injuries whatsoever within our said Counties, County of the Borough, and Town and County, and to hear and determine the premises and to deliver the Gaols of our said Counties, County of the Borough, and Town and County, of the Prisoners being therein, and to take all the Assizes, Juries, and Certificates before whatsoever Justices arraigned within our said Counties, County of the Borough, and Town and County. AND THEREFORE WE COMMAND YOU that at certain dates and places which you shall appoint for this purpose you and any two of you as aforesaid shall make diligent enquiries about the said injuries and offences, and hear and determine the same within our said Counties, County of the Borough, and Town and County, Doing therein what to Justice does appertain according to the Law and Customs of England, saving to Us the amerciaments and other things from thence to Us accruing AND WE COMMAND AND EMPOWER you to do in the execution of this Commission all things which have hitherto been lawfully done in obedience to Our Commission, of Oyer and Terminer, General Gaol Delivery, Assize and Association, and Our Writs of Association and Si Non Omnes, AND WE WILL that this Commission shall be deemed to be a Commission of Oyer and Terminer, a Commission of General Gaol Delivery, and a Commission of Assize.

In witness whereof we have caused these our Letters to be made Patent. Witness Ourself at Westminster the twelfth day of December in the sixteenth year of Our Reign."

(L S) SCHUSTER

When at the opening of the Commission in a County Town the Clerk of Assize "reads it short" he does so more or less in the terms following:*

George the Sixth by the Grace of God of Great Britain Ireland and the British Dominions beyond the Seas, King, Defender of the Faith, to the Honourable Sir Hugh Fraser, Knight, Justice of the High Court of Justice [When naming the Judge he turns and bows to him, and the Judge returns the salutation with his three cornered hat.] To such of our Counsel learned in the Law who are authorised by our Royal Warrant or by the Warrant of our Lord High Chancellor to be of the Commission, And to the Clerk of Assize and Circuit Officers of the North Wales Circuit. Greeting. Know ye that we have assigned you to enquire more fully the truth of all offences and injuries whatsoever within our County of Chester and to deliver the Gaol

* See *Stage and Bar* (1939) by George Bancroft, the very experienced Clerk of Assize of the Midland Circuit, at p. 219.

thereof and to take all the assizes juries and certificates within our County of Chester.

And therefore we command you that you shall make diligent enquiries about the said offences and injuries and hear and determine the same and take all the assizes juries and certificates doing therein what to Justice does appertain according to the laws and customs of England.

In Witness whereof we have caused these our Letters to be made Patent. Witness ourself at Westminster the twelfth day of December in the sixteenth Year of our Reign.

God Save the King

Index

Index

Index

Index

Index